MAN'S ECONOMIC ENVIRONMENT

McGRAW-HILL SERIES IN GEOGRAPHY

EDWARD J. TAAFFE AND JOHN W. WEBB,
  Consulting Editors

Broek and Webb A Geography of Mankind
Carlson Africa's Lands and Nations
Conkling and Yeates Man's Economic Environment
Cressey Asia's Lands and Peoples
Demko, Rose, and Schnell Population Geography: A
  Reader
Detwyler Man's Impact on Environment
Eliot Hurst Transportation Geography: Comments and
  Readings
Fryer Emerging Southeast Asia: A Study in Growth and
  Stagnation
Kolars and Nystuen Geography: The Study of Location,
  Culture, and Environment
Kolars and Nystuen Human Geography: Spatial Design
  in World Society
Kolars and Nystuen: Physical Geography: Environment
  and Man
Lanegran and Palm An Invitation to Geography
Mather Climatology: Fundamentals and Applications
Murphy The American City: An Urban Geography
Pounds Political Geography
Raisz General Cartography
Raisz Principles of Cartography
Starkey, Robinson, and Miller The Anglo-American
  Realm
Thoman and Corbin The Geography of Economic Activ-
  ity
Trewartha An Introduction to Climate
Trewartha, Robinson, and Hammond Fundamentals of
  Physical Geography
Trewartha, Robinson, and Hammond Elements of Ge-
  ography: Physical and Cultural
Trewartha, Robinson, and Hammond Physical Ele-
  ments of Geography (A republication of Part I of the
  above)
Van Riper Man's Physical World
Watts Principles of Biogeography: An Introduction to
  the Functional Mechanisms of Ecosystems
Yeates An Introduction to Quantitative Analysis in
  Economic Geography
Yeates Quantitative Analysis in Human Geography

MAN'S ECONOMIC ENVIRONMENT

EDGAR C. CONKLING

State University of New York at Buffalo

MAURICE YEATES

Queen's University
Canada

McGRAW-HILL BOOK COMPANY

New York St. Louis San Francisco Auckland Düsseldorf
Johannesburg Kuala Lumpur London Mexico Montreal New Delhi Panama
Paris São Paulo Singapore Sydney Tokyo Toronto

MAN'S ECONOMIC ENVIRONMENT

1 2 3 4 5 6 7 8 9 0 D O D O 7 9 8 7 6

Library of Congress Cataloging in Publication Data

Conkling, Edgar C
    Man's economic environment.

    (McGraw-Hill series in geography)
    Bibliography: p.
    Includes index.
    1. Geography, Economic. 2. Land. 3. Industries,
Location of. I. Yeates, Maurice, joint author.
II. Title.
HF1025.C773   330.9   75-22469
ISBN 0-07-012408-6

This book was set in Helvetica Regular by Black Dot, Inc.
The editors were Stephen D. Dragin and Susan Gamer;
the designer was J. E. O'Connor;
the production supervisor was Thomas J. LoPinto.
R. R. Donnelley & Sons Company was printer and binder.

CONTENTS

ACKNOWLEDGMENTS

The authors wish to express their appreciation to Mrs. H. Phelan for the skill and good judgment she demonstrated in typing and proofreading the manuscript of this book.

The illustrations were prepared in the Cartographic Laboratory at Queen's University under the direction of Dr. Henry Castner.

Edgar C. Conkling
Maurice Yeates

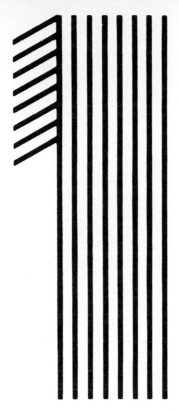

THE NATURE OF THE ECONOMIC ENVIRONMENT

When man looks at his environment, there are certain aspects of it that he considers especially important. These are the economic activities that supply the things he needs and wants and, at the same time, provide him with an opportunity for earning the income required to pay for them. For primitive peoples the economic environment is hardly separable from the physical environment, from which they obtain their food, shelter, and clothing in the most direct fashion. There is little division of labor in the folk society. Nearly everyone participates in extracting basic raw materials and foodstuffs from the forests and fields, and most members of the group have some role in converting these materials into directly usable forms—grinding grain into meal, weaving fibers and sewing skins into clothing, and making rudimentary tools, weapons, and shelters.

By contrast, the economic environment of modern society is exceedingly complex. There is an elaborate division of labor, not only between individuals and groups but also between different areas: communities, regions, and countries. The growing specialization of people and places inevitably makes them increasingly dependent upon each other and it creates ever higher levels of spatial interaction. In the most advanced societies the only economic enterprises that require direct contact with the physical environment are the first stages of production, that is, the extractive activities—agriculture, mining, forestry, grazing, and fishing. Ultimate consumption may take place hundreds or even thousands of miles from the sources of the raw materials, often with several intermediate stages of processing between.

This elaborate system has given modern man a far higher level of productivity than primitive folk find possible. In other words, we are able to get more units of output from the same number of units of land, labor, and capital. The system therefore provides each individual with a larger quantity of goods and services and thus produces a higher level of material comfort, a higher standard of living.

Despite these substantial advantages, however, the very complexity of our contemporary economic environment raises problems. Because it requires such intricate interdependence, the system is more subject to malfunctioning if one part of the chain fails. This arrangement also has an unfortunate tendency to exaggerate inequalities between peoples and places. Clearly, if we are to solve these problems of the economic environment, we need to learn more about it. Indeed, we must know as much as possible about the workings of this system if we are to make the day-to-day decisions required to keep it functioning and if we as individuals are to find a satisfactory place for ourselves within it. This is very different from the folk society, where all the decisions have already been made generations before and are given to its members through the accumulations of custom and tradition.

Although ideally every member of modern society should try to understand his economic environment and its many spatial ramifications, some persons, because of their special roles in the system, bring to this study different purposes and distinctive viewpoints. Most directly involved is the businessman, the entrepreneur or manager of a productive enterprise, upon whose decisions the success of the undertaking relies. As representatives of society at large, officials in the various arms of government have many reasons for knowing as much as possible about the economy. Among such agencies are planning commissions, taxing authorities, legislators, and even the military. The ordinary citizen should have a general knowledge of such matters for the conduct of his personal affairs and for casting his ballot intelligently at election time. Finally, there is that group of people whose duty it is to put the whole matter into an understandable framework and to convey this information to others. These are the academicians—regional scientists, geographers, economists, historians, political scientists, sociologists, and so forth.

SOME IMPORTANT QUESTIONS

Depending upon his place in society, each person has a list of questions about certain facets of the modern economic environment. Some of the most pressing of these questions have to do with the allocation of land, which is becoming more and more scarce as people increase in numbers and the intensity of their use of the land grows. What is it that determines how land is to be allotted to the many would-be users and contending land use types? Is there a basic principle that governs this allocation?

Whether it applies to rural or urban land, this most basic question is of interest to the academician, but it is even more immediately pressing for a number of other people. The farmer asks this question as he looks for the most appropriate location for setting up a dairy farm or a vegetable farm, or (if he already has a plot of land) as he tries to decide what is the most logical crop to produce in a particular place. He can readily determine whether or not a given piece of land has the necessary physical requirements, using fairly straightforward tests; but he must take into account a number of more subtle considerations as he tries to discover whether it is the best economic location.

Similarly, the shopkeeper has to decide upon the location that will attract the most customers for his particular type of merchandise, or, in some cases, decide what merchandising strategy is best for a specific location that happens to be available. From a different vantage point, acting for the community at large, the planning commission or zoning board must continually try to determine which land use type is most appropriate for a given area. If the board should decide to reserve that area for a specific use—residential, commercial, or manufacturing— will such a use prove economically viable in that location? Will it be compatible with neighboring uses?

Questions of this sort become especially urgent during periods of growth or change. For instance, the farmer must ask how his locational decisions are likely to be affected by changes in the size, makeup, or income of the urban population to which he sells his produce. He must also try to anticipate the effects of innovations in agricultural technology or of new transport developments. In the city, business-men and planners alike must try to understand why people and economic enterprises are moving to the suburbs. Why, they ask, are some activities more inclined to move than others? Where do businesses locate when they reach the suburbs? It is also important for them to find out why population characteristics— such as average age, income, and density—vary from one part of the city to another. Where should a firm that relies mainly upon female labor locate its establishment and why? These are a few of the issues of land use allocation that we shall be considering in Chapters 2 and 3 of this book.

Chapters 4 and 5 consider the location of manufacturing. For the academician attempting to refine his theories, the planner concerned with the economic health of his region, or the business executive looking for a site that will minimize costs and maximize profits, the principal question is: What are the basic considerations that affect the location of industries? Accepting the premise that manufacturing is essential to regional development, the planning commission asks why some areas attract industry more readily than others. They also need to know why industries tend to cluster together in certain places and to discover what kinds of industries are most likely to attract other activities.

How is the location of manufacturing affected by new developments in industrial technology, raw-material supply, innovations in transportation? In addition to these questions, entrepreneurs and regional planners must anticipate the probable locational effects of rising energy costs and the depletion of resources. In assessing their own growth strategies, national planning commissions have been studying the experiences of other countries, asking such questions as: Why has Japanese industry grown so fast? How and why did the nature of Japanese output change in character in such a short time?

The next major topic, appearing in Chapters 6 and 7, is the location of tertiary activities—retailing, wholesaling, personal and public services, the professions, and a number of others. This subject attracts increasing attention because tertiary activities now employ a majority of the labor force in most advanced countries. As the immediate source of supply for our needs and wants, tertiary activities play a central part in everyone's daily life; their locational pattern has an impact on where we live and work and where we enjoy our recreation. For urban and regional planners, as for academicians, the first questions are: Why do tertiary activities have such strong clustering tendencies? What governs the size and spacing of such clusters and of the population centers for which they form the nuclei? How do the number and variety of tertiary functions differ in service centers of different sizes? Government officials, among others concerned with urban problems, need to know what it is that causes such centers to grow and change. Why, they ask, are the larger places exerting such a strong attraction upon migrants from rural areas? Why are the larger metropolises growing at the expense of smaller centers?

Implicit in many of these questions is the suggestion that transportation bears a close relationship to the location of production. In exploring this relationship, Chapter 8 asks a question often voiced by planners: How can we analyze the essential characteristics of a transport network so as to be able to forecast its future growth and development? Pursuing this further, how can we predict the future impact on agriculture, manufacturing, and the services caused by changes in the transport system? How do the various transport modes—water, road, rail, and air—differ in their locational impact? These are some of the things that official agencies need to know if they are to anticipate the effects of their planning decisions. The importance of such questions is all the greater because such a high percentage of regional development funds ordinarily goes to transport improvements—at least 40 percent in the average less developed country. These same issues are obviously vital to merchants, manufacturers, and farmers operating in the affected areas, to legislators, governors, and other political leaders who must allocate the necessary construction funds, and to the ordinary citizens whose employment opportunities may be affected. A similar problem that is (or should be) of direct concern to regulatory agencies, is the probable locational effect of their rate-setting practices upon competition among carriers and upon the location of economic activities.

Chapter 9 takes up a closely related subject: trade, which can be considered as the flows of merchandise through transport systems. International trade has become a subject of intense public controversy as a result of recent world events that affect the economic welfare of nearly everyone. Of all the questions asked by academicians, political leaders, and citizens alike, the most fundamental are these:

Why trade? What do countries (or regions) gain from an exchange of goods? What determines the kinds of goods to be exchanged? How does trade affect the location of production? Addressing these questions at a time when the problems of trade are paramount in most people's thinking, we are reminded of the extent to which world prosperity is linked to the rapid rise in trade since World War II. As we see countries attempting to insulate themselves against political and economic events in the Middle East and other troubled parts of the world, we are led to ask additional questions: Why and how do governments interfere in trade? How do ideological differences affect trade? These matters of growing importance to nations are, of course, of at least equal concern to the companies directly engaged in exporting and importing and to the transport agencies that carry that trade.

Finally, in Chapter 10, we come to the subject of development, which has a bearing on all the topics considered thus far. Regardless of their particular levels of advancement, countries around the world present their governments with developmental problems. Planning officials and students alike are concerned with these questions: How do regions and nations grow and develop? More particularly, why do some grow faster than others? Is there a predictable sequence of events in the developmental process? What happens to agriculture, manufacturing, and trade as these changes occur? Is there a meaningful spatial pattern of countries (and regions) at various levels of development? Why do the disparities between rich countries and poor ones persist so tenaciously? We must gain some understanding of these things if we are to solve the many problems of areas that lag in their growth and development.

LOOKING FOR ANSWERS

In this preview of things to come, the reader will have noted that certain common elements have been constantly repeated. These repeated elements are fundamental to the analyses that follow. One common feature in all the subjects to be covered is the similar roles of the factors of production: capital, labor, and land (both in the sense of space occupied by an enterprise and as a source of raw materials). These factors combine in a variety of ways, and each economic activity has its own mixture of them. In addition, each activity usually presents a variety of ways in which these factors of production can be substituted for each other.

Another recurrent theme is the ordering effect of distance and transport cost, as these affect the accessibility of an activity to its sources of raw materials and energy and to labor and markets. Indeed, one modern writer (Isard, 1956) has devised a way to treat transport cost like one of the more traditional factors of production. Following his method, it is possible to substitute "transport inputs" directly for capital, labor, and raw materials (land) in the locational analysis. The role of distance is seen in several persistent tendencies that yield distinctive forms of spatial interaction. One of these is *focality*, the tendency for economic activities to focus upon some center of maximum intensity. Away from that center, the level of intensity decreases systematically with increasing distance in all directions. Another is *clustering*, the tendency of related activities to form concentrations within a limited area. In some cases even activities not functionally linked may be attracted to each other in this way. Spatial economic interaction thus assumes a number of characteristic forms.

It is our aim in this book to look for such commonalities: spatial regularities, repetitive elements, things that are true *most* of the time. These represent the first step toward understanding; they are essential for discovering answers sufficiently reliable for making useful predictions. Decision makers of all kinds must be able to anticipate with some degree of confidence the probable effects of their decisions. To the extent that we succeed in discovering commonalities, we are able to propose spatial theories: theories of the location of agriculture, manufacturing, and the services, theories of transportation and trade, and theories of the spatial dynamics of growth and development. As this suggests, by *theory* we simply mean generalized explanations of common underlying processes.

As an aid to understanding these ideas, we shall be examining each major topic in two parts. First we shall review some of the principal theories that have been developed as an explanation for the common locational tendencies of a given class of economic activities. We shall then note some representative examples of existing spatial patterns that express these common features in the economic environment around us. In each case the section devoted to real-world examples will present a number of empirical studies undertaken to test theoretical notions and will also provide a broad overview of spatial regularities to be found in the world patterns of each activity. This will give us an opportunity to see how well existing theories explain reality and to discover what is still lacking and in need of more study.

The main emphasis in this introductory text will be upon *economic* theories of location. This is not to deny the existence of some significant noneconomic elements in locational decision making. Undoubtedly some decisions are made without the benefit of full knowledge of all available alternatives; some are also influenced by such noneconomic considerations as cultural heritage, personal ties, and even personal whims. These noneconomic issues, however, present complications beyond the scope of this first book in location, particularly since the study of noneconomic locational influences is still in its initial phases. Thus far it has not progressed sufficiently to give rise to a cohesive theory that can be stated succinctly in these few pages.

Another reason for the emphasis of this book is that the economic factors in most cases provide a major part of the explanation. This is well illustrated by a study of the relationship between these two sets of locational considerations. In his analysis of agriculture in eight Swedish counties, Wolpert (1964) discovered that farmers of that region were not obtaining the full benefit possible from their holdings. By comparing the returns that could have been expected from optimal use of the land in each case with the kind of use to which it was actually put, he was able to measure the lost income that might be attributed to the human element in decision making. Despite the problems of disseminating knowledge of the latest agricultural technology throughout the region, together with the inertial effects of decision makers satisfied with the traditional ways of doing things, the average farmer was able to achieve two-thirds of the income of which his acreage was capable.

No doubt a similar study would show that farmers in the United States corn belt achieve an even higher percentage of potential earnings, considering the elaborate arrangements for spreading technical information in the region, the eagerness of farmers to accept new ideas in this area unencumbered by centuries of tradition, and the much greater capital investment at stake. If this is true of North American agriculture, where the family farm is still prevalent, a much closer approximation to optimality can surely be expected among corporate enterprises, whose management must annually confront a meeting of profit-hungry stockholders.

Finally, there is another set of reasons why the ultimate spatial form of the economic environment is unavoidably logical. Accumulated experience in the world of free enterprise has shown that personal considerations and mere whims can lead the decision maker only so far before disaster overtakes his enterprise. To the degree that the entrepreneur has incomplete information about his alternatives, this merely introduces a chance element into the undertaking; those who guess right have the greatest success and survive the longest. Every serious downturn in the business cycle produces an inexorable shake-out of enterprises that have suffered from economically unsound decision making. It should be emphasized again that the noneconomic elements should not be passed off as inconsequential; they are merely too complex for easy treatment, they need more study before they can be fully understood, and they provide a comparatively minor addition to the total explanation. Those persons wishing to read further on this subject, or on other topics introduced in this brief text, will find a number of additional readings listed at the end of the book.

LAND USE THEORY

One of the most basic of all geographical problems is how land is allocated among the many human activities competing for it. What is it that determines whether a given piece of land will be used for rural or urban purposes? If an urban activity is to occupy it, is there some way of predicting what kind this will be—retailing, manufacturing, wholesaling, or residential? If the plot of land is assigned to a rural use, what crops or animals will be produced there? Implicit in these questions is the assumption that there is some logic underlying the arrangement of land uses in earth space. In an effort to discover that logic and to answer the kinds of locational questions we have asked here, a growing body of land use theory has evolved.

As its name implies, this body of theory is focused upon land as a factor of production. In this context, land is regarded partly in terms of the amount of space that is occupied; but it is also viewed as a source of many of the things that human beings need, such as minerals and plant nutrients. This factor of production has a role in all economic activities. Each of these activities occupies at least some space, although some require more than others. As a whole, the greatest consumers of land are the rural forms of production, such as agriculture, grazing, and forestry. Urban functions usually occupy relatively much less space; but even for commercial, manufacturing, and residential uses land is an important consideration, in view of its scarcity in the crowded city environment.

Several general characteristics of land are important from the standpoint of location theory. One of these is its limited supply. In the world as a whole there is only so much land available for human use, and for this reason the would-be users of this land compete with each other for control of particular parcels, especially in fully occupied areas. Land may be viewed in terms of either *physical* space or *economic* space. Physical space refers to the total amount of land area that is available. In this sense, land has a fixed position in the earth's system of coordinates, and a given plot bears definite, unalterable distance and directional relationships to all other places on the globe.

Economic space refers to two characteristics—quality and location. Some sites enjoy special advantages with respect to quality that make them attractive to certain prospective users and consequently more valuable to them. In the case of rural activities, a given plot may be regarded more highly than others because it is capable of yielding a greater output at a lower production cost. Land *quality* is thus an expression of all those intrinsic physical attributes that affect productivity, including the nature of its soil, the configuration of the landscape, the presence of valuable rocks and minerals or of biotic resources, and prevailing climatic conditions. For its success, each of the primary activities requires land having specific qualities, some of which may be competitive with other desirable characteristics of the same plot. In central Illinois, for example, fertile soils are underlain by seams of valuable coal, the exploitation of which may preclude the use of that land for agricultural purposes. Generally speaking, human control over the quality of land is limited. In some instances man is able to alter or improve soils, to overcome diseases afflicting plant and animal life, or to restock biotic resources; but man cannot yet bring about a concentration of minerals or significantly alter climatic or weather conditions. Urban land uses are also affected by particular qualities of land, such as drainage conditions, climate, and slope; but, on the whole, the specific requirements of these activities are less demanding than those of primary forms of production.

Economic location refers to the utility of a piece of land because of its location in relation to other lands. Economic location is a function of accessibility, measured in terms of the cost, time, and effort required to reach a given spot. This characteristic is subject to change, however, as transport innovation in particular tends to alter distance relationships. Economic location also varies in importance with the type of activity. This is especially true of urban land uses, but it applies to rural uses as well. The effect of distance to market is felt differently by each branch of primary activity, owing to variations in the transportability of the product. Because it keeps well, wheat can be shipped by slower, relatively less expensive means than lettuce or fish; mineral ores require virtually no protection from the elements and can be shipped more cheaply than most food products. For this reason, some types of primary production are more strongly attracted to market than others. Distance and land quality may exert opposing locational pressures in a given instance, however, as in the case of vegetable production in California. There the advantages of climatic and soil conditions outweigh the cost of shipping produce to markets in the northeastern United States.

Agricultural land use theory originated in the nineteenth century, whereas the corresponding urban theory is a product of the twentieth. The two are closely related, however, since the basic problem is the same and so also is the approach to solving it. The main distinction is the greater complexity of the urban situation and the differing responses of various urban activities to the same influences. We shall, therefore, treat rural land use theory first, since the basic elements of the theory are more easily viewed in the relatively simpler agricultural context; afterwards we turn to the application of these ideas to the competition among land uses in the city.

THEORY OF RURAL LAND USE

The problem of agricultural location is affected by a number of characteristics peculiar to rural land use. Most forms of primary production, first of all, are *extensive* in their use of land; that is, they require large quantities of land relative to the other factors of production—labor and capital. Only a single type of rural land use can normally occupy a given plot at any one time, and a basic minimum area is required for each type. Space requirements are not the same for all primary activities, however. Forestry and fishing occur over great expanses of the earth's surface, as do the pastoral pursuits and such agricultural activities as commercial grain farming. Vegetable gardens, fruit orchards, and some kinds of mining, on the other hand, make small space demands. How extensively a given plot of land may be exploited for a particular purpose is subject to a certain amount of control on the part of the proprietor. He may choose to farm a small acreage of expensive land but fertilize it heavily and use efficient machinery or hire extra laborers in order to obtain a maximum output per acre. In effect, he is substituting capital and labor for land. There are economic and practical limits to the extent to which the farm manager can *intensify* his production in this manner, however, as will become apparent in the pages which follow.

SIZE OF ENTERPRISE

The *size of unit output* is another aspect of primary production that affects its character and location. By comparison with factories, the ordinary farm produces a very minute proportion of total world output. Since a given manufacturing establishment may account for a large percentage of the motorcars or washing machines entering the world market, the industrialist must take careful account of the effect his planning decisions may have upon the total supply of such products and thus upon the price structure. The farmer, however, knows that his output of wheat or corn represents only an insignificant part of all that is grown; he therefore ignores the effects that any change he may make in his own production will have upon the total. The same can be said of graziers, fishermen, and foresters, but it is less true of most mine operators, whose problem is usually similar to that of manufacturers.

Because of this the primary producer tends to adjust slowly to price changes, especially to falling prices; when he does react, he often does so excessively. The cumulative effect of all such producer decisions may be an alternation between periods of shortages and glutted markets, a problem that is particularly severe for many less developed countries. With all their vacillations, however, the markets for most primary commodities provide the nearest approach to perfect competition to be seen in the modern economic world. Another effect of small unit output is to limit the division of labor within an individual enterprise. It also tends to increase the importance of middlemen such as grain elevator operators, commodity traders in the great world market centers, and others who collect, store, or process primary goods and channel their flow to consumers.

NATURE OF DEMAND

Another problem for the agricultural producers is the *nature of demand* for food commodities. It has been found that as a population's income rises, there is a less than proportionate increase in the demand for food.* Even when there are changes in the demand for such commodities, the response of producers is tempered by the perishable nature of most foodstuffs, which require specialized transport equipment and elaborate marketing arrangements that cannot always be provided at will.

The location of primary production is further influenced by spatial variations in the character of demand. Consumption patterns of primary commodities reflect cultural, economic, and other human characteristics that differ from one place to another. Religious taboos, distinctions between rural and urban tastes, and differences in income and level of development all help to determine the location of production. If anything, the effect is more immediately apparent and the influence more direct in subsistence economies, where, for example, a preference for rice in a given district will produce a local emphasis upon that crop by the farmer consumers of the area.

SPECIALIZATION VERSUS DIVERSIFICATION

The tendency of certain agricultural enterprises to be either *specialized* or *diversified* in their output likewise affects location. Specialization, that is, concentrating upon the production of a single commodity, is advantageous to the entrepreneur because it permits him to acquire expert knowledge and experience in his chosen line and to benefit from the efficiency of specialized labor and machinery and well-organized marketing arrangements. Furthermore, he is able to

*See Chapter 10 for a discussion of Engel's law of consumption, which holds that poor families spend a larger proportion of their income on food than well-to-do families do.

produce that commodity for which his area is best suited by reason of climate, soils, and other physical factors. For some enterprises, however, diversification—obtaining several commodities from the same producing unit—is preferable. By not placing all his eggs in one basket the operator reduces the risk of total failure, is able to distribute his work load more evenly throughout the year, and obtains a steadier income. Another advantage of diversification is the saving in transport cost from a farmer's growing his own intermediate products such as field beets for feeding cattle or corn for fattening hogs. Moreover, by planting several crops in rotation he is able to maintain the fertility of his soil. If he is producing short-season crops such as vegetables, he may also be able to increase his income by growing more than one crop on the same plot in a single season.

NONECONOMIC INFLUENCES

Finally, there are several noneconomic considerations that are locationally important. Foremost among these is the human factor. Farm managers vary widely in their entrepreneurial skills, their motivations, and the extent of their knowledge. Some of them are swayed in their decisions by such things as custom and tradition, prejudice, and any number of other influences that prevent them from realizing the full potential of their land.

Governmental interference in the decision-making process of primary producers is another noneconomic influence that is playing an ever larger role. Agricultural and pastoral activities probably feel the impact of political measures more than most forms of primary production. Because these pursuits usually represent a way of life for the producers, they are hedged about by a multitude of traditional social attitudes, sentimental in nature and having much political potential. Moreover, governmental action for the protection of primary producers is sometimes regarded as necessary because, with their small unit output, they have a poor bargaining position against middlemen and may be forced to sell their products at widely fluctuating prices. To varying degrees, certain primary activities may be considered essential to the national welfare and thus subject to political intervention in the form of price controls, subsidies, quotas, tariffs, special credit arrangements, and other types of assistance and restriction.

DYNAMIC ASPECTS

Change is an ever present feature of primary production in technically advanced countries. Population growth, innovations in transportation, advances in production technology, and increases in real income are among the dynamic aspects affecting location. Better production techniques, for example, may make it possible to exploit mineral deposits, soils, or biotic resources that were previously regarded as useless; or they may increase the yields of old resources to such an extent as to decrease the area required for their exploitation. By reducing the cost of moving commodities to market, transport improvements may expand the area that can be profitably utilized. An areal expansion may also result from a rise in demand due either to population growth or to an increase in real per capita income.

Acceptance of change is not automatic, however, in any society. Resistance to new ideas is a common problem of underdeveloped regions, but inertia is far from unknown in even the most highly developed countries. Entrepreneurs may fail to take advantage of innovations because they already have too much invested in old machinery and equipment or simply because they have not managed to keep abreast of new developments. For this reason, contemporary patterns of production nearly always reflect in some measure the conditions of an earlier period as well as those of the present.

This list of locationally significant characteristics of rural land use, important as it is for understanding the locational problem, does not tell us how these features relate to each other nor does it explain how the allocation of rural land is ultimately determined. For this we turn to the location theorists, who have attempted to supply a logical answer to this question. Rural land use theory has tended to emphasize agricultural location, although grazing and forest-products industries have received some attention as well. By extension, however, agricultural land use theory can be applied to other primary activities as well.

CLASSICAL THEORY OF RURAL LAND USE

Agricultural land use theory has been centered upon the role of distance as a locational determinant. An important place in this theory has been given to the concept of rent as it varies from one place to another. This we might expect from the dominant position of land in the economics of agriculture. In common with other economic activities, the locational process in the field of agriculture can be observed at any of three levels: (1) the individual establishment, (2) all establishments producing a given commodity or combination of commodities, or (3) all establishments producing all commodities and combinations. Agricultural theory has traditionally been concerned with the two higher levels of aggregation, which make for easier generalization. In the usual approach to the agricultural location problem, it has been assumed that the operators already occupy their sites and are to select that land use which will yield the maximum return for each unit of area. The entrepreneur is regarded as an "economic man," having a perfect knowledge of all the alternatives open to him and always acting in his own economic best interests. Recognizing that the real situation contains too many variables for simultaneous comprehension by the human mind, the theorist usually begins with the simplest case, an idealized situation which provides laboratory conditions similar to those under which the chemist works. Thus only the variables which are thought to be most important are considered at first, all others being held constant by means of limiting assumptions to achieve a closer approximation to the complexity of the real world.

The starting place of the theory of agricultural location, and indeed of all location theory, is the work of Johann Heinrich von Thünen (1783–1850). From his experience as a farmer on the north German plain, Thünen had observed cases where two plots of land in different locations but similar in their physical characteristics would be used for unlike purposes. Suspecting that such incongruities might be caused by differences in length of haul to market, he set out to determine the role of distance in forming the rural land use pattern. Specifically, he wished to find laws governing the interaction of agricultural prices, distance, and land use as farmers sought to maximize their income.

Rent Thünen began his analysis by setting up a case in which the only variable was distance to market; all else was at first restrained by simplifying assumptions. The model he conceived consisted of a country having no connections with the rest of the world and occupying a level plain with uniform soils and climate. Centered on the plain was the only urban market in the country, a city situated in the midst of salt and iron mines and surrounded by agricultural and grazing lands. There was complete interdependence between the urban center and the rural territory tributary to it. The city supplied manufactured goods to the rural inhabitants and served as their market, while the farmers and graziers provided the food required by the urban dwellers. The rural territory was encompassed by a wilderness occupying land identical in its physical characteristics to that which was inhabited. This wilderness was presumably used only for hunting and trapping, but it could provide room for expansion of the production area if food requirements of the "isolated state" should grow. Transport facilities were uniform throughout the plain, and thus all parts of the state had equal access. This condition resulted from the absence of improved arterial routes and the fact that all goods were moved by horse-drawn carts or human porters, or transported themselves. Finally, Thünen stipulated that agricultural labor should everywhere be uniform in its productivity and cost, with equal real wages prevailing in all parts of the state. He considered such wages to represent either the payment made to hired workers or an equivalent amount paid by the farmer to himself for his own work.

    With the assumptions implicit in the above, Thünen managed to eliminate a number of variables that complicate the real world. The effects of international trade he removed by isolating his state from other countries, and distortions caused by competition among domestic trading centers he eliminated by having only a single urban center. He disposed of variations in production expense by assuming a uniform physical environment and equal labor costs. Differences in access to market for reasons other than distance he removed by means of a uniform transport system, the primitive nature of which resulted in a transport cost directly proportionate to distance. Thus the city's rural tributary territory was initially uniform throughout except for distance from the market center. Despite this uniformity, however, variations in transport cost from one location produced a differentiated land use pattern. Transport cost in this case reflected not only the expense of overcoming the friction of distance to the market but also the bulk, weight, and perishability of the commodities moved.

It was through the rent mechanism that transport cost influenced the spatial pattern of land use. As the income to the principal factor of primary production, land, rent played a central part in the Thünen scheme, just as it does in modern agricultural location theory. According to this view, the spatial pattern of agricultural production results from a process of competitive bidding among prospective rural land uses for occupancy of a given site. That type of production which is capable of yielding the highest net return per unit of land on a particular parcel of ground will make the highest bid for the use of that plot. Land uses unsuccessful in their bid for the first piece of land will be relegated to other locations, where they in turn are able to make the highest bid. Note carefully that it is the net return (income less expense) per *unit of land* (acre, hectare, etc.) upon which calculations are based, not the income per bushel or other measure of weight or volume.

At this point, it is important to specify what Thünen and other theorists mean by rent. The rent of common usage is more properly designated *contract rent*, that is, an amount actually paid by a tenant for the use of property belonging to someone else and in accordance with mutually agreeable terms contracted between them. The kind of rent to which Thünen referred was more specific— *economic rent*, which is *the surplus of income accruing to a unit of land above the minimum income required to bring a unit of new land into use at the margin of production*. At the margin, land is capable of yielding a return just sufficient to cover expenses. Land bearing a heavier burden of cost or having a lower income-producing capacity than that at the margin will not be used, whereas land having cost or income-yielding advantages superior to those of the marginal land will earn a surplus. The difference between the income-earning potential of one piece of ground and another may result from variations in fertility, distance from market, or any of several other possible distinctions.* In the Thünen model, of course, the difference is distance.

To illustrate this concept, we may take the example of an area producing only one commodity, wheat, the price of which is set in the marketplace by the interaction of supply and demand. A farmer's income per acre is therefore equivalent to the amount received in the market for the wheat grown on that acre minus (1) the cost of production per acre and (2) the cost of transporting that quantity of wheat to the market. It is apparent that in a one-crop case there is at any given point in time only one quantity that varies, namely, the cost of transporting the product to market. Since the farmer near the city pays less transport expense than one at the outer limit of production, his net return per acre is greater, the difference being *economic rent* (see Figure 2-1). This condition is apparent to all other farmers, however, and they bid up the amount they will pay for the use of land closest to the market. Thus the competition for the more desirable locations causes the income differential to be eliminated as the nearer land becomes correspondingly costlier. In this manner, economic rent is converted into ordinary contract rent.

---

*Ricardo is credited with having originated the concept of economic rent based on fertility differentials.

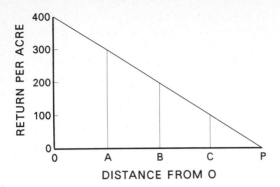

FIGURE 2-1 ECONOMIC RENT.

Economic rent can be calculated by the following formula (Dunn, 1954, p. 7):

$$R = E(p - a) - Efk$$

where

> R = rent per unit of land
> k = distance to market
> E = output per unit of land
> p = market price per unit of commodity
> a = production cost per unit of commodity (including the farmer's payments to himself for his own labor)
> f = transport rate per unit of distance per unit of commodity

If in the previous example we assume that a wheat farmer located 25 miles from market obtains a yield of 60 bushels per acre, has production expenses of 75 cents per bushel, pays 3 cents per mile to transport the grain to market, and receives a market price of $2 per bushel, then the economic rent accruing to an acre of that farmer's land can be derived by substituting in the formula as follows:

$$R = 60(\$2.00 - \$0.75) - 60(\$0.03 \times 25)$$
$$= \$75 - \$45$$
$$= \$30$$

Rings If we extend the above argument to a case where several crops or systems are in competition for use of the land, we can see how a differentiated pattern of agricultural and pastoral production evolves. Through the bidding process described earlier, the most desirable land nearest the market is preempted by those crops or agricultural systems capable of extracting the highest return from it. The progressively cheaper land at a greater distance is less demanding and is consequently relegated to uses that cannot compete for the prime locations near the market. The result is a zonation of production which, under conditions of uniformity, assumes the form of concentric rings around the urban center.

Figure 2-2 illustrates this ring formation with a hypothetical case in which three land uses compete for space. Potatoes, having a high yield per acre and commanding a good price in the market, would in this example yield the highest economic rent per acre ($600) if grown immediately adjacent to the center. This bulky product, however, is expensive to ship, as indicated by the steep decline in its economic rent curve with distance from market. Consequently, it is feasible to grow potatoes only to point *R* on the diagram. Wheat has a per acre yield lower than that of potatoes, providing an economic rent of only $400 if grown at the market. Although wheat is thus unable to compete for the close-in area, it is nevertheless cheaper to ship than potatoes and its economic rent line is therefore less steep. For this reason wheat becomes more profitable than potatoes at point *A* (even though potatoes could yield a net return as far out as *R*) and remains so until *S* is reached. If produced at the market, wool and mutton would provide only $100 per acre in economic rent; however, the wool is relatively light in weight, the sheep can walk to market, and the transport costs of this type of land use are consequently less than those of either potatoes or wheat. Beyond point *B*, then, grazing becomes the dominant land use, occupying the remainder of the land to the margin of the productive area at *P*. If, in this three-dimensional drawing, the figure *OPL* is rotated about its vertical axis *OL*, we see the creation of three concentric zones of land use about the market at *O*. In general, we may note that the slope of the rent line is affected by the cost of transportation, determined by relative bulk and weight in this case, but also subject to influence by other considerations such as perishability.

FIGURE 2-2   FORMATION OF LAND-USE ZONES AROUND A CENTRAL MARKET.

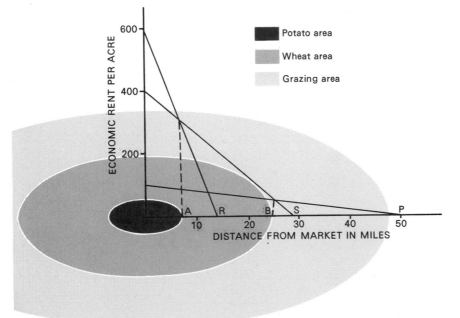

Intensity Another important aspect of Thünen's model has to do with the locational effects of variations in intensity. It will be recalled that the producer can increase the amounts of capital and labor (the variable factors) that he applies to a unit of land (the fixed factor) and thereby increase his output. Thus a farmer may intensify his operations by using more capital in the form of machinery, fertilizer, herbicides, or insecticides or more labor for soil preparation, weeding, thinning, or selective harvesting of crops. In areas of diversified farming, a common method of varying intensity is the use of rotation systems in which more or less land is devoted to the main cash crop—for example, corn in the midwestern United States or wheat or barley in Western Europe. In this case the result is reflected in the output of the major crop obtained from the total acreage of a particular farm.

If farmers can increase their output, and hence their gross return, in this manner, it may be asked why all farmers do not intensify their production to the fullest extent. The answer is that there are some practical limits to this expedient; variable factors can be added in increasing amounts only up to a certain level. Beyond that point, total output does not grow sufficiently to pay for the additional inputs and, indeed, may well begin to decline as workers become so numerous that they get in each other's way, too many machines pack the soil, or excessive concentrations of fertilizer poison the crop. This limitation on the intensity of land use is referred to as the *law of diminishing returns* or, sometimes, the *law of diminishing marginal productivity*.

How this principle works is illustrated in Figure 2-3. In this example a farmer begins by applying two units of capital and labor to an acre of land and is able to harvest 5 bushels of wheat. Next season he tries four units of variable inputs on his acre and is rewarded with 17 bushels, an increase (marginal physical product) of 12 bushels. Overjoyed, he then applies six units of capital and labor for a 16-bushel increase in output (plotted as the marginal physical product curve). The following year he uses eight units of variable inputs but is disappointed with an increased

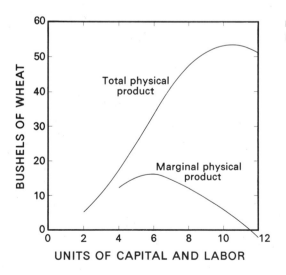

FIGURE 2-3 LAW OF DIMINISHING RETURNS.

output of only 12 bushels. Diminishing returns have begun to set in, as can be seen by the downturn in the marginal physical product curve. Undiscouraged, he then tries ten units, but output rises by only 6 bushels. The next year, using twelve units of capital and labor actually results in a 2-bushel drop in output. The added fertilizer and manpower have actually reduced the farmer's yield, and the marginal physical product curve has accordingly dropped below zero.

So long as this principle is expressed only in units of output (bushels of wheat), all farmers of a given region are affected equally under the uniform conditions we have assumed. If, however, we take into account that after paying transport costs the farmer close to market receives a higher net or "farm gate" price than the more distant farmer, then we find that the law of diminishing returns affects each differently. It can be shown that the most favorable level of intensity is much lower for the farmer receiving the lowest farm gate price than for one receiving a higher price. In other words, the farmer close to market can produce the same crop more intensively than one at a distance can. Likewise, in an area of diversified farming the most intensive farming systems are nearest the market. Since a greater unit output means that more of the crop has to be transported per acre, the rent curves of the more intensive systems are steeper than the others.

It should be noted that these comments on the locational effects of intensity can be applied with certainty only to comparisons of different ways of growing the *same* crop or combination of crops. They cannot be used for comparing very different kinds of operations, such as wheat farming and vegetable farming. The reason for this is that, as we have observed previously, the slope of the rent curve is also affected by differences in transport rates due to the characteristics of particular crops. All we can safely say is that crop or crop system with the steeper rent curve will always be closer to market.

Thünen's application Thus, Thünen's ideal state assumed the form of concentric zones of rural land use surrounding the urban market. The hypothetical rural pattern derived in this manner was composed of crops and other forms of land use then typical of his own district on the north German plain, as were the physical and technological conditions that provided the setting for them. He recognized that another environment could produce a different set of results, but he maintained that the fundamental principles were generally applicable.

Employing the assumptions listed earlier, Thünen derived the pattern of land use shown in Figure 2-4. The first ring was devoted to what he termed "free cash cropping," that is, *market gardening* and *fluid milk production*. Because of their highly perishable nature, fresh vegetables had to be grown as close as possible to the market, where they could be taken promptly and in prime condition. This type of agriculture, with its large output of valuable produce per acre, yielded a high return but incurred heavy transport costs. Consequently, its rent curve dropped very steeply away from the urban center.

Forest products occupied the second ring. From a modern viewpoint, this would appear to be a peculiar use for such expensive land. In Thünen's time, and under the assumptions prevailing in the isolated state, however, this was logical,

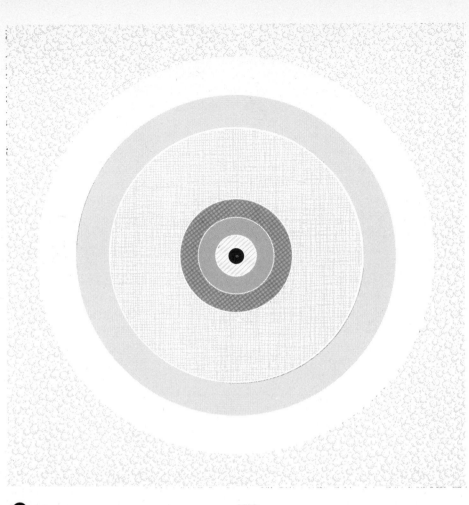

- ● The town
- ⬚ Horticulture and dairying
- ▨ Forestry
- ▨ Crop rotation without fallow
- ▦ Crop rotation with fallow
- ▨ Three-field system
- ☐ Grazing
- ☐ Wilderness

FIGURE 2-4 THÜNEN'S ISOLATED STATE: INITIAL ASSUMPTIONS.

especially since wood was the principal fuel and the basic raw material for building construction. Moreover, because it was exceedingly bulky and costly to ship by the primitive transport media upon which the country depended, the rent curve for this type of land use dropped quickly away from the center. Low production cost added further to the feasibility of tree farming in this ring. Thünen was able to confirm from his own calculations the logic of such a location in nineteenth-century Germany.

Rings 3, 4, and 5 were all used for crop rotation systems, the chief cash crop in each case being rye. The three rings differed from one another mainly in the intensity of their cultivation, which diminished outward from the center. As intensity of cultivation in the three zones decreased outward from the city, there was a corresponding drop in production costs per acre, especially in labor requirements, thereby compensating for the additional transport-cost burden of these outlying areas. Thus in the Thünen model there was a substitution of costs, with transport cost replacing production costs.

In the most distant part of the ideal state, the sixth ring was allocated principally to *livestock ranching*. Cash income was derived mainly from the sale of animal products in the "town." Unlike the bulky and perishable animal products of the first ring, however, these were highly transportable types such as butter and cheese, meat animals, and presumably wool. Crops grown in this remote region were partly for the feeding of the human and animal populations of the area, but they also included a number of industrial crops. Locally produced grain, for example, was converted into alcohol, which is high in value and greatly condensed in volume. Other industrial crops were flax fiber, clover seed, and oil seeds, all cheaply transported to market. Then, as today, the grazing industries and industrial crop production were pushed into more distant areas by other forms of production that could outbid them for the better locations. On its outer extremity, this sixth zone was bounded by the *wilderness*, a resource that could be exploited at some future time when the demand for agricultural commodities in the town should require an outward expansion of the productive area.

Thus we have the isolated state of Thünen with its concentric pattern of land use resulting from the variation of only a single element—distance from market. As a practical farmer, Thünen was fully aware of the multitude of other variables affecting the spatial arrangement of the rural landscape. By relaxing his original limiting assumptions one at a time, he next proceeded to add new ingredients to his test-tube situation to see how each would alter the rings.

Modifications to the classical model Among the more restrictive of Thünen's original simplifying assumptions were those which specified equal access to all parts of the state. Thünen himself noted the potentially distorting effect of such arterial routes as navigable waterways, improved roads, and railways, and he proceeded to relax his initial transport assumption. Observing that important cities generally have access to navigable water, he introduced a stream into his isolated state. Thünen's conception of the alterations this would make in the original pattern appears in Figure 2-5. Because agricultural commodities could be hauled directly to the river's edge and thence moved to the town by inexpensive barge or boat, each zone of production became elongated in a direction roughly parallel to the stream. Note that zone 1 was least changed in shape. A horse-drawn or poled barge was no faster than wagon transportation, and the water route was thus of little benefit to growers of perishables, for whom the important factor was time.

In Thünen's modified state the wood zone extended in a narrow band for some distance in each direction from the city, but it no longer enclosed zone 1 on the landward sides. Because the transport cost of wood was very high in relation to its

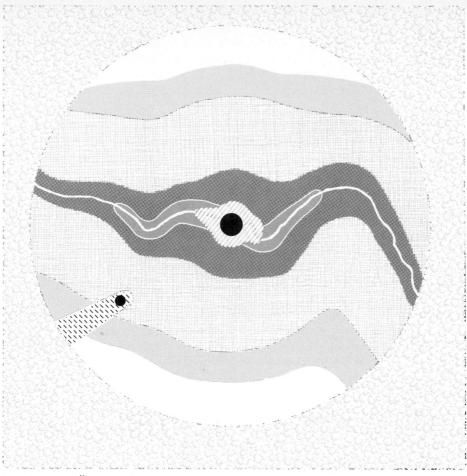

FIGURE 2-5 THÜNEN'S ISOLATED STATE: EFFECTS OF NAVIGABLE WATERWAY AND SATELLITE TOWN.

value, the riverside location had a particularly strong attraction for this form of production, as it does in modern Canada and Brazil. Indeed, it is probable that Thünen underestimated this effect. Rather than approaching close to the town, it seems more likely that the woodlots would have been situated at some distance upstream and downstream. Moreover, since there was demand in the city for only a finite amount of agricultural produce, we might expect the zones of production to become narrowed and the isolated state as a whole to assume an attenuated shape. Both of these modifications appear in Figure 2-6.

Although Thünen did little more than acknowledge the possibility of adding rail and highway routes to his state, we may consider their probable effects. As in the case of water transportation, arterial land routes would have caused the zones of production to be stretched out lengthwise parallel to the movement of traffic, as

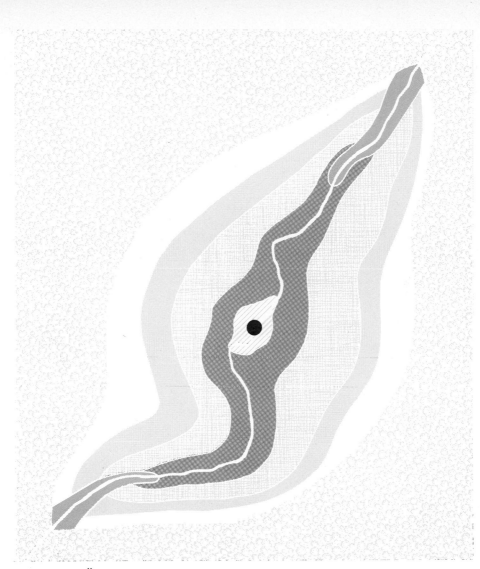

FIGURE 2-6 THÜNEN'S ISOLATED STATE: MODIFIED SHAPE AND NEW LOCATION OF FORESTRY.

seen in Figure 2-7. A further modification could have been expected where access points, such as rail sidings (or expressway interchanges in modern times), were widely separated along the route. Under these circumstances we might have found the development of Thünen rings, or at least supply areas of some dominant crop, centering upon each point of entry. Evidence of this is to be found in western Anglo-America, where wheat production focuses upon elevators positioned at intervals along the railways.

Another of the original assumptions that Thünen subsequently removed was

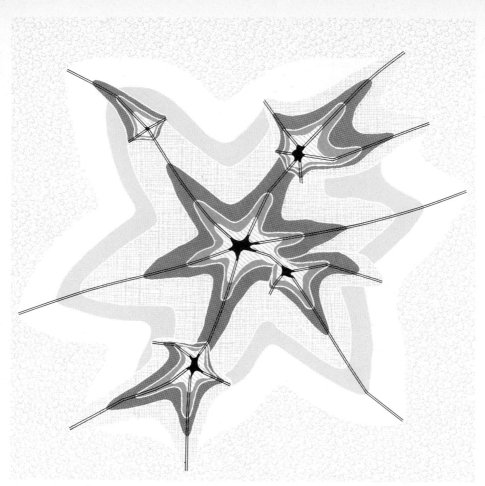

FIGURE 2-7 THÜNEN'S ISOLATED STATE: SEVERAL COMPETING CENTERS AND ARTERIAL ROAD SYSTEM.

the provision of only one urban market. His conception of the changes a second populated place would cause is shown in Figure 2-5. Because of the small size of his satellite, it had only a small tributary area, apparently with production of the zone 1 type. According to Thünen, the supply area of this village would have been elongated away from the major center, much like the tail of a comet, reflecting the lower level of demand and consequently of prices for locally grown produce in the smaller place. If several larger satellites had appeared on the plain, the resulting pattern of agricultural production would probably have looked more like that of Figure 2-7, which allocates a greater variety of crops to each satellite. In this example the tributary areas vary considerably in size, reflecting differences in population. Observe also that the agricultural supply areas dependent upon smaller urban places are in some cases completely enveloped by the areas served by the major center.

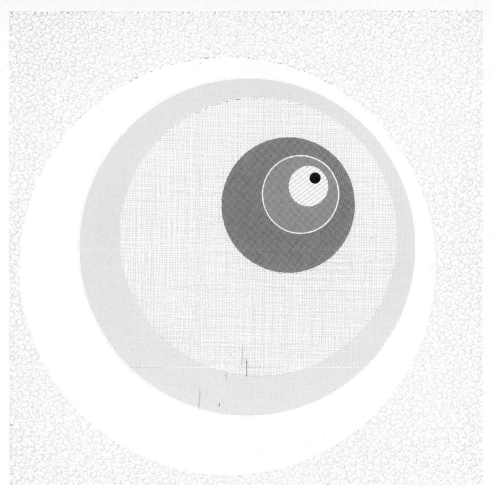

FIGURE 2-8 THÜNEN'S ISOLATED STATE: VARIABLE PRODUCTION COSTS.

In order to eliminate spatial variations in production costs, Thünen initially assumed a uniform physical environment and constant labor costs. He subsequently contemplated the effects of differing climates, soils, topography, and labor. If one part of a region enjoys more favorable conditions than another—whether because of lower wages, more efficient workers, richer soils, flatter, better-drained land, or other advantages—we should expect the zones of land use to be broadened as in the lower left-hand quadrant of Figure 2-8. In an area having rough terrain or some other production cost disadvantage, some land use zones would probably contract or disappear altogether. The upper right-hand quadrant of the figure illustrates such a condition.

Among other modifications Thünen considered was the introduction of foreign trade, taxes, and subsidies. Although these variables are too complex for adequate treatment here, we may note briefly a few of their possible effects. For example, rising foreign demand for a particular crop would likely expand the area of its cultivation, an effect produced in the wheat-growing regions of Anglo-America by the world grain shortages of the mid-1960s. Conversely, a crop experiencing heavy import competition would probably suffer a contraction of the area devoted to its domestic cultivation. If a protective tariff were to be imposed upon such imports (see Chapter 9), thereby curtailing the supply from abroad, the cultivated area should return to its former size. Subsidy payments aiding a particular type of production may be used by governments either to increase the area under that crop or to restrict it. An example of the latter was the United States soil bank program, which compensated farmers for retiring land from production. Taxes could be expected to have the effect of reducing the cropped area generally, whether or not the farmer was able to pass the tax on to the consumer.

One final feature of Thünen's theory that should not be overlooked is his treatment of the spatial patterns within individual farms. There he found the influence of distance much the same as at the national level. In the isolated state the price of a commodity was set in the marketplace, but transport charges were deducted from that figure before it reached the farmer's hands. A farmer's transport costs did not end at his front gate, however; he also had to bear the cost of daily trips between farmstead and fields. The result noted by Thünen was a tendency for more intensive, high-value production to occur near the farmstead and for those land uses requiring less attention to take place in the more distant fields.

Evaluation of the classical model   Some criticism of Thünen's contribution comes from persons who misunderstand its purpose and methodology. As a result, they interpret his ideas too literally, believing that his concentric pattern must be duplicated everywhere in all its original detail or forfeit its validity for this present age. Others are too impressed by his initial assumption to pursue the argument to the point where he relaxes those assumptions.

Nevertheless, theoreticians agree that Thünen's work contains a number of defects. Even though his basic principles are widely accepted, it is felt that he erred in certain particulars. Some writers believe that Thünen's thinking was affected by his personal involvement in managing a particular enterprise and that he was thus too caught up in the details of his own business. This preoccupation with his own empirical data, it is thought, prevented him from developing a complete general theory of agricultural location and carrying his argument to its final conclusion. Thus he neglected to develop a definite principle for locating the boundary between adjacent rings of land use and he was not sufficiently explicit on the basis for determining the content of each ring. His comments on the relationship between bulk or weight and value of product were especially vague.

Some feel that Thünen was mistaken in neglecting the effects of length of haul on transport rates. Although those effects might not have been important for the primitive transport media he chose for his model, the railway age had arrived at the time he was writing and the changes it was bringing to the transport rate structure could have altered his production rings. In common with other agricultural theorists, including more recent writers, Thünen also did not take sufficient account of procurement costs, such as those for machinery, equipment, and various other manufactured goods purchased from the city (although he did include one such input—the fertilizer used in his first ring). However, this was much less of a consideration in his day than it is now.

Reservations have been expressed concerning his assumption that all farmers in the isolated state were intent upon maximizing their incomes. In fact, only the better-trained, more highly motivated operators have such goals; many of the rest desire only to continue in their inherited way of life, satisfied with less than their full capabilities, and placing more importance on leisure. Moreover, there is customarily a lag in the dissemination of information, causing a delayed adjustment to change. Indeed, inertia could prevent the appearance of any sort of spatial order if it were not for the fact that continued change may forcibly bring the farmer's attention to the need to alter his methods or lose his capacity to support his family and himself. Most rural communities provide examples of inefficient farmers who are eliminated in the struggle for survival in a dynamic modern world. It is because of the human factor that borders between belts of production tend to be blurred, forming transition zones rather than lines. Although this is an important consideration in the analysis of any locational problem, we cannot fault Thünen for omitting from his model this complex factor so difficult to measure.

EXTENSIONS TO THE CLASSICAL MODEL

The errors and omissions time has revealed in Thünen's work detract but little from the total worth of his ideas, which were very advanced for the age in which he lived. His conception of economic rent as the basic determinant of the agricultural pattern underlies the work of many modern writers, who have continued to build on the foundation he laid. Some have further developed the theory by verifying, clarifying, and extending Thünen's notions; others have applied this modified theory to empirical situations in order to test and refine it further.

One of the most influential classical theorists of the present century was Theodor Brinkmann, whose ideas anticipated much of the work of later writers in this field (Brinkmann, 1935). He examined the effects of increasing the demand for agricultural products, changing technology, and differences in entrepreneurial qualities.

An increase in the demand for agricultural products would force the urban population to draw upon an area of greater radius for its agricultural needs. Such a rise in demand could result from an increase in population size or from rising per capita incomes, although he observed that the effects of income changes are limited by the operation of Engel's law. Demand also would be affected by removing the assumption of the region's isolation from the outside world, which would then permit foreign trade. Increased exports of agricultural goods would cause a rise in their prices and a corresponding expansion of the rings in which they were produced.

An increase in the general level of technology would bring a number of changes having an impact upon agriculture in particular. For one thing, there would be a higher degree of processing of farm commodities. Farmers would also be adversely affected by the substitution of industrial commodities for agricultural raw materials (as, for example, the substitution of nylon yarn for cotton or linen). The introduction of mechanical energy would influence farming operations as tractors displace animal power, eliminating the need for large acreages of such animal feed grains as oats. The separation of conversion activities from the farm would also increase. Thus with the introduction of centrally located creameries farmers would no longer churn their own butter but instead would have to ship their milk or cream in the liquid (and more perishable and bulky) state.

Certain technological advances would affect farming techniques directly. There are several kinds of agricultural innovations, and each has its own effects. Some reduce production costs, resulting, in the end, mainly in benefits to consumers in the form of lower prices for agricultural goods. Others increase the yield per acre, which tends to increase the attraction of the market for any type of production so affected. Finally, there is the introduction of labor-saving devices. Brinkmann observed that as agricultural technology advances, there is a general tendency for an increased substitution of capital for labor, since simple farming techniques emphasize the use of human labor while more advanced methods make greater use of capital.

Some of the most profound changes in agricultural location have resulted from innovations in transport technology. These changes have included a long-term downward trend in transport rates, the introduction of cheaper transport media, increased speed of haulage, and the invention of specialized equipment. Brinkmann noted that the general effect of transport innovation has been to level out regional differences, especially in the farm gate prices received by farmers. This proportionately reduces the force of the market attraction for agricultural production and brings a corresponding drop in the slopes of the rent curves. As transport costs thus become relatively less, other locational influences gain accordingly in importance. This is especially true of differences in soils, slope, climate, and other physical conditions, which become increasingly important in locational decisions. Some products benefit more than others from certain transport innovations. Perishable goods especially have gained in transportability through such innovations as refrigerated ships, trucks, and railway cars. This has enormously extended the range of some types of production, as shown by the large exports of butter, cheese, and chilled meats from New Zealand to the United Kingdom.

In his treatment of differences in entrepreneurial qualities, Brinkmann antici-pated many of the ideas that have gained prominence in recent times. Removing Thünen's economic-man assumption, he found, helps to account for a number of seemingly irrational locational decisions. Many farmers are impelled by noneco-nomic motives, some accept new ideas more quickly than others, and certain of them are more affected by tradition and custom. The farm operator who is more highly motivated or more skilled than his neighbors may be able to increase his net return by finding ways to reduce production costs or by obtaining higher prices for his merchandise through exceptional bargaining skills. Some types of farming—dairying, for example—call for greater managerial skills than others; but Brinkmann found that farmers tend to gravitate toward those types of production that best fit their individual capabilities. He showed further that the greatest opportunities for the exercise of individual initiative are in those areas closest to the market or where physical conditions are best. The superior manager enjoys what Brinkmann calls "entrepreneurial profits," extra income due to his greater-than-average skills. Such an individual also has a wider latitude of choice in selecting a location for his farming operations than ordinary farmers do.

CONTEMPORARY MODELS OF RURAL LAND USE

The classical model has a number of features that remain useful to the modern analyst; hence its persistence as a tool for teaching and research. Nevertheless, it has its limitations (Harvey, 1966, pp. 364–365), due especially to some of its underlying assumptions. One of these is the implicit idea that technological changes bring immediate and automatic adjustments in the land use pattern. The classical model also ignores the ways in which unit costs may be affected by changing market size. Most disturbing of all has been the assumption that all farm operators are economic men. To the extent that this is not the case, the usefulness of the classical model as a means for predicting the effects of change has been reduced. For these and other reasons, therefore, several promising alternative approaches to the agricultural location problem have recently been developed.

Interregional equilibrium models One way of explaining spatial variations in the use of land is to look upon the various regions and localities as areal units engaged in producing and exchanging goods with each other. This approach is borrowed from trade theory (Ohlin, 1933), which holds that each district will concentrate upon producing and exporting those commodities for which it has the greatest advantage relative to other areas and that it will import those goods for which its advantages are relatively less. This comparative advantage may be due, for example, to superior soils, climate, or labor skills, or it may be due to lower costs of various kinds.

Analyzing a locational problem from this viewpoint inevitably requires the introduction of a great many variables relating to the characteristics of the regions involved. These include such things as population size, per capita income, yields, joint products, production costs, and transport costs. A technique that has proved especially useful in such analyses is linear programming. This is a mathematical technique that sets some specific goal, such as maximizing profits or minimizing costs, and makes a number of assumptions about such things as expected changes in demand, costs, and other conditions at some future date (see, for example, Judge and Wallace, 1958; Heady and Skold, 1965; Skold and Heady,

1966). In addition to solving the main maximization or minimization problem, linear programming produces a second, or dual, solution that can be interpreted as a measure of economic rent at each location (Stevens, 1961, 1968). This technique has proved especially valuable for predicting land use patterns. However, like the classical model, to which it bears a close conceptual relationship, it is deterministic; that is, it describes conditions as they "ought" to be. To many modern theorists this is still inadequate, since it does not give sufficient weight to the human element.

Nondeterministic models Mainly as a response to the need for a more realistic treatment of the locational effects of human differences, several nondeterministic approaches have been introduced with some success. Behavioral models drop the assumption that farmers are economic men motivated by the desire to maximize their profits and possessed of a full range of skills and a complete knowledge of alternatives. Wolpert's studies of Swedish farmers, for example, attempted to measure the locational effects of human behavioral characteristics (Wolpert, 1964). In this work he distinguished between those farmers who were merely "satisficers," that is, satisfied with less than the maximum possible income, and those classed as "optimizers," who sought to obtain as much income as they could.

Some theorists have stressed the way in which an innovation in agricultural techniques spreads through a farming population (Hägerstrand, 1952, 1953, 1969). Certain individuals ordinarily receive ideas before others, owing to superior access to information, better education, greater alertness, or other circumstances. Such persons in turn spread the word to those with whom they come into contact until the innovation comes to be accepted by most of the population.

Other writers have been concerned with the problems of uncertainty that confront the farmer and the ways in which he copes with these. He must consider the effects of unpredictable weather conditions, fluctuating market prices, and a number of other circumstances that he cannot accurately foresee. Keeping in mind the growing requirements and the range of possible prices and yields of the crops that his land is capable of producing, he must plot a strategy that gives him the greatest probability of succeeding against these uncertainties. The approach used by theorists for solving this problem is referred to as "game theory."

In the next chapter we shall examine some of the real-world evidence of the operation of some of the forces basic to the classical model of land use, together with certain applications of the contemporary models. First, however, let us consider briefly how some of these ideas apply to other forms of primary production.

LOCATION OF OTHER PRIMARY ACTIVITIES

For the most part, rural land use theory is still directed mainly toward the location of agriculture, including animal industries. Although Thünen included a forest-products zone in his isolated state, this was actually a form of tree farming rather than forestry of the usual sort. The locational problems of primary activities other than agriculture have thus been neglected by most theorists; but existing theory nevertheless has considerable applicability to most of the extractive industries, including mining, fishing, and forest products.

How some of these concepts can be used for analyzing the location of mining is suggested by Figure 2-9. In the drawing, three mineral deposits A, B, and C are shown at varying distances from the market O. We may presume that the mineral is iron ore and that deposit A is in eastern Pennsylvania, B is in Minnesota, and C is in Venezuela, and that the market is represented by steel mills at Pittsburgh.

At an initially low level of demand for steel, the nearby Pennsylvania ore deposits are adequate to supply the needs of the mill. At this level of operations the transport cost curve RS shows that it would be economically feasible to go as far from the mills as point S for ore. Subsequently, however, the demand for steel rises to the point that the supply of ore in Pennsylvania is not sufficient. A shortage develops and the price of iron ore rises. This is reflected in an upward and parallel shift in the transport cost curve to R'S', which now permits exploitation of the more distant Minnesota deposits at B. At a still later date, important innovations in the transporting of ore are introduced, perhaps efficient new bulk carriers with automatic loading equipment. The reduced unit costs of ore haulage are reflected in a decrease in the slope of the transport cost curve to R" S". As shown in Figure 2-9, the drop in transport costs is so great as to permit ore to be obtained at delivered prices even lower than before. Equally important, the margin for ore procurement is extended outward to make it possible to tap new sources of the mineral at C.

Although the case illustrated here considers only the effects of transport cost at various distances, the analysis could be altered to take into account differences among the competing deposits in the quality of their ores and in the costs of extracting and processing them. The point to be emphasized is that if all ores are of the same quality, the nearest deposits will be exploited first, but the range of

FIGURE 2-9 TRANSPORT COST AND MINERAL EXPLOITATION.

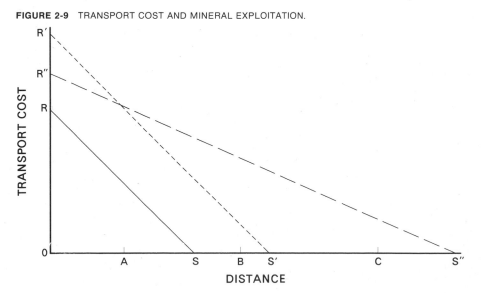

procurement can be extended by a rise in demand (and thus market price) or by a reduction in transport costs or by a combination of these.

If, on the other hand, quality varies widely, nearby poorer deposits would still be used first should the slope of the transport rate curve be particularly great. As the slope falls, differences in the quality of deposits assume an increasing relative importance, making more distant high-grade ores more attractive. This is seen in the large-scale development of rich iron deposits as remote from markets as those of Liberia and Sierra Leone in West Africa or even those of western Australia. This principle is analogous to the agricultural location problem, where physical differences, such as variations in soils or climatic conditions, become relatively more important locational determinants as transport costs decline.

By extension, these same ideas can be applied to forestry, as shown by the increasing exploitation of forest resources of Central America, Brazil, and Borneo in competition with more accessible areas. Similarly, we may point to the fact that the fishing banks off the coasts of the heavily populated eastern United States, Western Europe, and Japan are rapidly becoming depleted as a result of overfishing, while rich banks off the southern shores of Africa and South America receive little attention.

URBAN LAND USE

Most of the discussion concerning the theory of rural land use has revolved around a market mechanism and the competition of various potential users of land for specific locations. This approach has been developed by a number of writers concerning urban land use in an attempt to discern those forces that may explain the processes by which certain locations within an urban area are occupied by certain economic activities (Wingo, 1961; Alonso, 1964; Lowry, 1964; Nourse, 1968). The market approach builds directly upon the rural land use models discussed in the previous section, but, as has been succinctly expressed by Bourne (1971, p. 133), this is but one approach and, by itself, it is limited. A second approach is concerned with the behavior and decision-making processes of the population residing in the urban area, and these many and varied decision-making processes result in patterns and intensities of land use that are extremely complex (Yeates and Garner, 1971). As the scope of this volume is purposely limited to the economic aspects of the location of economic activities, the discussion in this section is devoted to the market approach and its application to urban land use (Alonso, 1960).

A SIMPLE URBAN LAND USE MODEL

Assuming the existence of a surface that is flat, homogeneous with respect to transportation facilities in all directions, and equally useful for all types of urban development, a distribution of land uses that is directly similar to the zonal patterns of Thunen's model can be derived. As in Thünen's case there is one market, the center of the city, which is the *locus of minimum aggregate travel costs* for the entire urban area. That is, if a map were constructed of the total costs of transportation of every point to all other points in the area, this would be the point of lowest total cost. All business activities wish to locate at that point, for they will then be in the center of their entire market area and will thus maximize their sales opportunities. All employment opportunities are thus found at the center of the city, and all workers also wish to locate as close as possible to their places of work in order to minimize the costs and time spent in daily commutation.

The result is that all these potential users, business and residential, compete for the central locations, with those activities capable of realizing the greatest profits per unit of land occupied outbidding all the other potential users and thereby preempting the most central locations. The potential profit, however, for each economic activity varies with the location with respect to the center of the city. For example, consider the location of banks, bus terminals, and salesmen. Banks make money by looking after other people's money and lending that same money to others at interest. They, therefore, desire locations that will maximize their number of potential customers—both depositors and borrowers. Consequently, they are able to pay very high prices for locations at the center of the city, which is 0 in Figure 2-10; but they are able to pay very little if their volume of business is small, which it would be at 1. Thus the "ability to pay" curve, or potential economic rent curve, for banks is very steep, as depicted in Figure 2-10.

Bus terminals also require central locations, for they wish to locate centrally to their entire market area, but because they consume quite large amounts of land for parking, servicing, and waiting rooms, they are not able to pay the same high price for a position at 0 as banks. Alternatively, though their total sales and profits may well decline to zero if they locate at 2, this decline is less steep than that for banks.

FIGURE 2-10 ECONOMIC RENT CURVES FOR FOUR DIFFERENT TYPES OF ECONOMIC ACTIVITY: BANKS, BUS TERMINALS, SALESMEN, AND AGRICULTURE.

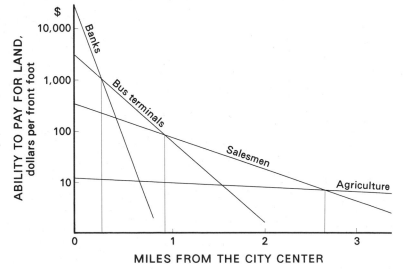

Thus the economic rent curve for bus terminals is less steep than that for banks (Figure 2-10). Salesmen working in stores in the central part of the city would also like to minimize the expense of the journey to work and the time wasted in daily commuting. They, therefore, would also like to locate centrally if possible, but given the relatively fixed nature of their income, they are not able to pay very high prices for such locations. The price that they are able to pay for a position at 0 is, consequently, very low. On the other hand, their satisfaction with residential locations at 1 and 2 is just a little less than at 0, for the difference in satisfaction is moderated only by the actual increased costs of transportation and the value that the salesman puts on his time spent in commuting. Thus the ability-to-pay or economic rent curve for the salesman is very shallow, and he is, in fact, willing to pay more for land at locations 1 and 2 than either banks or bus terminal operators.

If the ability-to-pay or economic rent curves are superimposed one upon the other, the by now familiar situation of those activities with the steepest curves capturing the central locations is apparent. The boundaries between adjacent zones are defined by the intersection of the two highest economic rent curves at a given location. Furthermore, if these curves are rotated around the locus of minimum aggregate travel costs (0), concentric zones of land use will emerge, with banks in the innermost zone, then bus terminals, and finally the residences of salesmen.

Land use and land values There are, of course, many thousands of different types of potential users of land in urban areas, and each of these has its own particular ability-to-pay curve, and in some cases a number of economic activities may share the same type of curve. Therefore, the occupant of a particular location is, theoretically, that use which can gain the largest returns from that location and pay the highest price. The price is expressed in real terms by the value of the land at that location, which, in the urban case, *includes the value of the building placed upon it*. This is because an alternative user for that particular site has to purchase not only the land but the building to gain that location. If he wishes to change substantially the use at that location, for example, to change from an industrial use to residential, then he will have to purchase the land and property, and then demolish the property in order to develop anew. It is for this reason that private redevelopment in urban areas is usually limited to a few dramatic instances in which either the predeveloped property has negligible value, or very large increments in profit can be realized by an immediate change in use.

Therefore the ability-to-pay or economic rent curves, when superimposed upon each other, outline a general profile of land values within an urban area, with the important observation that the value of the building placed upon it is also reflected in the value of the land. Theoretically, of course, the value of the building is related to the intensity of use that is possible at that site, though when aesthetic and historical values are injected (as they should be), this relationship is not so obvious. However, in general, the land value profile will diminish with distance from the locus of minimum aggregate travel costs, and the shape of this profile will depend on the shape of the individual economic rent curves. The highest values are at the locus of minimum aggregate travel costs, and this becomes the peak value location for the entire urban area.

A nonhomogeneous transport surface   Although there are many roads and many channels for communication and movement of goods in most urban areas, the transport surface cannot be regarded as homogeneous. Some parts of the city are serviced by certain modes of transportation that are especially useful for a particular kind of economic activity. Locations along railroad tracks, for example, are particularly useful for industrial activities that use railroads for the transportation of their inputs and the distribution of their outputs. Even roads vary in their carrying capacity and speed, with the major urban arterials being specifically designed or adapted for the movement of trucks, buses, and automobiles. Thus the transport surface is not homogeneous, and though there may be one locus of minimum aggregate travel costs, there may also be a number of other foci of lower travel costs for subareas within the city (such as at the intersection of arterials), and valleys of lower transport costs along the lines etched by the arterials.

Thus an accessibility surface which represents for each location the total costs of transport to all other locations within the urban area is, theoretically, the *inverse* of the land value surface. Berry (1963) presents such a land value surface (Figure 2-11), which is the inverse of an accessibility surface based on road transportation

FIGURE 2-11   THE LAND VALUE "CIRCUS TENT."

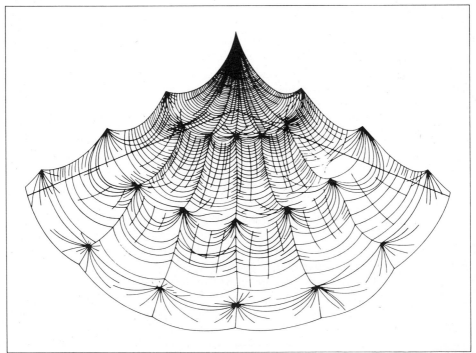

focusing upon one peak value location, a number of minor foci at the intersections of urban arterials, and ridges of higher values along the arterials connecting the peak value location and the minor foci in a grid pattern. The illustration would become much more complex, of course, if it took into account the many different channels of transportation in the city.

Distribution of the people Although it is fairly easy to visualize the bidding mechanism and resulting locational decision of business and industrial enterprises, it is difficult to envisage the same system operating with respect to households because one has to replace the concepts of turnover and profit with one of satisfaction. In terms of ability to pay, however, it is apparent that the preceding discussion would lead to the conclusion that the competition for locations close to the areas of greatest accessibility would lead to greater intensities of use, as measured by population density, on this higher-valued land. A corollary to this would be that this higher-valued land would be occupied by those with the ability to pay high prices, that is, the higher incomes.

The basic proposition, that higher population densities are found on the higher-valued land (plus buildings), is generally true, discounting the hollow core effect where business and commercial activities preempt almost all residential use (Newling, 1969). The corollary, however, is not true, for an examination of the central parts of most urban areas indicates that many central locations are occupied by the lowest-income families and persons of all, and at one edge of these, or grouped within them, are enclaves of the wealthy living in apartments or town houses. The reason for this juxtaposition is space and quality. The lower-income groups reside in these central locations because accommodation is relatively cheap per room. It is cheap because the living quality of that room is poor, and the room is small (large rooms may be subdivided) so that the actual space occupied by a person is minimal. The higher-income groups consume more space and reside in more luxurious surroundings, occasionally in new buildings, and frequently in old but well-maintained structures. Thus the poor live at higher densities for a given value of land than the rich, who are, in effect, spending their greater income on more expensive space and higher-quality housing.

Decline in strength of the locus of minimum aggregate travel costs During the last hundred years there have been many innovations in transportation within urban areas (Yeates and Garner, 1971, chap. 8). The sum total of the impact of these innovations has been that it is now possible to move fairly freely over a large part of the urban area. Concomitantly there has been a general reduction in the number of hours worked during the week and rising real incomes due to greater productivity. This increased affluence and available time have made it possible for the urban population to cater to tastes it had hitherto been unable to indulge in. One of the most far-reaching has been the desire for more living space by the middle classes with families, who form the bulk of society in North America. Another has been its need for an expression of independence, symbolized by the single-family home. The result of these, and many other trends, has been a decrease in the desire for locations close to places of work, and therefore a "flattening out" of the population density curve. The spread of population since 1945 at the periphery of urban areas has been particularly dramatic, for the new single-family homes have had to be constructed on available land which is usually found only at the edge of urban areas.

This fact alone would lead to the conclusion that the relative attractiveness of locations for commercial and business enterprises near the locus of maximum accessibility to the entire population would diminish. With a population becoming increasingly spread out, some economic activities can relocate and tap a segment of a market from a peripheral location. Furthermore, new and exciting forms of retailing are possible with large sites and new stores, such as an enclosed regional shopping center. Thus the locus of minimum aggregate travel costs is no longer the only location for a large number of business enterprises. Retailing activities have tended to decentralize as urban areas become larger, though the larger office buildings still tend to locate in the central part of the city. This decentralizing of retailing activities has been accentuated by the fact that the middle and upper incomes have been those most able to purchase homes in the peripheral areas, and these constitute the bulk of the potential market for many types of retailing activity.

Finally, along with the decentralization of retailing activities and the employment generated by these stores has been the location of new industrial plants, and the relocation of some older industrial plants, at the periphery of urban areas. This movement is in response to a number of factors, among which the desire for cheaper land and the apparent willingness of workers to commute relatively large distances by automobile are among the most decisive. As more and more job opportunities are created at the periphery of the urban area, more and more people wish to move to the jobs, and so the tidal wave of metropolitan expansion continues apace (Blumenfeld, 1954).

The theory of urban land use based on simple marketing principles can therefore be used as a persuasive model for detailing the economic processes concerned with locating land uses within urban areas. Though many other noneconomic factors such as personal preferences, discrimination, attitudes toward publicly financed transport systems, zoning, and so forth, should be taken into account, it is interesting to observe the degree to which economic forces of the type detailed in the simple urban land use model still operate. The model may not focus quite so strongly upon the arrangement of land uses around a single center, but the general underlying principle of relative accessibility is still remarkably robust. A multicentered model is, in effect, a rather obvious extension of the single-centered example.

SPATIAL PATTERNS OF LAND USE

In the classical model of land use, distance is taken to be the basic ordering influence, as the previous chapter has shown. Whether expressed as transport cost, as time, or in some other form, distance is the ultimate arbiter in the competition among land uses and land users for the best location, both in the city and in its rural hinterland. With a number of crops or urban activities striving for the most central location, the final allocation is decided on the basis of the slopes of their rent curves, the prime locations going to those land uses having the steepest curves. The amount of slope is in turn affected by the relative transportability of commodities or the relationships between transport and nontransport costs, including degree of intensity. Theoretically the ideal spatial arrangement resulting from this set of conditions is a system of concentric zones surrounding some focal point.

This outcome depends, however, upon the limiting assumptions that underlie the classical models. When any of these initial conditions is relaxed, the concentric pattern can be much disturbed. Land use zones become attenuated along major transport arteries, separate rings form around competing centers, and irregularities appear with variations in physical conditions. The ideal form can also be affected by changes in population size, nature of demand, or production and transport technology.

What remains of the ideal pattern once real-world conditions are admitted in this way? Does distance, in fact, have the theoretically expected influence that Thünen claimed for it? A century and a half after Thünen is it possible to find concentric zones in the rural and urban landscapes? If a fundamental order does indeed persist, what has modern technology made of it? Then too, what of the classical assumption of economic man, the decision maker who is regarded to be wholly rational, fully informed, and motivated only by economic considerations? To what extent does this accurately describe the farmer, householder, or businessman we know? To the extent that any of these persons proves to be a "noneconomic man," what kinds of locational effects should be expected to follow?

RURAL LAND USE

In looking for answers to these questions, we first attempt to find real-world indications of the locational influence of distance in the rural landscape. We are particularly interested in any signs of zonation, as well as effects of change and of noneconomic human behavior. After exploring these questions, we may then take a global view of major types of rural land use.

SOME EMPIRICAL STUDIES

The evidence comes from empirical literature of both the past and more recent times. Some of these studies have been directed specifically at the locational problem, while others supply incidental information on this subject although originally intended for other purposes. The clues are from many parts of the world: from both technically advanced and underdeveloped lands, and from the Orient as well as from the West.

Distance and agricultural location Some of the earliest confirmation of the anticipated distance effects of rent and intensity on land use comes from a period not long after that during which Thünen wrote. A study of nineteenth-century agriculture in Ontario (Norton and Conkling, 1974) used data from the 1861 Canadian census to explore the locational influence of distance from Toronto, which was then, as now, the central focus of the entire region. This was a pioneering period in Upper Canada, and settlement of outlying areas was still in progress. Using information from 618 sample farms in twenty-three townships of Toronto's hinterland, the study found that land values declined systematically with increasing distance from market. Altogether, 42 percent of the variation in land values could be attributed to Toronto's influence, while another 10 percent was related to distance from lesser urban places in the area. Arterial transport routes existed in 1861, but in their primitive state they appeared to affect land values only slightly. Indeed, so important was the influence of distance that even variations in the quality of the land did not greatly affect its price.

Distance from Toronto also influenced the output of major crops per unit of land area. For the chief commercial crops the effect was that of declining yields away from the urban market. This was especially true of winter wheat, which showed a strong negative correlation with distance from Toronto. A seeming paradox, however, was the increasing output per unit of land area of certain other crops as one moved away from the city. These were spring wheat and the root crops, such as turnips and potatoes, commodities that were used for the subsistence of local populations almost everywhere. As their output continued to rise outward from the city, a point was eventually reached where these became dominant and the commercial crop, winter wheat, virtually disappeared. This point could be regarded as the extensive margin of Toronto's supply area at that date. Beyond lay the pioneer fringe, where transport cost was too great at existing prices and under primitive road conditions for local output to reach market economically.

The study thus confirmed the expected effects of distance on land values and land use even in very early times; but it also indicated that, in a rapidly growing pioneering economy, farming activity does not necessarily end abruptly at the extensive margin as it did in the long-settled area of northern Germany described by Thünen. Beyond the margin, farmers were planting their newly cleared fields with crops needed to sustain themselves and their animals until such time as improved transportation or higher commodity prices might cause the margin to move out beyond them.

Taking a wider view of agricultural location, distance exerts an influence at the continental and even the world scales. Thus, for example, Thünen noted that world wheat prices in his time were set in London, the principal global market of the day. This is generally still the case 150 years later. As the major wheat importing and consuming area, Western Europe draws its supplies from all parts of the world. Prices elsewhere are derived from those in Europe, and any difference represents the cost of moving the wheat from producing areas.

The effect of this relationship is illustrated by the Canadian grain trade (Simpson, 1968). The wheat and other lesser grains originate principally on prairie farms in the Canadian west, from which they are trucked to local "country" elevators for cleaning, grading, and storage prior to loading on freight cars for the trip to elevators at ports on the Pacific or Lake Superior. In the latter case there is a further journey by lake vessels ("lakers") usually to storage facilities on the St. Lawrence, from which they are loaded on oceangoing vessels for shipment abroad. At each stage in this journey the local price is roughly equivalent to that at the next higher stage less transfer costs (terminal charges for processing, storage, and loading and unloading, as well as insurance and freight). Thus, next to London, the highest prices are those quoted at Montreal or other St. Lawrence ports, followed by successively lower prices at Lakehead, the country elevators, and, finally, the prairie farms, which receive the lowest prices of all.

Zonation of agricultural production The influence of distance on commodity prices, land value, and intensity of production has been noted at different scales by many observers; but what are its effects on the competition among different kinds of crops? Do these form distinct land use zones in accordance with our theoretical expectations? Zonation of agricultural production was observed in a classical study of the influence of Louisville, Kentucky, on farming within its surrounding area (Arnold and Montgomery, 1918). This case is of particular interest because of certain features closely resembling Thünen's. The fifty farms selected for the study were found in four distance zones: under 8 miles from Louisville, 9 to 11 miles, 12 to 14 miles, and over 14 miles. It was found that contract rent and land value dropped off steeply in succeeding distance zones from the city. A rapid decline in fertilizer use similarly occurred. As in Thünen's state, manure was purchased in the city, where it was produced by the draft animals of that period, and most of it was used within the first distance zone. Those farms closest to Louisville were principally engaged in vegetable production for the urban market, while those at a somewhat greater distance were mainly dairy farms. Beyond were other farms devoted to the field crops and mixed farming typical of agriculture generally in that section of the United States.

A number of observers have noted a concentric pattern of rural land use in Europe, centering upon the main urban and manufacturing concentrations of southeastern Britain, the Low Countries, and adjacent lands. One of the earliest of such studies (Jonasson, 1925) described an arrangement that largely holds true today. Its main features are an inner belt of horticulture and dairying, immediately adjacent to the core area of urbanization, followed by succeeding zones of less and less market-oriented types of farming and an increasing component of pastureland. The outermost zone is the main location of Europe's forests, reflecting the changes in accessibility since Thünen's time.

Although European agriculture has become modernized considerably since World War II, there are still sizable remnants of peasant agriculture from an earlier era. Among other places these are found in Brittany and the Massif Central of France, in Bavaria and Switzerland, and especially in the Mediterranean lands. This type of farming is characterized by nucleated agricultural settlements, whose inhabitants cultivate fragmented holdings in the surrounding area. Studies of such settlements in southern Italy, Sicily, Sardinia, and parts of Spain indicate that farmers customarily use the nearest land for those crops requiring the greatest labor and the most frequent visits. Typically a first ring is devoted to small plots of vegetables, olives, and grapes; beyond this are zones mainly sown to cereals, the proportion of fallow land and pasture increasing with distance from the village (Chisholm, 1962, pp. 59–67).

The underdeveloped world supplies many similar examples of concentric zonation. A study of Indian agriculture (Ahmad, 1952) found spatial patterns of this type in areas where cultivators live in nucleated agricultural villages surrounded by fragmented parcels of farmland. Characteristically these parcels formed three land use zones centering upon the village, with each farmer having the use of at least one strip in each zone. The nearest zone consisted of the most productive, most heavily manured and irrigated land. Next came a zone of irrigated land devoted to the chief food crops, beyond which was an outer zone of poor fertility used for the dry cultivation of millets and fodder. The arrangement produced a centralizing effect that tended to minimize the total aggregate travel time for all inhabitants of the village.

Such patterns abound likewise in Africa. In Ethiopia, for example, despite the decidedly nonuniform physical environment, a zonation of rural land use has been noted surrounding the capital city, Addis Ababa (Horvath, 1969). Vegetables are grown as close as possible to the city in locations where irrigation water is available. The remainder of the nearest lands is occupied by eucalyptus forests, which are an essential source of wood for fuel and building materials in the city. Beyond the forest is an area of mixed farming, mainly semisubsistence in character, with commercial production occurring only in the most accessible portions. In this tropical land, commercial milk production was late to appear, and it does not take place in the same areas as vegetable farming. In an earlier time milk was obtained from one's own or a neighbor's cows, often pastured on grassy plots within the city itself. This activity was subsequently crowded out by urban growth, and a few dairies were established on the city's margins, with human porters used for marketing the product. More recently a UNICEF-sponsored scheme for milk-collection centers in the hinterland has been implemented, mostly in the cooler sections north of Addis Ababa. Drawing upon a farming area 3 miles in radius, each center trucks its milk to a central dairy in the city for processing and distribution. Today Addis Ababa obtains its milk supply from both the traditional, 2-mile walking zone and the modern collection stations.

Locational impact of change   Thünen's rings were a direct consequence of his limiting assumptions, which were intended to remove all influences other than distance. Real-world cases such as those just described are to be found in those places where the conditions specified by Thünen are best preserved. What happens when these assumptions are removed or modified? Much has happened in modern times to complicate the basic concentric arrangement, and the rate of change has been accelerating. Among these events have been changes in the demand conditions for agricultural products and innovations in both transport and production technology. The previous chapter indicated some of the theoretically expected effects of these changes; now we may look at the empirical evidence. Developments of this nature do not usually occur in isolation, however, and we shall therefore follow our examination of individual dynamic influences with case studies illustrating their combined effects.

Changes in demand   Spatial patterns of agricultural land use are much affected by changes in the demand for farm products, both the total quantity required and the product mix. An overall increase in demand can result from population growth or an increase in consumers' incomes. In either case the likely effect, as noted by Brinkmann (see Chapter 2), is an increase in the cultivated area through an outward expansion of the rings, or an increase in the intensity of production, or, more likely, a combination of the two. It is also possible, of course, for populations or their incomes to shrink, producing spatial effects just the reverse of those cited.

Changes in the structure of demand may be caused by changes in the characteristics of a population, especially incomes. Although prosperity at first brings a growth in total demand, once basic food needs are satisfied, further additions to demand become more selective. With a subsequent increase in income, the amount of starches consumed may decline absolutely as well as relatively, replaced by increasing amounts of animal proteins, green vegetables, fruits, and other more costly "protective" foods. The usual measure of this effect is the *income elasticity of demand*, that is, the amount of increase in demand for an item that a unit increase in income will generate. In Britain, for example, it was found (Gasson, 1966) that the income elasticity of demand for pears was 0.9, which is to say that for every 1 percent of increase in income people were willing to buy 0.9 percent more pears. The figure was likewise 0.9 for leafy salad vegetables, while for apples and oranges it was 0.8. By contrast, the root crops such as potatoes had income elasticities as low as 0.1. Another type of population change affecting demand for foods is a rising educational level, which tends to produce an increased consciousness of dietary quality. Structural effects may result from cultural changes, such as those following the immigration of a new type of people with different tastes. Thus, persons from India are likely to be vegetarians, blacks may require "soul foods," and Middle-Europeans may prefer rye bread to white. In the real world, demand changes are usually accompanied by technological changes, so that the two are not always easy to separate. Therefore, before looking at specific cases, let us first examine this latter type of development.

Changes in technology Agricultural location has been affected substantially by new developments in transportation, agricultural technology, and processing methods. By its nature, transportation is highly susceptible to technological advances, some of which affect agriculture in general, while others have a more direct impact on particular types of land use. In the long run there has been a persistent downward trend in transfer costs, both relatively and absolutely (see Chapter 8). Cheaper haulage costs, reduced transit time, and more efficient handling methods have benefited all modes of transportation. Theoretically their net effect (Brinkmann, 1935, pp. 46–49) would be to increase the relative influence of nondistance factors, causing location of production to conform increasingly to local comparative advantage. This results from the decline in the rent curve as local price differences are reduced, permitting more distant areas to be exploited.

Transport developments often favor certain commodities. Thus the increased speed and cargo-carrying capacity of modern aircraft have increased dramatically the range of perishables such as flowers and small fruits, as illustrated by the recent airlifting of California strawberries to New York, London, and Paris. Indeed, various forms of specialized transport equipment had appeared much earlier, as, for example, the refrigerated ships and railway cars that made possible the marketing of Australian and New Zealand butter, cheese, and chilled and frozen meats in Europe and North America. Meanwhile, bulk carriers, together with automated loading and unloading devices, had been developed for the efficient long-range transporting of grains and other bulk cargoes by water. These innovations have substantially increased the latitude of locational choice for production of those commodities that benefit most from greater speed or reduced cost of transportation. As a result these commodities can be grown increasingly in localities where physical and other conditions are most favorable for their specific requirements. As Brinkmann predicted, therefore, the principle of comparative advantage is assuming a greater locational role as the friction of distance diminishes.

At the same time, remarkable developments in agricultural technology contribute further to the derangement of Thünen's neat rings. Some of these innovations, such as the internal-combustion engine used in farm tractors, have been borrowed from nonagricultural sources, while others, such as the corn picker and the combine, have been designed for specific agricultural applications. Some have appeared in response to chronic labor shortages, others to rising demand. Often they result in an intensification of production, particularly as the level of capital inputs increases. Among the latter are new types of machinery and equipment; chemical fertilizers, pesticides, and herbicides; and improved seeds and livestock feeds and even redesigned farm animals. At the same time, new farming methods are introducing greater efficiency into agriculture.

These modern developments are often bringing dramatically higher yields. In Britain, for example, potato yields rose from 7 tons per acre in the 1930s to 9 tons in 1962 (Gasson, 1966, p. 27). Meanwhile, wheat yields increased from 18.5 hundredweight per acre to 28.1 hundredweight. As a result, the quantity of agricultural goods produced annually on British farms before 1945 can now be grown on half the acreage. In some cases—potatoes and other root crops in particular—yields rose faster than demand and the acreage devoted to them had to be cut, with only the most suitable land remaining in use. Thus agricultural innovations can contribute to the growing influence of comparative advantage in much the same way as transport innovation.

The continent of Europe has long been cited as a region of high agricultural yields, but a comparison of yields in the 1922–1924 period with those of 1967 (Baade, 1971) has shown that European yields have consistently risen sharply as the use of commercial fertilizers has accelerated. In the earlier years the higher yields were confined largely to the European heartland, centering upon the Low Countries and nearby Britain, northern Germany, and southern Scandinavia (Figure 3-1), as noted above. This area of high yields coincided closely with levels of fertilizer use (Figure 3-2), except for certain naturally rich alluvial areas such as the Po Valley of Italy. The rest of the Continent experienced much lower yields, and fertilizer use was correspondingly slight. By 1967 both yields and fertilizer use had risen markedly in the continental heartland, but the central area of intensive production had meanwhile expanded in all directions (Figures 3-3 and 3-4). Only the extreme southern and easternmost parts of the Continent had failed to participate fully in the general intensification, and even these areas had shown much improvement.

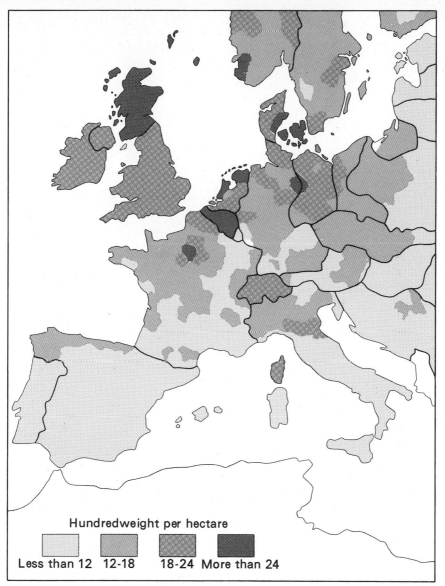

Hundredweight per hectare

Less than 12   12-18   18-24   More than 24

FIGURE 3-1 EUROPE: CROP YIELDS, 1922–1924. (FRITZ BAADE, 1972. "EINHUNDERT JAHRE STEI-GENDE ERNTEN DURCH DIE ANWENDUNG VON HANDELSDÜNGER," PAPER DELIVERED TO THE SEMINAR ON THE USE OF FERTILIZER AND ITS EFFECTS ON THE AGRICULTURAL ECONOMY, VATICAN CITY, APRIL 10–16. FIG. 1.)

Effects of changing technology and changing demand in the New World   During the period in which Thünen was writing, a new agricultural region was evolving in the New World, this one focusing upon the emerging metropolis of New York City. The changing agricultural land use patterns in New York's rural hinterland have

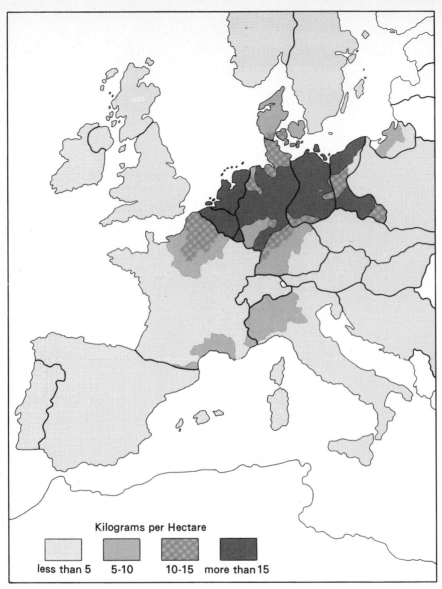

Kilograms per Hectare

less than 5   5-10   10-15   more than 15

FIGURE 3-2 EUROPE: INTENSITY OF USE OF FERTILIZER, 1922–1924. (BAADE, 1972, FIG. 2.)

been examined in a series of geographical studies covering the years 1800 through 1860. These studies were based primarily on a rich body of recorded information from books, records of transport agencies, newspaper files, farm journals, and other historical documents from that era, along with quantitative data from county records and the United States census of agriculture.

The study region included eighteen counties of western New York State, extending from beyond the Catskills and Adirondacks on the east to the Niagara

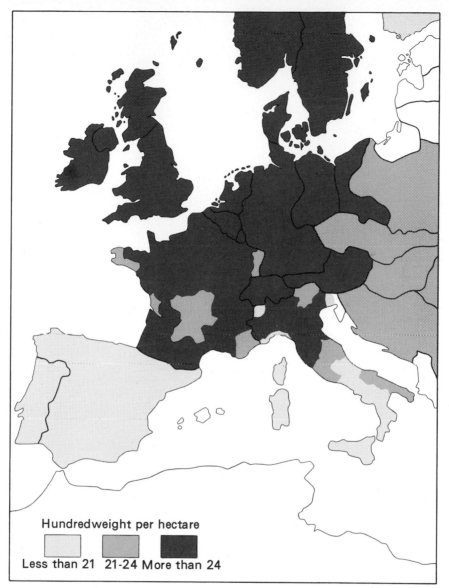

Hundredweight per hectare

Less than 21   21-24   More than 24

FIGURE 3-3   EUROPE: CROP YIELDS, 1967. (BAADE, 1972, FIG. 5.)

River and Lake Erie on the west. This area had previously been heavily forested, occupied only by Indians, hunters, and trappers, much like Thünen's wilderness. After the American Revolution and the defeat of Britain and her Indian allies, the region was entered by European settlers and gradually taken into the widening agricultural supply area of the eastern metropolis. Among the theoretical notions tested was the expectation that these conditions would cause concentric rings of land use to form and grow with the increase in demand and that this pattern would

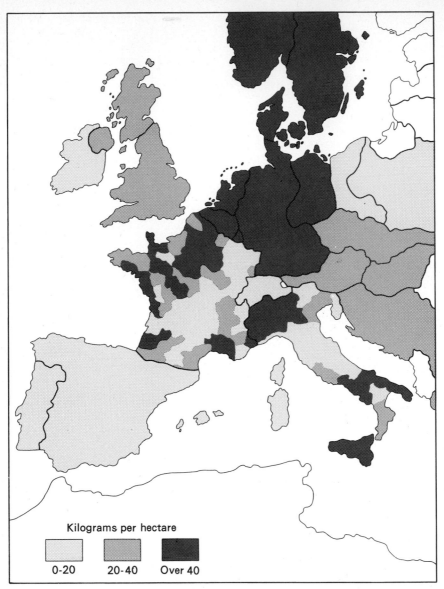

Kilograms per hectare

0-20   20-40   Over 40

FIGURE 3-4 EUROPE: INTENSITY OF USE OF FERTILIZER, 1967. (BAADE, 1972, FIG. 6.)

change in response to changes in the location of demand and the evolution of transport and production technology.

During this sixty-year period New York City asserted its dominance as the chief mercantile city of the East and gained a rapidly expanding role in both domestic and foreign trade in agricultural goods, making it the prime focus of commodity movements in the country. At the same time it was becoming a center for manufacturing, and this, together with its commercial functions, caused a rapid growth in the city's residential population from 60,515 to 813,669 within the time covered by the study. Thus, in addition to its role as a collection and distribution center for agricultural goods destined for other domestic and foreign markets, it was acquiring a sizable demand of its own. As a consequence the city was forced continually to extend its agricultural supply area farther and farther westward. The extensive margin of this supply area at any one time was determined by a combination of price (reflecting level of demand) and transport costs. Superimposed upon this secular trend were cyclical changes in demand. Wide fluctuations in demand, and thus price levels, caused temporary advances and retreats of the extensive margin during periods of financial boom or recession and times of war or peace.

The commodities flowing into the New York market included perishables such as vegetables and fluid milk; grains, especially wheat, the chief agricultural export funneling through the port; and animal products and fibers and other industrial crops. The historical evidence indicates that these goods were produced in a series of zones resembling truncated Thünen rings westward of the metropolis. As the margin advanced, these zones moved outward in a wavelike motion resembling ripples on a pond. A given farm in this western region underwent a sequence of land use changes as one after another of the waves of land use passed through its local area.

This effect has been noted in a study of the five-county area immediately adjacent to Buffalo at the western end of the region. Here the early settlement occurred mainly between 1800 and 1810. Records indicate that this part of the state was as yet beyond the extensive margin of New York City's supply area, isolated from the eastern market by the barrier of distance under conditions of primitive and exceedingly costly transportation. Consequently the farming population who occupied the land were forced to engage in subsistence agriculture, producing only for their own use as in the pioneering areas of Ontario cited earlier. Nevertheless, these farmers clearly operated under the assumption that their district would eventually be incorporated into an expanding area of commercial production.

The first tentative opportunities for commercial production occurred with the rising demand for their products resulting from the War of 1812, much of which was fought on the Niagara frontier. By the 1820s the region was able to participate fairly regularly in supplying the New York market. Farm output had changed little in character since the pioneering period, however; it included fruits, vegetables, cereals, and livestock. Both field crops and animals received little attention from the farmers in what was necessarily a low-cost type of operation here at the extreme margins of the supply area. Only certain selected commodities could bear the expensive trip eastward, and the remaining output continued to be consumed locally. The commercial products included meat animals, driven to market on the hoof, and stall-fattened en route, as well as hides and wool, commodities relatively low in bulk and high in value. In addition there were a number of industrial goods, including the plant stock fibers, hemp and flax, which, prior to shipment, received an initial processing that substantially reduced their weight and bulk. Locally grown fruits and grain were concentrated into valuable alcoholic beverages such as cider, brandy, and whiskey, which were readily transported. Occasionally even wheat made the eastward trip whenever wartime shortages made prices especially high. Between these times the extensive margin for this crop would then retreat eastward once more, as in 1819, when prices dropped precipitously. When political conditions permitted, some wheat made its way via Lake Ontario and the St. Lawrence River to the Canadian port of Montreal. With these exceptions, however, the five-county region was engaged in a form of rural land use very like that of Thünen's outermost ring.

By 1830 a rising demand in the East, together with a declining cost of transportation, had permitted the livestock–industrial crop zone to move farther westward, and the Niagara frontier district turned increasingly to a form of extensive mixed farming. The principal cash crop was wheat, grown with minimal inputs of labor and capital involving primitive implements, no manuring, and much fallowing of the land. Thus production costs were low, but so also were yields. Although there was still some marketing of livestock, this form of production was declining because of increasing competition from cattle produced more cheaply in Ohio and western Pennsylvania, now accessible to eastern markets by the same transport innovations that permitted this area to send its wheat to New York.

Mixed farming continued to prevail in 1840, but production methods had meanwhile increased in intensity. Wheat was still the main cash crop, but it now had to compete with wheat produced more cheaply in the Middle West, which benefited from continuing transport improvements. In the five-county area wheat was being produced in 1840 by methods requiring more labor, in particular a crop rotation system that included root crops (fed to livestock), regular manuring of fields, and the discontinuation of bare fallowing. With all the land thus in continual production at higher levels of fertility, yields rose substantially, but so did costs.

Wheat remained the chief cash crop in 1850 also, but by this time competition from the West had attained such levels that production on the Niagara frontier had been forced into still more intensive methods. This meant the introduction of improved rotation schemes involving new techniques, such as deep plowing and heavier manuring (including artificial fertilizers), and the introduction of new kinds of farm machinery. Thus the variable inputs, capital and labor, rose sharply, as the effort to increase unit output intensified.

The 1860s were apparently a period of transition during which the old patterns were becoming modified and some of the modern land uses were being anticipated. Wheat growers were also confronted with a serious invasion of plant pests and diseases. Mixed farming still prevailed, but it occurred in varying forms in different locations. The specialty crops prevalent in the region today were starting to appear in certain locations. Meanwhile there is evidence that the regular east-west zonation had been much modified by this date. Let us see why this was so.

Two developments were increasingly influential in shaping a new land use pattern by mid-nineteenth century. One of these was the appearance of regional markets that competed more and more for the agricultural goods that had formerly gone mainly to New York City. Many small populated places had arisen as the region developed, but these had had little effect on the agricultural pattern at first. As one by one they reached a certain threshold of population size, however, they were able to acquire agricultural rings of their own, especially those providing perishables such as vegetables and milk. Only four places had attained sufficient size in the eighteen-county area by 1860 to form their own agricultural supply areas to a measurable degree: Buffalo, Rochester, Syracuse, and Oswego.

The second important development was transport innovation. At the outset there had appeared two main routes of settlement, the Genesee Road, which reached Buffalo from Albany in 1815, and the Ridge Road, a link between Rochester and Lewiston completed in 1816. These were exceedingly primitive routes, however, and the cost of transportation to the head of navigation in Albany was $100 per ton. The isolation this imposed upon the western region was first broken in 1825 when the Erie Canal was completed from Albany to Buffalo, thus providing an all-water route linking New York City with Lake Erie. By 1828 the Oswego Canal was completed from Syracuse to Oswego, connecting the canal system with Lake Ontario. Other canals were subsequently added until a sizable network was in operation. For those areas served by the new system, the canals reduced transport costs by one-tenth of that of road haulage, to $10 from $100, and cut the travel time between Albany and Buffalo to only ten days, just half the previous time. In 1851 the New York and Erie Railroad reached the western end of the region, and in 1853 the New York Central was formed to join together in one statewide system a number of shorter early lines. These first railways did not as yet compete with the canals in cost; but they provided superior speed and remained in service throughout the year, whereas the canals were forced to close during the winter freeze-up.

Analyses of the agricultural census data for 1840, 1850, and 1860 (the first years for which they were available) show that transport innovations were indeed having profound effects on the location of agriculture. These studies indicate a decided attenuation of zones of land values and crop-and-animal systems along the transport arterials. At the same time, confirming Brinkmann's predictions, the steadily declining cost of transportation lent increasingly greater relative importance to other locational considerations, especially such physical conditions as soils, precipitation, drainage, and climate. The expected outcome of this latter development would be the appearance of distinct areas of specialization.

To explore this hypothesis, data for 325 townships in the western end of the state were examined (1) to determine the amount of location change in the land use pattern between the first agricultural census (1840) and the census of 1860 and (2) to measure the relative changes in the locational influence of distance, competing markets, and physical conditions. The census provided quantitative data on crop and livestock output; distances were measured to New York City, to the nearest regional market (Buffalo, Rochester, Syracuse, and Oswego), and to the nearest transport artery (water, road, or rail); and three land-capability classes were used to indicate variations in the physical environment.

The results showed that in 1840 the east-west component was still strong, that a fairly regular variation in land use still remained, with the most intensive and best-developed farm systems occurring predominantly in the eastern areas. At this date, fifteen years after completion of the Erie Canal, there had developed a strong attraction to transport arterials, especially the more intensive land use systems. Physical conditions as yet evidenced little discernible influence on the location of production, and the still-small regional markets showed no more (although Buffalo was beginning to show some slight attraction).

Confirming the historical information cited earlier, higher intensities prevailed in 1860 than in 1840; but by this time the best-developed types had begun to gravitate toward the four regional markets even as the pull to New York City was noticeably waning. Attraction to transport arterials remained moderately high. Meanwhile, farm types were becoming sorted out according to their particular capacities to compete for the more productive lands; and incipient areas of specialized agriculture were beginning to emerge, especially cheese production on the hilly, poorer land in the southwest.

Historical records indicate that later in the nineteenth century the areas of cheese specialization reached a high level of local concentration. Eventually, also, orchards, which had been nearly ubiquitous in earlier times, were gravitating to the climatically favorable shores of Lakes Erie and Ontario, following a trend foreshadowed by the analysis of the 1860 data above. Vineyards in time came to be localized in those areas having the special soil and microclimatic conditions demanded for high-quality grape production. Market gardening, already apparent around the four regional centers in 1860, was later to become even more firmly established and ultimately to be joined by truck farming of vegetables and small fruits for the New York City market in areas of certain soil types. In time also the fluid milkshed of New York City reached out into this western region, aided by introduction of that now venerable institution, the milk train.

To summarize, these studies tended to document the steadily declining influence of transport cost, as most of the territory came to be penetrated by modern faster and cheaper modes of transportation and improved facilities. They also confirm a corresponding ascendancy of comparative advantage as a locational influence, as shown by the rise of specialized production areas for cheese, perishables, intensive mixed farming types, and grazing in those areas particularly suitable to them. At the same time the principle of first choice is indicated in the location of vineyards and orchards.

A WORLD VIEW OF AGRICULTURE

The zonal patterns of agricultural land use tend to expand with the passage of time. One element causing this outward rippling of land use zones is a rising demand for agricultural commodities as urban populations grow in numbers and enjoy increasing incomes. A second factor is innovation, both in transporting farm products and in producing and processing them. Thünen's town is able to draw upon an ever-widening supply area as improved transport links and a general long-term decline in transport rates reduce the slope of the transport cost curve.

New farming methods increase the volume of output and reduce production costs, tending to depress market prices, while new processing techniques increase the transportability of the product.

Noting these tendencies, Schlebecker traced the evolution of a "world metropolis" (Schlebecker, 1960). In the ancient Mediterranean world, Athens was the urban focus for the agricultural collection system, but by the sixteenth century the principal market for agricultural goods had shifted to Western Europe. There the focus of demand was not merely one city but a conglomerate of several large population centers in southeastern England and the nearby Low Countries, northern France, and the Hanseatic ports. This world metropolis rapidly acquired a dense and highly urbanized population engaged in industry and commerce and reaching out well beyond the European continent for the food and industrial raw materials that these countries were no longer able to provide for themselves. Eventually the United States, Canada, and the southern continents were drawn into a vast global supply area. By the nineteenth century another urban concentration had formed in the northeastern United States and adjacent parts of Canada. This North American megalopolis acquired its own set of Thünen rings, which expanded quickly to include the entire continent and beyond. Thus the metropolis of Western Europe was joined by a similar urban cluster across the Atlantic to constitute the London–New York axis, the twin poles of today's world metropolis. In this way Thünen's isolated state has become the entire globe, linked together by a transport and marketing system that ensures a continuous flow of agricultural commodities from a worldwide supply area into the center.

Although the agricultural regions centering upon individual cities have become blurred by these developments, the global agricultural system still shows a certain zonation. This can be seen in the sources of Britain's food supply. Although that country's agriculture is modern and productive, it cannot supply more than a fraction of the needs of 54 million people crowded into a space equivalent to the combined areas of Illinois and Indiana. The remainder must be imported, and it is instructive to note which items are purchased abroad. First of all, these imports include virtually no fluid milk, which is produced domestically. However, domestic producers are able to satisfy only part of the demand for perishable fruits and vegetables, such as strawberries, cherries, plums, cucumbers, asparagus, and green peas. From 0.2 to 7.2 percent of these are imported, mainly from nearby European countries. Less perishable vegetables, fruits, and milk products (cabbages, onions, new potatoes, apples, and cream) are imported in larger quantities and come from greater distances, not only from Western Europe but also from North America, North Africa, and even remoter areas. More than half of Britain's cheese is purchased abroad and four-fifths of the latter comes from the farthest parts of the world. Grains and such industrial crops as wool and hides are, on the average, obtained from the most distant areas of all (Chisholm, 1962, pp. 97–105; Peet, 1969).

Given this global orientation of agricultural production with its focus on the London–New York axis, what are the locational characteristics of the main types of commercial agriculture today? In the following pages we examine briefly four categories: (1) the market-oriented production of perishable commodities; (2) relatively intensive types of mixed farming; (3) commercial grain farming, an extensive form of monoculture; and (4) activities characteristic of Thünen's outer ring.

Market-oriented production   Most of the commodities belonging to this class of production are either perishable or bulky or both. They tend to be very intensively produced, requiring high inputs of labor and capital, as well as a great deal of entrepreneurial skill. Historically these forms of production have occurred immediately adjacent to urban markets to minimize transport cost and transit time. Although to some degree this market orientation has continued to the present, there is an increasing tendency for such activities to become located according to the comparative advantages of particular areas. This confirms the prediction of Brinkmann, who cited this as one of the consequences of innovations in transportation (Brinkmann, 1935). Falling under this classification are (1) vegetables, small fruits, and flowers; (2) dairying; and (3) poultry farming.

Vegetables, small fruits, and flowers   Vegetable farming is a very large business, especially in the technically advanced countries. In the United States the farm value of these commodities (including potatoes and small fruits) is nearly $2 billion annually, a figure that is exceeded only by corn, hay, and cotton. They are also important to underdeveloped countries. Most urban places in Middle and South America have central markets for the sale of such produce, although even greater amounts are consumed by growers on their tiny subsistence plots.

These products come in a wide range of types, some highly perishable (lettuce, green onions, tomatoes, asparagus, cut flowers) and others much less so (potatoes, other root crops, and cabbages). They are mainly fast-growing plants, and it is often possible to harvest two or more crops from the same land in a single season. The yield from a single acre is thus high. Production methods are usually intensive, requiring much stoop labor, costly irrigation systems (even in humid climates), heavy applications of fertilizer, and much specialized equipment, including cold frames and hothouses. The systems of assembling and marketing such commodities are elaborate and well organized, and the services of various transporters and a hierarchy of middlemen are required at numerous collection and distribution centers.

Today there are two main types of growers as determined by their locational characteristics: market gardening and truck farming. Market gardening takes place close to a major urban center, and in most cases it is a seasonal activity. Individual enterprises characteristically occupy small acreages, grow several successive crops in a given season, and produce a wide variety of merchandise. Most rely upon quick transportation to jobbers and wholesalers in nearby urban markets, although much of the produce is sold to consumers directly off the farm. This is the type of free cash cropping that occupied Thünen's first ring.

A modern development, truck farming can be located at a considerable distance from the ultimate consumers. The location is ordinarily one with a particular advantage for such production, a superior climate or soil, for example. Truck farming has been made possible by modern processing techniques and the development of fast and cheap transportation. Unit production costs in such areas are sufficiently low to offset the extra outlay for shipment to markets. In other words, transport costs are substituted for production costs in the selection of such locations.

In Canada and the United States market gardening is still prominent around major metropolises, especially in those areas adjacent to the great constellation of coastal cities stretching from southern New England through New York, New Jersey, eastern Pennsylvania, and Delaware into Virginia. Similar concentrations are found farther inland, especially at the southern end of Lake Michigan, surrounding Chicago.

California is outstanding for its truck farming, accounting for very nearly two-fifths of the country's annual vegetable output as measured by value. To the obvious advantage of a year-round climate, which makes California the leading North American source of winter vegetables and fruits, is added the further asset of irrigation water from adjacent mountain ranges. Yields are high and California produce brings top prices in the eastern markets of the United States and Canada, to which it is linked by excellent rail, truck, and (increasingly) air service. In addition there is the rapidly expanding local market for produce in the growing cities of the West Coast. Florida is second to California in this type of agriculture, having a similar set of advantages.

In the Midwest of the United States and in southernmost Ontario is a special type of truck farming anticipated by Brinkmann. At selected points in this region of mixed farming, modern plants have been set up for the canning and freezing of vegetables and fruits. A processing firm contracts with farmers in the surrounding area to supply sweet corn, peas, lima beans, tomatoes, or some other fresh crop. Each farmer then sets aside perhaps 10 or 25 acres for this specialty crop while continuing to pursue his typical form of corn belt agriculture on the remainder, possibly 160 to 240 acres. Since the farmer cannot afford to divert much of his time for this vegetable crop, he uses highly mechanized methods in its production.

Other notable truck farming areas are the potato-producing districts of northeastern Maine, adjacent parts of New Brunswick, and Prince Edward Island. Parts of Idaho and Colorado are also devoted to this specialty. Truck farming of a more varied type is carried out on the muck soils of the Holland Marsh district north of Toronto and in the Essex Peninsula area east of Windsor and Detroit. The latter area has excellent lacustrine soils along the shores of Lake Erie and an unusually moderate climate for Canada.

In Western Europe Thünen rings of horticulture once surrounded all urban places of any size, and distinct remnants of these still remain around the larger places. As in North America, however, the modern trend is toward specialized truck farming areas. In Britain, for example, market gardening continues to persist around London, but it is changing in character (Beaverington, 1963) and much of the production is shifting to truck farming areas (Gasson, 1966). One truck farming area having particularly superior physical conditions is the Parts of Holland district of south Lincolnshire, where floriculture strikingly similar to that of the Nether-lands takes place. Tomatoes are grown mainly in sections of Essex, Kent, and Middlesex, which are among the few areas in Britain having sufficiently warm summers for this crop (Chisholm, 1962, p. 95). Across the channel in the Low Countries is a particularly intensive form of horticulture, especially in those sections of the Netherlands west and south of the IJsselmeer. The Mediterranean margins of the Continent have a subtropical climate that gives this area its important advantage in the production of winter vegetables, flowers, and fruits for sale in the northern countries. With its political fragmentation, Europe maintains an unusually large international trade in such perishables.

Some of the world's most intensive production of vegetables and fruits occurs in Asia, especially in Japan, where the industry is highly commercialized. It has been found that 80 percent of Tokyo's fresh vegetable supply comes from an adjacent market gardening zone that lies mainly within a 30-mile radius of the city center (Eyre, 1959). Intensity of production diminishes outward from this region, and the nature of the output changes as well, including a greater proportion of less perishable goods such as cabbages. Commodities of this type are shipped to Tokyo from as far away as the northern island of Hokkaido. Average farm size also tends to increase away from the metropolitan center. Similar spatial arrangements for vegetable production and supply have been found in Australia (Smith, 1966) and New Zealand (Hunt, 1959).

Dairying Brinkmann observed that animal products fall into two categories: those which are perishable and bulky, and thus are produced near their markets; and those which are compact and easily preserved and therefore suitable for produc-tion at a distance from the market. This distinction underlay Thünen's division of dairying in his isolated state into first-ring production of fluid milk and sixth-ring output of butter and cheese. These theoretical expectations are borne out in the real world except that the pattern is often modified by environmental conditions assumed away in the theoretical model.

Physical conditions, for example, may affect the competition between dairying and other forms of land use for a given area. Milk output per cow is usually reduced by excessively high temperatures or aridity. Cool, moist climates are thus better for the cows; they are also conducive to higher quality and better yields for the forage crops required for feeding them. Nevertheless, if local demand for milk is sufficiently high, dairying can be carried out under adverse physical conditions, though at higher production costs. Demand, in turn, is a function of income as well as population size. With their low per capita purchasing power, most underdevel-oped areas are unable to support important commercial dairying operations. A further consideration excluded from the simpler models is the effect of govern-mental price setting, sanitation standards and inspection requirements, and licensing arrangements. These are among the most pervasive noneconomic influences in the milk industry.

The character of dairying operations in the real world differs according to location and the form in which milk is marketed. Confirming theoretical expectations, fluid milk production within the urban supply area is intensive in nature, which is to say that the quantity of variable inputs per unit of land area is relatively great. Dairying of this type demands careful management and entrepreneurial skills of a high order. Moreover, to give the necessary close attention to the health and well-being of a high-quality dairy herd involves much labor. Many man-hours are also devoted to the careful handling of milk, since cleanliness and sanitation are essential to maintaining the low bacterial content specified by governmental standards for grade A milk. Additional human labor is consumed in growing the crops used for feeding the cattle. Dairying makes particularly efficient use of farm labor, being a year-round activity with no slack period. Finally, large amounts of capital are needed to operate a modern dairy farm. Much of this goes for elaborate mechanical equipment, such as milking machines, bulk cooling tanks, and mechanical feeders. The farmer must also proivde expensive accommodations for the animals if he is to comply with sanitary regulations in addition to his outlays for farm machinery and equipment.

The kind of dairying that takes place in areas remote from urban markets or in districts with rough upland terrain is of a different sort. Here the emphasis is upon what is termed "industrial milk," processed forms such as cheese and evaporated or powdered milk. As Brinkmann indicated, these commodities are more transportable and are produced under less exacting conditions. Less labor is required for crop production, the animals often being allowed to forage for themselves; and the absence of strict governmental supervision results in fewer demands on entrepreneurial abilities. Capital requirements are minimal. Hence dairying in the outer ring is an extensive type of land use appropriate to the cheap land it occupies. Today, as in the past, there is a tendency for areal specialization in this type of dairying. Particular products come to be associated with certain districts, and such localities acquire comparative advantages in their local specialties. Many old-world regions are famous for the traditional cheeses to which they have given their names, such as Roquefort, Cheddar, Caerphilly, and Emmental.

The milk-producing areas of the northeastern United States and adjacent parts of Canada illustrate several typical locational characteristics. Each major population center in this area of high per capita incomes draws upon its surrounding rural hinterland for the supply of fresh milk, and in some cases dairy cattle are stall-fed within the urban environs themselves. The areal extent of each such milkshed corresponds to the number of people to be supplied within the city, and traditionally those customers in the largest centers have had to pay the highest prices for milk transported over long distances.

So large and closely spaced are these urban milksheds that they tend to coalesce and overlap in the most densely settled sections, but dairying in this part of North America often extends beyond urban supply areas. A fairly continuous region of milk production, called the North American dairy belt, extends along both the Canadian and United States sides of the Great Lakes and eastward to the Atlantic coast. Within Canada this form of land use predominates in southern Ontario and Quebec as well as New Brunswick, Nova Scotia, and Prince Edward Island in the Maritime Provinces. The United States portion of the dairy belt encompasses most of Minnesota, Wisconsin, and Michigan, the northern parts of Illinois, Indiana, and Ohio, and the greater part of the New England and Middle Atlantic states. There is also a southward extension into Delaware, Maryland, and northern Virginia.

Several conditions favor this concentration of dairying. The dairy belt is adjacent to the largest urban concentrations in both countries: the American megalopolis along the Atlantic seaboard and reaching inland, together with the economic heart of Canada, which follows the north shore of Lake Ontario and extends eastward down the St. Lawrence to Montreal and Quebec City. In addition to markets, physical conditions favor dairying in this region, much of which lies north of the main area of mixed farming in North America. The growing season in the northern parts of the dairy belt is too short for many field crops, especially corn grown for grain. Consequently, the dairy farmers of this area devote their acreages to forage crops, small grains, and corn cut green for ensilage. Thus dairying prevails well beyond the urban milksheds in the cooler districts, such as those west of the Great Lakes and in the remoter parts of Ontario, Quebec, and the Canadian maritime provinces.

Throughout the North American dairy belt the cattle population is fairly evenly distributed, but distance to market tends to influence the ultimate use to which the milk is put. This is illustrated by a series of maps prepared for an Ontario Royal Commission Report. The first of these (Figure 3-5) shows that most of the southern part of the province was involved in dairying. The next map (Figure 3-6), however, suggests that those farms supplying fluid milk were more numerous in the area focusing upon Toronto. Note particularly the apparent influence of other centers in the eastern districts, Ottawa and Kingston, each with its own milkshed. Cream production (Figure 3-7) was prominent on the margins of the Toronto fluid milk region, especially in the north. Although cheese (Figure 3-8) was made in many parts of Ontario, it was most noticeable in an area lying between the Kingston and Toronto fluid milksheds; powdered and condensed milk production (Figure 3-9) extended into some of the remotest areas, such as the upper Ottawa River Valley. A hypothetical rent curve based on the traditional pattern of dairying in Ontario might look something like Figure 3-10, where the different uses for milk appear as successive Thünen rings.

In the decade since the appearance of the Royal Commission Report on which these maps were based, the dairy industry of Ontario has undergone some fundamental changes. Control of milk sales has been assumed by a quasiofficial agency, the Ontario Milk Marketing Board, which has equalized transport costs throughout the province. With all dairymen thus paying the same amount per gallon to milk haulers, regardless of distance to market, there is effective discrimination in favor of the remotest farmers. As a consequence fluid milk is now being produced in all areas, including those formerly devoted to industrial milk, and the famous Ontario cheddar cheese is now becoming scarce and expensive. Thus in Ontario the traditional concentric pattern of production is breaking down under the influence of political factors.

Similarly, the patterns of milk production in the American portion of the dairy

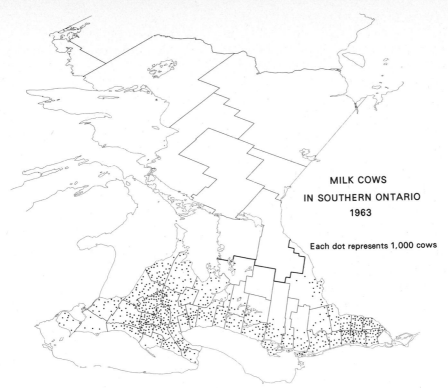

MILK COWS
IN SOUTHERN ONTARIO
1963

Each dot represents 1,000 cows

FIGURE 3-5   SOUTHERN ONTARIO: DISTRIBUTION OF MILK COWS, 1963.

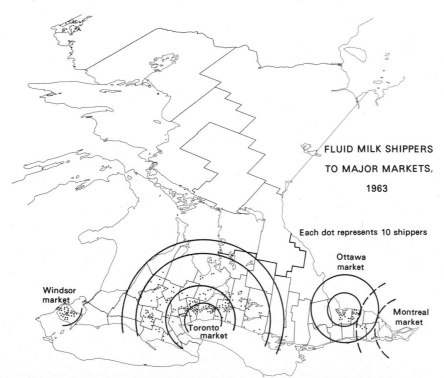

FLUID MILK SHIPPERS
TO MAJOR MARKETS,
1963

Each dot represents 10 shippers

Windsor
market

Ottawa
market

Toronto
market

Montreal
market

FIGURE 3-6   SOUTHERN ONTARIO: DISTRIBUTION OF FLUID MILK SHIPPERS, 1963.

FIGURE 3-7   SOUTHERN ONTARIO: DISTRIBUTION OF CREAMERIES, 1964.

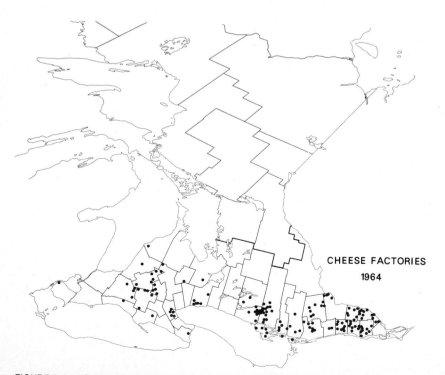

FIGURE 3-8   SOUTHERN ONTARIO: DISTRIBUTION OF CHEESE FACTORIES, 1964.

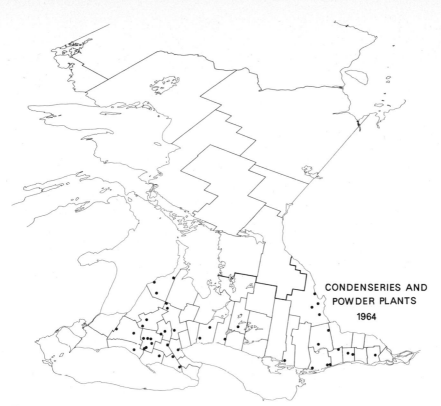

FIGURE 3-9 SOUTHERN ONTARIO: DISTRIBUTION OF CONDENSERIES AND POWDER PLANTS, 1964.

belt, which traditionally showed a close relationship to distance, are currently undergoing modification as control over the industry is increasingly exerted by governmental agencies. A comparison of theoretically ideal and actual supply areas for dairy products in the northeastern United States disclosed such a trend more than two decades ago (Bredo and Rojko, 1952). This has long been a deficit area, having to import part of its needs from states farther west (Canadian milk is excluded from the market). The supply varies with the season, however, and the months of May and June produce a surplus of milk in the area. The intensity of milk production, measured in pounds per square mile per day, is seen in Figure 3-11. The greatest intensity occurs mainly in those counties that supply the larger cities, especially New York and Philadelphia; the least is in the Appalachians and remoter sections of New England, both areas being outside the dairy belt as it is usually defined.

Figure 3-12 indicates the theoretical limits of the autumn milk supply areas of each major center in the study area (shown by dashed lines). These are calculated on the basis of prices received by farmers at each location after deducting transport cost by rail or truck. "Price contours" have been constructed to show the way in which farm gate prices vary spatially. The irregularities in this pattern result

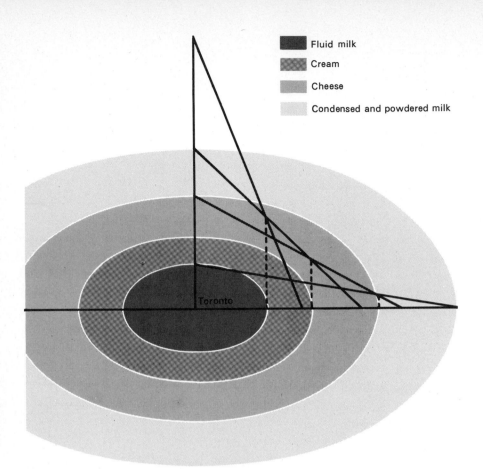

FIGURE 3-10 SOUTHERN ONTARIO: HYPOTHETICAL ECONOMIC RENT CURVE AND RINGS OF MILK, CREAM, CHEESE, AND PROCESSED MILK PRODUCTION.

from the nature of transport connections. The theoretical spring pattern also has been determined in the same manner, except that in this case the supply areas have been subdivided to indicate those counties that would be expected to provide fluid milk, cream, or industrial milk. On the basis of differences in price and transport cost, milk is supplied by the counties closest to market, cream comes from more distant areas, and industrial milk from the outer perimeters. For comparison the actual milksheds of selected eastern cities are also shown (Figure 3-13). A fairly strong resemblance to theoretically ideal supply areas is apparent, although there are distortions caused by political boundaries (reflecting differences in administrative control) and perhaps by some lag in adjusting to changing conditions. Note the overlapping of New York City's supply area with those of New England and Philadelphia.

Even more dense than the cattle population of the North American dairy belt is that of Western Europe. Collectively the latter region produces more milk than

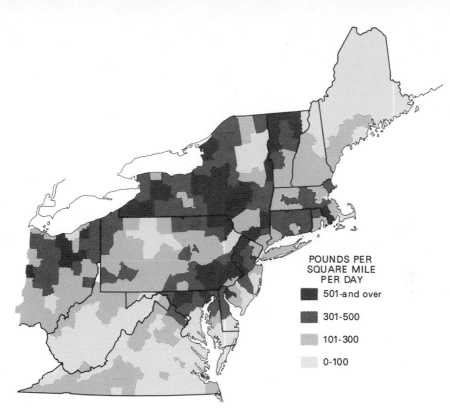

FIGURE 3-11   NEW ENGLAND: INTENSITY OF MILK PRODUCTION.

Canada and the United States, since it must serve one of the world's major concentrations of human population, which also enjoys a high per capita purchasing power. Although each of the major urban centers has its own milkshed, the Continent also has many areas noted for particular processed milk products, such as certain mountainous districts of Switzerland and Norway and upland communities in France. Some of these local specialties are made from the milk of sheep and goats as well as cows. The most concentrated region of milk production, however, is in the Low Countries, especially the Netherlands, and nearby southeast England. In this region, which coincides with the greatest European market, dairying is practiced intensively on expensive land, much of it laboriously reclaimed from the sea, lakes, and marshes.

The European pattern of milk production and marketing is undergoing changes similar to those of North America, as illustrated by the British experience (Chisholm, 1962, pp. 89–92). Until well into the nineteenth century, London and the other larger British cities obtained all their fluid milk from producers in their immediate vicinity, owing to the primitive means for transporting this perishable good. London's population today is eight times as large as it was in 1800 and has a much higher per capita purchasing power; consequently the city must draw upon a

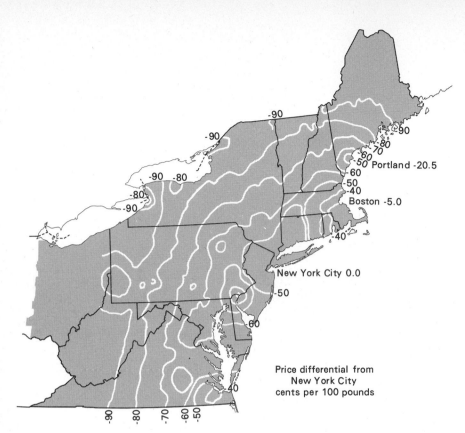

FIGURE 3-12 NEW ENGLAND: THEORETICAL LIMITS OF FALL MILK SUPPLY AREAS.

far wider area for its milk supply. The London milkshed has expanded to include much of southern England and Wales, aided by refrigeration and modern high-speed transportation. Urban populations elsewhere in Britain have likewise grown, and today most parts of the country are engaged in fluid milk production. As in Ontario, a Milk Marketing Board regulates the transfer charges paid by farmers, and retail milk prices have been equalized throughout Britain. Unlike the Canadian provinces, however, the British Milk Marketing Board encourages industrial milk production in peripheral areas. Nevertheless, many famous old cheese specialty areas have turned mainly to fluid milk, and the country now imports much of its cheese from the Netherlands, Denmark, and New Zealand.

Other forms of market-oriented agriculture A number of other types of rural land use vie for locations close to market. One of these is mushroom growing, which requires a high degree of skill and sizable outlays for the specially constructed buildings that house these unique fungi. Special soils and large quantities of organic fertilizer materials are needed too, as well as a great amount of hand labor. All this consumes very little land area, however, and mushroom houses are found

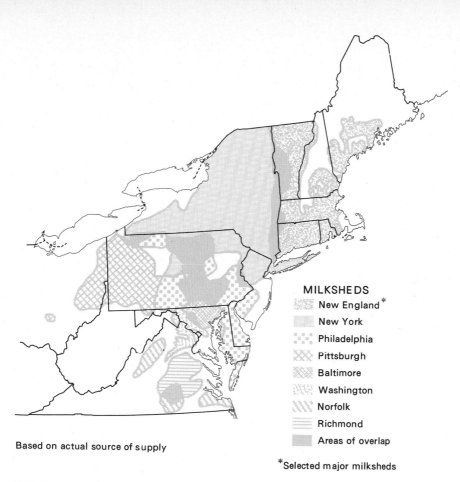

MILKSHEDS

- New England*
- New York
- Philadelphia
- Pittsburgh
- Baltimore
- Washington
- Norfolk
- Richmond
- Areas of overlap

Based on actual source of supply

*Selected major milksheds

FIGURE 3-13 NEW ENGLAND: "MILK SHEDS" OF SELECTED CITIES.

close to many metropolitan centers, which provide both ready markets and a good labor supply. An unusually large concentration of mushroom growers is to be found in southeastern Pennsylvania a short distance from Philadelphia (Merriam, 1962). Another market-oriented type of farming is floriculture, which is often associated with market gardening. Like vegetable growing, floriculture is labor-intensive and, in the case of greenhouse culture, requires much capital. Because many types of flowers mature quickly, yields are high. The product is perishable, especially cut flowers, and quick access to large urban markets is essential.

A third and very different kind of agriculture attracted to large markets is the poultry industry. This has become an unusually specialized activity in recent times. The dual-purpose hen has disappeared, replaced by birds carefully bred to give a large output either of eggs or of succulent meat. The egg layers make poor eating, and the meat birds or broilers are not good egg producers. An examination of the broiler phase of the industry will illustrate the unique characteristics of poultry farming in the modern world.

It would be difficult to find a more intensive form of rural land use than the growing of broilers. Specially designed housing is required to provide controlled temperatures and insulation from any outside noises that might startle the flock. The birds are particularly susceptible to epidemic diseases that can wipe out a flock overnight, and painstaking attention is therefore given to their health. Scientifically prepared feeds contain biotic additives and trace minerals, and elaborate precautions are taken to avoid infection. A quick turnover of birds is necessary, and the current general practice is "all in, all out," meaning that an entirely new batch of baby chicks is installed at one time and the complete flock is marketed at once when mature. This permits a thorough cleaning and disinfecting of quarters between batches. Production thus occurs in regular ten-week cycles. Little space is required for such operations, since less than 1 square foot is allocated to each bird and all feed is purchased off the farm. As this suggests, there is much emphasis upon efficiency, a response to a long-term decline in prices. Economies of large-scale production are likewise important, and it has been found that a capacity of 30,000 birds at a given time makes an ideal family-size production unit.

Transportation is an important consideration in this industry, not just because of the cost but also because of the problem of perishability. In terms of cost, half the total freight bill goes for procuring feed, while another 4 percent is required for obtaining baby chicks from hatcheries. The remaining 46 percent pays for live hauling of the mature birds to processing plants. For the broiler grower the immediate market is this plant, with which he normally has a contractual arrangement. It is important for the grower to locate close to such a plant because the birds undergo a 4 percent shrinkage of weight for every 100 miles they are transported, owing to losses from mortality, excreta, and transpiration. Because processing plants are themselves attracted to large urban concentrations, this represents one of the important reasons for the market orientation of broiler growers.

Another such influence is the natural affinity between broiler growing and market gardening. Interindustry linkages between these two forms of rural land use result in part from the large amount of fertilizer that is a by-product of broiler growing. It is estimated that 1,000 broilers can provide enough nitrogen for 1 acre of intensive vegetable cultivation. Labor requirements are also complementary, since the needs of the broiler industry are least during the midsummer period when vegetable growing has its peak requirements. Two of the most prominent areas where this relationship prevails are the Delmarva peninsula of Delaware, Maryland, and Virginia and the Niagara peninsula of southern Ontario.

Broiler production in southern Ontario is particularly market-oriented. Half the leading producers of broilers are within 25 miles of Toronto, and the greater part of the industry lies within or adjacent to the so-called Golden Horseshoe. This urban-industrial concentration, the most important in Canada, extends around the western end of Lake Ontario from Toronto to the Niagara River. The broiler growers and processors are mainly on the western side of Toronto, with the largest output of broilers coming from Lincoln County. The attraction here is the market gardening below the Niagara escarpment and the availability of feed from the rich agricultural area lying between Niagara and Windsor. Broiler growers have avoided the immediate environs of Toronto, however, because of the competition from other prospective users of this expensive land.

Mixed farming Beyond the zone of vegetables, flowers, milk, and poultry surrounding the market, we should expect to find a ring of mixed farming. Near each end of the North Atlantic urban-industrial axis there is indeed an agricultural concentration of this type. Mixed farming is a joint-cost operation in which crops and livestock are produced in combination, a diversified activity that provides the farmer with income from the sale of a number of commodities. This varied output is basically a result of soil management practices, but it also serves to provide the farm family with added security. It is a versatile form of agriculture, since the mix of crops and animals can be altered considerably in response to changing market conditions.

As practiced in the leading areas today, mixed farming is intensive, calls for skilled management, and is highly capitalized. Nevertheless, it employs far less labor per acre of land than the first-ring activities do. This labor is used efficiently throughout the year, although there are peak periods of work, especially during planting and harvesting. There has been a persistent long-term trend toward the substitution of capital for labor in mixed farming as technological innovations have appeared and as wages have risen. Yields are high and increasing, but the volume of output per acre still does not approach that of the first ring. As a result it is usual for the individual operating units in this type of farming to occupy much greater acreages than market gardening or dairying does.

Large sections of the mid-latitudes are devoted to mixed farming in those areas adjacent to the most populous districts of the wealthier technically advanced countries. These are regions of mostly good soils and fairly dependable precipitation. Much effort is devoted to preserving and enhancing the productivity of these soils, however, including scientific rotation of crops. In some places great expenditures have gone for land reclamation, draining and ditching poorly drained areas, and contouring steeper slopes for erosion control. Where land is particularly scarce, such undertakings have been elaborate. Mixed farming of the modern type is best represented today in the corn belt of the United States and Canada and the countries of Western Europe.

North American corn belt The principal zone of mixed farming in North America steadily shifted westward during the nineteenth century, always moving ahead of dairying and other more market-oriented types as the center of population migrated inland. Today it is the dominant rural land use in a large expanse of territory mainly south of the Great Lakes but also including the southernmost part of Canada, the so-called Ontario peninsula, which follows the north shore of Lake Erie from Windsor to Niagara. This characteristic form of agriculture extends southward to the Ohio River, and it reaches from Iowa and eastern Nebraska on the west to the middle of Ohio on the east.

Throughout this region the basis of the farm economy is corn, or maize, for which climatic and soil conditions of the area are particularly suited. Although native to the Americas, corn has now spread throughout the world; but in no other major area do yields equal those of the North American corn belt. On most farms the corn crop is converted into valuable animal products—hogs, beef cattle, and some lambs and sheep. In addition to the higher price these bring, there is a considerable saving from transporting the farm output in this concentrated form rather than having to move a bulky, low-value grain to market. Because the feed for the animals is produced on the farm, each such production unit is self-sustaining. Although animals are the chief source of income, there is also some return from the sale of small grains and occasionally from surplus corn.

Variable inputs per unit of land area in the corn belt are great. The farmers are well educated, skilled, and knowledgeable. Information on new developments in farming is communicated quickly by radio, television, and farm journals and technical reports from government agencies and universities engaged in agricultural research. There is an endless flow of scientific innovations in the breeding of plants and livestock, combating predatory insects and disease, and farm management and methods. Hybrid corn was one of the more prominent of such developments, but other improved plant types have performed similar miracles. Animals have been redesigned also, hogs having been bred for greater amounts of ham and bacon and beef cattle for top-grade meat cuts. Capitalization of the average corn belt farm is very great today. It is not unusual for an ordinary family farming unit to have an investment of $100,000 or more in machinery, equipment, and buildings. In addition to animal manures produced on the farm, soil building requires the purchase of large amounts of commercial fertilizer. Insecticides and herbicides must also be purchased and applied to the fields. As mechanization proceeds, the corn belt employs a diminishing number of farm workers, and the productivity of farm labor continues to rise steadily.

European mixed farming Taking a somewhat different form from corn belt agriculture in North America, mixed farming is the most widespread of the many types of agriculture found in Europe. The differences between mixed farming as practiced on the two continents are not as great, however, as they might appear at first glance. Although particular crops in the two systems may not be the same, they in fact perform similar functions in the farm economy, for the goal is to maximize output while maintaining a high level of soil productivity. As in North America, European mixed farming produces a diverse combination of crops and animals and is practiced with an intensity that is second only to that of the first-ring forms of agriculture to which it is adjacent. It is found in those areas of the British Isles beyond the dairying, vegetable, and flower-growing districts of southeast England. It is also the dominant form of agriculture on the north European plain, from the eastern provinces of the Netherlands eastward through Germany, southern Norway and Sweden, and Poland, into European Russia. In various forms it extends southward from the Low Countries into northern and central France and northern Italy. Much premium land in populous Europe is devoted to this kind of agricultural economy.

Traditionally European mixed farming was more intensive than its North American counterpart, since there have been more people to feed and less land to do it with, although this intensity systematically decreases away from the European heartland. Average yields have been higher, animal populations have been denser (much animal feed has had to be imported), and all available acreage has been carefully used. Farm operators are exceptionally skilled, relying as they do upon a depth of knowledge accumulated over a great many generations on the land. Until recently there has been no lack of manpower for farming activities, and in many parts of the Continent sizable farm populations lived in nucleated agricultural settlements within the main growing areas. Consequently European mixed farming has been more labor-intensive than North American agriculture, which has been short of labor from earliest times. With this abundance of workers European farmers tended to use less machinery than their American and Canadian counterparts, although the smaller average size of farming units has also retarded mechanization.

Today European farming is rapidly changing. Despite already high levels, intensity has been rising steeply in many areas. On a total acreage reduced by encroaching urbanization and industrialization, total European farm output has been growing rapidly since World War II. Between 1950 and 1971 wheat yields per acre rose by 94 percent, rye by 65 percent, and barley by 62 percent. Meanwhile there has been a remarkable increase in labor productivity. Typically, Germany's farm output per man-hour doubled during the period, while that of France has been going up at the rate of 6 1/2 percent per year, and similar rates are common elsewhere on the Continent. There are several reasons for this change. For one thing there has been a substitution of capital for labor, as rapid mechanization has replaced the diminishing supply of farm labor. The number of farm workers in West Germany, for example, fell 38 percent in a single decade. During the same ten-year period the number of tractors in the European Economic Community countries grew fivefold, and many other types of farm machinery, such as combines and balers, were added. Higher output per acre has also been achieved by the use of better seeds, larger amounts of chemical fertilizers, and improved livestock breeds. Average farm size has meanwhile risen substantially as formerly fragmented agricultural holdings have been consolidated, especially in traditional areas of peasant farming in Germany, France, and Sweden.

Outer rings in the modern world The types of rural land use described in the preceding pages were strongly attracted to market locations. Now we consider briefly a few examples of agricultural types having weaker ties to market. These were found in Thünen's remoter zones; today they are peripheral to the major centers of world commerce and industry. They are not able to compete successfully for prime agricultural land near the markets because of their low rent-producing capacity per unit of area. Their products are generally highly transportable, usually low in bulk in relation to their value, nonperishable, and easily stored and moved. Thus relegated to more distant locations with respect to other activities in the agricultural supply area as a whole, they have gradually been displaced by more market-oriented types and pushed ever farther from world centers by the processes described above in the example of nineteenth-century New York State. Not only have such forms of agriculture been driven to the margins of the continents of North America and Europe, but some have retreated to the farther parts of the earth.

This global expansion of Thünen's rings (as noted by Schlebecker) has occurred in response to growing world demand and has been made possible by falling transport rates, following advances in transport technology, and by declining production costs. Still another locational effect should theoretically be expected to result from lower transport rates, however. As Brinkmann noted, when the cost of moving farm commodities decreases, other locational considerations assume greater relative locational importance. For this reason the comparative advantages of different producing regions in many cases now outweigh the effects of distance. This means that activities of this sort are also being pushed out of the land of greatest productive capacity. Thünen's concept of economic rent is therefore losing in significance to Ricardo's definition based upon differentials in land capabilities. Crops now increasingly occupy the land most suitable for them, and the higher forms have first choice; lesser types are relegated to poorer areas that are often not the best for them. Whether it is distance or comparative advantage that governs, however, the same groups of activities are usually assigned poorer locations.

Some of the outer-ring forms of agriculture are exceedingly extensive in their use of land; indeed, some are among the greatest users of land. To some degree this results from their intrinsic characteristics, but it is also a result of the submarginal quality of the land into which they have been pushed. On the other hand, there are certain other outer-ring forms of agriculture that have high variable inputs, especially labor, despite the remoteness of their locations. Hence, today as in Thünen's time we must remember the caveat that intensity is not always related to market distance when different land use types are being compared.

Commercial grain farming The two largest areas of commercial grain farming are on the plains and prairies of North America and the steppes of the Soviet Union. Both are on the outer margins of mixed farming regions, and both are in areas of subhumid physical conditions. Their concentration in these places has not necessarily occurred because they are the most productive locations for grains. Although, paradoxically, some of the world's best soils are found here, rainfall is light and unpredictable, especially in those marginal areas referred to as the "dust bowl" in the United States and the "virgin lands" of the U.S.S.R. These crops are found here mainly because the small grains can grow under such conditions, albeit with low yields, whereas crops yielding higher rents are more demanding in their requirements. Other areas devoted to these land uses are in South Africa and eastern Australia and along the margins of the Argentine pampa.

Commercial grain farming is one of the more specialized types of agriculture. Characteristically it is a monoculture, with the entire productive acreage of a given farm devoted to a single small grain. The most important of these is wheat, a highly transportable commodity that has long been a major staple of world commerce. Despite the long distances over which wheat moves, however, its major growing areas require access to efficient, low-cost transport facilities. Indeed, certain of the most isolated wheat-growing regions must convert their grain into high-value animal products during periods of low grain prices. This form of agriculture is very extensive. Production costs are low, with few variable inputs per acre of land. Labor requirements are especially light, since only planting and harvesting are necessary, and in some cases even these seasonal operations are contracted out. Although farms are highly mechanized, the capital costs are spread over much total acreage. Little if any fertilizer is used, rarely is there a rotation of crops, and fallowing (dry farming) is common in the least humid areas.

Despite the characteristic richness of the soil, yields are quite low owing to the meager precipitation. The output per acre in these regions is much lower than the yields of small grains in humid lands where these represent a part of the mixed farming economy. The products of commercial grain farms are high in quality, however, including some of the choicer varieties of hard wheat used for making premium grades of bread flour. For all these reasons individual farming units in these areas have very large acreages, often thousands of acres in the United States, Canada, Australia, and the Soviet Union. Consequently the output per farm may be very great. In certain respects commercial grain farming is reminiscent of Thünen's three-field system. There is the same low level of variable inputs per acre and similarly low production costs; output per acre is also low. Another feature they have in common is fallowing, or resting, the land for a year or so between crops.

Commercial grazing   Extensive livestock production occupied the outermost ring of Thünen's isolated state, and it is similarly located in the present world. During the historical expansion of agricultural supply areas, a zone of grazing always moved ahead of arable farming. In the United States this is shown by the migrations of stockyard and meat-packing operations, an industry that has traditionally located on the marketward margins of animal-producing areas. During the earliest period meat-packing took place within the original Colonies, but as the agricultural system grew, the industry shifted westward to Buffalo and Pittsburgh, then to Cincinnati, Indianapolis, and Chicago, and finally to Kansas City, Omaha, and Denver.

Commercial grazing provides still another example of the principle of comparative advantage. Indeed, in this case it might even be termed the "principle of last choice," since most of the world's grazing has today been relegated to lands of the poorest quality as well as in the remotest locations. Because of excessive aridity or rough terrain the main livestock ranching areas are unsuited to crops but can graze animals. Still, these are by no means the most productive areas for animal rearing; far more animals per land unit could be produced on the better lands now devoted to crops. In the intermontane regions of the American West, for example, animal-carrying capacities are so low that more than 100 acres are customarily required to support a single beef animal. By contrast, the humid pampa of Argentina, a grazing land that has rich soils and ample rainfall but is remote from the world metropolis, requires as little as 2 acres per steer.

This form of rural land use is thus customarily found in areas submarginal for cropping. In Canada and the United States these are mainly the high plains and prairies, the western mountains, and the arid and semiarid regions between. This is the principal land use of the steppes, deserts, and tropical savannas of Central and South America, although, as noted earlier, even such favorable agricultural areas as eastern Argentina and adjacent Uruguay are devoted mainly to animal rearing. In South Africa commercial grazing is found on the high, dry central plateau. In Europe it occurs in two kinds of locations: along the southern margins of the Continent, especially Iberia, and in the uplands and rougher pasturelands of the British Isles and similarly low-quality land on the Continent.

The nature of the grazing industries varies with accessibility and the levels of development of the countries in which they are found. The American West is typical of commercial livestock rearing in a technically advanced land with superior transport connections to the major markets for animal products. Here it is very extensive in its use of land, taking advantage of the great amount of cheap land available for such purposes. Because of the low animal yield in such places, individual production units are extremely large, often thousands of acres. Variable inputs are very low since little equipment is used and few workers are needed, the animals requiring little day-to-day care. The largest outlay is for high-quality breeding stock, either beef or sheep (the two are not usually produced on the same ranch). The products are quite transportable, consisting of valuable live animals or compact bales of wool. A large proportion of the animals reared in the West are sold to corn belt farmers for finish fattening. The main exceptions occur in those fortunate places within the grazing region where irrigated agriculture is possible and supplementary feed can thus be provided for animal fattening. Irrigated alfalfa and sugar-beet pulp and tops are prime animal feed in such areas. A further requirement for this type of local animal finishing is ease of access to packing plants such as those in Denver or Omaha.

One final characteristic of commercial grazing industries is the prevalence of joint products. This is especially true of sheep ranching, which yields both wool and mutton or lambs. These are produced in essentially constant proportions on each ranch and provide the rancher with some intricate problems of planning, since the markets for meat and those for animal fibers are distinctly different.

Industrial crops Another group of rural land uses that appeared in Thünen's sixth ring were the industrial crops. These are agricultural commodities used as raw materials for industry, such as oil seeds (linseed, rapeseed, etc.) and plant fibers (cotton, sisal, and flax, among many others). Despite their usual remoteness from world markets, lands devoted to these commodities tend to be intensively farmed. The variable input normally used in greatest quantity is labor, plentiful and cheap in many peripheral regions, often underdeveloped countries. In those technically advanced countries where industrial crop production persists as a remnant of an earlier period, capital has ordinarily been substituted for labor. In addition to mechanization, it is usually necessary to use much fertilizer to maintain output of these soil-robbing crops. Much of the world's agricultural land is physically suited to such production, but relatively small acreages in total are required to supply a world demand that is either static or declining because of competition from synthetic substitutes. The products of such farming are supremely transportable when they leave the growing areas because of initial local processing to reduce bulk, often a labor-intensive operation. The commodities thus shipped are relatively valuable but small in volume and weight per unit of land area devoted to their production.

Cotton, the most important of the plant fibers, is a prime example of most of these characteristics. The first commercially significant growing areas of cotton were the Old South of the United States and the islands of the Caribbean. During the eighteenth and early nineteenth centuries these regions were on the outer margins of the world's agricultural supply area. The cotton farming economy was based on large and exceedingly cheap labor supply—African slaves. Initial processing on a large scale became possible with the appearance of the cotton gin, which removes the seed, two-thirds of the weight of the raw cotton. The cotton gin also greatly reduces the product's bulk by compressing the loose fibers into dense bales fastened with band iron. In this form cotton could be shipped cheaply over long distances to textile mills, first in Lancashire and later in New England.

Today the American cotton lands are no longer in the outer ring of world agriculture, and cotton farming has spread throughout the warmer parts of the earth. The industry continues to persist in the United States mainly because of an unusual combination of circumstances. First, growers have adjusted to the loss of low-cost labor and to intensified world competition by increasing their capital inputs. They have mechanized planting, tilling, and picking operations, and they are employing ever greater quantities of commercial fertilizers, insecticides, and weed killers. Second, increased exploitation of the joint-product nature of cotton fiber and cottonseeds has also helped. Today the seeds yield an increasing variety of commercially valuable products, including vegetable oil, cottonseed cake and meal (for animal feed), and linters (tiny hairlike fibers that adhere to the seed after the cotton is removed). Third, American growers are specializing increasingly in premium grades of cotton, particularly the long- and extra-long-staple cottons of the Southwest. Finally, and perhaps most important of all, cotton growers have enjoyed high government subsidies.

Cotton farming in the Soviet Union has assumed many of these same characteristics. There the crop is mainly grown under irrigation, emphasizes special types of fiber, is mechanized, and is subject to governmental intervention (most of the output is from state farms). Most of the other cotton lands are in underdeveloped countries, where there is much cheap labor. In West Africa and India and many other underdeveloped lands the cotton consists largely of low-grade, short-staple types. There are important exceptions, however: some of the world's premium grades of extra-long-staple cottom come from the irrigated valleys of Peru, Egypt, and Pakistan.

Plantation agriculture In addition to the activities described above, many other types of rural land use are to be found at a distance from the major world market although producing for that market. Among these are several whose locations depend upon some absolute or comparative advantage of the area in which they are found. A notable example is that broad class of rural activities referred to as tropical commercial, or plantation, agriculture. The absolute advantage in each case is a special set of climatic and soil conditions. Representative of crops of this type are sugar cane, banana, rubber, and the beverage crops—coffee, cacao, and tea.

It should be noted that these crops are not grown commercially in all possible locations; instead there is much regional specialization on the basis of comparative advantage. One such case is crude rubber production. Physical conditions in the rain-forest areas of tropical America, where the plant originated, are quite similar to those of Southeast Asia, where the major output occurs today. The main rubber-producing areas of the East have a decisive relative advantage in the nature of commercial control of the industry, accessibility to major sea lanes, and especially their large supplies of cheap, skilled labor. Meanwhile, corresponding regions in the Americas tend to specialize in tropical commercial agriculture of less labor-intensive kinds.

A somewhat similar case is that of tea, which comes from a plant that is adaptable to a number of physical conditions found throughout subtropical and tropical areas in both hemispheres. Nevertheless, by far the leading regions of tea production are in the Orient. One of the principal tea-growing districts is in southeastern China, which has physical conditions closely approximated in the South Atlantic states of the United States. Yet, attempts to establish such an industry in the latter location have failed, not because the plant did not grow well but because of inability to secure a labor force with the required skills at a competitive cost.

URBAN LAND USE

Thünen noted that the increasing levels of rent for agricultural land to be observed as one approaches the town merely anticipate a much steeper rise within the urban area, reaching a maximum at the town center (Hall, 1966, p. 133). This point of highest rents is equivalent to the "peak value intersection" (PVI) in the modern Western city. The pricing of urban land and its allocation among prospective uses and users can be viewed in fundamentally the same way as for rural property, namely, as a process of competitive bidding. Ideally this allots each piece of land to the highest and best use for that site (see Chapter 2). In both rural and urban areas this involves a substitution among costs and incomes, and in both instances the spatial effect is focal in nature. Distance from the urban center thus determines land values and produces a land use pattern of concentric rings, given all the limiting assumptions of the Thünen model. If this arrangement is to be regarded as the fundamental spatial structure of urban space, it must also be recognized that the introduction of variables other than distance can be expected to disturb the pattern. Some of these additional influences are static in character, producing variations from place to place on any given date, while others exert their spatial effects with the passage of time. The theoretical basis for this line of reasoning was reviewed in Chapter 2. Here we are to examine real-world evidence of (1) a fundamental zonal pattern of urban land values and use, (2) modifications of this ideal through the addition of other variables, and (3) the composite spatial effect of all these.

EVIDENCE OF THE THEORETICAL IDEAL

In most modern cities it is possible to distinguish certain centripetal influences upon land values and the locations of residential areas, commercial activities, and manufacturing, but the closest approach to the ideal occurred at an earlier date in North America. At the beginning of this present century the urban center was the point of convergence for all forms of transportation: railways, cable cars, street-cars, and rapid transit. Although recent events have complicated the pattern, the center still retains some of that attraction.

Land values The zonal arrangement reached its zenith in American cities about 1910, at which time land values dropped precipitously away from the PVI, to continue descending with increasing gradualness toward the margins of the urban area (Hoyt, 1933, p.337). The great contrast between central values and those on the periphery is shown by an early account of New York City (Hurd, 1924, pp. 133–159), although that city was somewhat exceptional in having two spatially separated PVIs, the highest being in the financial district and the other being the city's retail center. At that time land values on Wall Street averaged $35,000 per front foot as opposed to $5 per front foot for urban land at the city margins (and even this was twice the value of adjacent farmland).

Chicago's PVI has traditionally been at State and Madison Streets, which is the center of retailing. In 1910, the combined land values of the Loop (Chicago's central business district), with an area under 300 acres, represented 40 percent of the total for the entire city (Hoyt, 1933, p. 337). Values declined in all directions from the PVI at a rate that was fairly uniform logarithmically (Yeates, 1965).

Land use There is much real-world evidence to confirm the theoretical relationship between land values and land use. Certain activities can generate more rent than others at each site and thus tend to win out in the competition for it. The factors determining this outcome, however, vary from one class of land use to another and also within classes.

Residential land About two-fifths of total developed land in North American cities is allocated to residential uses. Several aspects of this class of land use tend to be arranged basically in a zonal manner. One of these is population density, which is highest near (but not usually in) the center and declines toward the margins. Closest to the center are usually found tall multifamily dwellings, with widely spaced single-family residences near the margins and various intermediate housing types between. The negative-exponential character of population density curves to be expected from this arrangement has been confirmed in many places, including Toronto (Latham and Yeates, 1970), Chicago (Winsborough, 1961; Rees, 1968), London (Clark, 1951), and Kingston, Jamaica (Newling, 1966).

Various characteristics of the population, such as median age and family size, have also been found to be related to distance from the city center. The life cycle of individuals and families is expressed in the age levels of the population; the presence of children in the home, in particular, influences the choice of residential location. Young families form in the close-in districts, but as family size increases, there is a tendency to escape to more spacious quarters farther out. Older couples, their children grown, in many cases return to the central area. Confirming these tendencies, it has been found (Hoover and Vernon, 1959) that the median age varies considerably between the inner and outer residential zones. Children are underrepresented in the core and especially few are of school age. Mainly the population in such areas consists of single adults and childless couples, the aged being overrepresented. The Chicago experience verifies this also (Rees, 1968). Moreover, the disparity in ages between the core and the suburbs seems to be increasing. A spatial analysis of Toronto's population confirms that the smallest families in that city are closest to the central business district (CBD) (Murdie, 1969).

Commercial land uses   The various classes of commercial land use—retailing, finance, offices, and so forth—have been found to assume a zonal arrangement with respect to distance from the PVI. In their analyses of eight CBDs, Murphy and Vance (1955) discovered that the innermost zone adjacent to the PVI is predominantly allocated to retailing, with a much lower percentage of space devoted to office uses. As one moves farther away from the PVI, however, the percentage of space occupied by retailing diminishes progressively, the proportion given over to offices grows, and, nearer the outer margins, certain non-CBD uses begin to appear.

A more recent study of Dubuque, Iowa (Yeates and Garner, 1971, pp. 353–359), indicated a close relationship between land use and land value within the CBD and disclosed a zonation of activities occupying first-floor locations. An inner area consisting of all sites with values higher than 25 percent of the peak value was found to be dominated by retail types, while services, finance, and office uses were generally absent. An outer zone including all locations with 25 percent or less of the PVI value showed increasing diversity of land use.

Manufacturing land use   Manufacturing occupies two zones within the city, one on the margins of the CBD and the other near the outer limits of the urban area. In the former area are those small, labor-intensive but low-wage firms making compact, high-value products; in the latter zone are the large, space-using establishments using great volumes of bulky, cheap raw materials and having a large output. Such a concentric arrangement of manufacturing was verified in a study of newly established firms in Chicago (Moses, 1968), where a concentration of small new firms was found at an average distance of 4 miles from the CBD and most of the large new establishments were observed at a distance of 11 to 16 miles from the CBD.

MODIFICATIONS TO THE ZONAL PATTERN

As we look at locational influences other than distance from the center, we discover that certain of these contribute to urban growth but do not necessarily disturb the concentric form. Other new variables, however, tend to change the concentric pattern. Those contributing to urban growth tend to be centrifugal, while those acting to disturb the ideal pattern may have a variety of spatial effects.

Growth of the city Among those influences acting to cause the metropolis to spread outward are population increase, resulting mainly from in-migration, and technological innovation of various kinds. Under ideal conditions, urban growth tends to cause an outward expansion of land use rings, as in the rural case. The process by which this occurs was described by Burgess for Chicago (1925) in the language of human ecology. Thus activities of an inner zone "invade" the next outer zone until eventually these and new land uses gain the ascendancy and "succession" occurs. Centrifugal tendencies of this type are to be found in each class of land use.

Changing population densities As noted earlier, there is confirmation for our theoretical expectation of a negative-exponential decrease in population density outward from the center. However, with the passage of time it has been found that the particular shape of the downward-sloping density curve changes. A comparative study of Pittsburgh, Pennsylvania, and Kingston, Jamaica (Newling, 1966) revealed that recent years have seen density curves become less steep. Especially in the United States, this trend can be traced to the suburbanization of populations associated with the life cycle of the family, racial conflicts of the inner city, the general rise in per capita incomes, and transport innovations, among other things.

A related change has occurred with respect to the point of highest density, the crest of the population wave, which has tended to shift progressively away from the center. Winsborough (1961) found, for example, that during Chicago's early years the central population density increased and then began to fall as residential uses were squeezed away from the center by commercial and manufacturing uses. Viewed in a three-dimensional sense, declining central densities could be likened to the forming of a hole in a doughnut.

Suburbanization of commerce and industry In 1910 the urban core of North American cities dominated both the production and distribution of goods and services, but this hegemony of the center has declined at least relatively during recent decades. Even as the residential population has been spreading outward, so also have secondary and tertiary activities. The CBD in particular has lost ground as it has been found too congested for auto-borne shoppers and as commercial firms have discovered the advantages of large-scale marketing in more spacious surroundings. Nevertheless, there has been a continuing and not entirely resolved conflict between centrifugal and centripetal influences, as a recent Chicago study has shown (Moses, 1968, pp. 63–64). An analysis of firm migration showed that the pull of the CBD is still strong for (1) finance, insurance, and real estate, (2) communications and public utilities, and (3) miscellaneous business services. For warehousing, transport services, and retailing the CBD tie was found particularly weak, and firms in these categories were most numerous among migrants from the center.

The evidence for both New York and Chicago shows that retailing in particular is declining in the CBD and growing on the periphery, although the ultimate demise of the CBD is belied by the clearly expressed determination of major mercantile chains to maintain their "flagship" stores in the center. Warehousing, which in earlier times relied upon proximity to inner-city rail terminals for intercity commodity movements, has now turned largely to truck transport and largely migrated to the city margins. It was found in Chicago (Moses, 1968), for example, that the origins of migrating warehouse firms were at a median distance of 3 miles from the CBD and that their destinations were at a distance of 10 miles. Chicago now has three times as many warehouses in the outer ring as in all the others combined.

Central office functions and banking operations have been reluctant to move, and the evidence for New York City (Hoover and Vernon, 1959, p. 99) indicates that only the smaller establishments tend to go to the suburbs. On the whole, such activities rely upon locations that are as central as possible to the total metropolitan area for the attracting of both customers and workers. In Chicago (Moses, 1968) it has been found that one reason for the CBD attraction for these activities is their dependence upon large numbers of female workers. Fewer women than men drive cars to work in that city, and the dependence of women on mass transit favored the CBD. Lunchtime shopping and after-hours recreation were also significant attractions. Indeed, many firms have been singularly unsuccessful in recruiting large female labor forces in suburban locations.

A similar picture is offered by manufacturing. Some decentralization of industrial employment has occurred in response to the long-term centrifugal effect of transport innovation, as the experience of Chicago shows (Moses and Williams, 1967). Like warehousing, many industries have shifted from rail to truck transportation; and, at the same time, some have experienced important innovations in materials-handling methods and production technology, including single-floor plant layouts, and a switch to electric motive power. This varies with industry type, however, and certain classes have been little affected by centrifugal forces. In the Chicago case (Moses, 1968) textiles and apparel, lumber and furniture, and food-processing firms have been especially hesitant to leave their inner-city locations. Firms of this type are labor-intensive, pay low wages, and hire large numbers of female workers. The advantages of the central areas for recruiting female industrial labor are the same as those for CBD service activities.

The conflict between centripetal and centrifugal tendencies in manufacturing location is affected, too, by the size and age of the firm. Studies in London (Martin, 1966), New York (Hoover and Vernon, 1959), and Chicago (Moses, 1969) have tended to confirm the "seedbed" hypothesis of firm growth and development. This views the inner zone of the city as an incubating area for new, small plants, which often depend upon leased space, rely upon close linkages with related firms, and must have a nearby supply of cheap labor. Some of these industries remain small and continue their inner-city locations indefinitely. Others outgrow their rental space and move to the periphery, where they can gain the full benefits of internal economies. Such firms are just as likely to migrate to locations on the outer periphery of the central city as to the suburbs. Confirmation of these tendencies has been provided by studies both in Chicago (Reeder, 1955) and in San Francisco (Lowenstein and Bradwell, 1966).

Departures from concentricity   Whereas the influences described in the previous section tended mainly to change the size of the urban system, several others are more likely to alter the basic form of the urban pattern. Some of the variables that have such an effect are variations in accessibility, innovations in marketing, and a number of social and political forces. Each of these tends to distort the concentric arrangement in various ways, though the basic economic processes that give rise to zonal patterns are usually still existent. In some cases they introduce a linearity or attenuation of land value and land use zones, and in certain instances they produce a clustering effect through either internal cohesion or external pressures or both.

Linear attenuations of zonal patterns   Arterial streets and highways, rail lines, and waterways provide faster and cheaper access, thus giving a special advantage to land adjacent to them. Rents of such land are bid upward, and the highest and best use occupies it. Activities benefiting from high accessibility tend to cling to routes of this kind as far as possible; hence the linearity of land use zones along arterials, especially commerce and manufacturing. Arterials frequently radiate outward from the urban center like spokes on a wheel, and urban growth at their outer margins tends to assume the form of sectors (Hoyt, 1939).

The effects of transport arteries on land values have been confirmed by Knos (1962) for Topeka, Kansas, and by Berry for Chicago (1963). The tendency of retail and service establishments to locate along routes reaching outward from the PVI has been observed in several communities. In some cases this type of land use may extend throughout all or most of the length of a major street on both sides in "strip," "ribbon," or "string" developments. These commercial activities, referred to as "urban arterial business," occasionally follow an important route beyond the limits of the city into the open country, where they become "interurban arterial business" (Berry, 1959). One large metropolis where this kind of commercial pattern is especially prominent is Los Angeles (Foster and Nelson, 1958).

Manufacturing enterprises likewise tend to locate along a main route of travel, whether rail, highway, or navigable water. Papermaking, food processing, refining, and various activities of like nature are prominent on the banks of the Thames as well as certain canals in the London metropolitan area (Martin, 1966). Sectoral growth of manufacturing has been studied in many other major centers as well. In Chicago Reeder (1954) found that when manufacturing plants move from the inner city, they tend to become located farther out in the same sector. At the outer margins of a city residential zones likewise tend to stretch farther along major highways and commuter rail lines, giving the often-noted star-shaped city.

Physical features may also take a linear direction and lend this form to land use zones. The crest of a ridge is often favored by high-income housing, for example; and, as Burgess (1925) observed, the slopes tend to be occupied by families in the middle incomes while the low ground remains for the less well-off. Hoyt (1939) stressed this characteristic of urban housing, which is particularly prominent in such cities as Montreal, Seattle, and Los Angeles. By contrast, commerce and manufacturing activities seek level land. A linearity of land use also appears along lake and ocean fronts, which, like elevations, are prized for high-class residential purposes. In many waterfront cities, like Buffalo and Montreal, such areas have already been preempted by commerce and manufacturing.

Clustering   Underlying the classical model of land use is the assumption of a single focal point for all activities. As cities grow in size and complexity and as the technologies of transportation, production, and distribution advance, this initial assumption becomes less realistic. In the large modern city many new points of focus for land uses of all types are appearing, with attendant effects on land values.

Competing with the original CBD, other concentrations of business activities are springing up to serve widely spreading residential communities. The same transport innovations that have contributed to the suburbanization of people have made possible the evolution of such shopping areas. A four-level hierarchy of shopping centers has been distinguished in Chicago; in descending order these are the CBD, regional centers, community centers, and neighborhood centers (Berry, 1963). This study also showed that commercial centers at each level exhibit distinctive characteristics including the number of centers of a particular type, the size of area served, their spacing, and the number of functions provided. Thus a city has only one CBD but several regional centers, even more community centers, and a great many neighborhood centers. While the CBD serves the entire metropolitan area, each successively lower level of center caters to a more restricted territory. As a consequence, neighborhood centers are separated from each other by comparatively short distances, but as one ascends the scale, the spacing of centers at each level becomes wider. The CBD provides a full range of functional types of commercial activities, but, as Garner's study (1966) of Chicago disclosed, certain of these activities are missing at the regional level, and still fewer are present in the community and neighborhood centers.

These same studies have also shown that each nucleated business area has its own PVI, away from which land values fall sharply. Related to this is an internal differentiation of land use types. Not only is there the concentric arrangement noted above for the CBD, but there is also a tendency for certain related activities to form clusters within a commercial center. This occurs at each level but is clearest at the higher ones. Mapping of such nucleations within Chicago's Loop (Berry, 1967) showed the retail district to be centered on State Street, the financial district on La Salle Street, a theater district on North State and nearby Randolph and Wabash Streets, and various other concentrations. In addition elsewhere in the city are such special areas as the automobile row. In each instance the commodities or services provided can be described as "shopping goods," since customers prefer to make comparisons before buying.

Political effects on urban land use patterns   The influence of political institutions on urban land use has been exceedingly pervasive but difficult to categorize in a simple way. Not only are governments important users of urban space for such things as institutions, the housing of administrative functions, and streets, roads, and parks, but they also affect nongovernmental land uses in a number of direct and indirect ways. Perhaps the most easily defined spatial effect of political entities is taxation, which appears to be mainly centrifugal. The suburbanization of manufacturing has been accelerated in such widely separated metropolitan areas as New York (Hoover and Vernon, 1959) and San Francisco (Lowenstein and Bradwell, 1966) by high taxes in the central city.

Zoning by municipal authorities, which first appeared in New York in 1916, seems in balance to have had a conservatizing effect on urban spatial structure, tending merely to freeze the existing arrangement in most cases, where such controls have been effective at all (Hoover and Vernon, 1959). Minimum-lot residential zoning in the suburbs favors wealthier families and retards intensification of land use in such areas. Where enforced, commercial zoning has tended to favor planned shopping centers rather than ribbon development. Zoning seems to have reinforced the tendency for manufacturing growth to occur in a sectoral fashion, adding new establishments on the outer margins of the areas where it originally became established. In other cases, however, manufacturing districts have become confined by zoning authorities to pockets surrounded by unlike land uses as the city has expanded.

Thus, the basic processes giving rise to concentric patterns of land use can be identified in both the agricultural and urban spheres. Naturally, many of the patterns appear complex, and it should be reiterated in this concluding paragraph that such complexities are to be expected. The general prevalence of the processes inherent in the economic rent model, however, are remarkable, and the local regional or world patterns that result are quite interpretable within this context. Those students who wish to delve deeper into agricultural or urban geography will tend to focus on departures from these overall patterns and the general theory from which they can be derived, but these departures should always be placed within the context of the rather simple spatial processes from which the concentric patterns are obtained.

INDUSTRIAL-LOCATION THEORY

Converting the raw materials of nature into useful objects is an activity that occurs in nearly every society from the most primitive to the most advanced. There is a decided contrast, however, between the rudimentary artifacts of an Amazonian tribe and the sophisticated products of a North American manufacturing center. Modern industry not only produces a different type of output but also employs a far larger proportion of the population, uses its workers in a more specialized fashion, and provides them with complex and ingenious machines powered by inanimate energy. For those countries fortunate enough to have well-developed industrial sectors, the outpouring of goods from their factories is a major source of prosperity. The material benefits of manufacturing are clearly recognized by those persons living in underdeveloped countries, where industrialization is often regarded as a panacea for every economic ill. Yet industry is strongly attracted to certain countries and to particular regions within countries, while it tends to avoid others. Why industries become located where they do is therefore a crucial question affecting the welfare of millions. The effort to find an answer for this question has produced a growing body of industrial-location theory.

EXPLAINING THE LOCATION OF INDUSTRIES

The basic elements of this theory derive from certain characteristics of manufacturing. The same factors of production that influence the location of primary activities (Chapter 2)—land, labor, capital, and entrepreneurship—also enter into the industrial-location decision; but these factors usually affect manufacturing in a different manner and are employed in other proportions than in agriculture. Manufacturing is also distinctive in having a number of social tendencies that cause the location of one firm to be influenced by the locations of other firms. In addition, industrial location is affected by a number of institutional factors, which are the organizational arrangements of human societies, and by the variable characteristics of human beings.

ROLE OF FACTORS OF PRODUCTION

In manufacturing location the factors of production sometimes play multiple roles. This is especially true of *land*. When regarded as a finite portion of the earth's surface, land is required by manufacturing in relatively small amounts in comparison with the needs of agriculture. Yet land differs in quality and price from one place to another, and certain physical attributes of a site may add to manufacturing costs. A particularly cold or hot climate, for example, may require extra outlays for insulation, air conditioning, or space heating. Otherwise the cost of land does not usually exert a major influence on the selection of a general region for production, although it may become an important consideration in the choice of a final site within the chosen region. Once a piece of ground has been occupied by a manufacturing plant, the cost of that land may thereafter be regarded as a more or less fixed item having little if any relation to volume of output or level of sales.

In its traditional economic sense, the term *land* can also be extended to include those raw-material and energy inputs that originate in the physical environment, however much they may have been processed and handled during the meantime. The sources of these inputs are distributed unevenly in earth space and often vary spatially in their quality, quantity, and unit cost. Some materials and fuels are therefore more accessible than others to the manufacturing site, and transport costs for procuring these needs must be added to their initial purchase price. The extent to which each of these inputs influences the locational decision depends upon its proportionate contribution to the final product.

Another factor of production, *labor*, also varies from place to place in its quality, quantity, and cost. For the most part these spatial variations in labor result from the imperfect mobility of people. Workers may be prevented by governmental restrictions from migrating to areas of greater opportunity; or, if free to move, they may choose not to do so because of social or cultural reasons. If a good supply of workers having a desirable set of qualifications thus becomes concentrated in a given area, this labor pool may prove a strong attraction to certain types of manufacturing.

In some cases *capital* is an important determinant of location. This term is used in many ways, both in common speech and in its technical applications. For our purposes two possible meanings are useful: (1) capital in the form of tangible assets such as machinery, buildings, and inventory; and (2) intangible forms of capital, including legal instruments (stock certificates, warehouse receipts) that represent claims to ownership of tangible goods and, more familiarly, money intended for investment in such assets. In either sense capital is required in varying degrees for all manufacturing operations. Its use entails a cost, payment of which takes the form of interest, dividends, or rentals. Some forms of capital are mobile, although there may be obstacles to their movement. Political barriers to the transfer of capital can have important locational effects, particularly at the international level. Some forms of capital equipment are physically difficult or even impossible to move. Thus capital is another factor of production that varies spatially in quantity and price.

In many industries it is possible for firms to vary the proportions of the factors of production used to make a given product. Like farmers, manufacturers can substitute transport costs for rent payments merely by choosing cheaper land at a distance from raw materials or markets. Similarly, industrialists can substitute capital for labor by introducing machinery to take the place of workers. It is also possible to substitute one type of raw material or fuel for another. These are but a few of the many options available to entrepreneurs for varying the mix of inputs for a particular line of production. When the possibilities for substitution are numerous, a greater latitude of locational choice is open to the producer.

NATURE OF THE PRODUCT

Certain characteristics of a firm's products may influence the location of its manufacturing facilities. In the first place, manufactured goods are more easily identified according to source than primary commodities are. Wheat, copper ore, and timber are sold by grade; their origins and the names of their producers are unknown to the final purchasers (although brand names are being given increasingly to citrus fruits and bananas). Most manufactured products, on the other hand, are stamped clearly with the name and trademark of the maker, who often spends large sums for advertising to influence consumer preferences in favor of his merchandise. To the extent that he succeeds in his sales promotion efforts, his customers will be willing to travel farther or pay more in transport costs for his products than for those of his competitors.

If a firm manufactures consumer goods—that is, if its products are in a form ready for use by the public at large—then the location of production will usually show a relationship to the spatial distribution of population. On the other hand, the making of producer goods—semimanufactured materials, supplies, and equipment—may or may not be attracted to markets. The demand for manufactured goods is usually more responsive to changes in consumer income or to changes in price than the demand for agricultural goods is. In other words, industrial products are said to have a greater *price elasticity of demand*. But even for manufactured items there is much variation in price elasticity from one industry to another. This is true especially of "luxury goods" as opposed to necessities.

INTERNAL ECONOMIES

The location of industries can be affected by some of the steps that are taken to reduce unit production costs within a single establishment. By making certain adjustments in operating methods, a firm can benefit from what is called *internal economies*. One way to accomplish this is through careful selection of the most efficient size of production unit. Every type of manufacturing activity appears to have an optimal size that applies to the individual establishment. The optimum may depend on the type of product made. Certain kinds of merchandise can be produced economically in large quantities at a single location, particularly if they are nonperishable and easily transported—radios, for example. Others are severely limited in the volume of output that is feasible in one place. Soft baked goods (breads and cakes) and other perishables that cannot withstand a long haul are of this latter type. Firms that wish to expand their markets for such goods must usually build branch factories rather than add to existing ones. The optimal size of establishment in a given industry tends to increase over time owing to improved techniques of production and transportation and to changing demand conditions.

An establishment has several inducements for operating as close as possible to its optimum and not to drop too far below it. These *economies of large-scale operation* have been classified under three headings (Hoover, 1948, pp. 78–80). The first is termed the principle of *massing of reserves*. It is necessary for each establishment to maintain a basic stock of raw materials, fuel, spare parts, and other items required to assure a steady flow of output and thus avoid costly delays. The storage expenses and the cost of capital tied up in such reserves can be a serious financial burden, but the size of the reserve maintained by a large establishment need not be much greater than that of a small one. The firm with one milling machine must carry most of the spare parts that are liable to breakage, but the firm with 100 milling machines can count on not having more than one or at most a few of its machines disabled for the same reason at any one time. When measured in terms of unit output, then, the large plant enjoys a substantial saving that is denied the small producer.

The principle of *multiples* provides a second set of economies of large-scale operation. Individual workers and machines can ordinarily be utilized most efficiently within certain lower and upper limits of output. An example of this is the steam engine, which, once set in operation, can power a large number of other pieces of machinery. If it is underused, much of its energy output is wasted; if it is overburdened, it refuses to function properly. A factory manager achieves the lowest unit operating costs by carefully adjusting the size of his output to take account of the imperfect divisibility of these basic elements in the process. Because individual men and machines contribute proportionately more to the operations of a small concern, it is more difficult to regulate production rates to their discrete capacity levels than it is in a large plant, which can distribute the load among many workers and pieces of equipment.

The third category consists of those savings that large factories may enjoy because of their ability to make *bulk purchases* of raw materials, equipment, energy, and services. They can also reduce transport costs by shipping and receiving in carload lots, and they can exert greater bargaining power to obtain better rates, terms, and prices in all their dealings with suppliers.

These and other internal economies can be achieved through the process of *integration*. The simple enlargement of a company's existing facilities or the merging of two or more firms competing in the same line of production can bring economies of scale in what is called *horizontal integration*. In other cases internal economies can be obtained through increasing the number of related operations taking place at a single location. This is true of those industries in which the processing of raw materials into finished products takes place in several stages. If a company is able to conduct several of its sequential operations at one location, it can obtain savings because of the increase in plant size and through eliminating certain costs incurred between spatially separated stages. *Vertical integration* of this kind is illustrated by the steel industry, which tends to integrate its smelting and refining operations wherever possible. The large integrated mill is able to save on transport costs between one operation and the next and on fuel costs, since the metal can retain much of its heat on short intraplant moves.

Vertical integration provides other benefits too. *Integrating backward*, an establishment can introduce preliminary stages of manufacture, thereby securing a more certain supply of raw materials and obtaining greater control over their quality and price. It is for this reason that some motorcar producers make their own steel. *Integrating forward*, the plant can be assured of a dependable, and perhaps enlarged, market for its products. This helps to explain the increased production of petrochemicals at petroleum refineries today.

EXTERNAL ECONOMIES

Relationships among different concerns also have locational effects. Generally speaking, intercompany relations may have either an attracting or a repelling effect on other firms. Under some conditions makers of standard consumer goods, such as bread or corrugated boxes, may seek to locate as far as possible from competitors so as to dominate a larger market. Many other types of manufacturing, however, achieve important *external economies* by locating near other producers, even competitors. For some companies this "social" tendency is due to the interdependence between suppliers and their customers. Substantial savings in transport costs can sometimes be realized by locating adjacent to another firm that is the source of a leading raw material or the principal market for a product. Thus steel mills may, on the one hand, attract concerns making the firebricks with which they line their furnaces; on the other hand, they may attract plants fabricating products from their steel. Such interfirm linkages are especially prominent in the chemical industry, where the by-product of one process may be a major raw material of another. Often firms in the same industry locate near each other to share the benefits of greater specialization. This is illustrated by the garment trades of New York and London, where a high degree of interdependence exists among shops specializing in cutting, buttonholing, and other individual operations.

Another reason for the clustering of manufacturing concerns is the complementary use of labor. This occurs particularly in districts where heavy industry uses predominantly male workers, thereby leaving a large reservoir of female workers available for employment in lighter industries such as electronics or textiles. Firms of the same type are sometimes attracted to a common location that has an established reputation for a particular product. The English chinaware industry, with its concentration at Stoke on Trent, is an example. Concentrations of this sort are further aided by the many service agencies that tend to spring up to provide for the specialized needs of the dominant industry in an area.

Many industrial concentrations are composed mainly of firms without direct links. The common attraction may be some transport feature, such as a seaport or an important road or rail junction point. As its population grows, a locality of this kind can be expected to provide a number of important *urbanization economies*, including financial institutions, transport agencies, utilities, and police and fire protection. Taken together, these various forms of internal and external economies have been termed *agglomeration*. This concept is one that has assumed an important role in the theory of location.

HUMAN CHARACTERISTICS AND INSTITUTIONS

From the interaction of the factors of production as modified by the particular characteristics of products and the agglomerating tendencies of industries, it would seem that we could arrive at a logical solution to the question of where manufacturing firms should locate their plants. In practice, however, production does not always take place at those locations that would seem best from a purely economic standpoint. A number of noneconomic considerations must also be taken into account, not the least of which is the effect of human institutions, and particularly their political institutions. Governments tend to interfere with the location of all economic activities, as we observed in the case of agriculture (Chapter 2); but political interference in manufacturing is especially apparent.

At all levels governments have a great stake in the industrial activities within their territorial jurisdictions. Manufacturing contributes importantly to the economic health and growth of countries, regions, and cities. In technically advanced countries it is a principal source of governmental revenue, a major employer, the main market for many primary commodities, and a leading earner of foreign exchange. Furthermore, it forms an indispensable basis for a country's military strength. Yet at the local level, certain types of manufacturing are poor neighbors, polluting streams and atmosphere, piling up unsightly spoil heaps, and raising a noisy clatter. For all these reasons, therefore, political bodies regularly interfere in the affairs of manufacturing concerns. Governments regulate, prohibit, entice, or assist industries in a variety of ways that affect their locations. The administrative devices used for these purposes include zoning, industrial development of lagging regions, and many kinds of taxing and licensing arrangements.

Even in those cases where governments do not interfere, the location of industries can be affected by the many characteristics of human beings as producers and consumers. The decisions of entrepreneurs are sometimes swayed by noneconomic motives, such as the value systems of the social or cultural groups to which they belong. Locational choices may be based on custom, tradition, or mere personal preferences. Likewise, the patronage of business firms may be influenced by the special traits of the buying public in a given area, their prejudices, whims, or perceptions.

DIFFERING APPROACHES TO A THEORY OF INDUSTRIAL LOCATION

This discussion of the influences affecting manufacturing location illustrates the complexity of the problem of the theorist. How can all these pieces be fitted together? How can the many elements be combined to determine the location of a given industry? What is the underlying spatial structure of the industrial pattern? Numerous theorists have attempted to answer these questions, and their approaches to the problem fall into distinct categories. The least-cost theory of industrial location is the oldest of the traditional approaches. This theory combines the various locational influences so as to determine that site where production can take place at a minimum total cost. A very different attack on the problem is made by the market-area analysis school. The locational process is viewed by this group as a search for that site where a firm can command the patronage of the largest number of customers and thereby maximize total revenue. Many of the more recent theorists have taken still other approaches. There is a tendency to develop more elaborate locational models and techniques for testing them, but in particular there has been an increased emphasis on the effects of human behavior in locational decision making.

LEAST-COST THEORY

The first efforts to develop a theory of manufacturing location were made in Germany, where Thünen had earlier presented his agricultural-location theory. Many of Thünen's notions apply to secondary and tertiary location as well as the primary, and his influence is especially apparent in the least-cost theories of manufacturing location. Several nineteenth-century German scholars attacked the problem of industrial location, especially William Launhardt; but the first person to attempt to develop a general theory of manufacturing location was Alfred Weber. Unlike his predecessors', Weber's writings were widely translated into English and became very influential in the United States, where the least-cost approach was subsequently to be developed further by a number of theorists.

Classical least-cost theory   Alfred Weber's major work on the location of industry appeared in 1909 (Friedrich, 1929). Following Thünen's lead, Weber looked for that location which would minimize costs and he gave little attention to the spatial nature of demand. Although he was interested mainly in manufacturing, his ideas also have implications for other branches of economic activity.

Weber's stated purpose was to develop what he termed a "pure" theory of industrial location, that is, one that could apply equally to any political or economic system. Elements found only in a capitalistic society were eliminated, as were those peculiar to socialism. It was his intention to discover the fundamental laws of industrial location and to learn how they operate. He was also attempting to develop a "general" theory, applicable to all types of industry. In the manner of Thünen, Weber derived his theory through the method of isolating analysis, singling out the major elements of location and eliminating all other complications by means of simplifying assumptions. The result was a deductive theory, that is, one that began with certain basic premises from which the details could be derived.

He insisted that his approach should not be expected to explain actual locations but to disclose those influences underlying all locations. For understanding particular locations he proposed to follow his general theory with a second work that would present a "realistic theory." This sequel, which was to be based on empirical study of German data, was never completed.

Weber defined *locational factors* as those "forces which operate as economic causes of location." These represented savings in cost that a firm could gain from producing in one place rather than in some other. The object upon which these factors act is the manufacturing establishment, or, as he termed it, the *locational unit*. In each case he was careful to compare only identical products.

Locational factors were classified by Weber in various ways. First he distinguished between *general* and *special* factors. General factors were those applicable to all industry, such as transport cost, labor, and rent; special factors were those pertaining specifically to a given industry—perishability, for example. Special factors were excluded from this general theory, together with all those peculiar to particular political, economic, or social systems.

Weber's second method of classification differentiated between *regional* and *local* factors. His regional factors, which established the fundamental locational framework of an industry over a broad area, were *transport cost* and *labor cost*. He regarded transport cost as the prime determinant, the factor which gave the basic orientation of industry. Labor cost he termed the "first distortion" of the underlying transport location. His local factor was *agglomeration*, a "second altering force" that caused industry to become concentrated at certain points within a region owing to savings from locating together. Under the heading "agglomeration" Weber included its counterforce, *deglomeration*. He regarded deglomeration as the tendency of industry to become dispersed from concentrated locations when the rent in such places rose too high because of congestion. He referred to agglomeration and deglomeration collectively as "every agglomerating tendency."

Before analyzing the locational process, Weber first isolated what he regarded as the basic causative factors by holding all others constant. These latter complications could then be reintroduced at a subsequent stage. The following were his initial assumptions, some of which are reminiscent of Thünen's model (Chapter 2):

1. The location of raw materials was taken as given, that is, fixed in space in a predetermined and known manner. He acknowledged that this was not in strict accordance with reality.

2. The spatial distribution of consumption was regarded as given. Furthermore, at the outset Weber took into account only one central buying point for each producing unit. He conceded that in reality the location of manufacturing influences the spatial distribution of labor and hence the pattern of consumption.

3. Labor had a given distribution, wages being fixed at any particular location but differing from one place to another. In each locality the supply of labor was unlimited at the prevailing wage rate. This assumed that labor lacked mobility and was unaffected by the location of industry.

4. Weber's transport system was uniform in all respects, and for simplicity he considered only one form of transportation, the railway. To achieve this uniformity, he adjusted weight and distance—the basic elements of transport cost—in various ways. Thus he attempted to compensate for differences in intensity of track use, size of shipment, terrain, roadbed, qualities of goods, and even the effects of the long-haul advantage. The result was "a mathematically flat plain," which he justified on the basis of German rate-setting practice of the time.

5. It was implicitly assumed that culture and economic and political systems were uniform.

With the problem thus simplified, Weber selected the theoretically best location for production, considering only one product at a time. The solution was mainly a geometric one, although an alternative mathematical solution was suggested as a proof and also for use in more complex situations. He arrived at the locational decision in three stages, beginning with the least-transport-cost location and adjusting this for each of the two other major influences.

Transportation Weber's theory gave an especially prominent place to *transport cost* as a factor of industrial location. The first step in his procedure disregarded all else and focused specifically upon finding that place of production which would minimize the total costs incurred in procuring raw materials and fuels and distributing the product to market. For simpler situations Weber used a *locational figure*, as illustrated in Figure 4-1. In this example the sources of two raw materials (or one raw material and one fuel*) and a single market are connected by straight lines, forming a *locational triangle*.

Since in each instance the problem was to find the point of least transport

---

*Weber made no distinction between materials and fuels, since their transport costs would affect location of production in the same way.

cost, the solution hinged upon the relative weights of the raw materials and products to be transported and the distances they must be moved. This in turn depended upon the characteristics of these materials, which Weber classified in two ways. When categorized by their "nature," materials were either *ubiquities*— that is, found nearly everywhere (wood, water, or brick clay in Weber's Germany)—or *localized materials*, found only in particular places (e.g., most minerals). Materials were also classified according to whether or not they lost weight in processing. "Pure" materials experienced no such loss, their entire weight being added to the product, whereas "gross" materials lost at least part of their weight. Fuels obviously belonged to the latter category, since essentially none of their weight entered the product.

After the materials had been thus classified, the locational triangle was used in the following manner. The place of production was joined to each corner by a line whose length was inversely proportional to the relative weight of the commodity to be transported to or from that corner. In Figure 4-1 these are the dashed lines connecting the production point *T* with the raw materials M_1 and M_2 and the place of consumption *C*. For more complex problems involving figures having four or more corners, Weber suggested the use of Varignon's frame, a device employing weights attached to strings (as shown in Figure 4-4). Only localized materials were considered capable of attracting production to their sources, since ubiquities, such as water, merely added to the pull of the market. Location, then, was affected by the proportion of the *weight of localized materials to a unit weight of product* (ton, kilogram, etc.).*

To demonstrate his method, Weber cited a number of cases indicating the locational effects of various possible combinations of material types.

1. *Ubiquities only.* The locational figure reduced to a single point, the market, since the materials were already at hand in the place where they were needed.

2. *Localized pure materials either alone or with ubiquities.* If only a single pure material was used, no change in weight took place in the processing. Production could therefore occur at the material source, the market, or anywhere along a line connecting these two points. If ubiquities had to be added to the one pure material, production would take place at the market. A product composed of several pure materials would also be made at the market. The addition of ubiquities in this last case would merely reinforce the market attraction.

3. *Weight-losing materials.* If a single weight-losing raw material was used, production would be at the source of that material. If ubiquities were added to it, manufacture would occur either at the material source or at the market, depending upon the proportion in which the materials were combined and the degree of

---

*This proportion gave a measure that Weber called the *material index*. If the weight of the product (unity) were then added to this value, this would give Weber's *locational weight*, which represented the total weight to be moved within a locational figure. A high locational weight indicated an attraction to raw materials, whereas a low value indicated an attraction to the market.

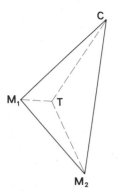

FIGURE 4-1 WEBER'S LOCATIONAL FIGURE.

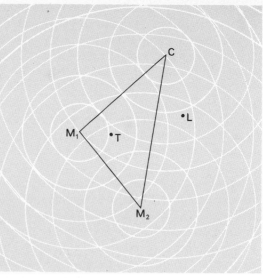

FIGURE 4-2 ISOTIMS.

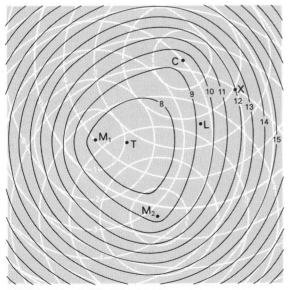

FIGURE 4-3 ISODAPANE METHOD FOR DETERMINING FEASIBILITY OF LOW-LABOR-COST LOCATION.

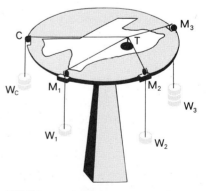

FIGURE 4-4 VARIGNON FRAME.

weight loss incurred. If several weight-losing materials were used, the decision depended on the balance achieved within the locational figure (perhaps determined with the aid of Varignon's frame). The addition of ubiquities in this latter instance might pull production to the market if those ubiquities outweighed all other materials combined.

From the above it will be noted that the use of the locational figure was necessary only where weight-losing materials were involved.

Labor   Weber observed that labor costs vary spatially, reflecting differences not only in wage rates but also in worker efficiency. He therefore treated this factor as "a first distortion" of the basic pattern given by the transport-cost relationship. The second step on his locational analysis, then, was to assess the relative effects of these two factors, transport cost and labor. By means of the mapping technique shown in Figures 4-2 and 4-3, he plotted the spatial variations in transport cost to arrive at a transport cost "surface." Labor costs at various locations could then be compared with the spatial pattern of transport costs. In Figure 4-2, which continues the example illustrated in Figure 4-1, the concentric rings radiating from each source of raw material M_1 and M_2 are lines connecting points of equal cost of procuring that material. Sometimes referred to as *isotims*, these lines are analogous to the contours that connect points of equal elevation on topographic maps. Similarly, the isotims centering upon the market C represent variations in the cost of distributing the product. In Figure 4-3 there are added a number of heavier lines, called *isodapanes*.* Isodapanes connect points of equal *total* transport cost, that is, the sum of all costs of assembling raw materials and distributing the product at every location on the transport-cost surface. Note that these isodapanes enclose a central area within which transport costs are less than $8. The lowest point inside this area is the least-transport-cost location, indicated by the letter T, as previously determined by Figure 4-1.

Let us next assume that at some other place in the region, point L, the cost of labor per unit of product is $3 less than at T, perhaps resulting from a surplus of workers caused by the closing of an established industry at L or an unusually high rate of population growth or a pool of particularly skilled workers at that point. Knowing that the transport costs of approximately $7 prevailing at T are the lowest in the region, we next look for an isodapane along which transport costs are $3 higher than those at T, thus exactly balancing the labor saving at L. This would be the isodapane marked $10. We find that the labor location L lies well inside this *critical isodapane* and that a net cost benefit would therefore be gained by an entrepreneur locating here. Had L been situated outside the critical isodapane, the additional transport cost would have outweighed the labor advantage. This, then,

*_Isodapane_ is from the Greek *isos* ("equal") and *dapane* ("cost"). The reader may wish to determine for himself how the isodapanes are derived. This can be done by summing all three isotim values where these are crossed by any one of the isodapanes. For example, at X on the $12 isodapane, the isotims read $2 + $5 + $5, which adds to $12.

is how Weber used isodapanes to determine the effects of deviating from a least-transport-cost location when there was an opportunity for a saving in labor costs at some other place. Isodapanes can also be constructed in such a way as to combine all kinds of costs that vary spatially. For example, this method could be used for assessing the feasibility of taking advantage of a local tax advantage, a subsidy, or tariff protection.

As Weber noted, labor costs are not equally important to all industries. As a convenient measure of the relative influence of labor in any given industry, he determined the average cost of labor required to produce a unit weight of product (a ton, for example).* Weber found that, in industries strongly attracted to low-labor-cost locations, establishments tended to become concentrated in a few places. He noted further that the long-term downward trend in transport costs would tend to increase the relative attraction of labor locations and thus accentuate the general tendency of manufacturing to agglomerate.

Agglomeration   In combining the effects of transport and labor costs, Weber had arrived at what he regarded as the general regional framework of manufacturing location. He then turned to the problem of determining how a location might be deflected *within* a region by the tendency of industry to agglomerate. In Weber's view there were two main ways in which a company could gain the benefits of agglomeration. First, it might increase the volume of output by enlarging its factory, thus gaining greater economies of large-scale production. Second, it might benefit from selecting a location in close association with other plants. As noted earlier, this "social" agglomeration would yield economies from sharing specialized equipment and services, greater division of labor, and large-scale purchasing and marketing, among other benefits.

Weber confined his attention specifically to what he called "pure" or "technical" agglomeration. Thus he omitted from consideration all types of "accidental" agglomeration, that is, industrial concentrations formed for reasons other than to take advantage of agglomeration economies per se. On such grounds he eliminated those agglomerations caused by the common attraction of industrial establishments to large concentrations of people or to ports, highway and railway junctions, and other transport features.

Deglomeration   The "weakening of agglomeration tendencies" he attributed to the competition for land, which becomes increasingly scarce and more expensive in areas of industrial concentration until high rents begin to outweigh the original

*Weber termed this the "index of labor cost." The higher the index, the greater the susceptibility of the industry to deviation from the least-transport-cost site in order to take advantage of labor savings. The feasibility of a given least-labor-cost location, however, is also related to the width of the interval separating the isodapanes—in other words, the rate at which transport costs increase. The more closely the isodapanes are spaced, the steeper is the transport-cost gradient. Consequently Weber found it more satisfactory to evaluate the effective pull of labor by determining the ratio of labor cost per unit of product weight to the total weight of all materials and products to be moved. This proportion Weber called the "labor coefficient."

advantages of agglomeration. His conception of these twin forces was thus much narrower than the usual view of them.

As a "second altering force," agglomeration could serve to divert manufacturing from either a least-transport-cost location or a least-labor-cost location, depending upon which was originally the dominant locating influence in a given instance. For an establishment that would normally be transportation-oriented, the savings from locating close to other firms might be sufficient to justify some sacrifice of transport cost. To determine whether or not such a diversion from the least-transport-cost site was feasible, Weber employed isodapanes in a manner similar to that previously used for weighing the counterattractions of transport and labor locations. First he ascertained the amount that two or more firms could save by agglomerating, then he determined that *critical isodapane* at which the economies from agglomeration would exactly balance the additional cost of diverting production from the point of lowest transport cost. Weber then constructed this critical isodapane around each production point as shown in Figure 4-5. Agglomeration would take place within the zone, or "common segment," created by the intersection of all the isodapanes (the shaded area of Figure 4-5). Note that every part of the common segment lies inside the critical isodapanes of all three firms.

The exact location of the new site within the common segment would depend upon which of the original producing units had the greatest volume of output. This largest factory would deviate from its original location just far enough to avail itself of the agglomeration advantages. The smaller units could exert less influence and would have to accept a common location as dictated by the dominant firm. For example, if P_1 has the largest output of the three, the agglomeration site to which

FIGURE 4-5   LOCATING A CENTER OF AGGLOMERATION.

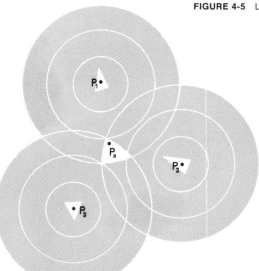

all will move might be at P_A. The new location of the three plants might bring them within range of new, cheaper raw-material deposits, and they could achieve still further savings in the form of transport cost. This added advantage from agglomeration could also attract still other companies that might otherwise have been unable to afford the move.

If the industry in question should happen to be one having a strong attraction to locations offering savings in labor cost, then the geometric solution would not apply. Because agglomeration and labor-cost savings could both cause deviations from the least-transport-cost location, these two influences might conflict. The decision would then go to the one that provided the greater savings. Weber indicated that the winner would more likely be the labor location, because that is a place where "accidental" agglomeration could be expected as a result of a concentration of population or the presence of special transport features. "Pure" agglomeration, he felt, would prevail only with industries having very low labor requirements, such as oil refining or chemical manufacture. The main effect, then, would be to increase the tendency of industry to collect at only a few locations.

Weber contended that, on the whole, the most important savings from agglomeration would accrue to those industries that yield a high percentage of value added by manufacture, which is largely a function of the cost of labor and capital equipment. With this in mind, he measured an industry's propensity to agglomerate by the ratio of its value added to the total weight of materials and product to be moved.*

Other features of Weber's theory   Weber's first chapters dealt only with situations where production was completed in a single operation at one location. He observed later that many industrial processes can be split into several stages, especially in those lines of production in which transport costs are a high proportion of the total. The first stage—where the raw material often loses much weight—would be drawn to the source of that material. The beneficiation of iron ore is an example of this. In subsequent operations the material becomes increasingly pure, with the result that later stages are attracted more and more toward the market. Although each stage of a manufacturing operation is affected in its own way by the advantages of agglomeration, the deviation of one stage due to this cause affects all other stages. Weber noted a trend away from such separations between stages and toward the vertical integration of manufacturing operations. This tendency was reinforced by the great concentrations of capital that had begun to form even in his day.

Weber then cited a hypothetical example of how a newly occupied region might evolve in response to these locational influences. He showed how primary, secondary, and tertiary sectors would form and develop a mutual interdependence for raw materials and markets. He also traced the emergence of locational patterns, which would become increasingly interwoven as the economy matured.

---

*He called this the "coefficient of manufacture." The higher this coefficient, the stronger the tendency of an industry to agglomerate.

An assessment of Weber's theory   There is no question that Weber occupies a preeminent place in the historical development of location theory. His was the first serious attempt to formulate a general theory, even though it is doubtful that he fully succeeded in that respect. Most subsequent work in locational analysis is rooted to some degree in Weber's theory. Despite the lasting qualities of his work, however, his theory contains numerous errors and oversimplifications. The correction of these has been a major concern of many theorists who came after him.

Most criticisms of Weber's theory have to do with his treatment of transport cost, agglomeration, and demand. On the surface, Weber's method of deriving a mathematically flat plain seems a logical way to simplify the problem of analyzing transport costs. After all, in adjusting commodity weights and travel distance to even out irregularities in the transport system, he did manage to avoid most of the obvious real-world complications. Some of these mathematical adjustments, however, do not accomplish what he intended. Certain transport features affect location in important ways that are different from the predicted results of Weber's locational figure. This problem has been cited by several theorists, most notably by E. M. Hoover, whose treatment of this problem appears below.

Much attention has been given also to the defects both in Weber's conception of agglomeration and in his method of analyzing it. He has been accused of intermingling three very different types of agglomeration economies without noting their basic distinctions. These three include (1) large-scale economies within a single establishment (savings in fuel and use of equipment, for example), (2) localization economies for all firms of a single industry at one place (specialized services, common pool of labor, etc.), and (3) urbanization economies of all plants of all industries (utilities, transport services, and other facilities found in an urbanized area). Although Weber cited these various advantages of industrial concentration, he seemed unaware that each category has its own peculiarities and locational effects, which require that they be studied separately (Hoover, 1937, pp. 90–91).

Weber's isodapane method of finding the agglomeration site has been criticized for its assumption that, if the first firm moves to the place offering agglomeration advantages, the others will automatically join it. Certainly there is no assurance that all the companies will agree upon an exact location within the common segment. Weber's geometric approach to agglomeration is thus regarded as inadequate.

The most frequent complaint against Weber's theory is its failure to consider the nature of consumption, which is by no means always focused on a single point, nor is it unlimited in amount. His theory thus remains a special case and fails to attain the full status of a general theory of location. As later writers have pointed out, there are many buying points for most products and this can greatly influence a firm's choice of location. Price changes also affect the level of demand for a product and thus the extent of the area over which a seller is able to attract customers.

Weber's theory is therefore no longer considered wholly acceptable in its original form. Many of its basic notions are sound, however, and, with modifications, the Weber approach remains useful for determining the general area within which a firm's minimum-cost location lies. Most of all, the theory continues to offer valuable insights into certain aspects of the locational process and to provide the basic vocabulary of location theory.

Modern refinements to least-cost theory   The theory of manufacturing location has continued to develop in recent years as more economists and geographers have turned their attention to the subject. Since Weber's time, most writers have tended to maintain a more balanced view and to draw upon a wider range of locational factors in building their theoretical models than their predecessors did. A few of the more recent theorists in the line of descent from Weber are reviewed briefly in the remainder of this section. Nearly all of them have treated the demand factor more realistically than Weber did, but each has nevertheless contributed importantly to the further refinement of least-cost theory.

Spatial variations in supply and demand   A prominent place among modern theorists is held by E. M. Hoover. Although he is usually considered a least-cost theorist, he has given much attention to the spatial aspects of both supply and demand in his two major works (Hoover, 1937, 1948). Both theoretical approaches have been stressed in his treatment of transport costs, production costs, and agglomerating advantages. All these he has related to the locations of individual firms, the development of industry patterns, and the problems of communities and regions.

The dynamic aspects of the location of economic activity have also been prominent in his work, including the location effects of short-term changes—depressions and booms—and long-term trends, including technological change. Hoover has applied these ideas to the problems of the unequal development of regions and particularly "distressed areas." An important place has been given in his writings to numerous influences excluded by Weber from his pure theory, especially political considerations.

Hoover has been given much of the credit for calling attention to certain of the locational effects of the structure of transfer costs and of rate-making practices (see Chapter 8). He has shown how Weber's locational triangle would be affected by introducing the long-haul advantage, a significant characteristic of modern transport media. If transport costs were directly proportional to distance, as in Weber's treatment, then the locational effect on a firm having a single raw-material source and one market would be as shown in Figure 4-6. In this example the costs of assembling raw materials are represented by the straight line extending diagonally upward from the source *M*, and the costs of distributing the product are shown by a similar line originating at *C*, the market. Summing the freight costs represented by the two diagonals produces the horizontal line appearing at the top of the diagram. The line of total transport costs is horizontal because in our example distribution costs and procurement costs are equal, indicating that a pure material is being used. Under these conditions location can take place at the raw-material source, at the market, or at any place between, as Weber predicted.

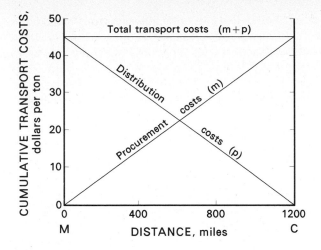

FIGURE 4-6 LOCATION OF PRO-
DUCTION WHEN TRANSPORT
COSTS ARE PROPORTIONAL TO
DISTANCE.

Had a weight-losing material been used, the line would have tilted upward to the right because of the greater cost of procurement. As a result the least-cost site of production would in that case have been at the location of the raw material.

Hoover has pointed out, however, that modern transport rate curves do not look like those shown in Figure 4-6. Instead of starting at the origin O, they tend to begin higher up the vertical axis as in Figure 4-7. The reason for this is that transport agencies today incur high terminal costs (for loading and unloading merchandise, preparing bills of lading and invoices, and other charges) at either end of the journey and these are independent of the distance traveled. The transport cost curves have also developed a greater degree of curvature than formerly (see Figure 4-7). This is due to the high fixed charges for equipment and maintenance and the greater efficiency in the use of vehicles and equipment on long hauls than short ones. This means that the most expensive miles covered are

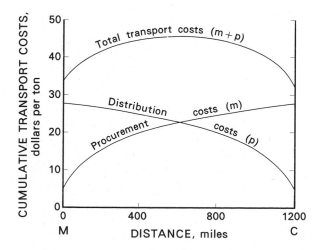

FIGURE 4-7 LOCATION OF PRO-
DUCTION WHEN TERMINAL COSTS
AND THE LONG-HAUL ADVANTAGE
ARE CONSIDERED.

those nearest the starting point; farther out the cost per mile drops steadily. In Figure 4-7 both procurement and distribution cost curves have assumed these characteristic forms, and the total transport cost curve develops a decided arch. Clearly the least-transport-cost product site lies at either end of the journey but nowhere between, Weber's predictions notwithstanding. This diagram helps to explain the many industrial concentrations found at the terminal points of railways, water routes, and other transport centers.

Other nodes in transport networks also tend to become centers of industrial agglomeration, especially junction points, transfer points, and other places where the journey is interrupted for any reason. The structure of transport rates paid by manufacturers and other patrons of transport agencies has also acquired a number of special characteristics in modern times. These have important locational consequences, as will appear in the chapter on transportation (Chapter 8).

Spatial variations in costs   The role of location theory in industrial geography has been defined by D. M. Smith, who has stressed the fundamental importance of theory as a basis for empirical research (Smith, 1966). Smith has introduced a number of graphic techniques, including "cost isopleths," or "cost contours" (Figure 4-8). These are lines joining places of equal cost, the latter being the sum of all costs that an establishment might incur at any place in the region. When used in the same manner as isodapanes, cost isopleths provide a convenient method for studying the effects of deviating from the least-total-cost site.

Also shown in Figure 4-8 is Smith's space-cost curve, which represents a section taken through a cost-isopleth map. The angle of this curve at any one point indicates the gradient of total costs as they rise from the least-cost site. Smith has shown how space-cost curves may be used for measuring the locational effects of agglomeration economies, differences in entrepreneurial skill, changes in costs resulting from subsidies, and changes in prices (Figure 4-9).

Variations in costs with changing scales of production   Among the many other important contributions to least-cost theory are those of Leon Moses, who has suggested that other theorists did not deal with one of the principal ingredients of the locational problem, namely, the variations in unit costs of production with changing scales of operation (Moses, 1958). Moses noted that theorists have set out to find the least-cost site before considering how unit costs may be affected by large-scale economies and other variables in the production process. The three problems of optimum output, optimum combinations of inputs, and optimum location are inseparable, however, and must therefore be solved simultaneously. He then proceeded to develop a graphic method for solving this problem.

Although geometric methods are valuable for gaining an understanding of locational problems, their very simplicity limits their applicability in the complex real world. For this reason mathematical models are increasingly being introduced into locational analyses. Harold Kuhn and Robert Kuenne (1962), for example, have developed a technique for determining the location of the least-transport-cost point in Weber's locational figure. This method provides solutions for problems

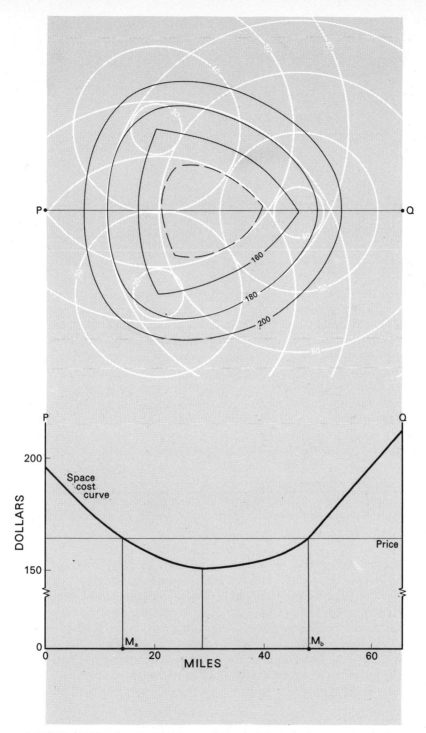

FIGURE 4-8 SMITH'S COST ISOPLETHS AND SPACE-COST CURVE. (DAVID M. SMITH. 1966. "A THEORETICAL FRAMEWORK FOR GEOGRAPHICAL STUDIES OF INDUSTRIAL LOCATION," *ECONOMIC GEOGRAPHY*, **43.** FIG. 3, P. 103.)

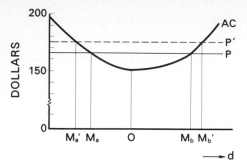

FIGURE 4-9 SPACE-COST CURVE: EFFECTS OF
PRICE CHANGE. (SMITH, 1966, FIG. 7, P. 110.)

involving any number of elements (i.e., raw materials and products) and any combination of weights.

MARKET-AREA ANALYSIS

As we have seen, there was but a single buying point in Weber's locational figure. All transactions were considered to take place in this market, with no limit to the quantity of product that would be accepted at the current price. The locational problem was merely to find that site where total costs were least, thereby permitting producers to maximize both sales and profit. Weber's generally unrealistic treatment of demand was questioned by a group called the market-area analysts. They developed a body of theory concerned specifically with the spatial distribution of demand and its effects on location (Greenhut, 1956). They held that Weber's one-market case was a special one and that the buyers of most products were scattered over an area. They maintained that if an individual buyer has a choice between two competing sellers, he will patronize the one that is closer to him. A producer's success therefore depends upon his locating near as many prospective customers as possible. The least-cost site will thus not necessarily be the best one. Although foreshadowed by some of the earlier German theorists, the market-area approach was first presented formally by Fetter, an American (Fetter, 1924).

Bases of market-area analysis This type of analysis as formulated by Fetter (1924) is based on the total value of sales that a particular location is able to command rather than the amount of territory to which these sales are made. However, if buyers are taken to be evenly distributed throughout the region, a given volume of sales can be considered the equivalent of a certain amount of territory. Two somewhat different meanings have been given to the expression *market area* in this context. It may be used to describe all buyers scattered over an entire territory or to the buyers of a particular firm and that portion of space they occupy. Thus we may speak of the market area *as a whole* or of the market area *of a firm*.

Analytical method The analysis begins with the following simplifying assumptions:

1. Buyers are distributed evenly in space and all have the same type and level of demand for a given product.

2. Competing products are identical in all respects and are indistinguishable in appearance.

3. Products are sold f.o.b. factory; that is, the buyer pays all freight charges from the plant.

4. Prices are based on the manufacturers' total costs plus markup that is the same for all producers. Thus any change in costs is immediately and fully reflected in the price charged the customer.

5. Freight rates are the same for all producers of the same goods.

6. Every firm occupies a location physically separated from its competitors, and each producer monopolizes the trade of those buyers who are closest to him. He is able to do this because of the savings in freight charges his customers obtain through purchasing from him instead of from one of his more distant competitors.

The theorist first determines the locational pattern that appears under these ideal conditions. He then proceeds to relax the assumptions one by one to discover the individual effects of these added variables on the shapes and sizes of the market areas of firms and thus on the location of production.

The success of a firm's locational choice is measured in terms of the size of the sales territory it monopolizes, since the latter is directly related to volume of sales. Each producer therefore strives to gain some cost advantage over his competitors that will enable him to enlarge his own sales territory at the expense of theirs. Many such advantages are possible, but, as we shall see, all can ultimately be expressed in terms of either sales price or freight rates.

Figures 4-10 to 4-12 illustrate the shapes of the market areas of two competing firms under differing conditions. Figure 4-10 presents the ideal case, in which neither producer has a special advantage. The two market areas are therefore identical in size and are separated by a boundary *XX'* that forms a straight line equidistant from the two production sites. A customer situated at any point along the boundary would incur identical freight charges on shipments from either producer and would therefore pay identical delivered prices for the merchandise. A buyer anywhere to the left of the line would obtain lower delivered prices from *A* and would always trade with him; a buyer on the right can trade more cheaply with *B* and invariably takes his business to him.

In Figure 4-11 the producer at *A* has gained some cost advantage over the firm at *B* that permits *A* to reduce his f.o.b. price. For example, costs at *B* may have risen because of an increase in wages or a decline in the efficiency of labor, an increase in rent, a decline in the quality of raw materials, or an increase in the cost of procuring them. Or perhaps *A* has succeeded in streamlining his operations so as to reduce his costs. Whatever the cause, *A* has been able to enlarge his market area at the expense of *B*. As a result the boundary between the two areas, *XX'*, has moved to the right and now tends to curve around *B*'s location. Note that this boundary assumes the form of a hyperbolic curve, as suggested by Fetter.

In Figure 4-12 still other assumptions have been removed. *A* and *B* have each

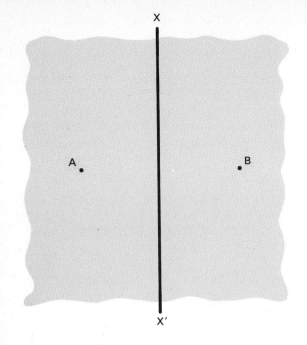

FIGURE 4-10 MARKET
AREAS OF TWO COM-
PETING FIRMS UNDER
IDEAL CONDITIONS.

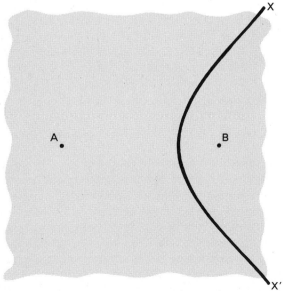

FIGURE 4-11 MARKET
AREAS OF COMPETING
FIRMS WITH UNEQUAL
F.O.B. PRICES.

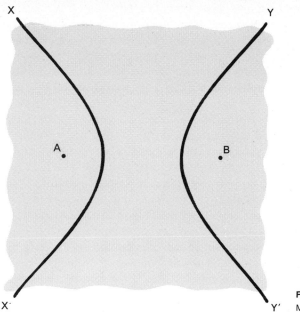

X   Y

A

B

X'   Y'

FIGURE 4-12   OVERLAPPING MARKET AREAS.

managed to invade the other's territory, thereby weakening the competitors' monopolies over more distant customers. This may have been accomplished by absorbing part of the freight, perhaps at the expense of nearer customers; or possibly it was achieved by some form of product differentiation, obtained by attaching brand names and distinctive labels to the packages. Whether or not there was any actual difference in quality, customer preferences would develop in such a way as to create a *zone of indifference*. In Figure 4-12 this is the shaded area lying between *A*'s extreme boundary at *YY'* and *B*'s absolute limit at *XX'*. Within the twilight zone some customers choose to buy *A*'s product while others prefer *B*'s.

Knowledge of any of these conditions (or even the suspicion of them) may influence *A* or *B* to move his place of business to a different production site in order to gain a new advantage or to overcome some disadvantage with respect to his rival. Under some conditions the two may end up side by side sharing the same market area.

Role of market-area analysis The market-area method is a useful analytical device for the study of those industries where products are standard and transport costs are sufficiently high to represent a substantial part of the delivered price. The approach has considerably less utility where market areas of competing firms cover an entire country. In the latter case, transport costs are ordinarily an insignificant item and standard delivered prices prevail.

One of the most useful applications of this theory is in the analysis of *supply areas*. These are similar to market areas except that in the market area a product is distributed over an area from some central point, whereas in the supply area commodities are brought together at one place from many sources. The collection of agricultural commodities customarily results in the formation of supply areas. Farm production units are usually numerous, are spread over a wide area, and sell identical commodities to a few centrally located buyers. Because farmers can minimize their time and transport costs by taking their products to the nearest agency, agricultural supply areas ordinarily assume regular shapes centering upon the collection point.

A familiar example of a supply area is the urban milkshed, the territory supplying fluid milk to a population center (see Chapter 2). Another example is provided by the grain-collection systems of the subhumid commercial grain-producing areas of midcontinental Canada and the United States. Figure 4-13 is a map of the grain supply areas of country elevators in a small section of the Canadian prairies. Situated at intervals along the rail lines, these elevators (shown by dots) receive grain from the growers and clean, grade, and store it until time for shipment to ports on the Pacific Coast, on Hudson Bay, or at the head of the Great Lakes. The grain supply area surrounding each elevator is composed of the farms upon which the elevator operator depends for his business. Note that these elevator hinterlands are quite regular in shape, reflecting the farmers' efforts to minimize their travel when delivering grain. This regularity is evidence of the standard price that prevails at competing elevators, the identical nature of the commodity, and a physical landscape closely approximating the Thünen-Lösch requirements for uniformity. The patterns show certain imperfections, however. We can detect some overlapping of boundaries where farmers in marginal locations are influenced by considerations of personal friendships and animosities as well as local road conditions. There is also an apparent tendency for some of the supply areas to be elongated at right angles to the rail line. The open spaces are mainly pasturelands.

Our examination of these two approaches to the locational problem has shown that if Weber was one-sided in his emphasis upon the least-cost site and his neglect of demand, then the market-area analysts were equally biased in their concentration upon demand and minimization of the spatial aspects of cost. Each school of thought has tended to ignore the other despite the obvious complementarity of their theories.

RECENT CONTRIBUTIONS TO INDUSTRIAL-LOCATION THEORY

The least-cost and market-area branches of classical theory are both normative: that is, they present a view of industrial location as it "should" be rather than the way it necessarily is found to be in the real world. The viewpoint of normative theory has been succinctly stated by Lösch: "The question of actual location must be distinguished from that of the rational location. The two need not coincide. . . . The question of the best location is far more dignified than determination of the actual one" (Lösch, 1954, p. 4). For a growing number of geographers this rationale has not been a satisfactory one. They are interested particularly in finding explanations for actual spatial patterns, and the predictive powers of normative

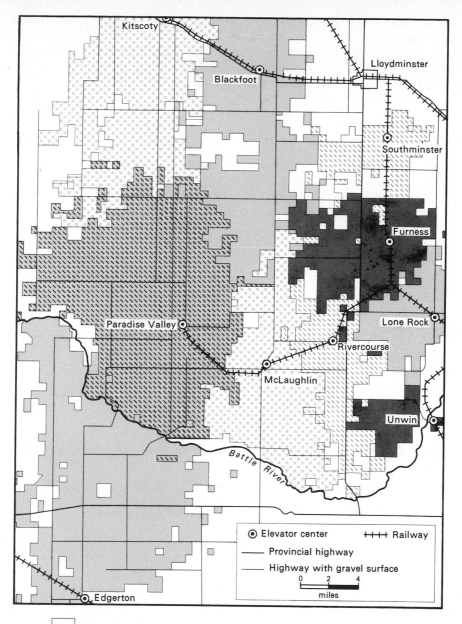

Other hinterlands and non-agricultural areas

FIGURE 4-13 SUPPLY AREAS OF COUNTRY GRAIN ELEVATORS ON THE CANADIAN PRAIRIES.

models have not been as great as they would wish. More often than not the gap between the rational and the actual has been found to lie in the realm of human behavior. Locations are the outcome of human decisions, and human beings are sometimes swayed by noneconomic considerations when making such selections. Therefore much of the recent work of location theorists has focused upon locational behavior and the nature of the decision-making process.

The firm as a decision-making unit One of the difficulties confronting the theorist at the outset is the complexity of the decision-making mechanism of the firm. It is difficult to generalize about this because there is such a wide variation in the ways in which businesses are organized. Decisions are made very differently by the small concern managed by a single owner-operator and by the company that is organized as a partnership. Even greater, however, is the distinction between these two and the corporation with its elaborate administrative apparatus. The decision-making machinery is also likely to vary with differences in firm size.

Traditional theory has been concerned with the problem of plant location, usually the selection of a new plant site. In addition there is the occasional need to relocate an existing plant. More frequently, decisions must be made as to whether or not an expansion or contraction of facilities should be made and, if so, at which of several branch plants the decision should be implemented. There is now an increasing awareness, however, that firms make other kinds of spatial decisions that can affect plant locations. They may have to decide on changes in sources and kinds of raw-material inputs or changes in product mix, or they may wish to reconsider their pricing policies. They may need to introduce new efficiencies through a reorganization of production, or to rule on whether or not to adopt an innovation.

Behavioral aspects of locational decisions Those who would develop a new behavioral theory of location are interested in overcoming several defects of the economic-man concept. Their attention has been directed particularly to the nature of entrepreneurial goals, the characteristics of the information-disseminating process, and the limits of entrepreneurial capacities.

Motivation Numerous locational studies have confirmed that the desire to maximize profits is by no means the only motive of entrepreneurs, but this varies from one type of firm to another (Mueller and Morgan, 1962, p. 207). In general, the owner-operator of a small business is the most likely to make decisions on less than wholly rational grounds. The large corporate enterprise will probably be the most sensitive to economic considerations, since the management are continually under stockholders' scrutiny.

Even the rationality of corporate decisions has its limits. There may be clashes of will between members of the upper levels of management, and sometimes stockholders and management have conflicting goals. Moreover, there is the difficult problem of defining precisely and objectively just what the optimal goal really is. Consequently, in firms large and small, decision makers can be better described as satisficers than as optimizers.

Spread of information Rarely do entrepreneurs have all the information they really need to make their decisions with full assurance. One problem is the length of time that it takes for information to be communicated: this has been found to vary with distance from the source. The effects of physical distance on the transmission of information have been widely studied (especially Hägerstrand, 1953), but there are also the barrier effects of cultural or social distance. Communication takes place much more readily between members of the same cultural or status group.

Many kinds of business information do not pass through regular communication channels but from person to person, which means the information arrives perhaps second- or third-hand. This results in time delays in transmissions, but, equally important, it increases the likelihood that the original message will arrive in distorted form. All this adds to the atmosphere of uncertainty in which locational decisions are made.

Entrepreneurial limitations The ranks of business management are subject to most of the frailties of mankind generally. One problem is the way in which information is perceived. Individual members of the management group may differ markedly in their interpretation of events, and the collective perception of the team may represent an unsatisfying compromise. Entrepreneurs not only vary in their ability to interpret but also differ in their capacities to act rationally. Entrepreneurial skill is a decidedly uncertain quantity. Moreover, there is the problem of entrepreneurial capacity in the case of the firm that has grown so huge that ordinary human minds cannot grasp all the complexities of the situation. Decentralization of decision making has been one response to this problem, especially in the automobile industry.

Entrepreneurial decisions are sometimes consciously or unconsciously colored by personal allegiance to one or another social, cultural, or ethnic group. Prejudiced attitudes can easily interfere with an objective choice. Finally, there is the problem of inertia, which affects many locational decisions. Once a locational choice has been made and acted upon, it becomes costly to uproot a company's facilities and move them to another place, even if the original decision was not a good one. Aside from the expense of moving, there is frequently a reluctance on the part of the management personnel to leave familiar surroundings for a new location (Mueller and Morgan, 1962, p. 430 et passim).

LOCATIONAL BEHAVIOR IN PERSPECTIVE

Clearly, the locational behavior of firms and the nature of the decision-making process are important ingredients in the locational mix and should not be disregarded even though they are difficult to incorporate in theoretical models.

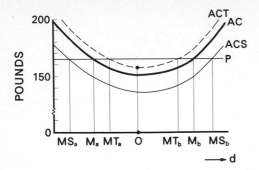

FIGURE 4-14 SMITH'S SPACE-COST CURVE: DIFFERENCES IN ENTREPRENEURIAL SKILL. (SMITH, 1966, FIG. 4, P. 105.)

Does this mean that normative models are no longer of any use, or that devising new behavioral models of location will be an impossible task? Here, Smith's space-cost curve provides assurance on both grounds.

Figure 4-14 illustrates the locational effects of variations in managerial skills. Spatial variations in cost for the industry as a whole are shown by the curve *AC*. From this it can be seen that, while *O* is the best location, the average firm can survive at any location between the margins at M_a and M_b. A company with superior management, however, can operate at the level of costs shown by the curve *ACS*. This extends the range of possible locational choice out to MS_a and MS_b, besides assuring a greater net return at any point in between. The poorly managed firm, whose curve is given by *ACT*, has a much-restricted latitude of locational choice from MT_a to MT_b. The space-cost curve can even be used to measure the extra cost that an entrepreneur would incur if he were to choose some site other than the least-cost location for reasons of personal satisfaction (Smith, 1966). These examples demonstrate the continuing value of least-cost theory as a norm against which to measure the dimensions of the human factor.

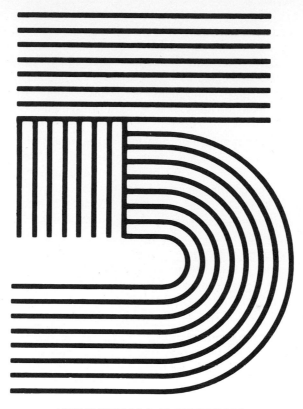

INDUSTRIAL PATTERNS

The large and growing body of literature on industrial location includes two main categories of theoretically based empirical studies, but the two are not mutually exclusive. The first group consists of studies carried out for academic purposes. Theoreticians find it necessary to test their hypotheses with real-world data if they are to develop models that are useful tools for analysis and prediction. Other academicians setting out to describe industrial landscapes may use theory as a conceptual framework for their regional studies. The second major group of empirical studies is intended to provide direct locational guidance to decision makers, including entrepreneurs who wish to find the best sites for new manufacturing facilities or to analyze marketing opportunities in new localities. Also in this second group are studies for the use of urban and regional planners, who usually regard manufacturing location as a key element in their efforts to solve the problems of communities, regions, or nations, and are always looking for better models to use for predicting the impact of their planning decisions.

As we sample this empirical literature, we shall be looking first of all for real-world evidence of the role played by each factor in the location of particular industries. Among the locational factors to be considered will be those of the classical and neoclassical theorists—transport cost, agglomeration, and labor—as well as certain factors neglected by earlier writers but needed for a more nearly complete explanation of existing patterns of production. The latter include noneconomic elements in the decision making of firms, influences imposed by the society and the state.

In addition to the location of individual industries, we are interested here in the locational considerations that cause many different industries to form spatial concentrations. At the lowest scale, the pattern of manufacturing within the urban community, we shall be drawing upon not only the concepts developed in Chapter 4 but also those of urban land use theory from Chapter 2. Moving to still higher levels of observation, we shall then examine regional, national, and global patterns of industrial concentration. In analyzing these broader patterns, we shall be interested in discovering the degree to which locational considerations coincide for a sufficient number of establishments to form industrial complexes. Increasingly important at these higher levels are the locational policies of global companies, national governments, and international bodies.

THE FIRM AND THE INDUSTRY

Classical and neoclassical theorists focused their attention upon the location of only a single establishment at one time. Recent writers have dealt increasingly with the firm, which may control a number of establishments engaged in one or many.stages of manufacture, or with the industry, that is, all firms making a given product or group of products. In this opening section we shall take in all these points of view, concentrating our attention in turn upon representative industries in which one or another locational principle is particularly prominent. As we shall see, however, it is hard to find an industry whose location does not simultaneously combine a number of influences.

TRANSPORT COST

Industries for which transport cost represents a relatively large part of the total outlay are generally those having to move much weight, either in procuring their raw materials and fuel or in distributing their products to market. For producers of this type there is a strong incentive to locate their processing facilities in such a way as to minimize the total expenditures for transportation. As the preceding chapter shows, for some manufacturers this means locating as close as possible to material sources and for others it requires a location close to the market or at some intermediate point, depending upon the distances involved and the relative weights to be moved in each case.

Yet, as Weber noted, there is a tendency for firms to fabricate a given product in a series of stages, with a different set of locational attractions at each stage. At any given stage an establishment's raw materials are in fact the finished products of establishments at some previous stage, and its products in turn become the raw materials for the next succeeding stage. Each stage has its own material index (see Chapter 4), which tends to diminish in the latter stages of manufacture. Consequently, the earliest stages of production are likely to be oriented to raw materials and the later stages to be market-oriented. An offsetting consideration for many such concerns is the opportunity to minimize total transport costs by locating successive stages in close proximity to each other. As we saw in Chapter 4, some companies achieve these savings by means of *vertical integration*—performing the various operations within a single establishment—while others choose to accomplish the same thing by locating close to suppliers and customers, thereby enjoying *external economies.*

None of these locational relationships remains fixed for an extended time, however. The balance in favor of one location or another can be tipped by transport innovations or changes in the transport rate structure. It can also be altered by the introduction of new processing techniques that change the weights of inputs relative to each other or to the product. A change in the structure of demand may dictate a new product mix, thereby causing a shift in the optimal location for processing facilities. All these locational problems are illustrated by the industries to be discussed here.

Iron and steel industry This most-studied of industries is a particularly good testing ground for location theory. Transport costs are clearly paramount to all others, in view of the large quantities of heavy, weight-losing, bulky, and cheap raw materials to be assembled—iron ore, fuel, and fluxing material—all plentiful but erratically distributed in the earth's crust. The product is likewise cheap, but it too is heavy and costly to move to market. At the same time, the steel industry has moderately high labor requirements, ranging, in the successive stages, between 10 and 30 percent of value added by manufacture. Nevertheless, in the steel industry labor cost has not proved to be a very significant locational consideration within countries because of industrywide labor unions and wage rates. Between countries, however, wage differentials can be important (see Chapter 9).

The steel industry is an excellent example of the principle of agglomeration in all its variations. Economies internal to the firm are illustrated by the importance of savings from large-scale operations at a single establishment, through the use of reduction and refining vessels and by transporting materials and products in carload or shipload lots. Even though the material index for the process of reducing ore to metallic iron is much higher than that for refining iron into steel, a substantial saving in fuel is achieved by placing the two operations side by side, thereby eliminating the unnecessary reheating of the metal. Similar economies from vertical integration are achieved by converting the coal to coke on the premises and by fabricating iron and steel products close by.

Most steel-manufacturing centers also exhibit external economies. Within the local community there are frequently direct linkages between the mills and their suppliers of firebricks and other inputs on the one hand and between the mills and their customers, the manufacturers of steel products, on the other. Moreover, the steel industry customarily benefits from close proximity to establishments with which it has no direct ties, as a result of access to common transport facilities, labor pools, and various service agencies—all of which is described under the expression "urbanization economies." The manufacture of iron and steel is a highly social industry, and its tendency to attract other industries gives it a special role in the growth and development of regional and national economies. This in turn causes the industry to be subject to political intervention through taxation, subsidization, regulation, or even nationalization.

Changing orientation of iron and steel manufacture   The individual roles of the various locational factors in this industry become even clearer as we view their changing interrelationships during the past two centuries. Since the middle of the eighteenth century iron and steel production has undergone technological changes that have shifted the emphasis from one raw material to another, altered transport arrangements, and affected the usefulness of different material deposits. Old sources of iron ore and fuel have been exhausted and new ones found even as important changes in demand for the product have been taking place.

   Before the industrial revolution the principal fuel for ironmaking was charcoal, while much of the ore was obtained from such convenient sources as "bog iron." Both of these materials were virtually ubiquitous in early Britain and the colonial Americas, as in other ironmaking regions. Because making charcoal requires large amounts of wood, those forested areas that had easy access to markets were favored by the early iron industry. One such ironmaking district occupied the upstream tributaries of the Allegheny and Monongahela Rivers, which flow together at Pittsburgh to form the Ohio River.

   With the appearance about 1750 of the blast furnace, which made possible the use of coal (in the form of coke) in the smelting process, coalfield sites suddenly became the favored locations for ironmaking. This locational attraction was all the more compelling because the primitive cold-blast furnaces required enormous quantities of fuel. Much coal was needed also for the subsequent working of the metal—"puddling" for wrought iron, making crucible steel, and fabricating into the various products. Because only certain grades are suitable for conversion into metallurgical coke, not all coalfields were able to attract the industry. In Britain the chief areas were the north outcrop at the heads of the valleys of the South Wales coalfield and the West Midlands coalfields centering upon Birmingham. One of the principal areas in the United States was the Pittsburgh district, drawing upon the Connellsville coking coal of the Monongahela Valley. Despite the important economies in coal use introduced by Nielson's hot blast, the attraction of coalfields remained overwhelming until the middle of the nineteenth century, reinforced by the vertical integration of ironmaking concerns and the concentration of iron-fabricating companies in those same areas.

   The period between 1856 and 1939 was one of further important technological developments in the industry, bringing radical locational shifts. First came the Bessemer converter, a fast, cheap way to make steel in large quantities, followed soon by the open-hearth furnace, also a large-scale method but one that yielded a superior product as well. These new methods of steelmaking were very economical, but they required vast quantities of high-grade, phosphorus-free iron ore. Because most British ores are high in phosphorus, this caused the nation's steel industry to migrate to coastal sites, where high-grade nonphosphoric ores could be imported from Spain.

In the United States the problem was concerned not with ore quality but with availability of ores in the quantities demanded by the new furnaces. Discovery of the huge, high-grade Lake Superior deposits provided the solution but also gave rise to a new set of locational arrangements. As in Britain, the new sites were at break-of-bulk points, this time along the southern shores of the lower Great Lakes, where Lake Superior ore could be unloaded directly into the mills, there to be joined by coking coal brought from the middle Appalachian fields by rail. New steel mills at Gary, East Chicago, Cleveland, and Buffalo thus minimized total transport costs both for procuring raw materials and for serving the rapidly growing Middle Western markets. At the same time, a large steel mill sprang up at Baltimore, a tidewater location where imported ores could be combined with the Appalachian coal to serve the east coast market. Meanwhile, the Pittsburgh-Wheeling-Youngstown concentration of steel products continued to do very well, with their local coal, Lake Superior and local ores, and large local markets.

Thus the second century of the industrial revolution produced these shifts in the location of steel mills. First it increased the attraction of sources of iron ore, especially at tidewater and other break-of-bulk sites. Second, it increased the pull of the market, further aided by greater use of scrap metal (generated in large urban concentrations) and the addition of by-product coking ovens, which served the industrial markets for chemicals.

Current trends In the years since the Second World War a number of other developments have occurred to bring still further locational shifts. One of these has been the need to find new sources of ore to replace the high-grade deposits, particularly those of the Lake Superior ranges, that had been exhausted by the drive to win the war. Exploitation of remote deposits became more feasible as the price of ore rose and new techniques for handling and transporting bulk cargoes were devised. Perhaps more important was the development of a technology for upgrading ("beneficiating") the abundant low-quality ores and converting them into more convenient and economical forms by sintering or pelletizing. Meanwhile, steel-mill technology has made important advances as well, particularly with the basic oxygen furnace, which has greatly reduced the time required to convert a batch ("heat") of steel. This has had a twofold effect: substantial economies in fuel consumption and an enormous increase in steel-mill capacity. The resulting economies of scale have been further aided by the introduction of much larger steelmaking vessels.

We are therefore able to see several locational trends in the steel industry today. One of these is the growing tendency to select tidewater or break-of-bulk locations for new mills, as typified by Britain's Spencer works at Llanwern on the

Bristol Channel, France's Usinor mill at Dunkerque, United States Steel's Fairless works on the Delaware River, Bethlehem Steel Company's Burns Harbor plant at the lower end of Lake Michigan, and the huge mills concentrated on the shores of Japan's Inland Sea. These and many other new installations were sited to receive water-borne cargoes of ore, which now account for an important part of the total tonnage of commodities entering international and domestic trade.

Another locational trend is the growing attraction of markets; for the steel industry, this means large concentrations of manufacturers using steel in their fabricating operations. It is significant, for example, that each of the break-of-bulk locations just mentioned happens to be located within or near a large manufacturing complex requiring much iron and steel as a raw material. The Burns Harbor, Indiana, mill is typical of the group, situated as it is immediately adjacent to the Chicago metropolitan area, one of the largest and most diversified concentrations of industry in the world. An important element in this marketward trend is the changing structure of transport rates, which assesses higher charges on processed items than on raw materials. Also contributing to this locational shift are the increasing efficiencies in the transporting of bulk cargoes of ore, fluxing materials, and fuels, the reduced weight of these raw-material inputs through the use of new beneficiation techniques at the mine, and greater efficiencies in fuel use made possible by the introduction of oxygen.

Weberian analysis of steel-mill locations In those instances where the spatial pattern of markets and raw-material sources is sufficiently uncomplicated, the steel industry lends itself particularly well to the use of Weber's geometric approach to locational analysis. The Mexican steel industry was the subject of one of the best-known studies of this sort (Kennelly, 1954–1955). At the time, integrated steel mills existed in only two locations, Altos Hornos, at Monclova near the Texas border, and Fundidora at Monterrey, in the same general region of Mexico but some distance southeast of Altos Hornos (Figure 5-1).

Ore for the two mills came from several sources but mainly from Durango in the Sierra Madre to the southwest. Coal was obtained from Sabinas north of Monclova, while a supplementary fuel, natural gas, was available by pipeline from Texas. Still another energy source, oil, was obtainable from Reynosa and Tampico. Another raw material, scrap, could be either imported from the United States or secured domestically from Mexico City or Monterrey. Mexico City was the principal market for the finished steel, while Monterrey took most of the rest. Given this combination of markets and raw-material sources, the twofold problem of the study was to find the minimum-transport-cost point for steel manufacture and to determine how well the two existing plants were located.

The first step was to ascertain the minimum-transport-cost point (MTP) on the basis of weight and distance. Assuming uniform accessibility and ignoring the existing route structure, a point P_1, fairly central to the location figure, was determined. When the current rail network was introduced into the calculations, the MTP moved 140 kilometers northeastward from P_1 to P_2. Actual freight rates were then substituted for weight and distance, with the result that the higher rates

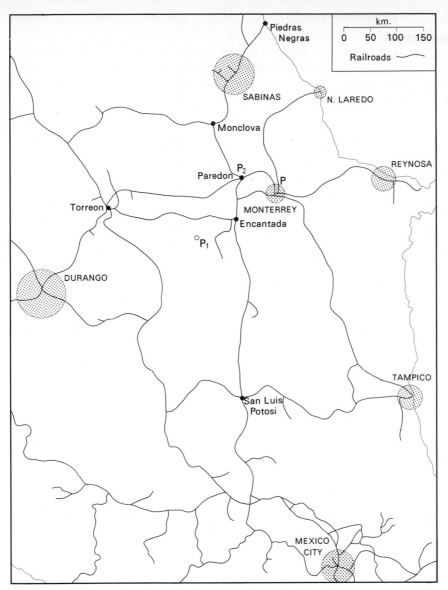

FIGURE 5-1 LOCATION OF STEEL MILLS IN MEXICO. (ROBERT A KENNELLY. 1954, 1955. "THE LOCATION OF THE MEXICAN STEEL INDUSTRY," *REVISTA GEOGRAFICA,* **15**:109–129; **16**:199–213; **17**:60–77. MAP 4.)

on finished steel increased the market pull. Following this procedure caused the MTP to shift to point *P*, which coincided with the location of Monterrey. Applying the Varignon frame to the analysis merely confirmed the empirical results previously obtained by trial and error, as did the use of isodapanes.

However the MTP was calculated, therefore, Monterrey proved to be the best location for an integrated iron and steel industry in Mexico, while Altos Hornos was shown to be less well located. With a material index of 4 and a locational weight of 5, the Mexican steel industry was influenced largely by transport cost rather than by other locational considerations and it was oriented largely to raw materials. With the punctiform character of its material and market locations, the industry thus provided an appropriate subject for the application of Weber's techniques.

Paper industry Another transport-oriented industry that is susceptible of this kind of analysis is paper manufacturing. In this case, however, the pull of raw-material sources is less clear, especially when the particular locational requirements of the different kinds of paper are considered. This is true even though essentially the same machinery is used in each case, whether the final product is newsprint, kraft (for bags), wrapping paper, paperboard (for boxes), or fine papers (book and writing papers). The chief raw material is wood pulp, made by a variety of chemical or mechanical processes; in addition, fine papers contain rags, cotton linters, and kaolin (for filler).

The greater part of the paper industry is oriented to raw materials, and much of it is vertically integrated, with pulp making and paper manufacture occurring at the same site. This segment of the industry is characterized by very large establishments, which achieve economies of scale with the aid of huge machines operated in continuous production runs. Aside from chemicals, the chief input is wood, a bulky material that loses much of its bulk and weight when processed into pulp.

In the United States and Canada much of the paper is manufactured in or near the principal remaining forested regions. The world's leading area is the southeastern United States, with its rapid rate of tree growth and sustained-yield forestry practices. Other important areas—all peripherally situated with respect to the main centers of population and industry—are the Pacific northwest (British Columbia, Washington, Oregon, and northern California), northern and western Ontario, Quebec, and the Maritime Provinces. The forested Scandinavian lands of Norway, Sweden, and Finland bear a similar functional and locational relationship to their European markets.

Exceptions to this general pattern are two special branches of the paper industry—manufacturers of fine papers and paperboard—both of which are attracted to market locations. The rags, cotton linters, kaolin, and pulp from which fine papers are made are assembled from many places by the paper mills, which are not usually integrated operations. From the standpoint of the mills these ingredients are therefore considered "pure materials" in the Weberian sense; that is, they do not lose weight in processing and exert little locational pull. Manufactured in short runs or batches with the aid of relatively small machines, fine papers rely upon skilled labor, more plentiful in heavily populated areas, which are also their main markets. The transport-rate bias against finished products further accentuates the market orientation of this segment of the paper industry.

The paperboard industry is also a batch type of operation, its finished product consisting of boxes made to order and specially printed for individual customers such as the manufacturers of bottled or canned beverages. One reason for the market orientation of paper box manufacture is the nature of the product, which is bulkier and more costly to transport than its raw material and hence has a short shipping radius. For these reasons, and also because of its competitive nature, this and other segments of the packaging-products industry are appropriate subjects for the market-area approach to locational analysis, as we shall see in a later section.

Case studies More representative of the paper industry generally, however, is newsprint manufacture, which accounts for much the largest share of total paper output. An excellent example of the locational influences encountered by this industry is the *Chicago Tribune*'s Canadian subsidiary, the Ontario Pulp and Paper Company. In 1911 the *Tribune* was expanding rapidly and needed an enlarged source of newsprint. The usual practice of that time was to divide this type of production into two distinct and locationally separate stages. The pulping operation took place close to the forests because of the bulky, weight-losing nature of the raw material; converting the pulp into newsprint occurred in the market area because paper was too readily damaged by the crude transport techniques then in use. This dictated a Canadian location for the initial stage and an American location for the final stage.

Prompted by a newly enacted Canadian export duty on unprocessed pulp, the *Tribune* departed from the traditional locational practice. The company decided to build a single vertically integrated mill in Ontario and to acquire its own fleet of lake vessels specially equipped to give cheap, damage-free transport for the finished product. Rejecting a raw-material site in the forests of northern Ontario because of high development costs in that remote area, the *Tribune* chose to locate its new plant at Thorold, situated at the extreme end of the Lake Erie water level on the Welland Canal (Figure 5-2). Here the pulping-newsprint mill could draw upon cheap Niagara electricity, a local pool of labor with a tradition of papermaking skills, cheap water transportation for both the raw material and the product, abundant process water, and direct rail access to Appalachian coal. Instead of drawing upon northern Ontario forests, the company obtained its wood from its properties along the shores of the lower St. Lawrence.

Although intervening years have brought a number of changes in the cost and sources of energy and raw-material inputs, methods of transport, and location of markets, the Thorold plant is still logically situated. The locational relationships, including the punctiform nature of sources and markets, still constitute a classical example of Weber's locational figure. Moreover, it demonstrates the advantages of a break-of-bulk site and of both internal and external economies.

Another case, this time involving a country's entire paper industry, is the well-known example of the Swedish paper industry (Lindberg, 1951). It was noted, first of all, that in the Swedish paper industry procurement costs for wood rise with increasing scale of production because it is necessary to extend the average distance in order to tap additional forested areas. Because of a material index of 3,

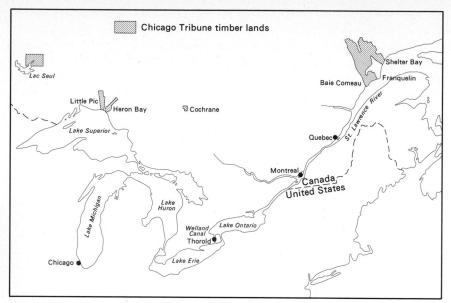

FIGURE 5-2 SOURCES OF PULP-PAPER FOR THE *CHICAGO TRIBUNE*.

an integrated pulp and paper operation would have to locate at the raw-material source; if the two steps are separated, the pulping operation would be at the raw-material source and papermaking at the market.

Following Weber's geometric technique, "isovectures" (lines of equal total transport cost, equivalent to isotims) were constructed for the spatially distributed forest resources of Sweden, a separate set being produced for each paper mill. Transport cost curves were calculated for each mill and other costs were added, including those for procuring coal, sulfur, limestone, and other raw materials, and for marketing the paper.

The resulting map of total costs provided a guide to the least-cost locations for the Swedish industry. Because the raw material, wood, is a relative ubiquity in forested Sweden, and because the nation's principal markets are overseas, the appropriate location for the paper industry is along the coasts, that is, on the marketward side of the raw-material region.

Other industries with high transport costs   *Metal trades*   Numerous other cases of high-transport-cost industries could be cited if space permitted. The other metal-processing activities, such as copper and aluminum, are generally like the iron and steel industry in being multistage operations with high material indices in their initial stages. Few of these other metal trades, however, have the vertical integration at one site or have achieved the external economies so typical of the steel industry.

Most copper comes from exceedingly lean ores that must undergo initial beneficiation at the mine before moving to subsequent stages of smelting, refining, and fabrication, each closer to the market than the preceding one. Although the chief ore of aluminum, bauxite, is generally richer than copper ore, aluminum processing passes through a similar sequence of stages. Until recently the refining stage of aluminum production, which yields the pure metal, did not fit the usual market-oriented pattern of later operations because of its extreme energy demands; however, aluminum refiners have recently found it possible to obtain the necessary large blocks of electricity within the principal market areas. New aluminum refineries are therefore locating more in accordance with theoretical expectations.

Petroleum refining Petroleum refining, on the other hand, is a high-transport-cost industry that is at least as vertically integrated as steel. It too has a history of changing locational tendencies. For several decades after the first oil well was drilled in 1859, the only marketed products were kerosene and a few other lighter fractions. At least half the crude oil brought from the ground was of no commercial use, giving the industry a material index of 2 or more. As a result refining took place at or near the raw-material sources.

At the turn of the century the coming of the automobile age greatly increased the quantity of petroleum products demanded but did little to change the structure of demand because the principal new product, gasoline, was another of the lighter fractions. Between the two world wars, however, demand gradually became more balanced as ships, trucks, and locomotives converted to diesel power, using a heavier petroleum fraction. Consumption of fuel oil for heating purposes also grew, taking still other heavy fractions. Meanwhile, advances in refining technology permitted the extraction of larger quantities of lighter products from each barrel of crude, and the growing petrochemical industry consumed nearly all that was left. By 1945, therefore, 90 to 95 percent of the crude oil was converted into marketable products, the remainder being consumed as refinery fuel. The material index of the oil-refining industry thus fell to 1.05 or less.

With its chief input now essentially a pure material in the Weberian sense, refining could theoretically take place at the source of the material, at the market, or at any break-of-bulk point in between. The major markets of North America have acquired their own refinery complexes as have those of Europe, where coastal sites are preferred for direct receipt of the crude from tankers from the Middle East. A trend toward market orientation developed, partly because of the transport economies enjoyed by giant supertankers bearing a single homogeneous commodity and partly because the oil companies felt that the great amount of capital invested in a large refinery was more secure in the home country than in the politically volatile Middle East. More recently the newly organized petroleum-producing countries have managed to reverse this trend by insisting that a larger proportion of their oil be refined at the source. The industry has effected important scale economies by building ever larger refineries, and it has increasingly integrated vertically by adding petrochemical facilities and the manufacturing of chemical products at the refinery site. Petroleum refineries have thus become the centers of large industrial complexes.

AGGLOMERATION

This brings us to a class of industries whose location is influenced to an unusual degree by agglomeration. We have already seen that this locational factor is important to manufacturing generally and is becoming more so as industries mature and become increasingly elaborate and interrelated. The significance of agglomeration is perhaps best demonstrated by the depressed economies of regions and countries that cannot offer this locational advantage to industries they would like to attract (see Chapter 10). Despite the acknowledged importance of agglomeration, however, it is difficult to measure; it is especially hard to separate the basic components of agglomeration from each other and from other location factors such as labor or capital.

Chemical industry   Of the many types of manufacturing whose location depends heavily upon agglomerative influences, one of the purest examples is the chemical industry. Although it is impossible to define this intricate activity with any precision, the U.S. Bureau of the Census identifies a threefold division of chemicals and allied products: (1) basic chemicals, (2) chemical products to be manufactured further, and (3) finished chemicals ready for ultimate consumption. The basic chemicals include acids, alkalies, salts, and organic materials that are made directly from plentiful, cheap, and simple elemental raw materials such as salt, air, limestone, coal, petroleum, soybeans, wood, milk, cotton, or sulfur. Chemical products to be manufactured further (chemical intermediates) are the synthetic fibers, plastic materials, and other commodities made from basic chemicals. Finished chemicals are the drugs, cosmetics, soaps, paints, fertilizers, and so forth into which chemical intermediates are converted for direct use by consumers. As this suggests, the purpose of the chemical industry is to synthesize, or build up, new substances by combining simpler ones.

Because most chemical production is highly automated and therefore has unusually low labor inputs, its agglomerative tendencies are more easily distinguished than those of many other activities. Yet its study is complicated by the many successive stages required to obtain an end product. Moreover, several commodities can often be jointly produced from one class of raw materials, and the various intermediates can be combined and recombined in innumerable ways.

In a typical petrochemical–synthetic fiber complex it is possible to discern all the different types of agglomeration. *Scale economies* are particularly important; indeed, many kinds of chemical production have thresholds so high that only the largest, most advanced national economies can provide a sufficiently large market to support them adequately. *Localization economies* are also clearly evident in such complexes, where many companies engage in similar or related forms of production and rely upon direct linkages with neighboring plants for their chemical intermediates. Similarly prominent are *urbanization economies*, the benefits gained by industries of all kinds, whether related or not, merely because of their spatial association. In chemical manufacturing many industries are drawn together by their sharing of a common source of basic raw materials and common transport facilities.

A Canadian example   The large petrochemical complex at Sarnia, Ontario, illustrates all these locational characteristics (Figure 5-3). Sometimes called Canada's "Chemical Valley," this concentration of industry owes its origins to an oil refinery established here at an early date by Imperial Oil to process crude obtained from a small oil field in Lambton County. With the exhaustion of local petroleum supplies, the refinery began to import crude from the nearby Lima-Indiana field of the United States. Subsequently the Sun and Shell companies also built refineries at Sarnia to serve the growing Toronto market without having to pay tariff on imported refined products.

Chemical production began at Sarnia during World War II, when the Canadian government constructed its Polymer plant to produce synthetic rubber. At the close of the war Polymer was joined at this location by a branch plant of the Dow Chemical Company and subsequently by other firms, including Fiberglass, St. Clair, Ethyl, Du Pont, and Allied chemical companies. Dominance of the nearby Toronto market was ensured by chemical imports from across the adjacent American border. This location, with its excellent connections by pipeline, rail, and water, provided easy access to such raw materials as crude oil and coal. This

FIGURE 5-3   OIL-PIPELINE NETWORK FOR SARNIA.

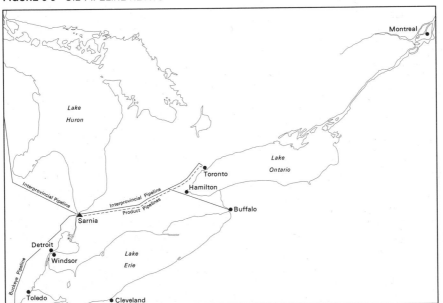

location provided abundant local supplies of salt and process water, together with easy access by pipeline, rail, and water to sources of crude oil, coal, and other inputs.

Interplant linkages among the chemical producers at Sarnia are exceedingly complex; the same hydrocarbons are often repeatedly recycled in ever-changing forms. In-plant linkages are also elaborate and a single plant may yield hundreds of products. There are vertical linkages, where the various stages in the manufacture of a single product take place sequentially in several plants; horizontal linkages, where components made by a number of plants come together ultimately for the manufacture of a given commodity; and diagonal linkages, where one firm makes a chemical used repeatedly in the various stages of manufacturing another item.

These linkages between and within plants have many advantages. One is the saving in cost and danger of long-distance haulage of hazardous, volatile, or corrosive chemicals. Other benefits come from face-to-face contacts among managers and technicians of different firms, common access to specialized services, and the reputation of the area for production of this type. This combination of locational attractions is reinforced by the enormous capital investment in plant and equipment that has accumulated here.

The Sarnia complex is duplicated by similar concentrations of chemical production elsewhere in Canada, particularly at Montreal and in the Alberta oil fields. Even larger complexes of this type appear at such locations as Ashtabula, Ohio; the southern shore of Lake Michigan; the Texas Gulf Coast; and the Thames estuary, Southampton Water, and the Merseyside districts of Britain.

LABOR

Spatial variations in labor cost represented Weber's "first distortion" of the basic locational pattern, the latter having previously been determined by transport costs (Chapter 4). Empirical studies have indeed confirmed that differential labor costs affect the locations of certain industries. Such labor cost differentials result from the imperfect mobility of workers from regions of low wages to those of higher wages. The mobility of labor is particularly restricted between countries, with their increasingly strict immigration laws; but labor does not move freely between regions within countries, or even between communities, where the barriers are of a more intangible, psychological sort.

How important is labor as a locational determinant? In manufacturing, the labor input, expressed as a percentage of total value added, varies substantially. In low-labor-cost industries the amount attributable to wages and salaries can range well below 10 percent; in high-labor-cost industries such outlays may rise to 20 or even 50 percent. Yet, the evidence seems to indicate that today few industries are greatly influenced in their locations within countries by wage differentials. More important in most cases are such things as the availability of an adequate supply of the needed skills or the general work attitudes of the labor force. Two industries whose locations have been much influenced in the United States by labor considerations are the shoe industry and rubber tire manufacturing.

Shoe industry According to Weber's own estimates, the shoe industry has a material index ranging between 1.05 and 1.08. Although this indicates a virtually pure material, transport rates are higher on the finished product, suggesting a net attraction toward the market (Hoover, 1937). The most important locational influence of all, however, is the labor input, despite increasing mechanization of the industry.

In his study of this industry, Hoover (1937) noted four main periods of development in the United States, to which we might add a fifth. During the first period, from 1630 to 1760, shoemaking was a local handicraft occupation. It was therefore ubiquitous in its spatial distribution, its pattern coinciding closely with that of early colonial population. Each village had its own craftsman who used local raw materials to fashion shoes from start to finish. With the appearance of larger population centers, the industry began to concentrate in eastern Massachusetts, Philadelphia, and New York City, where some division of labor among shoemakers occurred. This spatial pattern was an orientation to markets rather than to labor.

Between 1760 and 1860, the second period brought a greater subdivision to shoe production, as workmen in the three main areas of concentration became increasingly specialized in their operations. Because it is easier to learn to make one part of the shoe than the whole, specialization provided the opportunity either to reduce standards of labor skill or increase the quality of workmanship. In fact both of these occurred, causing the industry to split into two branches, one concentrating on high-quality shoes skillfully custom-made to individual measurements, while the other specialized in cheaper shoes made in a range of standard measurements and styles and warehoused for general sale.

The custom manufacture of shoes continued its old market-oriented pattern. There was no standardization of products, nor was there much division of labor. The wholesale branch of the industry, however, became increasingly attracted to large supplies of labor. As each worker was required to learn only one operation, skill requirements fell; but quantity production of cheap, standardized shoes required large numbers of such workers. Most wholesale production relied upon the old "putting out" method. A central shop stocked materials for distribution to workers, who performed the actual labor in their homes, each executing by hand a particular task and returning the item to the shop for further processing.

A further spatial division of the industry was based on the availability of complementary labor. For example, in the eastern Massachusetts district, most male workers along the North Shore were sailors and fishermen, leaving a surplus of female labor for shoemaking. The principal product, therefore, was lightweight women's shoes, which required much sewing. By contrast, along the South Shore, which had few harbors, most male workers were farmers. Because of the short growing season in that area, the men found part-time employment in the shoe industry, where they did the heavy work while women performed the lighter tasks. Hence the local specialty became men's boots and shoes.

Even with the appearance of the railways and the beginning of the westward movement, the eastern areas retained their dominance of the industry. The principal reason for this was their large supply of labor with a century's accumulation of shoemaking skills. Except for a few local custom craftsmen, the western areas had no skilled workers and had little surplus labor for manufacturing in general. As so often happens with the penetration of modern transport into new areas, the railway merely reinforced the concentration of production in the eastern core area (see Chapters 8 and 10).

Near the end of the period a number of events began to alter the locational relationships within the shoe industry. By the middle of the nineteenth century the center of gravity of the market had moved farther westward, where surpluses of labor had begun to appear. Meanwhile, the older areas of concentration in the East were finding local supplies of raw materials increasingly inadequate and were having to procure these from more distant sources. At the same time, the introduction of new machines reduced skill requirements. They also brought increasing consolidation of manufacturing in central shops—the first modern shoe factories. The hold of eastern shoe manufacturers on the industry began to weaken.

The third period, from 1860 to 1900, was one of continued mechanization of shoemaking. The McKay sewing machine (1860) completed the transition to factory operation. Aided by the presence of a large number of German immigrants, Rochester and Cincinnati acquired shoe factories, and in time so did Detroit, Chicago, St. Louis, and Milwaukee. Factories sprang up in still other places that had concentrated markets and surpluses of labor. By the end of the century the eastern centers of shoemaking had lost ground relatively; they responded by specializing in light, high-quality shoes made from fine imported leathers. For this kind of manufacture they had a monopoly in the essential labor skills. Thus the midwestern centers came to specialize in heavier, cheaper shoes mass-produced from local hides.

Between 1900 and World War II, a fourth period brought a new series of events that caused further reorientation of shoe manufacture. As machines became more sophisticated, it became possible to make fine shoes of even better quality and higher style. Fashion gained a bigger role in shoe sales, necessitating quick style changes and giving increased emphasis to market accessibility. With the declining competitive position of eastern manufacturers in the growing markets of the interior, the latter turned to the export market—until even that was lost during the Great Depression of the 1930s. Meanwhile, unionization of labor, which had begun in the 1870s, continued to gain momentum in this labor-intensive industry, contributing to the further decline of production in the East.

The general pattern that evolved during the first half of the twentieth century still prevails in the current, or fifth, period. The older centers of the East rely upon their advantages in labor skill and reputation to emphasize high-style shoes, whose production is seasonal, occurs at a relatively small scale, and is subject to strong union pressure. By contrast with this unstable element in the shoe industry, the midwestern manufacturers have a much steadier production of the more standard types of shoes. A new element that has appeared in recent years has been the incursion of imported shoes into the American market—at both ends of the price range. The cheapest shoes (sneakers, etc.) must now compete with even cheaper imports from Hong Kong, Taiwan, and South Korea, while the more expensive lines must compete with high-style, handmade shoes from the United Kingdom, France, and Italy. Thus the labor factor has experienced a resurgence in a new form and at the international scale.

Rubber tire manufacture   The development of the American rubber tire industry demonstrates the difficulty of separating the factors of agglomeration and labor, both of which have affected its locational pattern. Originally specializing in bicycle tires, the rubber companies of Akron, Ohio, managed to dominate automobile tire production throughout the first third of the present century. Their pioneering efforts in tire making gave the Goodyear, Firestone, Goodrich, and several smaller companies an early start in the production of original-equipment tires for the automobile industry of nearby Detroit. Large tire orders resulting from the exploding market for vehicles prompted the Akron firms to introduce mass-production techniques, thereby gaining important economies of scale. With their low unit costs, they were able to drive most of their non-Akron competitors out of business. By 1935 Akron employed two-thirds of the nation's rubber workers and contributed three-fourths of the value added by manufacture (Sobel, 1954).

In addition to economies of scale and other agglomerative advantages, Akron's initial locational attraction for rubber tire manufacture included the large local pool of skilled workers. This permitted the Akron firms to use complex machinery with high levels of labor productivity and low unit costs despite the high wage rates prevailing in the area. Akron companies also benefited from their proximity to Detroit and their centrality with respect to the market for replacement tires: more than half the country's motorcars were registered within 500 miles of Akron in 1930.

Akron's labor-cost advantage ended abruptly in 1934, when the rubber workers' union succeeded in its organizational efforts there. Union-imposed restrictions on labor output, such as a six-hour day and work-sharing arrangements, caused the productivity of Akron's workers to drop below that of the rest of the country. In response to this development, the tire manufacturers rapidly decentralized their operations until by 1938 Akron accounted for only one-third of the total hours of rubber workers in the nation. Although unionization ultimately spread throughout the country, equalizing wage rates, the differential labor costs of the 1930s had a lasting effect on the industry's locational pattern. Reinforcing this spatial distribution in the postwar period was the emergence of large regional markets for original-equipment tires for the automobile industry, which has also decentralized in recent years. Meanwhile the remaining production in Akron has focused on highly engineered rubber products, following the lead of the eastern shoe-manufacturing regions under similar conditions.

MARKET-AREA ANALYSIS

The growing tendency for rubber tire production to locate with respect to spatially distributed regional markets leads us to consider the empirical evidence for a different approach to locational analysis—that based on the theory of market areas. As we noted in Chapter 4, industries for which this type of analysis is appropriate tend (1) to be highly competitive, (2) to serve cutsomers scattered over a wide territory, (3) to make fairly standardized goods, and (4) to produce goods that have a limited range of distribution because of perishability or because they gain weight in processing.

Container manufacturing   One of the best examples of such industries is the manufacture of containers—cans, bottles, and boxes. It is one of the most competitive of industries. There is very little to differentiate the products of one container firm from those of another, since all rely upon the same standard raw materials, designs, and production equipment and processes. Moreover, because they sell directly to manufacturers who use these items to package their own commodities, they must deal with the purchasing agents who consider only the product's technical specifications and are not to be swayed by advertising claims for differences that do not exist, as is common in the consumer goods market. The market for containers is spatially distributed, particularly the food and beverage industries, which are essentially ubiquitous. Cans, bottles, and boxes all gain much bulk in their manufacture and are therefore costly to ship.

The locational influences at work in the container industry are shown by the circumstances that brought can-manufacturing firms to the Eden Valley area of western New York (Figure 5-4). The Eden Valley is a prime truck gardening district, producing large crops of vegetables and small fruits on its rich, glacially deposited soils. The five food-processing concerns of the Eden Valley formerly obtained their containers outside the area from the three major can companies—American Can Company, National Can Company, and Continental Can Company—all of which manufactured their cans in plants centrally located with respect to very large regional markets. Concentrating their production in this fashion permitted the can manufacturers to enjoy important economies of scale.

Two related events changed this locational pattern. One was the substantial increase in the output of a number of vegetable-growing areas, and the other was the recognition by one of the container firms that a competitive advantage could be gained by siting smaller can-manufacturing operations within the individual gardening areas. The increased market penetration would more than offset the losses in scale economies. It was this reasoning that caused the Continental Can Company to construct a plant at North Collins, in the Eden area. Immediately Continental captured the entire Eden Valley market, thereby forcing its competitors to follow its example if they were to avoid permanent loss of the important sales to be made in the district. The National Can Company took this course of action; the other major company, American Can Company, did not.

In setting up operations in the Eden Valley, the two can companies had to take into account these locational considerations. (1) The market for cans is large and spatially distributed, including not only the five processing plants in the valley but also many others scattered throughout western New York. (2) The raw materials are compact and cheaply shipped (the customer pays the freight). One of these materials, sheet metal, tin-plated or lacquered, is procured from the large

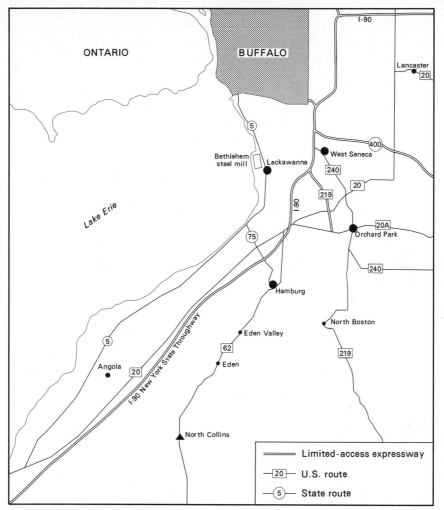

FIGURE 5-4 LOCATION OF CONTAINER MANUFACTURING IN THE EDEN VALLEY SOUTH OF BUFFALO.

Bethlehem Steel Company mill in nearby Buffalo. The other material is can ends, which come ready-made from central feeder plants in the old regional centers (Marion, Ohio, in the case of National Can). In making the ends, economies of scale are too important for decentralization and the ends are inexpensively shipped in compact packages. (3) The packing plants obtain the cans f.o.b. factory, which means that the customer pays the freight. (4) The finished cans are very bulky and incur high transport rates. (5) Labor costs are important, but wage rates are standard in this nationally unionized industry.

Because of the competitive situation this set of conditions imposes, the two can-manufacturing plants in the Eden Valley have complete control of the local market, which they share between them. By failing to join them at this location, the other of the "big three" can producers, American, has forfeited the western New York market. The two can producers in the Eden area are located centrally in their market areas and very close to each other. This arrangement is duplicated in many other places, as, for example, on the outskirts of Toronto, where the major can manufacturers have chosen adjacent sites.

Motor vehicle assembly Each of the major location theories offers a useful framework for viewing the spatial pattern of motor vehicle manufacture, but the theory of market-area analysis provides special insights. This is particularly true if we are concerned with the locational problems of a single manufacturer such as General Motors, which has twenty-two assembly plants in the United States. In this latter case we are dealing with a commodity that, for a given vehicle model, is truly uniform regardless of where it is produced.

Automobile manufacture is an extremely competitive industry. In the battle for the American market only four domestic producers have managed to survive: General Motors, Ford, Chrysler, and American Motors. Despite the large stakes, entry of a new firm into the industry is difficult if not impossible in view of the enormous capital investment required to establish the required degree of vertical integration, the necessity for a large national and international dealership organization, and the importance of a well-established reputation for the product.

Vehicle manufacturing as a whole is a multiple-stage operation. For some highly integrated corporations it begins with processing raw materials—products of the mine and the plantation. At the next stage these metals, fabrics, and other commodities are shaped into the various component parts of the vehicle: carburetors, generators, distributors, windows, stampings (body panels, hoods, etc.), and a great variety of others. At the end comes the assembly operation, which consists of bolting, welding, and positioning parts and subassemblies to form the completed vehicle. Our main interest here is in the last of these stages.

It is important for assembly plants to have good access to establishments making parts, considering that each vehicle contains between 12,000 and 20,000 parts coming from a large number of suppliers. Yet, as viewed by the assembler, these parts are pure materials—that is, not subject to further weight loss. Following Weber's argument, therefore, vehicle assembly is not bound to the sources of its materials, the parts. Because the finished product is bulkier and more subject to damage in transit than its component parts, it is more costly to ship the vehicles to market than it is to procure the parts. Although it is the buyer who pays the freight, the manufacturer must minimize distribution costs if he is to remain competitive with rival sellers. Thus the assembler can increase total revenue by locating centrally within his market area, and the industry as a whole is strongly attracted to large concentrations of population.

Despite the key locational role of the market factor, other influences are also operative and in some instances are critical. By comparison with other industries vehicle production is only average in its use of labor. Yet differential labor costs can be vital in this highly competitive activity, where it is necessary to account for every penny. At various times and places labor has been a serious problem and labor-management relations have been volatile. In this thoroughly unionized industry, wage rates are fairly standard throughout a given country; but labor *costs* can vary substantially because some areas are more troubled with labor unrest than others.

Agglomeration, in all its manifestations, likewise exerts an influence. Large-scale economies are essential in the industry today because high capital outlays must be spread over as many units of output as possible. The least slump in production levels can cause unit costs to rise dangerously. Here lies the special advantage enjoyed by the giant firms—and the principal explanation for the struggles and high mortality rates of smaller companies.

Historical changes in the spatial pattern of motor vehicle assembly in the United States lend emphasis to some of these locational influences and particularly to the role of the market. When the industry began, early in this century, innumerable small firms sprang up in the country's main manufacturing centers. Within a few years the industry had dwindled to insignificance everywhere but in Detroit. There has been much speculation about Detroit's success—its preexisting marine-engine, metalworking, and carriage industries, the local concentration of venture capital, and the presence of an active group of entrepreneurs such as Olds, Ford, Haynes, and Duryea—but one of its most important advantages is often overlooked: its centrality with respect to the national market. At a time when motorcars were essentially handmade and relatively expensive, the American population was much smaller and poorer than today. Hence the number of potential buyers was not large enough to support several production centers.

By midcentury all this had changed. As the industry matured, mass-production methods had reduced costs even while per capita incomes rose. As a result vehicle sales doubled and redoubled until at last individual regional markets became large enough to support their own assembly plants. Decentralization of the industry was further hastened by the greater militancy of unions in the Detroit region, where there was greater resistance to new labor-saving machinery than in other parts of the country. The "big three" automobile makers had also reached the limits of their entrepreneurial capacity by this time and had begun to decentralize decision making by giving more authority to plant managers. World War II also brought governmental pressure upon this and other key industries to spread their operations more widely for greater safety in the event of air attack.

The contemporary pattern of vehicle manufacture in Canada lends emphasis to some of these locational tendencies of the industry. Today Canada's assembly plants are still concentrated in the center of the national market, and the province of Ontario alone has about nine-tenths of the total output. The Toronto metropolitan area takes one-seventh or more of all new cars and trucks produced, and the area within a 200-mile radius of the city takes at least one-fifth more. Not only do Toronto and southern Ontario provide the largest market, but the city offers a large pool of labor with an industrial tradition.

The Canadian motor vehicle industry has one chronic problem: its national market is too small for optimal economies of scale. With a total population only slightly larger than that of California or New York State, the country can support only one major concentration of vehicle production and that only by means of a high tariff on imported cars and parts. A partial solution to this problem has been found in the Canada–United States Automobile Agreement (see Chapter 9).

FOOTLOOSE INDUSTRIES

Increasing numbers of industries are being given the label "footloose," implying that they are entirely free of locational constraints. This characteristic derives partly from the fact that their transport costs are low in relation to the value of the product. Their apparent locational freedom is also associated in many instances with a high degree of automation and a high technological content. The expression "footloose" is misleading, however, because in fact very few industries are wholly lacking in locational needs; even high-technology industries entail important external linkages, as the following example shows.

Electronics   Often cited as a typical footloose activity is the electronics industry, which uses compact and essentially pure materials to make products that are valuable and have strong technological requirements. Not only does it incur low transport costs, but it has only minimal fuel and power needs. Nevertheless, the electronics industry has important manpower needs, which substantially influence its location.

In those branches of the field devoted to durable consumer goods, such as radios and television sets, the nature of manpower requirements changes as the manufacture of a given product passes through the developmental phases into the maturer ones. The innovative phases actively seek areas where high-level scientific research is taking place; indeed, some of the more complex products, such as those for military use, are permanently attached to locations of this type. The production of goods for industrial or consumer use ultimately reaches the point where it has become sufficiently routine for most of the work to be done by semiskilled or unskilled workers. For these products the strongest locational attraction is therefore to large numbers of production workers, especially female labor.

These locational traits were confirmed by a study of New England's electronics industry (Estall, 1963). Electronics manufacture became established in that region at a time when most industry of the area was in decline. It began with the manufacture of radio and television components and expanded rapidly as it entered into wartime production of radar, telecommunications, industrial control and computing systems, and missile control and guidance systems. These sophisticated products required a great amount of research and engineering. The focus for this kind of activity was Boston, where the main attraction was the availability of scientific personnel at Harvard and M.I.T. and in private research laboratories. For the less skilled tasks associated with this kind of production the region provided a large pool of female labor. A remarkable concentration of establishments engaged in research and development exists along Boston's circumferential highway, Route 128.

On the outer fringes of the greater Boston area and extending into other parts of New England are firms manufacturing the better-established electronics products. Here the availability of large numbers of production workers is the prime requisite. For those goods in which mass-production methods have become thoroughly developed, the main areas of United States production have moved even farther inland, especially to the Midwest.

In Canada the principal center for high-technology electronics production is Toronto, which also dominates the commoner forms of electronics manufacture. The advantages of this location for the former type are illustrated by a firm making sophisticated electronic controls for the aviation industry. The company, which does most of its own research and development work, manufactures its products from such materials as electronic components, machined parts, metal fabricated parts, and other manufactured items, all of which are purchased. Half its employees are female production workers, while most of the remainder are highly trained engineers. Production labor accounts for only one-fifth of the value added, but the total outlay for all wages and salaries comes to very nearly half the value added.

Toronto is the prime Canadian location for high-quality labor of all types. Not only is it the economic heart of the country, but it also has the universities and technical training institutes to provide such skills. For the firm making aircraft control devices, this was a compelling attraction. Also important was quick and easy access to a large number of plants that made the various components and parts required in its equipment. Proximity to Toronto's large collection of such industries relieved the company of the need to maintain its own costly inventories of such items.

Not having to stockpile these materials also provided the firm with the flexibility to respond quickly to changing product demand in a rapidly changing field. Its customers for aviation controls were aircraft assemblers and parts manufacturers, as well as commercial airlines. Although transport costs were a minor item, access to customers was especially vital. For speedy delivery, air shipment was necessary; hence the firm's choice of a site adjacent to Toronto's international airport. From this point the company could quickly dispatch controls and spare parts to customers anywhere in Canada, the United States, or elsewhere in the world.

Electronics manufacture is thus not truly a footloose industry in the full sense of the word, despite frequent claims to the contrary. It has locational needs of a compelling nature, including the immediate availability of very special kinds of personnel as well as an adequate supply of production labor. Even though transport cost is not an important locational determinant, ease of access is important. Viewed in this manner, it seems unlikely that many so-called footloose industries can be accurately given this label.

INDUSTRIAL CONCENTRATIONS

One thing emerging from the preceding pages is the social nature of manufacturing—the strong attraction that most industries have for other industries. We have seen that this attraction is not limited to the direct linkages between related industries but includes also the common needs of different kinds of manufacturing for ready markets, labor supply, and transport and other services. Because of these social tendencies, industries form concentrations, which can be observed at several different scales. At the local level, clusters of industries develop within urban areas; on a broader scale, clusters of industrial cities produce manufacturing districts, such as the Mohawk Valley district of New York State. In turn, groups of manufacturing districts may form belts of manufacturing, which sometimes spill over international borders. Examples are the North American manufacturing belt, shared by Canada and the United States, and the Western European manufacturing belt, comprising southern England and neighboring areas on the Continent. A trait common to all levels of concentration is the tendency to focus upon a central core where manufacturing activity reaches a peak, and away from which intensity of production diminishes in all directions.

This section takes a broader perspective; the succeeding section will look at local concentrations. To gain a better understanding of these patterns of manufacturing, we shall be asking why each major concentration came into being and what are its main characteristics. At each scale we shall look to location theory for answers to these questions. In many instances we shall also find clues in the historical development of concentrations: the existence of some initial locational advantage such as access to raw materials, markets, capital, or a transport feature, or perhaps the presence of unusual entrepreneurial skills. More often the answer will lie in a combination of all these. When a region gains a head start, it is difficult for other late-coming regions to counter it, especially since the pioneering area will have acquired a number of external economies over the years. This question underlies many of the problems of development to be discussed later in Chapter 10.

A WORLD VIEW OF MANUFACTURING

From the international perspective, the spatial pattern of manufacturing offers many contrasts (see Figure 5-5). The first contrast is between the world center of industrial activity and those areas at a distance from it. At least two-thirds of the world's manufacturing employees work in Anglo-America, Europe, the Soviet Union, and Japan; yet these four great workshop regions contain only 28 percent of the world population. More to the point, these four produce at least seven-eighths of all the world's manufactured goods. Even the nature of production differs between this center and the periphery, as shown by the fact that the four leaders devote little more than one-quarter of their output to food, textiles, and clothing, whereas the outlying manufacturing areas put as much as three-fourths of their effort into these bare necessities. In the world industrial center a large part of the output consists of metals and metal products; on the periphery only a minor portion of the production is of this sort.

Another set of contrasts exists between communist and noncommunist countries. The communist lands of Eastern Europe, the Soviet Union, Cuba, China, North Korea, and North Vietnam contain an estimated one-third of the world's

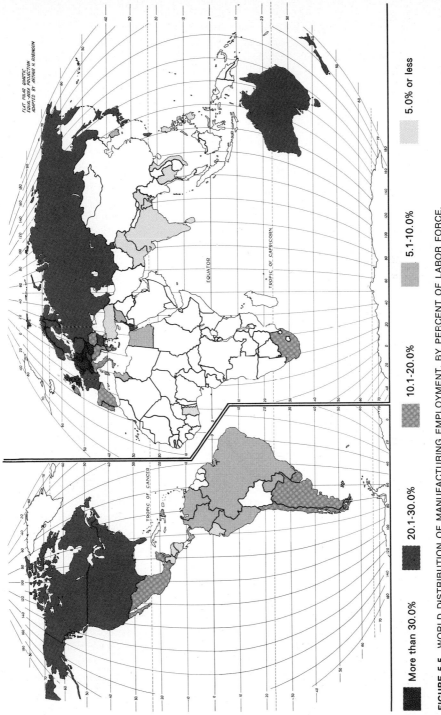

FIGURE 5-5 WORLD DISTRIBUTION OF MANUFACTURING EMPLOYMENT, BY PERCENT OF LABOR FORCE.

More than 30.0% 20.1–30.0% 10.1–20.0% 5.1–10.0% 5.0% or less

labor force; yet these centrally planned economies account for almost two-fifths of all manufacturing workers. This is true despite the large work force that each communist country employs in agriculture, especially in Asia. One of the reasons for such a large industrial work force is the emphasis of state planners on manufacturing. The services in communist countries are limited to only the barest minimum share of available labor, by contrast with the two-thirds or more that the United States and Canada employ in this manner. As we shall see, however, the centrally planned economies generally obtain a much lower output per industrial laborer than the more advanced noncommunist countries.

Another way in which these two groups differ is in the structure of their manufacturing. Communist industry stresses basic metals and other producer goods, including basic chemicals; it provides only a minimal supply of consumer goods, particularly consumer durables such as motorcars. The main goal is to achieve a forced growth of national economies and to bolster military strength. Noncommunist production, on the other hand, follows the dictates of the market-place, which results in a proliferation of consumer goods of all kinds.

Thus world manufacturing provides two basic dichotomies, one center-periphery in nature, the other ideological. In addition to these differences, there is a range of nonideological differences in the philosophy regarding the role of government in economic affairs. Let us examine some of the world's leading manufacturing concentrations and note their characteristics.

Major industrial regions *North America* The United States and Canada consti-tute the most productive region in the world industrial heart. Although they have only 11 percent of the noncommunist world's labor force and only 20 percent of its manufacturing workers, this region accounts for more than 43 percent of all industrial output (1972). The United States alone produces 41 percent of the free world's manufactured goods, much of which is consumed by its own large and prosperous population. In addition to its great effective demand, the United States is comparatively well endowed with a wide variety of material resources; yet so high is the level of production and consumption that the nation finds its own supply of industrial raw materials inadequate, especially petroleum and certain metallic ores. Indeed, with only 6 percent of the world's people, the United States uses from one-third to one-half of its resources.

The United States manages to turn out a major part of this huge quantity of manufactured goods in one region (Figure 5-6). In 1971, 55 percent of its value added by manufacturing came from the states of New England, the Middle Atlantic (New York, New Jersey, and Pennsylvania), and the east north central area (Ohio, Indiana, Michigan, Illionis, and Wisconsin). Within these states lie most of the United States portion of the North American manufacturing belt. The region benefits from the momentum it gained as the cradle of American manufacturing; its accessibility by cheap water transport via the Atlantic ports and the Great Lakes; the dense rail and highway networks that focus upon it; its large deposits of high-grade coal; and the presence here of the nation's largest, most prosperous population.

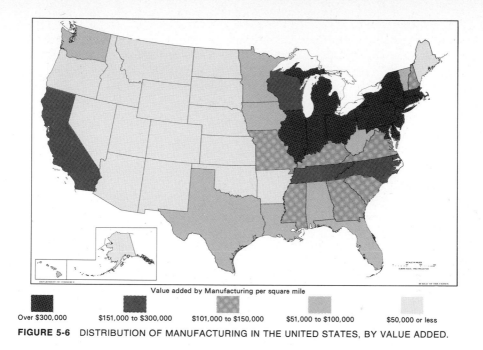

Value added by Manufacturing per square mile

| Over $300,000 | $151,000 to $300,000 | $101,000 to $150,000 | $51,000 to $100,000 | $50,000 or less |

FIGURE 5-6 DISTRIBUTION OF MANUFACTURING IN THE UNITED STATES, BY VALUE ADDED.

The manufacturing belt is not continuous but includes a number of important manufacturing districts, each with its distinctive character. Leading them all is the New York metropolitan area, the largest manufacturing center in the Western Hemisphere and one of the most diverse. Important also are the districts of southern New England, central New York State, and the Delaware River and eastern Pennsylvania. Farther west are the Pittsburgh–Wheeling–Northeastern Ohio and Southern Michigan–Northern Indiana districts. Finally, along the shores of Lake Michigan is the Chicago-Gary-Milwaukee district, second only to New York in total manufacturing employment.

Another major region includes the South Atlantic states, from Maryland southward to Florida, from which come one-eighth of the country's value added by manufacture. Originally an area of resource-based industries, it has attracted an increasing number of labor-intensive activities because of its large pool of pliable, nonunion workers. The Pacific Coast region ranks third, producing more than 11 percent of the country's output, three-fourths of this being in California. A fourth major region is the Texas-Louisiana Gulf Coast, where petrochemicals and nonferrous metal refining are prominent.

Canada's manufacturing is even more concentrated than that of the United States (Figure 5-7). The greater part of it is found along the Toronto-Montreal axis, which represents the Canadian continuation of the North American manufacturing belt. The principal focus is Toronto and the Golden Horseshoe, a crescent of intensive manufacturing activity reaching from Oshawa on the east to Hamilton, St. Catherines, and Niagara Falls around the western end of Lake Ontario. Although

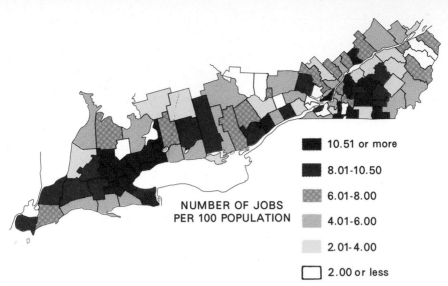

NUMBER OF JOBS
PER 100 POPULATION

■ 10.51 or more

■ 8.01-10.50

▦ 6.01-8.00

▨ 4.01-6.00

░ 2.01-4.00

☐ 2.00 or less

FIGURE 5-7 DISTRIBUTION OF MANUFACTURING EMPLOYMENT IN CANADA. (DATA FROM D. MICHAEL RAY. *DIMENSIONS OF CANADIAN REGIONALISM.* GEOGRAPHICAL PAPER NO. 49, POLICY RESEARCH AND COORDINATION BRANCH, DEPARTMENT OF ENERGY, MINES AND RE-SOURCES. FIG. 20.)

initially resource-based, the manufacturing of this region is now becoming more and more market-oriented and diverse, drawn to the growing population crowding into this most prosperous part of Canada. The diversity of manufacturing in this area is enhanced by the Canadian government's policy of restricting imports of foreign-made goods.

Noncommunist Europe   Second in output to North America, the great concentrations of manufacturing in western and southern Europe produce more than one-third of the goods manufactured in the noncommunist world and employ 36 percent of its industrial labor. Its area of most intense manufacturing activity focuses on southeastern England, the Rhine delta, and the valleys of the Rhine and Ruhr, and it extends outward to encompass much of north and central France, the Swiss plateau, northern Italy, and southern Scandinavia (Figure 5-8). Although manufacturing began in this region at a very early date, it lagged behind North America until after World War II, when it grew rapidly.

The United Kingdom was the locus of the first industrial revolution but has not participated in the general growth of Western Europe's industry in recent decades. Whereas the country produced 10 percent of all noncommunist manufacturing in 1958, it turned out only 6 percent of it in 1972. Despite its small area (equal to the combined areas of Indiana and Illinois), the United Kingdom's industries are remarkably concentrated. The largest grouping is in the London region (see below), which has the nation's biggest population and highest incomes and therefore attracts a great diversity of mainly market-oriented industries. Immedi-

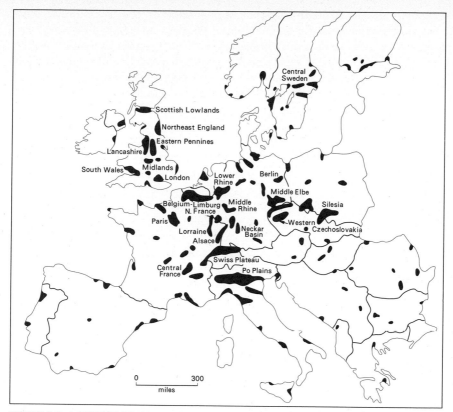

FIGURE 5-8 LOCATION OF MANUFACTURING IN EUROPE. (E. WILLARD MILLER. 1962. *A GEOGRAPHY OF MANUFACTURING.* ENGLEWOOD CLIFFS, N.J.: PRENTICE-HALL. FIG. 3-1, P. 132.)

ately adjacent to the London region on the north and northwest are the English Midlands, the next most active area of manufacturing, devoted especially to vehicle production and other engineering activities. Manufacturing in the old specialized districts along the country's periphery is doing less well, despite elaborate government programs. These include South Wales, the Lancashire and Merseyside districts, the northeast coast and Yorkshire, and the Scottish Midlands. The United Kingdom is counting on its North Sea petroleum to reverse its industrial decline, although the major impact of this oil development is still some years away.

On the opposite side of the English Channel, the Rhine Delta and Rhine-Ruhr concentration occupy parts of Belgium, the Netherlands, Luxembourg, and northwestern Germany. These areas, which contain some of the world's highest population densities, employ at least one-third of their work forces in manufacturing. Although local markets are thus very large, the area's dependence upon foreign markets is unusually high. It is well located to receive raw materials and ship goods through the great ports of Rotterdam, Amsterdam, and Antwerp, and it has immediate access to nearby supplies of coal and iron ore. Surrounding it are the most populous and prosperous nations of Western Europe, with which it has direct access by a dense network of railways, highways, and waterways. Virtually every type of production is represented here, but basic metals, engineering, chemicals, and textiles are especially prominent. Germany's manufacturing also includes a district in the middle Rhine Valley and others in the Neckar and Saar basins, and along the Baltic coast, centering upon Hamburg.

France's industrial growth, which has accelerated in recent years, has now placed it ahead of the United Kingdom. Paris and the Paris basin predominate, but the north of France continues to be important, as do Lorraine, with its basic metals, and central France, focusing upon the rubber and chemical complex at Clermont-Ferrand.

Switzerland has a long manufacturing tradition and a prosperous citizenry with accumulated skills of a high order. Although a third of the labor force is engaged in manufacturing, the country must still import labor from Italy. The product emphasis is upon highly engineered goods, valuable products capable of bearing transport costs from this interior location. Italy, on the other hand, got a late start in manufacturing but has developed rapidly, especially in the north. Genoa and the Po Valley cities of Turin and Milan have acquired important concentrations of metallurgy, chemicals, textiles, and engineering, including motorcars. More recently yet, Spain, Portugal, Greece, and Yugoslavia have likewise experienced a burst of manufacturing.

Meanwhile, on the northern margins of the Continent, Scandinavian industry continues to specialize in products that reflect the region's physical resources and peripheral location. With a long tradition of manufacturing based on an abundance of iron ore and forests but a meager supply of fossil fuels, Sweden produces highly engineered goods, including precision steel, fine glassware, and paper. Danish industry is likewise growing, despite a lack of domestic raw materials and fuels. Norway, on the other hand, has acquired important electrometallurgical industries based upon plentiful hydroelectricity and appears likely to attract additional energy-using manufactures because of her important North Sea oil discoveries.

Eastern Europe and the Soviet Union The U.S.S.R. and her communist neighbors in Eastern Europe constitute the third largest industrial concentration. The national planning agencies of these countries accord top priority to investment in manufacturing and allocate one-fourth of the labor force to this type of production, despite their unusually large numbers of agricultural workers. Their use of manufacturing labor is inefficient, however, as shown by the fact that the Soviet Union produces only slightly more than half as much industrial output as the United States with a work force half again as large. In addition to their industrial emphasis, communist planners have stressed basic metals and producer goods generally. Thus, although the U.S.S.R. lags behind the United States in total value of manufacturing, her steel production is about the same as that of the United States.

Communist central planning agencies not only determine what will be produced but where. In the U.S.S.R., which is the world's largest nation in total land area and is thus well endowed with mineral raw materials, the main locational problem concerns distance and transport cost. The population is concentrated west of the Ural Mountains, whereas many of the raw materials are east of the Urals in Siberia, resulting in exceedingly long rail hauls. Nevertheless, there are important iron, manganese, coal, and petroleum deposits in the western areas, which also contain the principal centers of manufacturing. The Soviet manufacturing belt extends from the Baltic Sea at Leningrad eastward to the Middle Urals and southward to the Black Sea (Figure 5-9). Within this large area the relatively diversified central manufacturing region, focusing upon Moscow, predominates. In the south is the Ukrainian metallurgical region, an old area of iron and coal mining, and on the east is the Middle Volga region, with its hydroelectricity and petroleum. Lesser concentrations of Soviet industry occur in the Caucasus, in the Kuznetsk Basin of southwestern Siberia, and in the Tashkent area of Soviet Central Asia.

Japan Among the individual manufacturing nations of the world, Japan ranks comfortably in third place behind the Soviet Union. Her industrial output, now greater than that of West Germany, the United Kingdom, or France, is about half

FIGURE 5-9 LOCATION OF MANUFACTURING IN THE SOVIET UNION. (RICHARD LONSDALE AND JOHN THOMPSON. 1960. "A MAP OF THE USSR'S MANUFACTURING," *ECONOMIC GEOGRAPHY*, **36**:42. FIG. 2.)

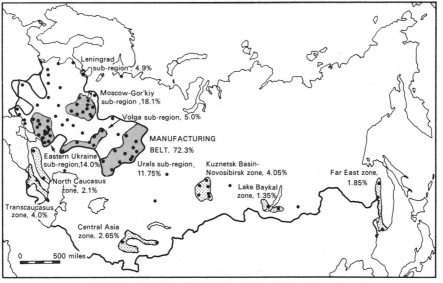

AREAS OF MANUFACTURING CONCENTRATION IN THE SOVIET UNION

Boundary of Soviet manufacturing belt

Sub-regions of Soviet manufacturing belt

Outlying zones

• Centers with an estimated 0.25%
or more of total Soviet manufacturing

All figures in percentage of U.S.S.R. total

that of the U.S.S.R. and growing rapidly. This California-size island nation is ruggedly mountainous and has little level land except along the coasts. The country is very poor in industrial raw materials, with few metallic minerals, little good coal, and virtually no petroleum. Nevertheless, Japan has a large population—about half that of the United States—and a skilled labor force, one-quarter of whom are in manufacturing.

Although Japan must import most of her raw materials and fuels from distant sources and ship her products equally far, her manufacturing output is very large. The stereotype of Japan as a labor-intensive producer is no longer true; today the country has a shortage of labor, is experiencing rising wages, and is automating extensively. Japan's recent success can be attributed to superb organization by a skilled entrepreneurial group enjoying close government cooperation; the intelligent mobilization of investment capital; and efficient use of skilled labor. Another important contributor has been Japan's marketing strategy. Foreign sales of Japanese goods are essential to pay for needed imports and to generate growth, but the country's domestic market is more important than generally realized. Surprisingly, only 10 percent of national output is exported, by comparison with 35 to 40 percent for the Netherlands and Belgium.

Japanese manufacturing is diverse. An efficient, productive group of basic industries rely on economies of scale from gigantic refineries, steel-making vessels, electric generating stations, and chemical works. Japan's shipyards lead the world. Better known to most people, however, are her consumer durables— cameras, television and radio sets, motor vehicles, and so forth. Despite Japan's small land area, her manufacturing forms a dense concentration around the margins of the Inland Sea on the main island of Honshu (Figure 5-10). Outlying parts of the country are mainly agricultural and more lightly peopled than the crowded industrial district. With all her recent prosperity, Japan's industrial future is endangered by the high cost and uncertain availability of much-needed oil imports.

Lesser concentrations of manufacturing Only 12 percent of the industrial production of the noncommunist world occurs outside the four main regions described above. In several places, however, there is locally significant production, and a few areas are experiencing industrial growth. Although, as we have previously observed, much of the production in outlying areas is resource-based or consists of processing for local needs, some new trends are appearing.

Latin America In 1972 Latin America contributed less than 6 percent of the manufactures of the noncommunist world. However, certain parts of Latin America are developing quickly: the two brightest spots in an otherwise lagging area are Mexico and Brazil. Despite rapid rates of population growth, both countries are surging forward, successfully mobilizing their important natural and human resources. Venezuela's development is likewise proceeding steadily, based upon large supplies of petroleum and iron ore. Meanwhile, however, the older industrialized Latin American lands—Argentina, Uruguay, and Chile—are lagging, mainly because of social and political problems.

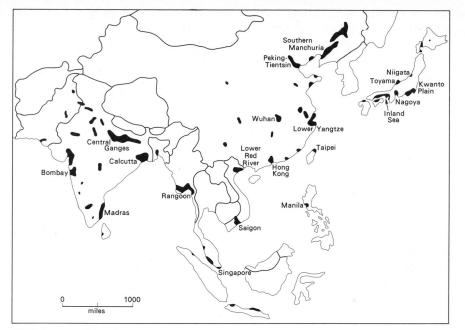

FIGURE 5-10 LOCATION OF MANUFACTURING IN SOUTHEAST ASIA. (MILLER, 1962, FIG. 5-1, P. 236.)

Africa and Asia In the large and populous African continent, only the Republic of South Africa is enjoying industrial growth of any consequence, her main assets being a large and diverse natural endowment. In South Asia, several countries are increasing their industrial production. The largest producer of the region is India, whose reserves of iron ore and coal are substantial and of good quality. Retarding her growth, however, is an acute shortage of capital and the presence of a huge, unskilled, and poorly fed population, whose low per capita income provides a meager local market. On this uncertain base, India has achieved a respectable production of basic metals, cheap mass-produced textiles, and a growing list of other producer and consumer goods.

An interesting parallel to India is communist China, whose 850 million people have a per capita gross national product estimated at less than $100. Still largely an agricultural land, China has only recently discovered how large and varied her mineral resources are—metallic ores, coal, and petroleum. Before the communist takeover in 1949, China's modern forms of manufacturing had been developed mainly by foreign capital and entrepreneurship. It was concentrated in the northeast, principally in the coalfield areas of Manchuria, in Pacific Coast port cities (notably Shanghai), and at major river ports on the Yangtze.

With Mao Tse-tung's assumption of power, the communist Chinese began a drive to develop the interior, following the guidance of Soviet advisers, who placed a Soviet-style emphasis on basic industries. Within a decade the Chinese communists had broken with the U.S.S.R. and had begun a reorientation of their industry, this time stressing the needs of agriculture for such items as tractors, irrigation pumps, and agricultural chemicals, and reducing the costly effort to develop the country's interior. China's rulers are hampered by a severe capital shortage and a desperate need to feed a huge and growing population. Their strategy consists in part of using masses of laborers to create capital goods—dams, irrigation works, roads, railways, and factories. Manufacturing output is rising and the nation's former isolation from the noncommunist West is ending as the Chinese begin the importation of machinery, equipment, and materials required for industrialization.

Certain other newly industrializing Asian lands are assuming the former Japanese role as suppliers of cheap labor. In Hong Kong much of this development is under the direction of indigenous entrepreneurs, but in such countries as Singapore, Malaysia, South Korea, and Indonesia multinational corporations based in Europe, Japan, and North America are providing the managerial skills and capital. The products of these new industries are the customary mass-produced textiles and inexpensive clothing and footwear, but they also include electronic components and appliances.

Australia and New Zealand Australia and New Zealand are remote outliers of the advanced world—occupied by transplanted Europeans who have adapted to new surroundings and conditions. In both countries industrialization is proceeding steadily. In addition to resource-based activities such as meat-packing and milk processing, they are receiving investment by multinational companies in factories producing for both local and foreign markets. In each country the role of foreign enterprise is arousing controversy.

TRENDS IN WORLD MANUFACTURING

Growth Until disrupted by the energy crisis of 1973, world industrial output had grown almost continuously in recent decades. Between 1963 and 1972 noncommunist production rose by 16.4 percent, while that of the centrally planned economies grew by 20.7 percent, although beginning from a lower base. Of the major noncommunist countries Japan achieved the most rapid growth, 29.7 percent between 1963 and 1972, which is more than twice that of the United States. As a whole, the industries of Western Europe grew at or near the world rate, except for France, whose growth was higher than average, and Britain, whose growth slowed. Almost all the countries on the periphery of the European Continent developed industrially between 1963 and 1972, as they at last began to partake in the general prosperity of the Continent. Most of the less developed countries lagged badly in their industrial growth; but, as we have seen, Mexico, Brazil, and a few others did very well.

Economies of scale In general, those major countries enjoying the fastest industrial growth made maximum use of their opportunities to reduce unit costs through large-scale production. This was true of Japan, Western Europe, and the Soviet Union. Meanwhile, the often-repeated predictions that bigness would reach its limits and bring diseconomies of scale failed to materialize, as the leading areas continued to grow larger and expand their leads. In many parts of the noncommunist world, multinational corporations contributed to this increase in the scale of production.

Energy crisis Currently, however, many national growth strategies are going awry because of the crisis in energy. Most of the world's leaders have little or no petroleum of their own, especially Japan and many Western European lands. In each case, recent industrialization has occurred on a basis of cheap, plentiful supplies of imported petroleum. The fourfold rise in the price of Middle Eastern oil may retard the growth of many of these countries.

There is a growing possibility that manufacturing may undergo a reorientation to sources of petroleum. Nations that export petroleum are beginning to use the opportunity to acquire their own industries: steel mills, petrochemical plants, fertilizer factories, and even automobile assembly plants are starting up in Saudi Arabia and other Middle Eastern countries. If this should continue on an important scale, it would replicate the migration of industries to coalfields during the eighteenth century.

Some of the more important effects of high fuel costs may be felt in peripherally located nations. Countries remote from world markets become effectively even more remote because of the reversal in the long-term trend toward declining transport costs. Does this mean that such countries as New Zealand and Australia will have to turn to closer markets for their exports and to produce a greater number of their own needs? If so, the net result would be an increase in national self-sufficiency and a corresponding decline in standards of living.

INTRAURBAN LOCATION OF MANUFACTURING

Where manufacturing is likely to locate within the city is an important question for the geographer, but it is also a matter of more than casual interest to the planner and the entrepreneur. Yet we do not find explicit answers to it in the industrial-location theory of Weber and other classical writers reviewed in Chapter 4. The problem of the classical theorist was to locate the individual firm, or, more precisely, the establishment. After selecting the appropriate general region, he then looked for the particular locality (town or city) where costs are minimized or where revenues are maximized, depending upon which branch of theory he was using.

After choosing the final location, he treated it as unidimensional, in other words, as though the establishment occupied no space. This approach avoids the questions of precisely where to site the firm within the selected urban area, and it provides no information about the general spatial pattern of all industries within the city.

Nevertheless, classical theory does give some implicit help with the problem by providing two of the ingredients needed for a solution—the locational roles of labor and of agglomeration. To learn how these determinants operate within the urban setting, however, we must return to the theory of urban land use (Chapter 2). It will be remembered that urban land use theory examines the locational decisions of many firms in the aggregate as it views zones or districts of similar land use. It regards the locational problem as one of competition for space among many contending land users and land uses. Considering the social nature of industry, this aggregative approach is certainly appropriate.

One aspect of the intraurban problem of industrial location that assumes a prominent place is the center-periphery dichotomy. On the one hand are centripetal forces tending to pull certain activities toward the urban center, and on the other are centrifugal forces attempting to draw them out to the margins of the urbanized area. We saw in Chapter 2 that some industries are therefore more inclined toward inner-city locations, while others are more likely to be in the suburbs, depending upon the balance of tradeoffs between labor and nonlabor costs in each case. A second feature of the intraurban locational problem is the tendency for industrial districts to grow outward from the center along arterial transport routes or other linear features. Finally there are the clustering tendencies of industries resulting from the various kinds of savings they can affect by locating close to each other. Beyond these considerations based on the economics of location lies still another set of influences of which even the first location theorists were aware: the policies of governmental agencies.

MANUFACTURING IN THE METROPOLIS

Although the locational characteristics of manufacturing within an urban setting are similar regardless of the size of the city, they can be seen most clearly in the major world metropolis.

London The archtype of the great European metropolis with a very long industrial tradition, London is also the political capital of the United Kingdom and was once the control center of a vast global political and commercial empire. The economic consequences of this political role are all the greater because Britain has a highly centralized form of government. London is the largest city in the country: approximately one-fifth of the entire population of England and Wales live within greater London (the officially designated metropolitan area), and one-fifth of all the people in the United Kingdom as a whole (including Scotland and Northern Ireland) live in the "London region" (greater London plus seven adjacent counties of southeast England; Figure 5-11).

Growing out of these and other characteristics are a number of powerful locational attractions that London offers to manufacturers. Of prime consideration to a great many industries is the size of the local market; a London firm has immediate access to the nation's largest concentration of consumers, who also happen to have Britain's highest per capita incomes.

The metropolis also provides a labor pool consisting of one-fifth of all the manufacturing employees in England and Wales, a diverse collection of highly skilled workers with a long industrial tradition and including many specialties not found elsewhere in the British Isles.

London's function as a major transport center is of vital importance to the many industries wishing to distribute their productions to a national market. As the

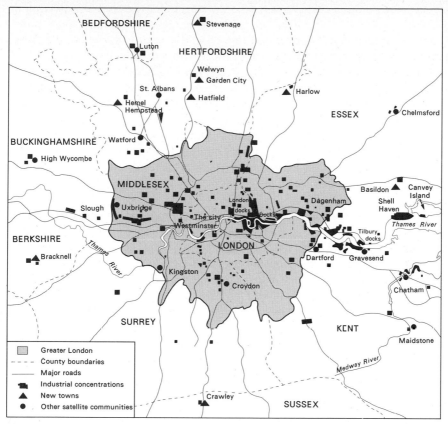

FIGURE 5-11 LOCATION OF INDUSTRY IN THE LONDON AREA.

leading port of the British Isles and one of the largest in the world, London performs a break-of-bulk service for the entire nation. Focusing upon the port is the entire domestic transport network, whose major arteries radiate from the center like spokes on a wheel. The domestic network includes a road system dating to the Roman era, an ancient and elaborate system of inland waterways, and a dense system of railways. London is likewise the focal point for international airlines, for which it is a principal gateway to the European continent, and the domestic airline system.

As the center of national administration, London is the best location for firms relying upon government contracts, particularly since the country nationalized its steel, coal, and most transport industries. London is a preeminent financial center, not just for Britain, but for much of the world. As one function that remains intact from the period of imperial greatness, the city's financial community continues to be a prime source of loan and investment capital. London also remains a center of science and learning, culture, and style. Its large universities, medical centers, theaters, orchestras, and art and design schools—in association with a great many other amenities—make it a most pleasant and exciting place to live. Thus London has a great many unique attractions for industries and for the people who work in them.

Even so, London has features that repel some kinds of production. With so many people and such a variety of activities crowded into a limited area, it has become exceedingly congested, its land in very short supply and costly, and its streets and roads badly congested. One consequence of crowding is a cost of living so high that many foreign-based enterprises must add a "London differential" to their employees' salaries. Nevertheless, industrial wages tend to be higher than elsewhere in Britain, partly because of tight union control. By no means least of the forces acting to repel industries from London has been a government policy, dating from the 1940s, that favors decentralization of employment from the largest centers—and especially London.

London's place in British industry Despite these negative aspects, London's positive attractions cause it to lead the nation in many major industrial categories. In a detailed study of manufacturing employment in greater London, Martin (1966) found that the leading employer was the engineering industries, which as a group accounted for 23 percent of all the engineering workers in England and Wales. Many subcategories of this major industrial group had much larger proportions of the total, however. In the electric lamp and electronic tube, office machine, heating and ventilating, and refrigeration industries, London had half or more of the workers in all of England and Wales. In addition, London had between 40 or 50 percent of all the workers in the wireless and telephone apparatus, other electrical goods, electric cable, gas meter, and printing machinery industries.

The second largest group of London workers were those in clothing manufacture, who as a group represented 28 percent of all England and Wales. Within this category, the metropolis employed more than half the women's tailoring workers and those in "other tailoring" (including theatrical costumes). The next largest employers in greater London, in order, were paper and printing (37 percent of England and Wales); food, drink, and tobacco (23 percent); vehicle manufacturing (15 percent); wood and furniture (31 percent); metal goods (17 percent); miscellaneous industries (37 percent); chemicals (24 percent); and instruments and precious metals (49 percent). In each of these major groups, individual subcategories, often of a specialized nature, represented a much larger share of the national total. Examples are office fittings (over half the workers in England and Wales in this industry); pens, pencils, and stationery goods (62 percent); photo film (75 percent); toilet preparations (74 percent); scientific instruments (53 percent); surgical and dental instruments (62 percent) and many others. On the other hand, a number of industries did not show up well in London. Among these were textiles; primary metals; and bricks, glass, and stone.

Summarizing these results, we find that the industries best represented in greater London had one or a combination of the following locational traits. They (1) were *labor-intensive*, requiring workers with a high order of skills, capable of performing delicate, intricate, or very specialized tasks; (2) produced *consumer goods*, especially "shopping goods," such as women's tailoring; (3) were *port industries*—sugar refining, flour milling, or chocolate manufacture; or (4) were uniquely *specialized*—one-of-a-kind industries such as theatrical costumes, film manufacture, and toy production. Characteristically, the industries poorly represented in London were (1) those requiring a large pool of *cheap, unskilled labor* (London labor is too costly); (2) *space-using or heavy industries* (land is too scarce and expensive); or (3) those oriented to domestic raw materials (generally lacking in London).

Spatial pattern of London industry   The spatial arrangement of manufacturing in London exhibits center-periphery, sectoral, and clustering tendencies similar to those of other cities; but it is also affected by certain physical features, notably the Thames River, and by the city's great age. One effect of age is the density pattern of industrial employment, which reaches its peak in the center and declines steadily outward in all directions (Martin, 1966). As we saw in Chapter 4, the usual pattern of newer centers is for manufacturing employment to be low in the center and to form concentrations in the second and in the outermost zones. The activities best represented in London's central manufacturing district are small concerns having strong interfirm ties, high labor inputs (especially skilled labor), high value added, and (peculiar to London) a long tradition in the area. The city center is also the preferred location for firms for which the greater London area is itself the main market.

Some of the oldest industries of London's near east side district are clothing and furniture manufacture. Also prominent today are makers of tools and instruments. There is a tight cluster of medium and small instrument firms near the center, including manufacturers of medical and dental instruments and scientific instruments. These concerns are strongly attracted to London's market and skilled labor and have close ties to specialty glass manufacturers. The smaller toolmaking establishments likewise focus on the near east side for some of the same reasons.

In the clothing trades, the center contains a concentration of small and medium-size tailoring and dressmaking establishments. Many of these specialize in only one operation and must have close links with other firms performing complementary operations. All of them require skilled labor and benefit from personal contacts with each other in the event of style changes. There is further advantage of proximity to the mercantile houses in the fashionable West End shopping district. Although most men's ready-to-wear clothing manufacturers have been repelled from the district by high labor costs and are much better represented in Yorkshire and Scotland, London's central manufacturing district still retains its attraction for firms making the highest-quality men's suits. One important advantage is the availability of workers having the skills necessary for the great amount of handwork these garments require. Those manufacturers of ready-to-wear suits remaining in London are mainly outside the central garment district, in a sector extending northeastward toward the city margins. There is a tendency for these firms to increase in size as their distance away from the center increases.

As this indicates, London industry displays very strong agglomerative tendencies. This is especially true of the smallest shops, which derive external economies from spatial association with each other. Also important, however, are the reputation of the area for certain kinds of production, access to a large labor pool and to specialized services, and common use of public facilities. In addition to the linkages among small firms, many small establishments have a functional dependence upon larger ones, from which they draw raw materials or upon which they rely as customers.

The largest establishments are more locationally independent because of an ability to provide their own internal economies. By means of horizontal and vertical integration they can achieve considerable self-sufficiency. Yet, like the small concerns, many large industries concentrate in particular districts because of common locational needs of other sorts.

These agglomerative inclinations are by no means confined to the central area. There are some important interfirm linkages among the vehicle, instrument, metal smelting, and general metal goods concerns elsewhere in the city. For example, the small and medium-size transport equipment plants tend to be associated together in areas south and west of the main manufacturing cluster. Although there is much interdependence among the vehicle parts suppliers, body builders, and assemblers in these smaller size categories, the large integrated automotive firms are locationally independent. With their need for much space, they are located at a distance from the center on both the far east and west sides of the urban area. Notable among the east side firms is the large Ford plant at Dagenham, Essex.

The engineering industries as a group bear a particular stamp in London. Here most of them produce intricate machinery, often in shorter model runs; few make standardized metal goods, which are manufactured elsewhere in Britain, mainly in the Midlands. London's electrical engineering firms, which are characterized by an unusual amount of research and development, are fairly scattered in the metropolis, although they tend to favor the outer suburbs on the west and southwest. The larger tool concerns are mainly close to the aircraft and vehicle plants and to other engineering firms. The smaller general engineering firms, such as ball-bearing producers, are closely tied to their customers, especially the larger makers of electrical goods, tools, vehicles, and other metal goods.

As we might expect from what has been said earlier about the nature of the industry, chemical production in London has powerful and intricate interfirm ties. The strongest connections of all are among the producers of chemical intermediates, who form the main bonds that unite the industry as a whole. Chemical production is located principally in the central and eastern parts of the metropolitan area. Spatially associated with the chemical industry is food processing. This does not necessarily represent direct functional ties, but rather a common need for transport facilities and water.

Indeed, transportation provides one of the most compelling linkages among London's manufacturers. For example, electrical engineering firms making such bulky items as transformers and generators concentrate near waterways and arterial highways, as do larger firms in the general engineering group. Some of the most prominent port industries are the larger chemical plants, situated along the Thames Embankment and the canals, where they make use of both the transport facilities and process water. The food industry was originally on Thamesside, and the sugar-refining plants are still there. Transport needs are paramount in the food industry; as firms outgrow their inner-city sites, they seek new locations on arterial roads in the western suburbs.

With all its agglomerative tendencies, London manufacturing is currently undergoing a decentralization. In recent years there has been a movement of industries from the metropolitan area of greater London into the outer reaches of the London region, which includes, in addition to London itself, the counties of Hertford, Essex, Kent, Surrey, Sussex, Hampshire, and Middlesex. During this time industrial employment in the London region has actually grown faster than that of the nation as a whole. The movement of industry from metropolitan London into surrounding counties represents in large measure a deglomeration of the type described by Weber, that is, a response to the rising cost of increasingly scarce land in the urban center. Evidence for this is provided by the prominence of large space-using manufacturers among the firms leaving London. Another important reason for the decentralization is government policy, which favors this trend and helps to enforce it through its issuance of licenses to build or remodel.

An examination of the list of industries participating in the move to the periphery of the London region shows that most firms choose new locations in the same sector from which they are moving. For example, vehicle manufacturing on the periphery has grown most rapidly in the northeastern sector, suggesting the influence of the Ford factory, which lies in that direction. Wood and clothing industries have also moved northeastward from their old locations on the near east side. The engineering industries, which are prominent in all the outlying areas, are especially so in the northwest and southwest. The chemical industry has moved eastward along the Thames but has also gone to Southampton Water in the south.

The new industrial concentrations of the periphery have occurred mainly in two kinds of areas. The first of these is the new towns, whose development is sponsored by the government. The other consists of estuarine locations—sites alongside the deepwater channels of the Thames and Southampton Water. Especially attracted to the latter have been the oil-refining, petrochemical, paper, and cement industries.

From this brief summary we have seen a number of locational tendencies affecting the spatial structure of manufacturing in London. These same tendencies have also appeared in many other large metropolises, most notably New York City (Hoover and Vernon, 1962). The net effect of opposing centrifugal and centripetal forces in each case has recently been to increase relatively the amount of manufacturing in outlying areas. In London as elsewhere, certain types of manufacturing initially have a strong cohesiveness, which produces tight clusters of related activities. As firms grow in size, however, many become self-contained and no longer need close neighbors. In both London and New York some industries have expanded in sectoral fashion, especially those attached to waterfront areas and other linear features. Governmental actions have had important locational impacts in most large cities, although in Britain these result from deliberate policy decisions while in the United States they are mainly the unintended by-products of measures originally designed for different purposes.

CENTRAL PLACE THEORY AND TERTIARY ACTIVITIES

Central place theory is a theory of location with respect to one aspect of tertiary activity (Berry and Pred, 1961, p. 6). Tertiary activity, in general, involves both production and exchange for the purposes of consumption. In the production sense, tertiary activity is concerned with the provision of services which are consumed in the same way that food is manufactured and consumed. In the exchange sense, tertiary activity involves the whole range of facilities that are used to overcome the friction of distance—the system of communications and transportation required to mesh society together.

The economic geographer is therefore concerned with two different aspects of tertiary activity. One aspect involves the description and analysis of tertiary activities such as retailing, wholesaling, public service provision, and so forth, which arise as a result of the demand for services by people. As people are distributed quite widely over the surface of the earth, this understanding of the spatial distribution of tertiary activities is conveniently arrived at through the derivation of general principles relating to the nature of the demand surface and the politicoeconomic aspects of supply. This chapter is concerned primarily with tertiary activity in the productive rather than the exchange sense, for the transport and communications media are considered in Chapter 8.

The discussion of tertiary activities, and in particular central place theory as it pertains to the location of these activities, is divided into two parts. The first part is concerned basically with a brief review of the range of tertiary activities and a discussion of theoretical rationale for the central place model. The second part, Chapter 7, presents some of the operational definitions and empirical evidence relating to the concepts discussed in this first part.

TERTIARY ACTIVITIES

A general discussion of tertiary activities on a world scale is necessary for two main reasons. In the first place, the range of types of tertiary activity is very broad, and many of these types are used by, or come in contact with, people during their daily routine. Second, the proportion of employed persons in the world concerned with tertiary activites is quite large but varies considerably from country to country. It is to these two aspects that we address ourselves in this section.

TYPES OF TERTIARY ACTIVITIES

There are many different facets of tertiary production. In the United States, a country with an extremely large proportion of its labor force concerned with tertiary activities, the Department of Labor divides tertiary employment into four main types. The discussion below will follow this classification with minor modifications.

Distributive occupations The first type of tertiary activity is concerned with the distributive trades; it includes all persons involved with wholesale and retail activities. A business concerned with wholesale activities purchases goods in large lots from a manufacturer, breaks them down into smaller lots (a process which can involve repackaging), and sells the smaller lots to retail firms which sell directly to the consumer (Vance, 1971). Wholesale firms therefore tend to be specialized and locate where there are a number of retail outlets for particular types of goods. Thus, whereas wholesale firms are less obvious in our everyday life, retail activities impinge upon us directly, for they include such services as drug, food, and clothing stores, restaurants, movie houses, banks, and so forth.

Marketing in Canada The magnitude of distribution or marketing through whole-salers and retailers is very large. Moyer and Snyder (1967, pp. 2–6) indicate that (1) the value added by marketing in Canada approaches the value added by manufacturing, (2) for every dollar the Canadian consumer spends on finished goods, roughly 52 cents is accounted for by marketing activities, (3) approximately one Canadian worker in five is directly engaged in distribution, and (4) there are as many persons directly engaged in the marketing of goods as employed in the manufacture of goods. The interesting question that arises from these facts is whether marketing costs too much, for the trend would appear to be for the costs of distribution to increase still further.

Financial world   A second type of tertiary activity involves persons concerned with finance, insurance, and real estate. The importance of this group is directly related to the wealth of countries, for stockbrokers, insurance agents, investment advisers, and so forth can exist only where there is considerable wealth. In fact, the very high personal income and consumption found in the wealthiest countries of the world has resulted in an extremely complex set of financial systems which result in significant geographic differences. This is well exemplified by differences in banking between the United Kingdom, the United States, and Canada.

United Kingdom   In the United Kingdom, commercial banking is dominated by five large companies: Barclays, Lloyds, Midland, National Provincial, and Westminister. The reason for this domination is that branch banking is permitted throughout the country, the result being that small banks through time have been purchased by the larger banks. The head offices of these five banks are located in the City of London in close physical proximity to the Bank of England. The Bank of England is, in effect, a *banker's bank* for, since it is banker for the government, deposits in this institution are the most secure of all deposits, and the credit of the institution is the greatest. Thus the branch banks will hold reserves in the large regional banks, and these will hold reserves in the head office bank in the City of London, and this will, in turn, hold credits in the Bank of England.

The importance of branch banking as a system to the geography of economic activity is that it gives rise to a dispersal of financial employment among many centers and a clustering of banking establishments within settlements. The system of branch banking allows banks of all sizes to exist, for the size is related to the demand for banking. Therefore, it is not uncommon to find branch banks operated by a single clerk in small villages. Clustering occurs because each of the "big five" is competing with the others, and as each has to provide a similar service for the same range of customers, competition forces them to locate in close proximity. Therefore, there is a proliferation of small branch banks, which are connected to larger regional banks, which are in turn connected to the central headquarters in the City of London. Thus, there is a series of clusters at all levels in the banking system, a locational characteristic related directly to the institution of branch banking.

United States   In the United States, branch banking is usually not permitted, California and New York State being notable exceptions. The net result is the development of a pattern of bank location substantially different from that in the United Kingdom. Once a bank is established in a particular area, other banks find it difficult to enter and compete, for they do not have a large parent bank upon which

Boundaries of
Federal Reserve districts

Boundaries of
Federal Reserve branch territories

⊛ Federal Reserve bank cities
• Federal Reserve branch cities

FIGURE 6-1 FEDERAL RESERVE DISTRICTS AND SUBREGIONS.

to depend. Thus commercial banks tend to be dispersed within urban areas, and very small banks with one or two tellers are almost nonexistent.

The banker's bank is the Federal Reserve Bank of the United States government, and the single commercial banks use this facility through the twelve regional Federal Reserve banks established by the federal government. The twelve Federal Reserve regions and subregions, with the cities in which the regional banks are located, are presented in Figure 6-1. All the Federal Reserve districts are supposed to be almost equal in population size, though population migration west and south may have created an imbalance in recent years. Subregions served by Federal Reserve branch cities have been established within districts that are excessively large.

Canada Banking in Canada differs from that in the United States in that branch banking is permitted. The Bank of Canada in Ottawa is the central bank, and commercial banking is dominated by the Canadian Imperial Bank of Commerce, the Bank of Montreal, and the Royal Bank of Canada. As a consequence, branch banks of varying sizes are found within almost every settlement in Canada.

Our discussion has concentrated on commercial banking as a service activity, for it is this aspect that commonly enters our everyday lives. There are many types of financial institutions involved with the monetary aspect of the economy. These include security and commodity exchanges, insurance companies, brokerage houses, and the like. Financial concerns are all highly specialized activities, and they tend to locate in the large cities. Taking North America as a whole, Kerr (1965, p. 177) has suggested that relative employment in financial activities (financial employment related to total employment by urban area) is greatest in New York, followed by San Francisco, Dallas, Toronto, Atlanta, Minneapolis, and Montreal, in that order. If total employment in financial activities is taken into account, then New York and Chicago emerge as the two leading centers.

Government activities   A third type of tertiary activity involves persons concerned with the *civil service* or government activities. This category includes all employment in local, provincial or state, and central government activities. Therefore, all teachers (except those employed by private institutions), income tax officials, political representatives, and persons involved with government agencies (such as the FBI and CIA) are included within this category.

This aspect of tertiary activity is supported directly by taxes, and it is an employment grouping that is increasing in numeral importance. From published information* it can be estimated that in the United States the employment in federal, state, and local government activities (excluding defense) has increased its proportional share of the total labor force (including the armed services) over the last forty years. Whereas approximately 6 percent of the total labor force was employed in such activities in 1930, this proportion increased to 7.6 percent in 1940, 9.4 percent in 1950, 11.5 percent in 1960, and 14.4 percent in 1967. An entertaining reflection on these figures is that an increasing share of the electorate have an important direct economic stake in policies that concern such employment.

Personal service   The fourth type of tertiary activity includes all those activities that can be described as personal service. The most important subcategory within this group is medical and hospital services. The greater the wealth of an individual, the more he is able to spend on services that purport to safeguard his physical health. As a consequence, in the United States, there are almost as many persons employed in medical and hospital services as there are in selling food. Other important service industries within this group are hotels, laundries, and the entertainment business.

WORLD DISTRIBUTION

A substantial proportion of the working population of every country in the world is concerned with tertiary activity. The actual proportion appears to depend very much on the level of development, for we would expect employment in tertiary occupations to be lowest in the underdeveloped countries and highest in the more

*U.S. Bureau of the Census, *Historical Statistics of the United States, Colonial Times to 1957*, Washington, D.C., 1960, pp. 72 and 709–711; and U.S. Bureau of the Census, *Statistical Abstract of the United States, 1968*, Washington, D.C., 1968, pp. 215 and 223.

developed parts of the world. This is because the effective demand for the output of tertiary activity exists only in areas where primary and secondary activity is highly productive and employment is extremely specialized. The greater the degree of specialization, the more an individual has to depend on other producers in the economy. The greater the productivity of a nation, the more wealth (in terms of money) there is to spend on the output of other producers in the economy. Thus the proportion of the labor force employed in tertiary activities should be related to the average income of a country.

The presence of such a relationship is indicated in Figure 6-2. The data pertain to the 1960s, and the countries have been selected to make the tertiary productive occupations as comparable as possible. There is a definite tendency for the proportion of persons employed in tertiary production to increase as the wealth of a country increases (wealth measured by per capita income), but the tendency is not entirely regular. Thus the relationship between level of economic development and tertiary production is general with specific variations.

CENTRAL PLACE THEORY

The presence of a large tertiary sector in an economy of a nation therefore depends upon the level of demand. Consequently, an essential concern becomes the effect of the spatial distribution of demand on the location of tertiary activities. A set of propositions concerning the location of tertiary activities can be developed from the ideas introduced by W. Christaller (1933) and developed by Lösch (1938, 1954). These ideas form a part of location theory which is commonly referred to as "central place theory."

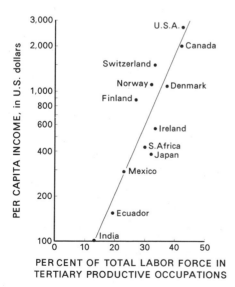

FIGURE 6-2 THE RELATIONSHIP BETWEEN THE PROPORTION OF THE LABOR FORCE IN TERTIARY PRODUCTIVE OCCUPATIONS AND PER CAPITA INCOME FOR SELECTED COUNTRIES.

SOME FUNDAMENTAL CONCEPTS

Central place theory (Berry, 1967) provides an abstract framework for analyzing two aspects of the space economy. One aspect concerns the location of settlements as service centers, that is, providers of services for themselves and the surrounding rural area (Garner, 1967). Thus, central place theory is important in the study of settlements in that it provides a rationale for the location of settlements as service centers. It does not, of course, provide a rationale for the location of other centers that are located where they are for nonservice reasons, such as mining towns, though mining towns, once established, may well perform a service function. The second aspect of the space economy upon which central place theory casts considerable light concerns the allocation of tertiary activities among settlements. It is in this respect that the theory is important, and it is for this reason that the ensuing discussion concentrates upon the allocational rather more than the locational aspect of settlements.

Assumptions   A theory always involves assumptions, and central place theory is no exception. Most of the assumptions are similar to those postulated by Thünen with respect to elementary land use theory.

1.   The first assumption is the existence of a flat limitless plain. This assumption removes the real-world existence of physical variations which might affect the location of transport routes, settlements, and people. The "limitless" constraint removes the effect of boundary problems of any kind.

2.   The second assumption is that the rural population is spread evenly over the plain, and that each person has the same purchasing power and behaves similarly. The demand is therefore spread evenly, and no imperfections exist due to spatial variations in wealth. At the outset, however, each person is self-sufficing.

3.   The third assumption is a homogeneous transport surface. This implies that it is equally easy for a person to move in any direction.

4.   The first three assumptions constitute an initial stage in the development of a human-economic landscape. The evolution of this landscape is related solely to the development of tertiary activities.

All the above assumptions therefore permit the development of a set of postulates based on economic criteria related to tertiary activities.

Model of a single-business type   Suppose that on this plain a person decides to establish a bakeshop to sell bread. Two factors determine simultaneously whether a bakeshop can be established profitably. One factor is the minimum level of demand that it takes for a baker to operate. The other factor is the distance that people are prepared to travel to buy bread at a particular price. If people are not prepared to travel to the bakeshop to buy bread, whatever the price, then there is no way that the shop can exist profitably. If, however, the price is such that people are willing to travel to the shop, and the demand is such that it meets the minimum level of demand that it takes for the shop to operate, then that service can exist.

Businesses require different levels of demand in order to operate; the necessary level depends upon the costs of operation, which vary according to the type of business. Some businesses can run efficiently and offer goods and services at reasonable prices only with large operations and high-volume turnover. Such businesses, therefore, require a high level of demand in order to exist. Other concerns can make a profit and operate at a reasonable level of efficiency with a limited volume of sales. Also, the level of profit required is related to the volume of demand necessary for operation. If an entrepreneur is content with a profit sufficient to provide an average standard of living, he will not require the volume of demand considered necessary by someone with much higher expectations.

Threshold, business type, and establishments   The discussion thus far has introduced a number of definitional concepts. One is that a bakeshop will not exist unless a certain minimum level of demand is attained. This minimum level of demand is termed the *threshold* for a bakeshop. A bakeshop is a *business type* (*function*) or a type of tertiary activity, and if two bakeshops exist, there would be two *establishments* of a bakeshop business type (functional type). Thus, in general terms, threshold can be defined as the minimum level of demand required to support one establishment of a particular business type. As assumption 2 establishes a situation where each person has a similar income and propensity to consume, the definition can be rephrased to be: the minimum number of people required to support one establishment of a particular business type.

Range of a good   Another concept introduced by the bakeshop example concerns the distance that people are willing to travel to purchase goods and services offered by particular business types at certain prices. As an illustration of the general principles involved, the following discussion refers to Figure 6-3 and assumes that one business type offers one kind of good: in this case, a bakeshop sells bread. The curve illustrates a hypothetical demand schedule for bread. At price P_f quantity Q_c of bread will be purchased by an individual, but if the price of

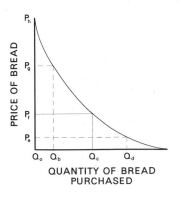

FIGURE 6-3 A HYPOTHETICAL DEMAND SCHEDULE FOR BREAD. IN THIS CASE IT IS ASSUMED THAT THE QUANTITY OF BREAD PURCHASED BY AN INDIVIDUAL DECREASES AS THE PRICE INCREASES. (AFTER LÖSCH, 1938, P. 73.)

bread rises to P_g, the individual will purchase less bread (Q_b). At price P_h an individual will purchase no bread at all (Q_0).

The geographic situation that is important in this example is that the people who buy the bread (who are similar and have the same demand schedules) are distributed evenly over a plain. Therefore, each individual has to travel to the bakeshop to make a purchase. As a consequence, each purchaser has to overcome the friction of distance, which involves a time cost, and so the *real* price of bread to an individual becomes the sum of the price at distance d (P_d) and the transport cost (t_d). In the discussion we assume that transport costs are positively related to distance.

If the price at the bakeshop is fixed (P_e), a person who has to pay t_f transport costs to get to the shop should pay a real price of $P_e + t_f = P_f$ and therefore purchase quantity Q_c of bread. A person living farther away and incurring transport cost t_g would pay $P_e + t_g = P_g$ and would therefore purchase only amount Q_b of bread. On the other hand, a person living next door to the bakery would incur relatively no transport costs (t_0) and would therefore pay only $P_e + t_0 = P_e$ for bread. As a consequence, the latter person would be able to purchase, for the same outlay, more bread than the other individuals.

To reflect the distance factor, Figure 6-3 can be redrawn to show real price increasing with distance (Figure 6-4). The limit of the service area of the bakeshop is set by the point where the transport costs are so high that no bread will be purchased at all ($P_e + t_h = P_h$). This is the maximum range of service area of the bakery. In general terms, the line demarcating the maximum service area of a good sold by a particular business type is defined as the *maximum range*, or *ideal limit*, of a good. It is the line beyond which no person will use a particular business type or function. As the demand is assumed to be evenly distributed over the whole plain (assumption 2), and the transport surface to be homogeneous (assumption 3), the service area of the bakery can be defined by a circle, the radius being t_h. For the bakeshop to exist at all, the threshold must lie within the maximum range of the good (Figure 6-5).

A central place A third concept that is introduced by the bakeshop example concerns the location of the shop. The bakeshop not only provides services for its region; it also provides employment for those individuals who work in the shop. Because most workers tend to try to minimize time lost in the daily journey to work,

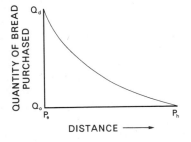

FIGURE 6-4 THE EFFECT OF DISTANCE ON THE "REAL" PRICE OF BREAD AND THE QUANTITY PURCHASED. THE CASE PRESENTED HERE ASSUMES THAT THE "REAL" PRICE OF BREAD IS EQUAL TO THE PRICE AT THE BAKER SHOP PLUS THE TRANSPORT COSTS INVOLVED (t). THE OTHER ASSUMPTIONS ARE THE SAME AS THOSE IN FIGURE 6-3. AS A CONSEQUENCE, THE QUANTITY PURCHASED DECREASES WITH DISTANCE FROM THE BAKESHOP BECAUSE THE TRANSPORT COSTS ARE ASSUMED TO INCREASE LINEARLY WITH DISTANCE. (AFTER LÖSCH, 1938, P. 73.)

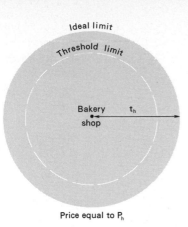

Ideal limit

Threshold limit

Bakery
shop • t_h

Price equal to P_h

FIGURE 6-5 THE ECONOMIC REGION OF A BAKESHOP. FOR THE BAKESHOP TO EXIST AT ALL, THE THRESHOLD FOR BREAD MUST LIE WITHIN THE MAXIMUM DISTANCE THAT PEOPLE ARE WILLING TO TRAVEL TO PURCHASE BREAD.

these employees will either live next door or in the general vicinity of the store. As a consequence, the bakeshop gives rise to an agglomeration of homes and buildings, which collectively are described as a settlement. This settlement is at the center of a region which it serves, and such a center is termed by Christaller a *central place*. A central place can therefore be defined as the center which serves an area larger than itself, and this area is the *complementary region* of that center.

A THEORETICAL MODEL

There is, however, a large area of the plain that remains unserved by the bakeshop. This area lies beyond the ideal limit that defines the complementary region of the store. The only way to fulfill this demand is by the establishment of other bakeshops over the plain. The consequent problem concerns the arrangement of bakeshops over the plain and the shape of the complementary regions pertaining to these services. In the ensuing discussion it will be assumed that each bakeshop established has the same threshold and ideal limit as the one described thus far.

Hexagons In Figure 6-6 it can be observed that if the ideal circular shape of a complementary region prevails, either there will still be areas where people are not served (case A), or the regions will overlap (case B). The latter case could well result in two or three centers competing for the same market area. The net result could be that the threshold value for none of the centers is attained. The most efficient shape can be observed to be that where the hinterlands take the form of hexagons, and the threshold limits lie within the perimeter of the hexagons.

The arrangement of central places that emerges under such ideal conditions would be geometrically predictable. As all complementary regions are of the same size and the same shape, the hexagons will interlock into each other in such a way that each central place is equidistant from six surrounding centers. In this simple case, central place theory is deterministic, for once the locus and range of two central places are known, the location of all other places is also known.

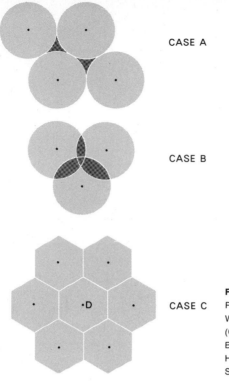

CASE A

CASE B

CASE C

FIGURE 6-6 THE IDEAL SHAPE OF COMPLEMENTA-RY REGIONS. WITH CIRCULAR HINTERLANDS THERE WILL BE AREAS WHERE PEOPLE ARE NOT SERVED (CASE A), OR THE REGIONS WILL OVERLAP (CASE B). THE MOST EFFICIENT SHAPE IS THAT OF THE HEXAGON (CASE C), IN WHICH ALL AREAS ARE SERVED, AND THERE IS NO OVERLAPPING.

The examples can now be extended by injecting a second function into the central place model. Suppose that a person decides to establish a drugstore. There will be a threshold size for a drugstore and a range beyond which people will not visit a drugstore (an ideal limit). The discussion will assume that the threshold limit of a drugstore lies within the ideal limit. Thus the same spatial processes prevail for both a bakeshop and a drugstore, and the only difference will be assumed to be in size of threshold and the range of the goods provided by the drugstore.

Assume that the threshold size for a drugstore is three times that for a bakeshop. A drugstore will therefore require a complementary region at least three times as large as that for a bakeshop. Thus, if the drugstore locates at place D in Figure 6-6c, its complementary region will be not only the complementary region for the bakeshop at D, but also the closest one-third of the regions of the six surrounding central places (as illustrated in Figure 6-7). The net result is hinterland for the drugstore three times as large as that for the bakeshop at D $[1 + 6(1/3) = 3]$.

Hierarchies The impact of the addition of this drugstore to the service array present at D is also extremely important. The drugstore will employ people as well as the bakeshop, and so the population of central place D should increase with the

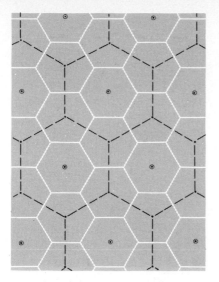

○ Central place containing a drugstore

· Central place containing a bakery shop

Complementary region of drugstore

Complementary region of bakery shop

FIGURE 6-7 A HIERARCHY OF CENTRAL PLACES. IN THIS CASE, A PARTICULAR HIGH-ORDER FUNCTION CAN SERVE AN AREA THREE TIMES AS LARGE AS THE AREA SERVED BY A LOW-ORDER FUNCTION.

added employment opportunities. As a consequence, D will be larger than the surrounding communities. With the addition of further business types and more people, the population size of the central place will itself begin to have an impact on its own tertiary structure, for the people living in the central place also desire goods and services.

The discussion concerning the addition of business types, and the impact of these additions on the population of the central place, introduces several more concepts that are extremely important in the analysis of the distribution of tertiary activities. The first concept concerns the threshold values of business types. Business types with high threshold values need large service areas and are therefore found less frequently than functions with low thresholds. As far as terminology is concerned, business types with high threshold values are described as high-order, and functions with low threshold values are described as low-order. Also, central places which contain high-order business types are described as high-order central places, and central places that have only low-order business types are described as low-order central places.

As the number of business types increases, the population of a central place increases, but the feedback of the effect of the population on the tertiary structure of the central place results in the proliferation of establishments among the lower-order businesses. Thus the population of a high-order central place might support ten bakeshops whereas the complementary bakeshop region might support only one such store. As a consequence, the total number of establishments of all functional types increases as the population of a center increases. However, the number of business types found in a central place increases with the population of a central place, but at a decreasing rate. This latter situation is reinforced in the real world by the fact that there are far fewer higher-order than low-order business types, and is illustrated in Chapter 7.

Thus another concept that has been developed from the discussion of the model of a multibusiness type is the hierarchy. The addition of the drugstore to a central place means that its complementary region extends into one-third of each of the six complementary regions of the lower-order bakeshop function. As a consequence, if there are 144 central places containing bakeshops distributed over the plain, 48 of these central places will contain a drugstore as well. These higher-order central places will be located so that each is equidistant from six surrounding central places that contain drugstores (Figure 6-7). In this particular example, a twofold discrete hierarchy of central places will develop. The discreteness of the hierarchy therefore depends upon the addition of business types or groups of business types at discrete constant intervals.

Urban growth and agglomeration The above discussion of the effect of the demand generated in the central place itself leads to the development of another extremely important concept in the theory of tertiary activities—the effect of urban agglomeration. The developed countries of the world are extremely urbanized, and the rate of urbanization is rapidly increasing. Indeed, it has been estimated that by the year 1980 nearly 80 percent of the population of the United States will be living in urban areas. The reasons for this great increase in urbanization have been discussed previously, but the impact is of great importance in this discussion.

An urban area is not just a provider of tertiary activities. By far the greatest part of the economic activity of mankind in the developed part of the world takes place in urban areas. An urban area can be a transportation center, a locus of industry, a mining town, and so on, and individuals and their families concerned with these activities have to be provided with services. Thus, all urban areas are to a degree central places (that is, providers of tertiary activities) as well as centers of other economic activities, and it is the growth of these other economic activities that primarily generates the growth of urban areas and the demand for more services (Yeates and Garner, 1976, pp. 78–102).

This trend is particularly reinforced by improvements in transportation facilities which make it possible for people to travel farther for goods and services without increasing their time costs. As an example of this, the interstate highway system in the United States favors the larger urban centers because the system has been designed to connect all towns of 50,000 or more people. Consequently, the range of a good (the ideal limit) is increasing, and as it does, the smaller central places that have few low-order functions are diminishing in number or declining.

Thus the tertiary structure of an urban area in the developed part of the world exists more and more to serve its own population, and other urban populations, and less and less to serve rural regions. As urban areas get larger, the tertiary structure of an urban area becomes more and more a reflection of its own size, and less and less a reflection of the size of its complementary region. Consequently, as an urban area grows, the tertiary activities found within it increase in number and size, and the feedback effect of the growth from this, and all other sources, has a continuous agglomerative growth effect.

Product differentiation Up to this point we have assumed that one establishment of a particular business type is involved with the sale of a specified good which has a certain threshold value. Therefore, each establishment of a given business type has the same threshold value, and each business type is associated with a particular threshold level. This is illustrated in Figure 6-8a, where C represents a business type with a low threshold level, B a middle threshold level, and A the highest threshold level. Of course, it is not necessary for each business type to have a different threshold level; in fact the hierarchical principle, when applied to business functions, suggests that a number of business types may have thresholds of similar values.

However, it is evident in the real world that establishments within a particular business type are not homogeneous; that is, they do not sell a good, or goods, that have the same threshold. Even though they may sell the same goods or services, some establishments may offer a different type, quality, or value of product. Thus, in the case of restaurants, the Campus Restaurant (frequently a "greasy spoon") may have a lower threshold value than Trader Vic's or The Beaver Room. As a result, each business type may well be associated with a range of thresholds rather than a unique threshold size as previously implied (Garner, 1966, pp. 117–120).

This situation is illustrated in Figure 6-8b, where the threshold values for a number of business establishments of business types A, B, C are assumed to be normally distributed and overlapping. The mean value for each business type

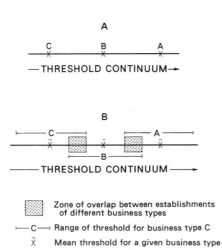

FIGURE 6-8 THE EFFECT OF THRESHOLD OVERLAP FOR DIFFERENT BUSINESS TYPES. IF THE THRESHOLD VALUES FOR DIFFERENT BUSINESS TYPES ARE AT DISCRETE INTERVALS, AS IN A, THEN A CLEAR HIERARCHY OF BUSINESS TYPES EXISTS. IF, HOWEVER, THERE IS A RANGE OF POSSIBLE THRESHOLDS FOR EACH BUSINESS TYPE, THEN SOME OVERLAP CAN OCCUR (B). (GARNER, 1966, P. 119.)

therefore expresses the most likely threshold for that type. Note, however, that the overlap is quite large—and particularly so in the case of *B* and *C*, indicating that central places (and their hinterlands) containing sufficient demand for business activity of type *C* may occasionally contain type *B* as well.

CHRISTALLER'S THREE PRINCIPLES CONCERNING THE DISTRIBUTION OF CENTRAL PLACES

Christaller considered that the location of central places and the allocation of activities among them are affected by three factors or principles. These are:

1. The marketing principle
2. The transportation principle
3. The administrative principle

Two of these principles are economic and one is political, but together or singly they are considered to determine the central place system. Under various circumstances one may dominate, but it is quite likely that the influence of each will be felt at various times during the historical development of a particular system.

MARKETING PRINCIPLE

The economic mechanism giving rise to a system of central places according to the marketing principle has, in effect, been described above. The optimum location for the central places is, as for all three principles, such that they are equidistant from each other, that is, on the lattice point of a set of equilateral triangles. The assumption in the example of the bakery and the drugstore was that the threshold value for a drugstore was three times that for a bakery. The result of this

FIGURE 6-9 CHRISTALLER'S THREE PRINCIPLES WITH RESPECT TO THE LOCATION AND HIERARCHY OF CENTRAL PLACES. (A) THE K = 3 MARKET PRINCIPLE; (B) THE K = 4 TRANSPORTATION PRINCIPLE; (C) THE K = 7 ADMINISTRATIVE PRINCIPLE.

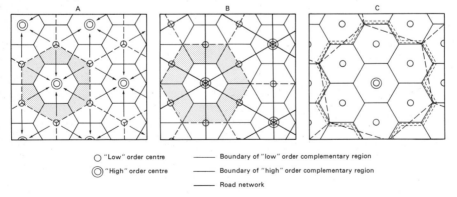

○ "Low" order centre	——— Boundary of "low" order complementary region
◎ "High" order centre	——— Boundary of "high" order complementary region
	——— Road network

assumption is that the complementary region for the drugstore is three times as large as that for a bakery and a two-tier hierarchy (as illustrated in Figure 6-7).

Christaller considered that the marketing principle operated spatially according to a rule of threes (his $k = 3$ principle), which gives rise to the situation described above. In Figure 6-9a a two-tier hierarchy (consisting of *low*-order and *high*-order central places) conforming to the $k = 3$ principle is illustrated, with the sample region indicating the proportion (one-third) of the complementary region of the low-order central place going to the high-order central place for the high-order business type. Notice that the diagram clearly indicates that the low-order central places are divided up into thirds as well.

TRANSPORTATION PRINCIPLE

If central places are located according to the transportation principle, then, according to Christaller, as many important places as possible will be on one traffic route between two important towns, the route being established as straight and as cheap as possible (Christaller, 1966, p. 74). Thus the central places will lie on straight traffic routes, and the intervals between central places will be of equal length. Therefore, if a low-order central place is to be established, it will be located halfway between the high-order places. Consequently, the complementary region of the high-order places will be four $[1 + 6(1/2) = 4]$ times that of the low-order places.

This $k = 4$ system for the transport principle is illustrated in Figure 6-9b. In the diagram the transportation lines connect the high-order places, and the low-order places are located halfway between. The sample region shows the six halves of the low-order complementary regions that are within the complementary region of the high-order central place. If the central places (regardless of hierarchy) are spaced as in Figure 6-9a, it is obvious that the size of the complementary regions of the high-order places will be larger, and that the high-order places are spaced farther apart. Also, each high-order central place has six routes focusing upon it.

ADMINISTRATIVE PRINCIPLE

A system resulting from the sole operation of the administrative principle rests upon the assumption that individual complementary regions must not be subdivided. Therefore, the hierarchy is built up by the addition of whole regions. In Figure 6-8c the same set of low-order central places and regions exists as in Figures 6-8a and b. If whole complementary regions are to be aggregated, the easiest method is to add to the high-order center the complementary regions of the six surrounding central places $[1 + 6(1) = 7]$.

Christaller therefore suggests that the administrative principle results in a $k = 7$ system. In Figure 6-9c the generalized boundary is shown in hexagonal form superimposed upon the boundary that amalgamates the six surrounding complementary regions, which has a wavelike appearance. If the administrative principle above were to operate, then this generalized hexagonal boundary would be the complementary region of the high-order central place. It is to be noted that with this $k = 7$ system the size of the high-order complementary region is much larger than that resulting from the $k = 4$ system, which in turn is larger than that of the $k = 3$ system. Furthermore, the high-order centers are spaced farther apart in the $k = 7$ system than they are in the $k = 4$ system.

The variation in k is therefore critical in determining the spacing between centers and the number of centers at each level in the hierarchy. For example, in the sample region in Figure 6-9a there is one high-order place and two [6(1/3) = 2] low-order places (giving a 1, 2, progression). In Figure 6-9b for one high-order central place there are three [6(1/2) = 3] low-order central places (giving a 1, 3 progression). In the $k = 7$ system (Figure 6-9c) for one high-order central place there are six [6(1) = 6] low-order central places (giving a 1, 6 progression). If the system were extended beyond a two-tier system, the progressions with respect to centers by size class would progress geometrically. For a four-tier system, in the case of $k = 3$ the progression would be 1, 2, 6, 18; for $k = 4$ it would be 1, 3, 12, 48; and for $k = 7$ it would be 1, 6, 42, 294.

LÖSCHIAN MODIFICATIONS

Our discussion of the theoretical basis for the central place model, which is based on the monumental work of Lösch (1954), reveals the basic criticism of the fixed k hypothesis. In our previous discussion, the k value, which was arbitrarily chosen to be 3, related to the increased threshold requirement for the second business type (the drugstore) that was introduced into the system. If this value can be arbitrarily chosen, then no particular value of k is sacrosanct. Thus, it can be argued with some considerable justification that while Christaller's three locational principles are interesting, they are but special cases of a more general situation. In fact, a large number of k values can be used, the only restriction being that the value must yield a hexagonal pattern of dominant and subdominant central places. The k values giving the ten smallest market areas are 3, 4, 7, 9, 12, 13, 16, 19, 21, 25, and of these Lösch (1954, p. 120) considers $k = 7$, 13, and 19 to be the most efficient, for in these cases settlements are not divided among several supply centers.

The impact of this particular modification is extremely important, and it is discussed in some detail by Lösch (1954, pp. 116–134). If many market areas of size $k = 3, 4, \ldots, n$ are laid down so that all of them have at least one center in common, and these hexagons are then rotated so as to achieve six sectors with central places containing many business types and six sectors containing central places with few business types, a pattern of city-rich and city-poor sectors can be obtained. The top half in Figure 6-10 illustrates the arrangement of this pattern, an arrangement which would be duplicated if the lower half were present. The properties of this pattern are that (1) the greatest number of locations coincide, (2) purchases are maximized locally, (3) distances are minimized between central places, and thus (4) the volume of shipments and the total length of transport routes are at a minimum. The top half of Figure 6-10 does not, however, take into

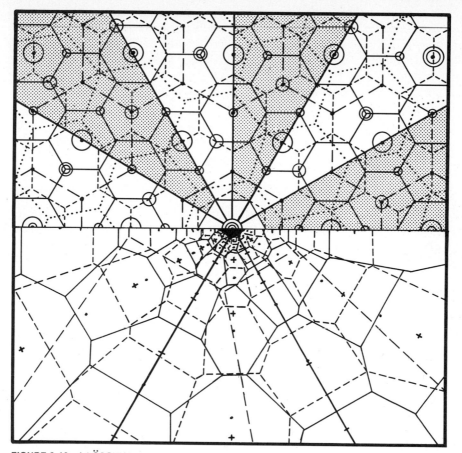

FIGURE 6-10 A LÖSCHIAN LANDSCAPE WITH ALTERNATING CITY-RICH (UNSHADED) AND CITY-POOR (SHADED) SECTORS AND AN EVEN DISTRIBUTION OF POPULATION (TOP) COMPARED WITH A PATTERN THAT MIGHT RESULT FROM AN UNEVEN DISTRIBUTION OF POPULATION RESULTING FROM AGGLOMERATION (BOTTOM). IT IS TO BE NOTED THAT IN THE TOP PORTION THE HIGHER-ORDER CENTERS RICH IN BUSINESS TYPES ARE INDICATED BY THE NUMBER AND SIZE OF THE CIRCLES AT A PARTICULAR LOCATION. THE LOWER DIAGRAM DISTINGUISHES THREE LEVELS IN THE HIERARCHY AND THE ORDERS OF THE CENTERS BY DOTS, CROSSES, AND SOLID BLACK. (AFTER ISARD, 1956, PP. 270 AND 272.)

account the uneven distribution of population that would result, for the size of the hexagons is predicated upon an even distribution of population. The bottom half of Figure 6-10 illustrates a pattern that might be due to the varying size of central places and the uneven distribution of population that would result from agglomeration forces.

The models postulated by Christaller and Lösch therefore result in markedly different systems (Haggett, 1965, p. 124). The fixed *k* constraint results in (1) all places at the same level in the hierarchy having the same business types, and (2) all

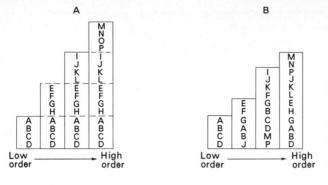

FIGURE 6-11 A CONTRAST BETWEEN THE ALLOCATION OF BUSINESS TYPES AMONG CENTRAL PLACES IN (A) A DISCRETE CHRISTALLERIAN HIERARCHY AND (B) A LÖSCHIAN SYSTEM.

higher-order central places containing the business types of the lower-order places (Figure 6-11a). The Löschian system results in less distinct hierarchical structure, for (1) settlements of the same size need not have the same array of business types, and concomitantly, (2) higher-order central places need not necessarily have all the functions of lower-order central places, though they will tend to have most of them (Figure 6-11b). One cannot expect, however, to find precise conformity to either the Christaller or Löschian system in the real world. A degree of variation will always occur simply because of such factors as product differentiation, and so it is never possible to determine which of the two systems is really the more applicable. It may be instructive, however, to examine some of the .empirical work in central place analysis, illustrate further environmental modifications, and compare the applicability of the two systems with real-world data.

CENTRAL PLACE THEORY: SOME EMPIRICAL EVIDENCE

The empirical work concerning central place theory and its various reformulations is voluminous. Much of the literature is cataloged and summarized in Berry and Pred (1961, 1965) and described in some detail in a later volume by Berry (1967). A large number of these studies concern the United States, but there are also numerous works covering various central place concepts concerning the United Kingdom (Bracey, 1962), Canada (Marshall, 1969), West Africa (Abiodun, 1967), India (Mayfield, 1967), Germany (Barnum, 1966), China (Skinner, 1964–1965), New Zealand (Clarke, 1968), Poland (Kielczewska-Zaleska, 1964), and South America (Snyder, 1962). These, and many hundreds of other examples covering many parts of the world, lend cumulative support to the basic concepts of the central place model, though there is little doubt that in numerous cases the research procedures and methodology may have lacked absolute rigor (Marshall, 1969, pp. 46–47). Therefore, with this general weight of evidence in mind, the ensuing discussion will be limited to a few examples located in North America, which, while they do not by themselves prove, nevertheless demonstrate the type of evidence that has accumulated in such large measure to support the basic tenets of the theory. These concepts can be discussed with respect to the allocational and locational aspects of the model, and the use of the model for analyzing change.

ALLOCATION

We have indicated previously that the allocational features of the central place model, that is, the distinction of business types among urban centers, are of particular importance to the economic geographer because he is concerned with the processes which result in the varying distribution of tertiary activities over the surface of the earth. The empirical analysis of these allocational aspects begins with the supposition of an isotropic surface, then notes and tries to include the distorting influence of real-world economic, cultural, and physical variations. For example, a few of our illustrations are taken from work in an area bounded by Lake Huron, Georgian Bay, and Lake Simcoe in Ontario, Canada (Yeates and Lloyd, 1970; Thoman and Yeates, 1966). This area (Figure 7-5) has an undulating surface consisting of morainic material, the only major relief feature being the Niagara escarpment, which rises up to 800 feet above the surrounding lowland as it follows the outline of the glacially sculptured southern Georgian Bay coastline before being obscured by morainic debris south of Shelburne. Outside incorporated centers, the density of population varies between 10 and 30 persons per square mile, with generally higher densities in the vicinity of Lake Simcoe. Most of the incorporated places act both as service and manufacturing centers, and, in fact, nearly all places with a population of more than 2,000 have some secondary industry within them. Thus, as the population of an urban center increases above 2,000 people, its tertiary structure is supported more by the secondary activity of the center and less by its region.

THRESHOLDS

A very important aspect of the theory of tertiary activities relates to an order of business types. From the theoretical discussion in the previous section it is suggested that an order of business types can be determined from threshold values. High-order business types have large thresholds and are found only in the largest urban centers, while the lowest-order business types are found in all centers of all sizes. The perimeter of an area around a central place which contains enough population (including the central place) to support a business type defines the *inner range* of the good sold by that particular type, while the *maximum range* (or *ideal limit*) is the line beyond which no person will travel to obtain that good. Thus the complementary region of a central place must lie between the inner range and the maximum range of the good for its associated business type to be in existence at that place.

Calculation of thresholds Ideally, it should be possible to obtain a list of all central places (i) and the number of establishments (E) of a particular business type (i) found in each central place:

$$_jE_i \qquad i = 1, 2, 3, \ldots, n$$

and rank these central places according to the population of each central place (P_i) plus that of its complementary region (R_i). For this jth business type there should be a number of central places which contain one establishment, and each of these should have the same value of $P_i + R_i$. All those central places with a value of less than $P_i + R_i$ will not have that business type, and those with populations greater than $P_i + R_i$ will have one or more. As noted in the previous chapter, the maximum range of a good may lie well beyond the inner range (or threshold limit), and so the value at which the second, third, and subsequent establishments of the jth business type enter a central places varies. Thus, in general terms

$$_jE_i = f_1(P_i + R_i)$$

where $j = 1, 2, 3, \ldots, m$ for m business types. In most research situations it is extremely difficult to measure R_i, and so the equation is usually modified to read

$$_jE_i = f_1(P_i)$$

This modification means that for business types in small central places the thresholds are usually underestimated, while in the larger central places, where the R_i component may be very small, the modification is not so serious. For this reason it is wise to use a method for calculating thresholds of a particular business type that takes into account the number of establishments in large as well as small centers.

Such a method for estimating thresholds was first introduced by Berry and Garrison (1958a); it can be illustrated with data obtained from the southern Georgian Bay area in 1966. The number of establishments of the optician business type (G for glasses) are plotted on a graph with respect to population, and the least-squares "best-fitting" line is fitted to the scatter of points. In this particular case, as in all the business types examined by Berry and Garrison, the best-fitting curve indicates an exponential relationship of the form

$$P = ab^G$$

which can be expressed in linear form as

$$\log P = \log a + \log bG$$

The linear form is presented in Figure 7-1a (all central places with fewer than 1,000 people excluded from the diagram), in which the population axis is on a logarith-

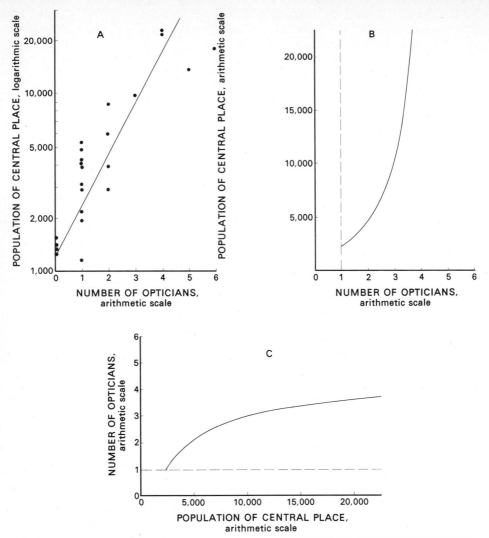

FIGURE 7-1 THE ESTIMATION OF A THRESHOLD VALUE FOR OPTICIANS IN THE SOUTHERN GEOR-
GIAN BAY AREA, 1967. (A) THE BEST-FIT LINE; (B) THE CURVE IN ARITHMETIC FORM; (C) THE CURVE IN
ARITHMETIC FORM WITH THE AXES SWITCHED FROM B.

mic scale while the optician axis is arithmetic. The nonlinear exponential equivalent of the straight line in Figure 7-1a is plotted in Figure 7-1b, and this form of this
curve illustrates quite clearly what an exponential relationship is: each additional
establishment serves a larger increment of population. For example, 2,300 people
are estimated to be the requirement for one optician, but 9,000 people are required
for three.

This particular relationship is placed in the correct form in Figure 7-1c, for the correct form of the equation is not $P_i = f(G_i)$ but $G_i = f(P_i)$. The traditional procedures of Berry and Garrison's analysis have been followed, however, in order to maintain continuity with their classic Snohomish study. The exponential form of the relationship between the number of establishments of a particular business type and the population of a central place, which is demonstrated most clearly in Figure 7-1c, has persuasive theoretical support. It is reasonable to assume that while 2,300 are required for the threshold support of one optician, that establishment will be able to serve more than that basic requirement. Thus, the second, third, and subsequent opticians to enter the central place usually will require progressively more people than the threshold for their support. It is clear, however, that while this may be a plausible rationale for the exponential form of the best-fit line, this need not always be the form of the best-fit curve. The ability to handle more than the threshold requirement is not always feasible in the same way for all service business types.

Threshold values of business types   Threshold values for a variety of business types have been calculated for many different areas in the world. Most such studies use the method described above, but a few use the Reed-Muench method (Haggett and Gunawardena, 1964). This method defines the threshold as the size of central place which divides a ranked list of all centers in such a way that the number of places lacking the business type above the division is equal to the number of centers possessing the business type below the division (Marshall, 1969, pp. 98–99). For our example we will use thresholds estimated by means of a best-fit line as described in Figure 7-1 in the previous section. The data are presented for two different regions: Snohomish County, Washington, and the southern Georgian Bay area in Ontario.

Berry and Garrison (1958a) have estimated threshold values for fifty-two different tertiary activities in Snohomish County. These estimates are presented arrayed along a single-line population nomogram in Figure 7-2, but it should be noted that one business type—sheet metal works—has been deleted from the tabulated fifty-two, on the grounds that it is more a secondary industry than a tertiary activity. On the same illustration (Figure 7-2), threshold estimates are also presented for thirty-six different tertiary activities in the southern Georgian Bay area. It is to be noted that the definition and names of the business types differ in a number of instances in the two studies, and in the Canadian study some business types are aggregates of similar tertiary activities. However, the definitions of twenty-one business types can be regarded as similar; these are listed in Table 7-1.

Table 7-1 illustrates that the threshold estimates in the two regions, though different in absolute values, taken together are quite similar. It is apparent that the range in values is much greater in the Georgian Bay area, and the rather different services offered by stores of the same type in the two areas also accounts for much of the variation. If the thresholds are ranked, however, it is clear that in general low-order business types in the Snohomish County study are also low-order

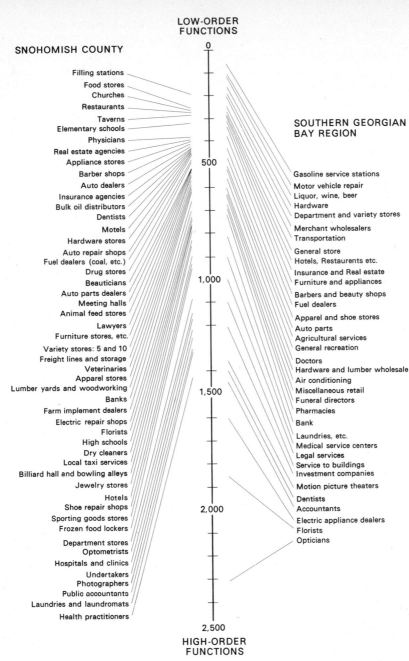

FIGURE 7-2 THRESHOLD VALUES FOR FIFTY-TWO BUSINESS TYPES IN SNOHOMISH COUNTY, WASHINGTON, AND THIRTY-SIX BUSINESS TYPES IN THE SOUTHERN GEORGIAN BAY AREA, ONTARIO, 1967. (DRAWN FROM DATA IN BERRY AND GARRISON, 1958, P. 150; AND YEATES AND LLOYD, 1970, P. 58.)

TABLE 7-1 THRESHOLD POPULATIONS FOR SELECTED BUSINESS TYPES IN SNOHOMISH COUNTY, WASHINGTON, AND THE SOUTHERN GEORGIAN BAY AREA, ONTARIO, CANADA

BUSINESS TYPE	SNOHOMISH COUNTY		GEORGIAN BAY	
	THRESHOLD	RANK	THRESHOLD	RANK
Gasoline service	196	1	110	1
Taverns (liquor, wine, beer)[1]	282	2	160	2
Physicians	380	3	590	13
Real estate (and insurance)	384–409	4	320	5
Barbers and beauticians	386–480	5	380	7
Oil fuel dealers	419	6	440	8
Dentists	426	7	1,350	19
Hardware	431	8	200	3
Drugstores (pharmacies)	458	9	660	15
Automobile parts	488	10	520	10
Lawyers	528	11	900	18
Furniture (and appliances)	546	12	340	6
Variety (and department) stores	549	13	210	4
Apparel stores (and shoes)	590	14	480	9
Farm implement (agricultural services)	650	15	530	11
Florists	729	16	1,850	20
Dry cleaning (laundries)	754	17	700	16
Sporting goods (general recreation)	928	18	540	12
Optometrists (opticians)	1,140	19	2,300	21
Hospitals and clinics	1,159	20	820	17
Undertakers (funeral directors)	1,214	21	650	14

[1]The name in parentheses is the term used by Yeates and Lloyd (1970).

business types in the Canadian study. In fact the Spearman's rank correlation coefficient, which indicates the degree of similarity between the two rankings, is calculated to have a value of +0.58, which tests as being significant at the .01 level. Furthermore, it should be noted that much of the variation is accounted for by the great difference between the rankings of physicians and dentists in the two areas. It can be conjectured that this may well reflect the relative shortage of this type of professional service in rural Ontario, though it should be noted that medical service centers have a lower threshold value in that area.

The spacing of the business types along the nomogram (Figure 7-2) also exhibits certain similarities. It is noticeable that although there are few real clusters of business types around discrete population values, nevertheless the higher-order business types are located farther apart along the nomogram than the lower-order types. In fact, twenty-nine tertiary activities in Snohomish County and sixteen in the southern Georgian Bay area have thresholds between 200 and 600, but only eight business types in the former region and five in the latter have thresholds between 1,000 and 1,400. Therefore, the proposition that there are fewer higher-order business types than lower-order types within a given range is also supported by these data.

INCREMENTS OF GROUPS OF BUSINESS TYPES

We have observed that one of the basic tenets of Christallerian central place theory is that there are cumulative increments of business types, with each higher-order central place containing all the business types of the immediate lower order plus a new set definitive of that particular order. It is apparent from the previous chapter that there are three ways that may be used to define an order of central places: population, the number of business types, and the number of establishments. Although the population of a place may well be concerned with basic activities other than those involving the tertiary sector, nevertheless it has a positive feedback effect on the array of services that are offered by the place. Thus the customer attractiveness of a place is enhanced and the range of the complementary region is extended. This process, therefore, raises the importance of such a central place relative to the order of the others. Consequently, although the population of a central place may be concerned with activities other than providing tertiary services to its complementary region, nevertheless population can be considered an important indicator of the order of a place.

Allocation of business types among urban centers in Snohomish County The Snohomish County threshold data are subdivided into five classes, each containing an equal number of business types, ranging from the lowest to the highest, according to the rank-size threshold estimates in Figure 7-2. These are:

Class 1: Filling stations to barbershops

Class 2: Automobile dealers to beauticians

Class 3: Automobile parts dealers to banks

Class 4: Farm implement dealers to shoe repair shops

Class 5: Sporting goods stores to health practitioners

The urban centers listed by Berry and Garrison (1958a, p. 150) containing 250 or more people (twenty-two in total) are also subdivided—into three groups according to population rank size. These are:

Group A: Seven urban centers ranging in population from 1,600 to 3,494

Group B: Eight urban centers ranging in population from 600 to 974

Group C: Seven urban centers ranging in population from 300 to 500

The proportionate number of business types of a given class found in centers of each size group are listed in Table 7-2. The table can be interpreted by reading either down the columns or across the rows. For example, reading down column B, if the eight middle-sized urban places each contained at least one of each of the ten business types in the lowest class, the percentage would be 100 percent. Instead, the entry indicates that the middle-sized group contained these lowest-

CLASS OF FUNCTION	URBAN CENTER GROUP	LARGE URBAN CENTER, PERCENT A	B	SMALL URBAN CENTER, PERCENT C
Low-order function	1	89	74	59
	2	68	39	24
	3	70	30	27
	4	57	23	16
High-order function	5	50	15	1

SOURCE: Data adapted from Berry and Garrison, 1959, p. 150.

order business types 74 percent of the time. Likewise, they contained the ten in class 2, 39 percent; the eleven in class 3, 30 percent; the ten in class 4, 23 percent; and the ten in class 5, 15 percent of the time.

If all functions were found in all centers, regardless of population size, all the proportions would be about the same. This is obviously not the case! Also, if the proportions fluctuated in an inexplicable fashion, one could also conclude that population is a poor indicator of the order of a place. If, however, the proportions declined, in a fairly regular fashion *down* the columns and *across* the rows, then one could conclude that population is a reasonably good indicator of the order of a place. This appears to be so in most cases, though there are a few questionable situations. The proportions do not decline regularly down column C, indicating that the group of smallest urban centers contains some places with quite high-order business types. This is confirmed by the fact that one central place in this group contains one of the highest-order business types [$1/7(10) = 0.014 = 1.4\% \approx 1.0\%$]. Also, although the proportions do decline down column B, the drop from class 1 to 2 is rather steep considering the small population range of centers included in this group. However, it can be concluded that the larger urban centers, which are usually the highest-order places, have the higher-order and most of the lower-order business types; and the smaller urban centers, which are usually the lower-order places, rarely have any of the higher-order business types but usually contain those of the lowest order.

Allocation of business types among urban centers in the upper Midwest The above conclusion is supported by the findings of Borchert and Adams (1963) in the upper Midwest of the United States. This area includes Montana, North Dakota, South Dakota, Minnesota, northern Iowa, northwestern Wisconsin, and the upper Michigan peninsula. In this study the authors determine those business types that are typical of the various orders in the hierarchy of central places. High-order central places are defined as those that have a certain mix of business types that are considered characteristic of such a level in the hierarchy, and the lower-order centers are also delimited by characteristic mixes of the different types. Thus, the population of the center is only incidental to the determination of its order, for it is the service characteristics of the place that are preeminent in the scheme of classification.

In the upper Midwest, four characteristic types of trade center are discerned, and eight classes of central places are suggested to exist in the hierarchical order of service centers. Each of these orders is characterized by a particular bundle of business types (Figure 7-3).

1. Gasoline filling stations and the tavern or lunchroom are typical of the lowest level of central place—the *hamlet*.

2. The next two levels are convenience centers which provide those services that are common necessities for everyday life. The *minimum-convenience* centers always have the two hamlet-level business types plus a grocery or general store, a hardware store, a bank, and a drugstore, as well as two of four other business types (see Figure 7-3). The *full-convenience* centers always have the ten business types found at the minimum-convenience and hamlet levels plus stores concerned with appliances or furniture, jewelry, men's or boy's or women's clothes, and a laundry or dry-cleaning establishment plus any three of five others.

3. The next two levels of central place are characterized by specialty activities for which customers make special trips and which frequently involve comparative shopping. These activities include camera stores, florists, radio and TV stores, and women's accessories. The *partial shopping* centers always have from four to eight of the thirteen specialty functions listed in Figure 7-3, while *complete shopping* centers have nine or more, plus all those characteristic of the convenience and hamlet levels.

4. Wholesale activities particularly characterize the highest level of central places. *Secondary wholesale-retail* centers contain all the specialty, convenience, and hamlet-level types, but they also have ten to thirteen of the wholesale activities listed in Figure 7-3 and over fifty wholesale establishments. *Primary wholesale-retail* centers have all the wholesale activities listed in Figure 7-3 plus over 100 wholesale establishments. *Metropolitan wholesale-retail* centers have all the wholesale activities and over 500 wholesale establishments. Wholesale establishments proliferate with size of urban center in the same way as retail establishments.

The general trend is for the number of urban centers in each class of central place to increase as the hierarchical order decreases (Table 7-3). In the upper Midwest the only metropolitan wholesale-retail center is Minneapolis–St. Paul. This class of center usually provides other important services for a large region as well as the retail and wholesale activities. In this class of center invariably are found the regional head offices of insurance companies and a large array of specialized medical facilities. Frequently, in North America, such centers contain also the

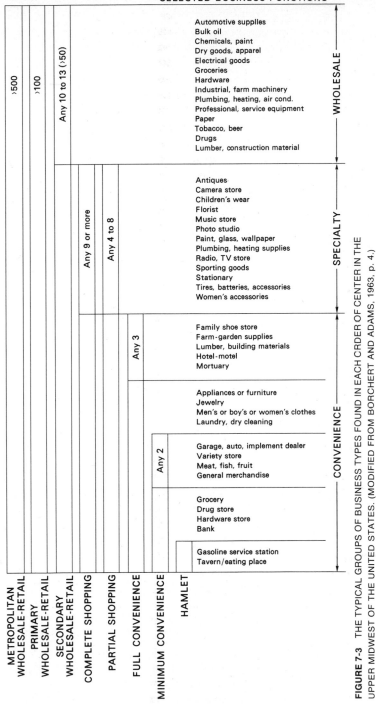

SELECTED BUSINESS FUNCTIONS

WHOLESALE
Automotive supplies
Bulk oil
Chemicals, paint
Dry goods, apparel
Electrical goods
Groceries
Hardware
Industrial, farm machinery
Plumbing, heating, air cond.
Professional, service equipment
Paper
Tobacco, beer
Drugs
Lumber, construction material

SPECIALTY
Antiques
Camera store
Children's wear
Florist
Music store
Photo studio
Paint, glass, wallpaper
Plumbing, heating supplies
Radio, TV store
Sporting goods
Stationary
Tires, batteries, accessories
Women's accessories

Family shoe store
Farm-garden supplies
Lumber, building materials
Hotel-motel
Mortuary

Appliances or furniture
Jewelry
Men's or boy's or women's clothes
Laundry, dry cleaning

Garage, auto, implement dealer
Variety store
Meat, fish, fruit
General merchandise

Grocery
Drug store
Hardware store
Bank

Gasoline service station
Tavern/eating place

CONVENIENCE

>500 — METROPOLITAN WHOLESALE-RETAIL
>100 — PRIMARY WHOLESALE-RETAIL
Any 10 to 13 (>50) — SECONDARY WHOLESALE-RETAIL
Any 9 or more — COMPLETE SHOPPING
Any 4 to 8 — PARTIAL SHOPPING
Any 3 — FULL CONVENIENCE
Any 2 — MINIMUM CONVENIENCE
HAMLET

FIGURE 7-3 THE TYPICAL GROUPS OF BUSINESS TYPES FOUND IN EACH ORDER OF CENTER IN THE UPPER MIDWEST OF THE UNITED STATES. (MODIFIED FROM BORCHERT AND ADAMS, 1963, p. 4.)

TABLE 7-3 THE HIERARCHY OF TRADE CENTERS IN THE STATES OF THE UPPER MIDWEST

CLASS OF TRADE CENTER	NUMBER OF TRADE CENTERS	MEDIAN POPULATION OF TRADE CENTER
Wholesale-retail	18	
Metropolitan	1	1,440,000
Primary	7	55,400
Secondary	10	32,200
Shopping centers	206	
Complete	79	9,500
Partial	127	2,500
Convenience centers	491	
Full	112	1,600
Minimum	379	800
Hamlets	1,820	160

SOURCE: Borchert and Adams, 1963, p. 2; and Borchert, 1963, p. 11.

regional head offices of financial concerns, such as brokerage companies and small stock exchanges.

To complete the theoretical analysis, it is necessary to postulate the existence of two or even three classes of central place of a higher order than the metropolitan wholesale-retail center. While a number of places, such as Pittsburgh, St. Louis, and Baltimore, offer a range of business types similar to that of Minneapolis–St. Paul, others offer an even wider range and even more specialized activities. For example, Los Angeles, Chicago, and Toronto and Montreal in Canada have a wide range of specialized activities of a financial and sales nature (such as advertising) which mark them as centers of national importance. Chicago has a large commodity market, and Toronto and Montreal have very active stock exchanges. New York, the highest-order center, has the largest stock exchange, in terms of total volume of stocks listed, in the world, and is the center of trading and marketing for North America. The theoretical highest-order center of all would be a central place that is the retail, wholesale, financial, administrative, and cultural center of the country. There is no such center in North America, for in both Canada and the United States the administrative capitals have been located purposely away from the financial centers. London and Paris, on the other hand, are good examples of such centers, for they are the retail, wholesale, financial, administrative, and cultural capitals of their countries, and, for a few decades, they were the highest-order central places for empires.

SOME ALLOCATIONAL MODELS

Thus it is apparent that although population cannot be used by itself to indicate the order of a place, nevertheless the number of business types (B) and the number of establishments (E) are related to the size of the population of the place (P) plus that of its associated complementary region (R). These relationships are useful in a planning context (see Chapter 10); they can be presented in symbolic form as follows:

$$B_i = f_2(P_i + R_i)$$
$$E_i = f_2(P_i + R_i)$$

Because of the previously mentioned difficulty of measuring R_i, the value of this term is usually disregarded.

Empirical models: southern Georgian Bay area   The models derived from these central place concepts involve an aggregation of spatially distributed data into regression equations in order to determine the best-fit relationship. For this reason they are referred to as cross-sectional models, and their interpretation involves problems that are similar to those that are derived from time-series data. Whereas with time-series models some of the problems have been attacked and partially solved, the problems of using cross-sectional data in statistical models are suspected but known only by intuition (King, 1969, pp. 157–162). It is necessary, therefore, to indicate that although the results may look extremely attractive, they must be interpreted with a degree of caution.

The first model suggests that the number of business types found in the ith central place is a function of the population size of the ith place, there being n settlements within the area. The parameters for the best-fit line derived from empirical data pertaining to the southern Georgian Bay area in 1964 and 1967 are presented in Table 7-4. These parameters prove to be highly significant for both time periods, and also quite similar—a finding that provides both useful substantiation for the research methodology and welcome support for the utility of the equations. The best-fit equation takes the general form

$$B_i = a + b \ (\log P_i)$$

and the relationship in 1967 is estimated to be

$$B_i = -56.26 + 28.12 \ (\log P_i)$$

TABLE 7-4   REGRESSION PARAMETERS RELATING BUSINESS TYPES TO SIZE OF PLACE: SOUTHERN GEORGIAN BAY AREA, 1964 AND 1967

YEAR	a	b	r	t_b	n
1964	−58.93	28.62	0.93	15.42	40
1967	−58.26	28.12	0.92	14.47	40

SOURCE: Yeates and Lloyd, 1970, p. 57.
Note: r is the correlation coefficient and t_b refers to "student's" t, which in this case indicates that the regression coefficient (b) is significantly greater than zero at the .01 level.

TABLE 7-5 REGRESSION PARAMETERS RELATING
ESTABLISHMENTS TO SIZE OF PLACE: SOUTHERN
GEORGIAN BAY AREA, 1964 AND 1967

YEAR	a	b	r	t_b	n
1964	−0.8097	0.8475	0.93	16.04	40
1967	−0.7234	0.8296	0.95	18.91	40

SOURCE: Yeates and Lloyd, 1970, p. 57.
Note: r is the correlation coefficient and t_b refers to "student's" t,
which in this case indicates that the regression coefficient (b) is
significantly greater than zero at the .01 level.

If we substitute a population of 150 into the equation, the associated number of
business types for a place of that size is estimated to be 3.63, or either three or four.

The second model, relating the total number of business establishments found
in a place to the population of the place, is also found to be highly significant if
both variables (E_i and P_i) are expressed in logarithms. The parameters for this
best-fit relationship are listed in Table 7-5, and again they indicate a high degree of
stability for the two time periods. The equation takes the general form

$$\log E_i = \log c + d\,(\log P_i)$$

and the relationship in 1967 is estimated to be

$$\log E_i = -0.7234 + 0.8296\,(\log P_i)$$

If a population of 150 is substituted into the equation, the associated number of
establishments for a place of that size is estimated to be either twelve or thirteen.

Classification Thus the relationship between population and number of business
types and number of establishments for forty places in the southern Georgian Bay
area for two time periods is quite strong. If

$$B_i = a + b\,(\log P_i)$$

and

$$\log E_i = \log c + d\,(\log P_i)$$

then

$$\log E_i = \log u + \log v\,(B_i)$$

The existence of such a relationship is indicated in Figure 7-4 (inset) for the
southern Georgian Bay area in 1967. In this diagram forty-six more places have

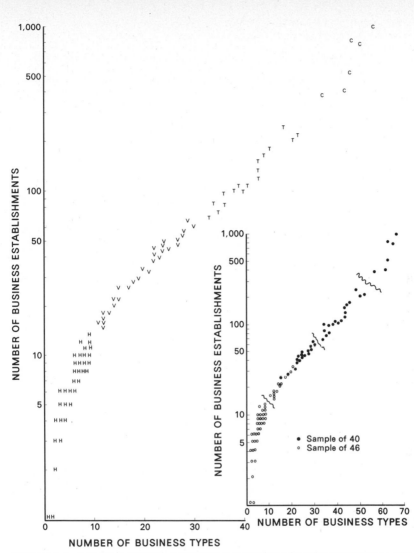

FIGURE 7-4 THE RELATIONSHIP BETWEEN THE NUMBER OF ESTABLISHMENTS AND NUMBER OF BUSINESS TYPES IN A CENTRAL PLACE: SOUTHERN GEORGIAN BAY AREA, 1967.

been added to the forty used above (Tables 7-4 and 7-5) for which there were data for two time periods.

This relationship between establishment and business type is found in many other studies in North America (Berry and Garrison, 1958a; Berry et al., 1962); it is used by Berry to determine the existence of a hierarchy on the basis of the "breaks" and the separate regimes that occur in what appears to be a continuous relationship. As the aggregation of data to graph form ignores the essential spatial aspect of the central place hierarchy and emphasizes the continuous nature of

TABLE 7-6 COMPARISON OF THE TERTIARY STRUCTURE OF CENTRAL PLACES IN THE SOUTHERN GEORGIAN BAY AREA WITH SOUTHWESTERN IOWA

	BUSINESS TYPES		ESTABLISHMENTS		POPULATION	
	GEORGIAN BAY	SOUTHWESTERN IOWA	GEORGIAN BAY	SOUTHWESTERN IOWA	GEORGIAN BAY	SOUTHWESTERN IOWA
Hamlets	1–19	1–8	1–13	1–10	50–460	10–170
Villages	11–30	9–26	15–65	11–45	220–1,300	170–400
Towns	34–51	27–55	85–240	46–120	900–4,000	400–1,700
Cities	55	55–100 (approx.)	370	124–400 (approx.)	8,000	1,700–9,000

SOURCE: Figure 7-4; Berry et al., 1962.

most size distributions, it is not surprising that in much of the evidence the separate regimes appear illusory. In this case it is postulated that three breaks exist (see Figure 7-4, inset), dividing the distribution into cities, towns, villages, and hamlets. It is interesting to note that with respect to their endowment of business types the classes are similar to those graphed by Berry et al. (1962) for southwestern Iowa (Table 7-6). Furthermore, it is entertaining to observe that the upper limits of population for the various classes in the Georgian Bay study appear to increase according to a rule of threes. The overlap in the population regimes (which may well also occur in the southwestern Iowa study, but cannot be interpolated from the graphs) indicates that there must be a number of cases in which the population of the complementary region is an extremely important determinant of the tertiary structure of the place. Also, there may be a number of instances where inertia has affected the rate of structural readjustment.

Location of central places and hierarchical ordering   Geography, by very definition, involves the analysis of spatial systems and the answering of the question. "Why are things located where they are?" It is impossible, therefore, to ignore the locational aspect of the hierarchical structure, for it is an important feature of the central place model. Equally, it is difficult to include these locational aspects, for the real world rarely conforms to the postulated isotropic surface, though Berry and Garrison (1958b, p. 111) have demonstrated the Löschian notion that "*whatever* the distribution of purchasing power (and whether in an open countryside or within a large metropolis) a hierarchical spatial structure of central places supplying central goods will emerge." Invariably, there are many features that distort patterns. In the southern Georgian Bay area, the lakes, which have served and are still serving as important transport arteries, are a focus for settlements; and many of these have become small industrial and ship-repair centers. Furthermore, the accelerating urbanization of the Toronto metropolitan region is engulfing the eastern portion of the study region and causing rapid growth and change in that area.

In Figure 7-5 we have plotted all those centers that have been classified as

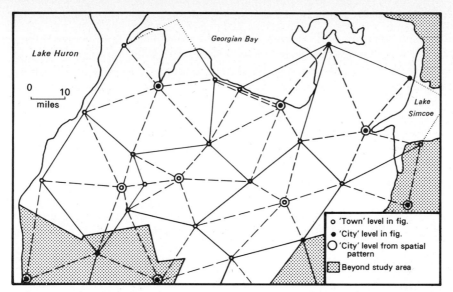

FIGURE 7-5 A POSSIBLE CENTRAL PLACE LATTICE IN THE SOUTHERN GEORGIAN BAY AREA.

"cities" and "towns" in Figure 7-4. It is apparent that the cities are clustered in the eastern part of the study area, where they are important small manufacturing centers as well as serving as centers of tertiary activities. Considering the many distorting effects, the lattice is remarkably regular, and the hexagonal complementary regions of the "city"-level centers are, on the whole, recognizable. The locations of these "city"-level places are predicated upon the assumption that Barrie (B) and Owen Sound (O.S.) are the subregional centers for the area, and therefore provide "city"-level activities as well. It is useful to note that the distortions of the real world result in only three of the six "city"-level centers as determined by spatial arrangement conforming to those defined graphically as "city"-level in Figure 7-4.

CONSUMER BEHAVIOR

All the concepts derived from central place theory rest upon the assumption that individual consumers behave, on the average, in a predictable fashion. In the context of our discussion these assumptions pertain to consumer travel behavior and the distances that individuals are prepared to travel for various goods. Huff (1960) postulates that the consumer travel behavior of individuals is related to (1) the characteristics of individuals, (2) the way in which they perceive the array of places to which they may travel, and (3) the individuals' image of the total friction of distance between residence and the places where they may acquire the desired good or service.

In a detailed analysis of a sample of the Iowa dispersed farm and nonfarm population, Rushton (1966) indicates that individuals do not necessarily shop at the nearest center where a good is available. Large centers at some medium distance appear to take precedence over small nearby centers in some instances. The explanation for this is that individuals perceive large centers as more attractive than small centers, even though both may provide the same tertiary facility, simply because large centers are known to have a greater range of choices and more opportunity for other activities as well. On the other hand, it is evident that these centers must be close; and the more necessary the purchase, the greater the likelihood that the consumer will minimize distance to be traveled.

Consumer behavior in the southern Georgian Bay area The more general accuracy of these observations is indicated by an examination of three desire-line maps that have been constructed for three services in the southern Georgian Bay area (Figure 7-6a, b, c). The services are: groceries, a business type (retail food) considered typical of the hamlet level; banks, considered typical of the village level owing to the institution of branch banking in Ontario which permits the larger banks to place one-teller branches in many centers; and opticians, considered typical of towns. The desire-line maps have been constructed on the basis of over 1,000 sample interviews taken systematically over the entire study area, and the lines represent the straight-line distance of the respondent's residence to the place usually visited for that particular service.

The desire-line map for groceries (Figure 7-6a), which include everyday general food items, predictably exhibits a plethora of places the respondents visit. Most people appear to go commonly to their closest hamlet, though it is noticeable that many persons residing close to large centers, such as Owen Sound, Barrie, and Orillia, tend to travel farther to these places, frequently bypassing their local hamlet, or even village. Presumably, as rural roads improve and automobiles become even more comfortable and their number increases, the desire lines to these larger centers will increase in length.

These same features recur for the village- and town-level examples: banks and opticians. As the order of the business type in the hierarchy increases, the lower-order centers disappear from the maps. Visually, this is less apparent between parts a and b of Figure 7-6 than between parts b and c because many of the hamlets are revealed by only a single desire line. The desire-line map for banks reveals a very discrete series of complementary regions for villages throughout the entire area, with the larger regions again focusing on the larger centers. The desire-line map for opticians (Figure 7-6c) reveals only those places with town-level functions; nearly all the villages (and all the hamlets) are ignored. Once again, the larger places have the largest hinterlands, and it is noticeable that a number of the desire lines focus off the map to the south and east. This focus is metropolitan Toronto, indicating that it is with the higher-order specialized services of this type

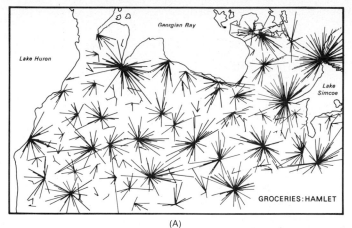

(A)

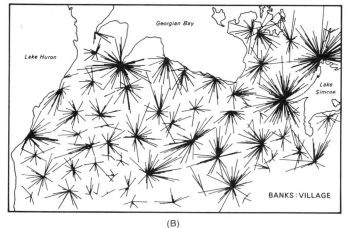

(B)

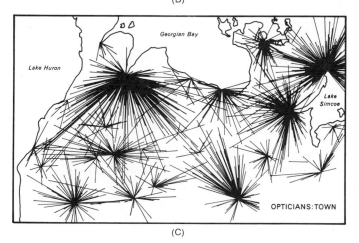

(C)

FIGURE 7-6 DESIRE LINE MAPS FOR (A) GROCERIES, (B) BANKS, AND (C) OPTICIANS IN THE SOUTHERN GEORGIAN BAY AREA, 1966. (THOMAN AND YEATES, 1966, PP. 82, 85, 88.)

that a large metropolitan area begins to exert its dominance over its complementary region.

POPULATION DENSITY AND TRADE AREA

Our examples, therefore, support the contention that (1) consumers tend to go to the closest center that provides the goods they are seeking; (2) they may bypass lower-order centers if there is a higher-order center within a reasonable distance; (3) the range of the good increases with the order of the good; and (4) the higher the order of the center, the larger its complementary region. The size of the complementary region is theoretically related to the population density or, more accurately, the purchasing power density of the area concerned. This is demonstrated with respect to four areas of different population density in North America in Figure 7-7. The four areas are:

1. The wheatlands of South Dakota, through which the population density is usually ten persons per square mile.

2. Eastern Ontario, which averages about fifty persons per square mile (Ray, 1967)

3. Suburban Chicago, where population densities range from 3,000 to 9,000 persons per square mile

4. Urban Chicago, where densities vary from 20,000 to 50,000 persons per square mile

The diagram relates the population served by a central place or its urban counterpart, the retail nucleation, to the trade area served. Central places serving a fairly large area (about 100 square miles) which contains a small population are in low-density regions, whereas those serving a fairly small area (about 10 square miles) which contains a large population are in high-density regions. The highest-density areas are the urban regions and the lower-density areas are rural. Thus a cross-sectional line running diagonally from the top left-hand corner of Figure 7-7 to the botton right-hand corner calibrates a change in density from low to high. Thus the diagram compares the service hierarchy in four regions of differing density and demonstrates a common structural relationship. The higher the order of the center, the larger the trade area and population served, and the relationship between these two characteristics appears to be remarkably similar in all four areas of differing density.

The lines indicating the upper limits of the different levels in the hierarchy are straight, signifying consistency, but they slope backward, suggesting that although trade areas increase in size with decreases in population density, they do so at a rate slower than the decline in population density. Berry (1967, p. 33) suggests that since individuals are willing to travel farther when densities are lower, the potential complementary region of places in low-density areas is larger than would be expected. As a consequence the higher-order business types in the lower-order

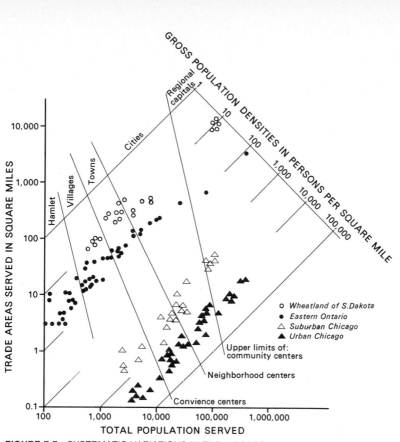

FIGURE 7-7 SYSTEMATIC VARIATIONS IN THE HIERARCHY. (RAY, 1967.)

places move up a level in the hierarchy, for the population is willing to go to the higher-order center for those types of goods. This has a feedback effect on the size of the lower-order centers, for as they lose these business types, they lose a proportion of their economic base, which in turn has a negative effect on the population of the place itself. Thus hamlets, villages, towns, and cities tend to be smaller in South Dakota than in eastern Ontario.

CHANGE

No geographic study is complete without an analysis of change and a discussion of its causes. This is particularly so in North America; for it is here that change, whether expressed in social, economic, or cultural terms, is inbred into the very fiber of society. In the ensuing discussion we outline briefly some of the more important processes that are considered to influence change in the allocation of tertiary activities among central places, and then discuss a few examples of change associated with these processes.

FACTORS INFLUENCING CHANGE

The catalysts of change are many and varied, and in any particular situation it is difficult to discern which of the many possibilities has had the greatest influence. Undoubtedly, one of the major factors influencing change in the structure of central places is migration, though the character of this migration has altered greatly in recent years. Other factors of similar importance involve transportation improvements and the changing life-style and tastes of society.

Migration   For much of the present century the dominant influence has been the sheer volume of rural-to-urban migration, which resulted in a change of North American society from predominantly rural before 1920 to predominantly urban after that time. This rural-to-urban migration has slowed in pace in recent years, however, as shown by the fact that whereas 538,154 persons moved from a rural to an urban location in Canada between 1956 and 1961, 494,734 moved from an urban to a rural location, leaving a net movement in an urban direction of only 43,420 persons (Kalbach and McVey, 1971, p. 98). The greatest volume of internal migration was between urban areas (1,552,521 for the five-year period), and in particular from the smaller urban areas to the larger ones.

Thus the massive rural-to-urban migration of the immediate past is being replaced in importance by an interurban migration in recent years, a migration that involves a movement from smaller urban areas to larger ones, which, parenthetically, includes a large proportion from urban areas in regions of economic distress to those of more vibrant growth. This latter situation is particularly disturbing not simply because of the greater-than-average movement from rural areas and the smaller towns in these declining regions, but because the individuals involved are from the most productive age groups and include the more aggressive and educated segment of the local population. As a result, two problems are created. The economically stagnant areas lose whatever little attractiveness they might have had for industry, and any chance that may have existed for rural redevelopment, for the residual population becomes polarized around the very young and the very old. This means that they become more dependent upon large inflows of assistance in terms of social services and general welfare.

But the problems are not simply confined to the declining areas, for the receiving urban areas become the recipients of large numbers of people who are employed intermittently in occupations that are very sensitive to cyclical fluctuations in the economy. The problems of cyclical unemployment are then compounded by the stresses and strains of the continuing adjustment process to urban and metropolitan life being experienced by the recent urban migrant. These difficulties have proved particularly apparent with respect to the poor Appalachian whites and the Southern small-town blacks who have moved in large numbers to the metropolitan areas of the United States in recent decades.

Transportation   The influence of innovation in transportation techniques and systems is discussed in some detail in the next chapter. In general, the real cost of transporting manufactured products and people per mile has decreased since the late 1950s. The widespread use of the automobile, improved roads, larger trucks, piggyback railroad flatcars, uniform containerization, for example, have all aided the efficiency of transport. Thus, the range of all goods and services, whether retail or wholesale, has increased, and the trade areas of the more competitive firms in the more attractive central places have increased in size. With respect to the consumer, it is important to note that the massive expenditure on the construction of four-lane limited-access highways connecting nearly all the major urban centers in North America, along with the general availability of late-model high-powered automobiles, has, in effect, made these large centers highly accessible to the great majority of the population.

Changing life-style   Life-style, in the context of this discussion, refers to the way in which individuals and families view themselves as consumers and the role of consumption in their lives. There is little doubt that the act of purchasing things or even participating in the purchasing, and the satisfaction to be gained from this act, have an important effect on the spatial behavior of individuals. At the outset it is important to note that, in real money terms, people are a great deal wealthier today than they were twenty or even ten years ago. They can, therefore, afford not only to purchase more things, but also to spend more money in the act of purchasing. As a consequence, they are prepared to drive farther, purchase a more comfortable automobile for this purpose, and visit places which provide them with greater pleasure while they are spending their money, although prices may be higher. Thus it is not uncommon to find people visiting a more expensive supermarket or air-conditioned shopping center to make purchases rather than a cheaper but old-fashioned grocery or department store.

In effect, greater individual wealth has permitted individuals in North America to view the act of purchasing as more than simply a necessity—as a recreation as well. Of course, even in decades past, shopping was a recreation, but only very occasionally, and invariably only for high-order goods. Today, shopping for goods of all kinds can become part of the act of recreation. As a consequence, multiple-purpose shopping trips, which are encouraged by the design of planned shopping centers, are common, and the customer is transported into a holiday atmosphere by the color, gaiety, and carefree ambience of his surroundings. The fact that purchasing has become a recreation for most people, and a family recreation at that, has had a tremendous impact on the structure of central places, for people are becoming even more willing to travel to the larger urban centers for quite low-order goods. This willingness is enhanced by the advertising industry which, through the media (particularly television), fosters the image of the larger urban area and, by omission, in effect deprecates that of the smaller town.

EFFECT OF CHANGE ON CENTRAL PLACE SYSTEMS

The empirical evidence with respect to change involves an analysis of an area for two or more time periods. Most studies we have cited are concerned with one time period; this reflects the difficulty of obtaining comparable data for a number of time periods for any one area. There are, however, a few studies of central place systems over a period of time (Berry, 1967, pp. 3–25; Hodge, 1965). We will utilize those concerning Ohio and eastern Ontario in the discussions (Brunn, 1968; Hodge, 1966).

Change in thresholds   Brunn (1968) reports a study of changing threshold values for thirty-nine business types that occurred for two time periods (1940 and 1964) in a random sample of thirty-two central places, varying in population size from 150 to over 4,000 in rural northwestern Ohio. This is not an area of economic decline—in fact it is one of the most prosperous farming areas in the United States—but this very prosperity has been associated with greater efficiency, larger farm sizes, greatly improved transportation, and along with it a decline in number of the rural farm population. As a consequence, the population is prepared to bypass these smaller centers and visit the larger ones for many of their services. Thus, in the selected sample, there was a general decrease in the number and variety of services available in these small trade centers from 1940 to 1964.

This upward movement of business types, which for a number of firms means movement to a higher-order central place, is reflected by significant general increases in thresholds. Of the thirty-nine services that appeared in the selected centers in 1940 and 1964, thirty-five had greater and only four had lower threshold values at the end of the time period. The most marked of these is the general store, which experienced a drop in threshold value of 184 (Brunn, 1968, p. 204). This is an example of a business type which tends to hang on in the small centers even though their population is declining and their trade area dwindling, and indicates that an "inertia" effect can result in certain stores staying in operation even though the threshold may be decreasing (Brunn, 1967). These are often of the "Ma and Pa" variety, and though they may stay in existence until the operators retire, they are rarely economical enough to be purchased either for the same or a similar use.

Change in the hierarchy   Decreases in threshold value, or a general upward movement of some business types to higher-order centers, must be reflected by changes in the hierarchy. Hodge (1966) has documented a number of changes of this type, one of which is for eastern Ontario. Table 7-7 indicates the percentage distribution of trade centers in 1951 and 1961 for two different time periods in seven different classes of central place. It is evident that the proportion of hamlets in eastern Ontario has declined, whereas the proportionate number of higher-order centers has either remained static or increased, with the minimum-convenience order of trade centers exhibiting the greatest increase. Thus, Table 7-7 indicates, in gross terms, a tendency for the lowest-order centers, which are located close to each other, to diminish in number; this is a reflection of the tendency of people to travel farther to higher-order centers for lower-order services.

A much more dynamic view of these changes can be obtained by examining the fluctuations within each class. Table 7-8 shows the amount of growth, decline,

TABLE 7-7 CHANGES IN THE PROPORTION OF TRADE CENTERS BY CLASS IN EASTERN ONTARIO, 1951–1961

HIERARCHICAL CLASS	1951, PERCENT	1961, PERCENT
Hamlets	53.9	49.2
Mininum convenience	18.6	21.4
Full convenience	10.0	9.7
Partial shopping	6.6	8.2
Complete shopping	5.9	5.6
Secondary wholesale retail	4.8	5.6
Primary wholesale retail	0.2	0.3
Total	100.0	100.0

SOURCE: Hodge, 1966, p. 187.

and stability within each class of central place. If there had been stability in the structure of tertiary economic activity in eastern Ontario between 1951 and 1961, all places would have remained in exactly the same relative order; there would be no change, that is, no movement of centers up or down the hierarchy, and each entry on the diagonal (indicated by italics in Table 7-8) would read 100 percent. The only example of such a situation in Table 7-8 is in the primary wholesale-retail class, which indicates that all places classified as primary wholesale-retail centers in 1951 were classified as primary wholesale-retail centers in 1961.

The figures in Table 7-8, however, reveal a much more complex picture. Of the trade centers classified as hamlets in 1951, 60.5 percent were still providing hamlet-level functions in 1961, but 33.1 percent had expired, 8.8 percent had expanded their service functions to become minimum-convenience centers, and 0.4 percent had become partial shopping centers. Thus, the numbers to the left of the diagonal indicate decline, and the numbers to the right indicate growth.

TABLE 7-8 CHANGES IN PROPORTIONATE NUMBER OF TRADE CENTERS WITHIN EACH CLASS GROUPING, EASTERN ONTARIO, 1951–1961

HIERARCHICAL CLASS	EXPIRED BY 1961	HAMLET	MINIMUM CONVE- NIENCE	FULL CONVE- NIENCE	PARTIAL SHOPPING	COMPLETE SHOPPING	SECONDARY WHOLESALE- RETAIL	PRIMARY WHOLESALE- RETAIL
New, 1951–1961		89.3		10.7		Growth		
Hamlet	33.1	*60.5*	8.8		0.4			
Minimum convenience	3.8	26.8	*63.5*	6.1				
Full convenience	4.6	2.3	25.6	*51.2*	16.3			
Partial shopping				24.1	58.6	17.2		
Complete shopping				3.9	26.9	*53.9*	15.4	
Secondary wholesale- retail				Decline		14.3	*85.7*	
Primary wholesale- retail								100.0

SOURCE: Hodge, 1966, p. 191.

Overall, it can be observed that the majority of centers are either on the diagonal or the left. Thus, the trade-center story for eastern Ontario is decline in all except the higher-order central places. This general within-class decline is related to two main factors discussed previously—transport improvements and economic stagnation.

The empirical evidence with respect to the allocation of tertiary activities among urban places therefore appears voluminous. We have discussed some of the evidence and a few of the more simple techniques used to demonstrate that these concepts can be tested, whatever the locale. The impact of cultural variations can be determined in a similar fashion. Murdie (1965) compared the shopping behavior patterns of old-order Mennonites and modern Canadians in southern Ontario, and found that the Mennonite group patronized the smaller local centers for high-order and low-order goods, whereas the modern Canadian visited more distant centers for high-order services. Similarly, the French Canadians in eastern Ontario shop in towns containing predominantly French-speaking inhabitants, and English Canadians patronize centers that contain primarily English-speaking people (Ray, 1967). The French- and English-speaking groups therefore bypass centers that are not in their linguistic and cultural milieu. Nevertheless, apart from these cultural variations, most of the studies indicate that the Christaller-Lösch deductions are tenable in a variety of situations.

TRANSPORTATION: THEORY AND PATTERNS

One characteristic of the human environment that will by this time have begun to stand out with special clarity is that those things which people need are highly concentrated in a limited number of places. Previous chapters have shown that physical resources are unevenly distributed, as are the facilities for converting them into objects useful to man. Moreover, human populations are themselves much denser in some places than others. Because locations of raw materials, productive facilities, and people often fail to coincide, it frequently happens that supply and demand are spatially separated. Matching the two thus requires the transporting of goods and people.

NETWORK ANALYSIS

A transport network consists of a given set of specific locations linked together by a number of routes to form an interconnected system (Kansky, 1963). The components of this system are thus a series of points (representing origins, destinations, and intersections) and lines (the routes). The network concept might be extended also to encompass the areas served by means of these linkages. All components of a network have definite locational relationships with each other, and it is with these that we are chiefly concerned here.

Simple as this arrangement appears, it may be asked why we wish to analyze transport networks. First of all, the simplicity is deceptive; internal relationships of a network can be quite complex. Second, the character of a network tends to determine the kind of impact it will have upon the economies of the localities it serves. The study of networks helps to explain which regions trade with each other and what goods they exchange, where urban populations receive their agricultural produce, where entrepreneurs are most likely to locate their manufacturing and service establishments, and a number of other important locational questions.

The nature of transport networks has immediate, practical implications for public policy. Careful planning is particularly essential in designing transport systems for newly developing areas, since transportation is a necessary accompaniment of development. A knowledge of network characteristics is important also for designing modifications and additions to existing systems in anticipation of new demands. The ample benefits of network analysis have been demonstrated by numerous studies, some of which will be cited in the next pages.

From this it should be apparent that we shall be reviewing network analysis from two standpoints, one a short-run view and the other a long-run view. This section is to treat short-run considerations, that is, the nature and development of transport networks as such. The long-run aspects, reserved for the following section, are concerned with the effects of transport networks in shaping the location and character of other activities. In the next few pages we are to view two short-run aspects: (1) the structure of networks, in both their present and predicted forms, and (2) the flow through networks, today and in the future.

NETWORK STRUCTURE

The *structure* of a transport network refers to the spatial arrangement of the parts of the system and the relationship between them. It takes a geometric view of such a system. Currently the study of network structure relies mainly on the theory of graphs, a valuable conceptual tool for describing networks and for comparing one network with another. Graph theory is used increasingly also for generating theoretical networks or duplicating the generation of existing networks in order to gain a better understanding of the processes by which transport systems evolve. This in turn is useful for forecasting transport development and thus offers important aid to the regional planner.

Transport networks and graph theory The mathematical theory of graphs is the foundation of graph theory as applied to transportation geography. By means of graph theory a network structure can be viewed abstractly; this makes it possible to measure and analyze systems objectively. This is done by breaking networks down into their basic elements, whose interrelationships can be more easily

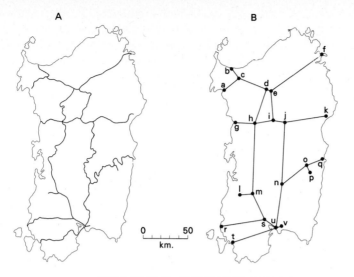

THE RAILROAD NETWORK OF SARDINIA

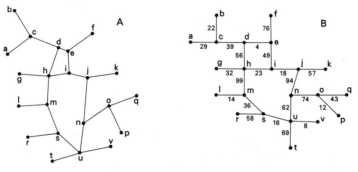

GRAPHIC SIMPLIFICATION OF THE RAILROAD
NETWORK OF SARDINIA

FIGURE 8-1 SARDINIA: RAILROAD NETWORK AND GRAPHIC SIMPLIFICATION. (KAREL J. KANSKY, 1963. *STRUCTURE OF TRANSPORTATION NETWORKS: RELATIONSHIPS BETWEEN NETWORK GEOMETRY AND REGIONAL CHARACTERISTICS,* RESEARCH PAPER 84, DEPARTMENT OF GEOGRAPHY. CHICAGO: UNIVERSITY OF CHICAGO PRESS. FIGS. 1 AND 2, P. 8.)

distinguished. An example of how the graph-theoretical approach works can be seen in Figure 8-1. Part *a* of this figure is a map of the railway system on the island of Sardinia, and part *b* represents a simplification of the network for graph-theoretical analysis. In this schematic view, the system is conceived as a series of points, consisting of major settlements (origins and termini) or route intersections, together with the lines, or rail links, connecting these points.

Although graph theory has only recently been adopted by geographers, it has been much used elsewhere for studying the essential characteristics of electric circuits, linguistic structures, nervous systems of human beings and animals, and social structure and social interaction. Indeed, one of the major advantages of viewing transport systems as graphs is that this makes possible direct comparisons with other kinds of systems, such as electrical or nervous systems, and expressing these relationships in common mathematical terms.

Properties of networks The degree to which a node is accessible to the rest of a transport system is a network property that has interested geographers much, since it is a useful indicator of the locational advantage of a center or junction point. This is a very practical problem for development planners concerned with the effects of their decisions upon various localities for which new transport arrangements are being designed. One rudimentary measure of accessibility is the *associated number*, which simply designates the maximum number of links required to reach all other nodes from that place.

The spacing of routes within a network is likewise of interest. Route spacing serves as an indicator of average distance between routes, and it also has some implications of directionality. Three typical spacing patterns are shown: (1) divergent (the common gridiron pattern), (2) random (routes going every which direction), and (3) convergent (tending to meet at some point). The spacing of routes in southwestern England has been analyzed and found to be largely random (Haggett and Chorley, 1969, p. 104). This is hardly unexpected for an area that has been continuously settled for a very long time and whose routes grew up early in largely unplanned fashion.

The concept of network *density* is also extremely important. By density is meant simply the total number of route miles (or kilometers) per unit of area. It is a very useful measure and is frequently applied at all levels of observation from local to world scales. Network density has proved to be highly correlated with other characteristics of areas, especially population density (Taaffe et al., 1963). As might be expected, therefore, the highest route densities of all occur in large cities, and especially in the most heavily populated sections. Network densities are also closely related to physical environmental conditions, which represented the traditional explanatory variable in early works on transportation geography. Route densities appear also to be a function of level of economic development, an aspect to be explored later in this chapter.

Forecasting network structure The regional planner who is preparing for a period of rapid economic growth must give special attention to the transport needs of his area. This can be difficult, since the future location and size of population centers are frequently not known. There may also be an imperfect knowledge of the distribution of resources and a severe shortage of capital for investment in the region, especially in those poorer lands where such planning is crucial. With such constraints as these, traditional engineering methods of transport planning can be too cumbersome, slow, and costly. Moreover, partly because of their costliness, they cannot be used to consider all possible alternatives, to anticipate the range of eventualities.

Network forecasting routines offer an attractive solution to this problem. They can be used to predict a number of possible future transport networks based on different sets of assumptions as to future population distributions and allocations of resources (Morrill, 1965). These routines take into account the previous experience of other areas in similar circumstances and also recognize explicitly the role of chance in the selection of routes. Chance may indeed be an important consideration, since fortuitous events tend to introduce an element of irrationality. Out of the range of alternative solutions supplied by such forecasting routines, it should be possible to select, at least for initial planning purposes, that prediction which seems most likely.

FLOWS THROUGH NETWORKS

Up to this point we have been concerned with networks as spatial patterns composed of nodes and the links that join them. Now we shall consider the flows through those networks—in other words, the movements of commodities or passengers within transport systems. As an aspect of network theory, this type of analysis owes much to the work of engineers dealing with flows through electrical systems. Flows are to be viewed here as a form of spatial interaction, since each individual flow moves between some origin and a destination within the network. The volume and character of flows thus reflect relationships between different regions—between those areas generating traffic and those receiving it.

As suggested earlier, the flow of commodities is equivalent to trade, a large and complex subject in its own right and one that we have saved for Chapter 9. Nevertheless, certain features of these flows relate specifically to network analysis, and it is these that we shall consider briefly here. First there is to be a discussion of various approaches to analyzing flows between regions, especially the gravity concept and programming techniques. Next to be considered will be constraints in transport systems, those features tending to reduce the capacity of systems to handle flows. Finally there will be a section on forecasting flows through networks.

Gravity concept One of the earlier approaches to explaining flows between regions was proposed by Ullman, who suggested that they be regarded as a form of spatial interaction (Ullman, 1957, pp. 20–27). Underlying this is the notion of *complementarity*. Complementarity refers to the differences in regions that give rise to an exchange of goods or travelers between them. Because of these differences, one region is able to provide a supply that satisfies a demand in the other region. Such complementarities may be due to differences in resource endowments of the two regions—either variations in physical resources or different resources of labor and capital. Indeed, complementarities often arise between regions that are basically very similar in resources but have acquired special advantages in particular lines because of economies of large-scale production in those specialties.

Another fundamental consideration is *distance*, which is of particular interest to economic geographers. In order to overcome the barrier of distance separating two regions, it is necessary to make expenditures of time and money for transportation. If these outlays are excessive, trade cannot take place. Distance is not a simple measure; it may be expressed not only in terms of time and cost but also in such forms as social distance. Because of this ambiguity in meaning, Ullman has suggested that instead of using the term *distance* we should substitute the expression *transferability*. By this he meant distance as measured in real terms: time, money costs, human effort, or whatever else best reflects the true impact of overcoming the separations between places (Ullman, 1957, p. 23).

Ullman has suggested also that the flows between two regions can be adversely affected if another source of supply happens to be closer to market than the first, therefore constituting an intervening opportunity (Ullman, 1957, p. 22). In other words, there is a tendency to procure one's needs from the nearest source of supply, a basic notion of central place theory.

The mathematical device most frequently used for empirically examining flows is the *gravity model*. This method of estimating flows among regions has been much favored by planners concerned with transport movements. The model is given by the following expression:

$$I_{ij} = k \frac{P_i P_j}{d^b}$$

where I_{ij} = amount of interaction
P_i = the size of the first center
P_j = the size of the second center
k = a constant representing the proportion of the population participating in that specific activity
d = the distance separating the two centers
b = some empirically derived exponent of distance

In words, this expression states that the interaction between two places is directly proportional to their size and inversely proportional to the distance that separates them.

Since first acceptance of the gravity model, a great many examples have accumulated to demonstrate its applicability to the analysis of flows. These include studies of migration, commuting, consumer shopping behavior, telephone calls, and commodity movements. An example of the use of a simple form of the gravity model for analyzing freight shipments is given in Figure 8-2, taken from the classic study by Zipf (1949). The diagram shows the total volume of goods moving by railway express between thirteen pairs of cities in the United States. In this case the vertical or Y axis represents weight of shipments and the X axis gives the gravity model formulation. A clearly inverse relationship between distance and interaction is indicated.

The example indicates a common situation: although the amount of interaction declines with distance, the rate of decline diminishes away from the central point of focus. In other words, the curve of distance decay becomes less steep at greater distances. This suggests that the true exponent of distance (b in the gravity model) is greater than 1 in each of these instances. There has been considerable

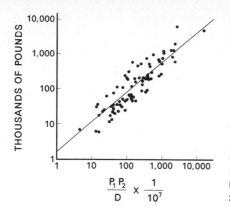

FIGURE 8-2 THE RELATIONSHIP BETWEEN THE AC-
TUAL MOVEMENT OF GOODS AND THE THEORETICAL-
LY EXPECTED VOLUME AS DERIVED FROM A SIMPLE
GRAVITY MODEL. (GEORGE K. ZIPF. 1949. *HUMAN
BEHAVIOR AND THE PRINCIPLE OF LEAST EFFORT.*
READING, MASS.: ADDISON-WESLEY PRESS. FIG. 9-
20A, P. 402.)

study of the different values taken by this exponent in different cases. For example, the exponent has been found to vary with the type of traffic and mode of transportation. Thus a higher exponent was found for travel by car than by air (Iklé, 1954). Membership in a particular social or economic class also appears to affect this exponent. This has been demonstrated by one study in which higher-income persons were found to be willing to travel longer distances (and, hence, to produce a gravity model relationship with a lower exponent of distance) than those with lower incomes (Olsson, 1965, p. 60). Differences in education and occupation produced similar results in another case (Huff, 1960). Technological advancement also appears to affect the rate of distance decay. This would seem to account at least in part for the tendency for the exponent of distance for airline travel in the United States to fall with the passage of time (Taaffe, 1962).

Distance-minimization concept A conceptually simple but particularly effective method for solving problems relating to flows through networks is linear programming. It is useful especially for determining the most effective assignment of flows from their origins to their destinations. Programming is applied to a wide range of problems where an optimal solution is needed, since it is an ideal way for discovering inefficiencies in any system. The term *programming* refers to the fact that the method entails solving a set of linear equations by following a predetermined "program."

In general, the technique is applied where something is to be maximized or minimized, subject to a given set of limitations or constraints. This makes it especially appropriate for solving what is often called "the transportation problem." In this problem the supply of a given commodity is known at a number of specified sources; also known are the demand at a particular set of destinations, the available transport routes, and a set of specified transport costs. The objective is to determine the minimum-cost assignment of transport flows from origins to destinations. It is usually subject to these constraints: total demand equals total supply, all individual surpluses are transported from their origins, all individual demands are satisfied, and all flows are positive (Garrison, 1959, pp. 471–476).

In a very practical application to a transportation problem, programming was used for assigning pupils to high schools in Grant County, Wisconsin (Yeates, 1963). The purpose of the study was to allocate students in such a way as to minimize the cost of providing bus transportation to and from their homes. This, in effect, established the optimal boundaries of each school district. Figure 8-3a shows the residential locations of the 2,925 students, and Figure 8-3b gives the locations of the thirteen high schools, together with the existing school district boundaries. Because the procedure used in this study required allocating pupils by square-mile sections, it was necessary to make an initial adjustment of these boundaries so as to conform with the sectional boundaries (Figure 8-3c). Transport cost was assumed to be proportional to distance, and the distance of each square-mile section from a school was measured by line of sight (desire line) rather than by the existing road network. Although this introduced some small distortion, its effects were of minor importance in view of the regularity of the typical Midwestern rural road pattern.

The pupils were then reassigned to the various high schools in such a way that total transport cost was reduced to a minimum. Figure 8-3d gives the results, including the revised school district boundaries that would be produced. Figure 8-3e compares this new set of boundaries with the old (adjusted) ones. A detailed survey of two of these districts indicated that this new arrangement would apparently reduce the average distance each pupil was transported by 0.3 to 0.4 mile. It was calculated that this would save the county school system several thousands of dollars in transport costs each year.

Forecasting flows Much of what has been said up to this point concerning the analysis of flows through networks suggests ways of predicting future flows, both their volume and spatial patterns. Such predictions require making a number of assumptions regarding future supplies and demands. Thus it is necessary to estimate the growth rates of residential communities, areas containing resources likely to be developed, industrial districts, and other important trip-generating areas.

There are several problems in anticipating future supplies and demands. Special difficulties are posed by short-term variations in traffic volume, which tend to be cyclical in nature, although long-run changes or secular trends can also be troublesome. One of the most vexing problems of transportation planning is the periodicity of flows. In order to cope with high traffic volumes at certain times, it is often necessary to invest heavily in expensive equipment and facilities that are used little at other times. Such variations in traffic may take place within twenty-four-hour periods or seven-day periods, or they may occur seasonally. This differs with the location of the route and the predominant purpose of the trips, whether

---

FIGURE 8-3 THE OPTIMAL ASSIGNMENT OF STUDENTS TO HIGH SCHOOLS: (A) RESIDENTIAL LOCATION OF STUDENTS: (B) ACTUAL HIGH SCHOOL BOUNDARIES; (C) FORMALIZED BOUNDARIES; (D) OPTIMAL BOUNDARIES; (E) COMPARISON OF THE FORMALIZED-ACTUAL AND OPTIMAL BOUNDARY PATTERNS. (M. H. YEATES. 1963. "HINTERLAND DELIMITATION: A DISTANCE-MINIMIZING APPROACH," *THE PROFESSIONAL GEOGRAPHER*, **15**:7–10.)

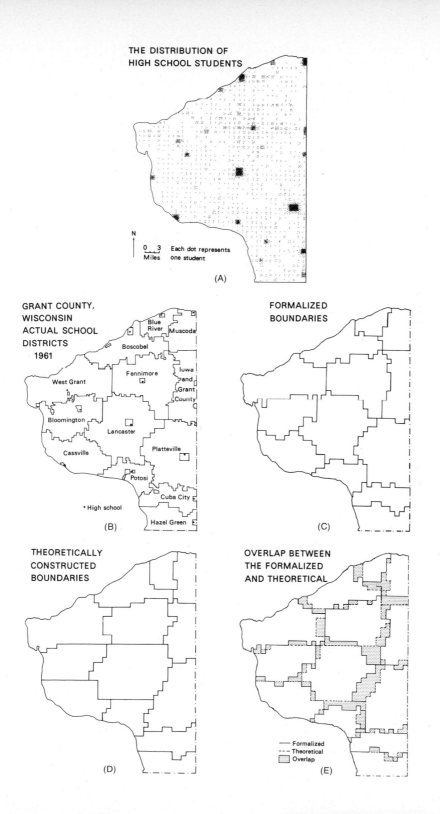

THE DISTRIBUTION OF
HIGH SCHOOL STUDENTS

N

0   3   Each dot represents
Miles   one student

(A)

GRANT COUNTY,
WISCONSIN
ACTUAL SCHOOL
DISTRICTS
1961

Blue
River   Muscoda

Boscobel

Fennimore

Iowa
and
Grant
County

West Grant

Bloomington

Lancaster

Cassville

Platteville

Potosi

• High school

Cuba City

Hazel Green

(B)

FORMALIZED
BOUNDARIES

(C)

THEORETICALLY
CONSTRUCTED
BOUNDARIES

(D)

OVERLAP BETWEEN
THE FORMALIZED
AND THEORETICAL

—— Formalized
---- Theoretical
▨ Overlap

(E)

commercial, commuting, recreational, or shopping. In certain fortunate instances there is a complementarity of timing between the different kinds of trips.

The most extreme variations of all take place from one part of the day to another. This is especially true in large metropolitan areas, where passenger traffic has a great deal of peakedness. Exceedingly heavy flows occur at the start and close of each workday, the evening rush hour being the worst time of all. Contrasting with these are the low periods of midmorning and midafternoon and the sharp falling off that takes place in the evening and into the small hours of the morning. The peakedness problem is a serious one for urban highway designers and traffic controllers, but it is even worse for the mass-transit agencies— commuter rail lines and bus companies. For these it imposes heavy cost burdens in the form of salaries for inefficiently used operating personnel and capital tied up in underused equipment and right-of-way. These difficulties lie at the root of many of the financial crises of urban mass-transit companies today.

There is usually a variation in traffic flows from one day to the next, also. Total traffic tends to be somewhat lighter during the first part of the week and to grow progressively heavier toward the end. For the most part, this reflects the shopping and recreational travel habits of the population and their influence on passenger movements. This weekly variation would be greater than it is if it were not for the offsetting effects of commercial vehicular traffic, both truck and rail, which is more evenly spaced. There are likewise seasonal fluctuations in passenger traffic. From a low period in midwinter, there is a gradual rise toward the latter part of the summer, with especially high peaks on holiday weekends such as the Fourth of July or Labor Day in the United States, or bank holidays in Britain. These variations may, of course, be attributed to the seasonality of recreational travel.

Over the long term there has been a steady upward trend for total traffic flows nearly everywhere in the technically advanced lands, but this differs among the various modes of transportation. The sharpest and most persistent rise in volume has been that of motor vehicle movements, especially cars and trucks. A counter-trend has been the deterioration of bus traffic in small and medium-size cities. There has also been a remarkably sharp upward trend in air movements, especially passenger traffic, although recently this industry has proved peculiarly susceptible to fluctuations in the business cycle. Although railway freight traffic has managed to maintain a modest growth despite serious competition from other transport modes, particularly motortrucks, passenger traffic has declined disastrously in the United States. Rail passenger flows in Canada and parts of Western Europe have been less affected, however; and railways are heavily used in parts of the Orient, especially Japan and India.

With data estimates of this type, transport planners have developed several techniques for predicting future flows. These rely mainly on the kinds of analytical methods described earlier, since ordinarily a technique that contributes to an understanding of the character and operation of networks also provides a ready means for forecasting. Thus two of the most used tools are the gravity model and programming, usually within a graph-theoretical framework. Network analysis and forecasting provide bases for understanding the impact of transportation on the location of economic activities, the relationship of transportation to regional development, and the evolution of present and future transport systems. These are the subjects to which we turn next.

LOCATIONAL EFFECTS OF TRANSPORT RATE STRUCTURES

From our discussion thus far it might be inferred that transport charges paid by the user—the shipper or the passenger—are directly proportional to the distance traveled. This is not necessarily the case; rate structures depart from the expected pattern in many ways that can influence location importantly.

The rates that users of transport services must pay reflect basically the costs incurred by carriers—the railway, truck, bus, canal, steamship, or airline companies—but the correlation is very imperfect. Moreover, the costs of carriers may themselves vary spatially in a complex manner. Let us examine the nature of transport cost structures and rate-setting practices and note the spatial irregularities these produce in the rate system and their effects on the location of economic activities.

PRICE DISCRIMINATION

Aside from the basic costs incurred by a carrier, a number of factors affect the amount such a firm can assess a customer for the use of its services. Chief among these are the nature of the demand for transportation, the kind of competition that is offered, and public transport policy (Daggett, 1955, pp. 299–300).

The demand for transportation services stems from the user's expectation that by moving his product from one location to another he will get a higher price for it. There is some evidence that the intensity of demand is greater for high-value products, perhaps reflecting the greater gain from transporting these as compared with low-value commodities. It has also been shown that the price elasticity of demand for transportation is determined by the price elasticity of demand for the product in question. In other words, if a rise in the price of the good sharply reduces the demand for it in a particular market, the shipper of that item will strongly resist any move on the part of the carrier to raise transport rates to that market. The demand for passenger transportation is somewhat similar to that for freight traffic, except that personal travel decisions are not always made on rational grounds; the desire to go to a particular place may be so strong that a rate increase is more readily accepted.

Where there is competition among carriers for the freight or passenger traffic of an area, the anticipated effect is to reduce the margin of profit received by transport companies from service extended to that district. Competition tends to force each carrier to adjust his rates more closely to his actual costs; indeed, to a limited extent rates may actually drop below costs in the battle for increased business. The intent is to recoup this reduced revenue in one locality with the higher margins obtainable in other areas where competition is lacking and a greater spread can be maintained between carrier costs and rates charged

shippers. Competition assumes different forms. There may be competition between carriers of the same type, as in the case of two railways with parallel tracks
between a given set of origins and destinations, such as Chicago and New York.
Parallel service is also common in the steamship trade and in air traffic service. In
modern times there has been increasingly intense competition among unlike
modes of transportation. A shipper in Chicago may have the choice of sending his
goods to New Orleans by barge, rail, or truck—or, if the goods are not too bulky, by
air.

The implicit assumption to this point has been that carriers are free to set their
own rates, to the extent that customers are willing to pay them and to the extent
that the rates will not be undercut by competitors. Today, however, carriers are
losing this independence increasingly, as governments become more involved in
the transportation business. One of the mildest forms of such intervention is
governmental regulation of carrier practices, including rate setting. In the United
States the federal government operates through a number of agencies, including
the Interstate Commerce Commission; and state governments and even some local
ones have likewise maintained licensing and regulatory bodies. This form of public
involvement stems from the view that government must act as arbiter among
competing carriers. It is further argued that government must fulfill its role as
guardian of the public welfare, ensuring fair treatment of travelers and shippers
and preventing discrimination against certain regions. Public revenue also depends heavily upon fees and taxes obtained in this manner.

LENGTH OF HAUL AND LOCATION

More directly related to problems of location is the tendency of carrier costs to fall
as *length of haul* increases. This effect results from the interrelationships between
two distinct types of costs, namely, *terminal costs* and *line-haul costs*. Every
shipment, regardless of the distance that it is moved, incurs a set of largely fixed
terminal costs that go to pay for such things as loading and unloading, weighing,
clerical work (preparing bills of lading and invoicing customers, for example),
switching, and car detention at each end of its journey. Line-haul costs, which
include outlays for fuel, equipment wear and maintenance, and crew costs, tend to
increase with distance.

Each type of transport mode tends to have its own cost structure. Terminal
costs and fixed costs are typically highest for water movements, as a result of the
expensive port facilities and equipment required; but the variable and line-haul
costs are usually lower than those of other forms of transport, partly because of the
minimal friction encountered from the water itself and also because little or no
right-of-way maintenance costs are involved. By contrast, terminal costs and fixed
costs are least for motortrucks, although their line-haul costs are highest. Railway
costs ordinarily fall somewhere between these two extremes with regard to both
types of costs. The net effect is suggested in Figure 8-4. Where all three modes of
transport are available to shippers, as in the routes lying between Chicago and New
Orleans, the shipper's decision in each case is influenced by the length of journey.
Figure 8-4 shows that for any trip within the interval from *O* to *A* (Chicago to Cairo,

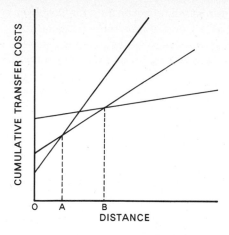

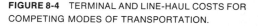

FIGURE 8-4 TERMINAL AND LINE-HAUL COSTS FOR COMPETING MODES OF TRANSPORTATION.

Illinois, perhaps), truck transport is cheapest. For trips of intermediate length terminating somewhere between *A* and *B* (Memphis, Tennessee, for example), railway would be least costly. Beyond *B* the longer journeys would be made most cheaply by water (such as barge to New Orleans).

So far, our discussion has assumed implicitly that line-haul costs rise at a constant rate from the origin. Except for the most primitive means of transport this is not usually the case. Ordinarily the cost per mile is greatest during the first few miles of the journey, after which unit distance costs gradually drop off. This results from the more efficient use of equipment, fuel, operating employees, and other economies associated with longer hauls.

This long-haul advantage frequently has important effects on the location of production. This is shown by Figure 8-5, in which curve *X* represents transport costs for procuring a raw material from its source at *A*, and curve *Y* gives costs for distributing the product to the market *B*. The problem is to find a place for production where the total outlay for transport costs will be minimized. This total for all possible sites between *A* and *B* is shown by the upper curve (*X* + *Y*), which

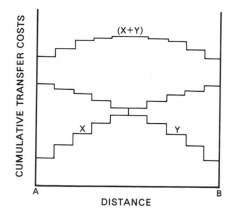

FIGURE 8-5 LOCATIONAL EFFECTS OF THE LONG-HAUL ADVANTAGE.

represents the sum of curves *X* and *Y*. Inspection of the total transport curve shows that the minimum-transport-cost sites are at either end of the journey, the source of the raw material at *A*, or the market for the product at *B*, rather than any place in between A and B. Thus the long-haul advantage favors production at terminal points.

Other features of the rate structure likewise affect location. One of these occurs at any point where a cargo must, for one reason or another, be transferred from one transport mode to another. This *break-of-bulk* problem is illustrated in Figure 8-6, which presents the hypothetical case of a demand for commercial fertilizer in the farming area of southeastern Pennsylvania. The basic fertilizer raw material, phosphate rock mined in Florida, is shipped by water from the port of Tampa, this being the cheapest means of transporting such a low-value, high-bulk commodity. Upon reaching Baltimore, the material is transferred to railway cars for the remaining, inland portion of the journey.

The problem is this: Where should the phosphate rock be converted into a refined form suitable for agricultural use? As suggested above, the long-haul feature of the rate structure would dictate manufacture in either Florida or Pennsylvania. In this case, however, there are two differences. First, there is the necessity for adding other ingredients in preparing the commercial product, especially sulfuric acid, which is obtained from production points in the Northeast. This favors fertilizer manufacture at the marketward end of the journey. Second, there is the additional set of terminal charges incurred when the phosphate is off-loaded at Baltimore, and further shipment by a more expensive mode. Thus, as shown by the solid line in the figure, transport costs rise sharply at Baltimore and continue to go up steeply until the final destination at Lancaster, Pennsylvania, is reached. The ultimate solution is to process the phosphate rock at the port of Baltimore, thus reducing the bulk of this raw material and making the saving in subsequent transport costs shown by the dashed line in the figure.

In other cases, this argument favors processing at some break-of-bulk point closer to the point of origin. For example, the lean Minnesota taconite ores move by rail or truck to loading ports on Lake Superior, where they are processed into

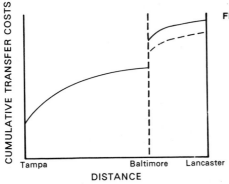

FIGURE 8-6   BREAK-OF-BULK POINTS.

high-grade iron pellets for further shipment in this more concentrated form by lake steamer to steel mills in the lower lakes region.

WORLD SYSTEMS OF TRANSPORTATION

In the preceding pages we have attempted to isolate those essential properties of transport networks that would permit us to forecast their growth and development, and we have looked for relationships between certain general characteristics of transport systems and the location of production. Now let us see how these elements are expressed in the world patterns of transportation. Although we shall be examining each type of transportation individually, it is essential to remember the additivity of transport modes. No single mode is wholly self-contained, especially in less developed areas. Again we shall summarize the essential characteristics of each type of transportation and then observe how their world patterns reflect the influence of population distributions, the interaction between places of supply and demand, relative levels of development, and degree of accessibility.

WATER TRANSPORTATION

In many parts of the world, water transportation was the first form of long-range commercial haulage to appear. It will be remembered that this is a cheap means of moving goods and people, especially over longer distances, partly because of the minimal resistance to traction afforded by water at moderate speeds and partly because many natural waterways require little or no cost for initial right-of-way development. Yet water transport has a number of disadvantages that affect the location of routes and the volume and composition of traffic. First of all, it is slow, at least until radical new types of carriers such as hydrofoils become more feasible commercially. In many cases it is also circuitous. This is especially true of inland navigation, which depends a great deal upon the nature of the terrain and of drainage systems; but even ocean carriers are often forced to take the long way between origin and destination where such barriers as land masses or navigation hazards intervene. Moreover, there are problems of seasonality, including periods of violent storms or freezing conditions.

Ocean shipping   With nearly 70 percent of the earth's surface covered by water, and with thousands of miles of ocean separating major continents, the world's merchant fleets account for a major portion of the total ton-miles of cargo moved by all forms of transportation. Our concern at this point is with the configurations and densities of ocean routes and the nature and locations of nodes (the ports) within the system.

Steamer routes   Despite the vast amount of water available for navigation, most ocean traffic is confined to a limited number of clearly defined routes; meanwhile, major expanses of water go unused by shipping. The greatest route densities lie between the highly developed regions of the earth—Europe, Anglo-America, and Japan—and the next heaviest densities connect these economic centers with their suppliers and markets in peripheral areas. The lightest traffic is that between underdeveloped countries. Many carriers maintain round-the-world services which start perhaps at New York, collect and distribute cargo at each of the Atlantic east coast ports of the United States, then cross the ocean to call at various European ports and thence through the Mediterranean to the Orient before crossing the Pacific on the return journey to the United States via the west coast and the Panama Canal. Thus, the world network of steamer routes is highly focal in nature, with the principal lanes centering upon the economic heartland and connecting its component parts. This network is also a center-periphery pattern, having its greatest concentration at the center and diminishing toward its outer margins.

The leading group of steamer routes are those linking the east coast of the United States and Canada with the ports of Western Europe. Other routes converge upon Anglo-America from a variety of points in the Caribbean, from the west and east coasts of South America, and from Oceania and the Orient. Reaching out from Europe are a great many steamer lanes leading to countries in the Southern and Eastern Hemispheres. When political conditions in the Middle East permit, one cluster of routes passes through the Mediterranean and Red Seas to ports along the coasts of Africa, south and east Asia, and Oceania. Others lead directly southward along the west coast of Africa and thence to the Orient. Europe also has regular ocean links to the Caribbean and to both coasts of South America.

World ports Just as the links in the world system of ocean shipping disclose a great deal of information about the nature of the pattern, so do the nodes in that system. These are the seaports, those places which supply facilities such as docks and quays for transferring cargo and passengers between water and land. Most seaports are situated in locations providing natural harbors, that is, protected deepwater anchorages for ships; but if there is sufficient traffic to warrant it, ports may be sited along coasts lacking such natural qualifications. In that case, breakwaters, dredging, and other necessary capital improvements may be supplied to remedy nature's neglect, as in the case of Los Angeles.

It is significant that the four largest ports in the world—Antwerp, London, New York, and Rotterdam—are located at either end of the North Atlantic routes. Many of the other larger ports are also situated along these same coasts: Liverpool, Hamburg, Marseilles, Le Havre, Philadelphia, Baltimore, and New Orleans, for example. In other parts of the world, many important ports are found where principal routes meet. Thus in the Orient, major steamer lanes converge upon Singapore and Hong Kong, both of which serve vital transshipment functions for their own regions.

Most ports have a reciprocal relationship with their hinterlands, that is, the territories from which they draw their exports and to which they provide imports. If several ports happen to be situated along the same coast, they may compete keenly with each other for a share of this business. This is true especially of New York, Boston, Philadelphia, Baltimore, Newport News, and New Orleans, all of which vie for the export and import trade of the American Midwest. As foci of trade, ports usually have additional commercial functions relating to the buying and selling of goods and the provision of a wide range of services to the international trading community, such as banking, insurance, customs house brokerage, and the like. As break-of-bulk points, ports likewise are much favored as sites for those types of manufacturing that engage in the refining and processing of imported bulky raw materials and the production for export of goods made from domestic materials.

Inland waterways Waterways used for domestic transportation take several forms. Some have been conveniently provided by nature, such as lakes, large rivers, and coastal waterways; others are largely man-made, such as canals and docking basins. Despite the advantages of water transport in general, as a cheap means of moving certain kinds of cargo, inland waterways have several disadvantages, particularly rivers and canals. Some of these difficulties have to do with the nature of the right-of-way. The barrier effects of certain terrain features and problems of water supply may severely reduce the choice of route location, and limitations on channel draft and width may restrict the capacity of vessels. Some rivers suffer from strong currents and navigation hazards, problems common even to such heavily used streams as the Rhine. Permanent solutions to these problems ordinarily require large capital outlays for engineering and construction.

Industrial heartland In some of the more industrialized areas of Western Europe and North America, water transport has reached a comparatively high level of refinement. Much engineering has been devoted to improving navigation on natural waterways and to building almost wholly synthetic canal systems. Many of the most modern river navigation projects have been conceived as only part of multipurpose development schemes. The Tennessee Valley Authority, for example, is responsible for power production, flood control, general regional development, and a number of other objectives quite apart from navigation. Inland waterways of most developed lands have been adversely affected by competition from other transport modes, and they have experienced an absolute decline in some places and stagnation in others. Throughout Europe and North America this competition has forced carriers to specialize. Whereas the early canals once carried nearly everything that moved, including package freight and even passengers, they have lost all but the bulky, low-value commodities, first to the railways and then to highway transport.

As measured by tonnage, the largest single component in the waterway network of Canada and the United States is the Great Lakes–St. Lawrence Seaway system, which provides low-cost transportation for the raw materials of the iron and steel mills sited along both sides of the lower lakes. Ores converge upon this great metallurgical region from both directions, coming from the Lake Superior deposits of Minnesota, Michigan, and western Ontario and from the Quebec-Labrador fields served by the lower St. Lawrence ports. This routeway is especially important for the eastward flow of grains from the Canadian prairies and from the Midwestern and Plains states of the United States. The importance of this system to

Canada is apparent from the concentration of economic activities extending along the northern shores of the lower lakes and downstream on the St. Lawrence.

Peripheral regions Outside the world heartland, most waterways are of the unimproved types. Among these are numerous large lakes, such as Victoria in East Africa, Titicaca in the South American Andes, and major rivers, such as the Yangtze (China), Mekong (Indochina), Amazon (Brazil and Peru), Magdalena (Colombia), and the Niger, Congo, and Nile Rivers of Africa. Despite their undeveloped nature, these routes are exceedingly important to the areas served, since they are often the main, or even the only, avenues of commerce. Existing roads and railways are often merely ancillary to these waterways. Man-made waterways are prominent in certain less developed regions, however, especially irrigation canals, which frequently perform a vital transport function. By contrast with the waterways of modern technically advanced areas, these routes carry all types of merchandise, including package freight and passengers. Water-borne commerce of less developed areas differs from that of North America and Europe also in its predominantly short hauls.

LAND TRANSPORTATION

In technically advanced countries, rail, highway, and transmission systems are not only highly developed but also highly competitive. This competition has reduced the relative importance of railways in many areas, and in some of it has brought an absolute decline, especially in passenger traffic. Highway transport has reaped much of this gain, but pipelines have captured some of it also, as have power transmission systems in an indirect way. Considering the close association between intensity of economic activity and the nature of transport networks, it is to be expected that the highest development of land transportation will have taken place in areas of technical advancement.

Railways In the struggle for business, railways have one important advantage: because of their more economical use of fuel and manpower they are more efficient than highway transport for moving large volumes over long distances. The competitive disadvantages of rail transportation are many, however. Although not so restricted by physical barriers as inland waterways, railways nevertheless incur high construction, maintenance, and operating costs in areas of difficult terrain. The Colorado Rockies, for example, have been penetrated only by Denver and Rio Grande Western, and this by means of expensive tunneling and long detours. Even in flat terrain, railways are at a disadvantage because of their lack of route flexibility. Unlike trucks, they are confined to a fixed network that requires much capital to build and is difficult to change. Fixed costs are high, as are maintenance costs, the latter alone representing two-fifths of total expenditures.

The world railway pattern discloses high densities and connectivity in the industrial heartland of northwestern Europe, northeastern North America, and Japan. The pattern is contrastingly sparse in peripheral areas, and many parts of Asia, Africa, and South America are nearly devoid of rails. There are important exceptions, however, to both of these generalizations, since areas of poor railway development exist within the heartland and enclaves of fairly high rail density are found in certain outlying areas. Many otherwise underdeveloped countries have districts engaged in highly commercial exploitation of local primary commodities, and some former colonial countries have inherited good railway systems. Furthermore, in several places remote from the original European heartland there are pockets of technical advancement, such as Australia, Argentina, Chile, and South Africa, that have extensive railway mileage.

Industrial heartland Even within some of the most highly developed countries there are regional differences in density, some areas generating much traffic and others very little. It should also be noted that railways tend to focus upon certain population and industrial centers that have a high degree of accessibility and to avoid areas that generate little traffic or act as barriers to movement. The railways of the United States and Canada are facing much competition from highway, air, and even water transportation, which are invading their traditional markets. Much of the short-haul business was lost to trucks some time ago, and the competition for long hauls is growing with the introduction of such innovations as the interstate highway system of the United States and Canada's Route 401 and Queen Elizabeth Way. Trucks have taken much of the perishable and package freight, leaving bulky, low-value commodities to the railways. Consequently, there has been an overall relative decline in rail freight volume and a considerable reduction in total revenues. Meanwhile, passenger traffic has been yielded to private automobiles, buses, and airlines. Several railway companies are being forced to merge, and little-used lines are being abandoned in both Canada and the United States.

Rail densities are highest in the North American manufacturing belt, which is shared by the two countries. Within this region, rail routes converge upon a number of important centers, notably Chicago, New York, Toronto, and Montreal. The United States and Canadian rail systems, as a whole, tend to focus upon this area, producing a decided east-west orientation of those routes linking the various parts of the manufacturing belt and connecting it with its hinterland in the western states and provinces. Railways in the southeastern United States, on the other hand, tend to have a north-south orientation, evidence of the strong ties between that region and the populous Northeast, to which it supplies both raw materials and manufactured goods.

Europe contains the densest railway trackage in the world (Ginsburg, 1961, pp. 60–69). The overall rail pattern suggests a concentric design, with the highest densities in the core area centering upon Belgium and Luxembourg and including West Germany and the United Kingdom. Track densities very nearly as high are found in adjacent Switzerland, France, the Netherlands, Italy, East Germany, Poland, Czechoslovakia, and Hungary. Peripheral European countries have railway densities decidedly lower than those at the core but nevertheless well above the world mean (Ginsburg, 1961). Some of these are highly developed countries, such as the Soviet Union and northern Scandinavia. Although railways are the most important form of transportation in the U.S.S.R., the territory of that country is vast and the population densities are much lower than those of Western Europe; moreover, the existing tracks are used with an uncommon intensity. The economies of Sweden, Norway, and Finland are concentrated in the southern portions of those countries, and with a few exceptions railways are absent from their arctic districts. However, many of the peripheral lands of southern Europe are largely rural and at much lower stages of development. The rail densities of Spain, Portugal, and Greece are thus distinctly lower than those in the heart of the continent. The lowest densities of all are in primitive Albania. Europe has a number of prominent rail hubs—London, Paris, and Moscow, for example—from each of which the routes radiate like spokes of a wheel.

Peripheral areas   It has been estimated that countries that occupy three-fourths of the earth's land area have railway densities below the world average (Ginsburg, 1961, p. 60). Most of these nations are remote from the industrial heartland, principally in Asia, Africa, and Latin America. The majority have low per capita incomes.

Yet within those regions are numerous exceptions, countries with high railway densities surrounded by others with poorly developed rail networks. This is true especially of Japan, a technically advanced land with an economy now third largest in the world. Like the Soviet Union, Japan has emphasized rail transportation and continues to use her dense railway network intensively and efficiently, not only for freight but also for passenger service. Other exceptions in Asia are less developed countries, former colonies whose railway systems were constructed by an imperial power for purposes of commercial exploitation. Britain, for example, provided the Indian subcontinent with an excellent rail network which has been inherited by India and Pakistan. Similar development occurred in the former British colonies of Ceylon (Sri Lanka) and Malaya, and also in Taiwan and Korea during their period of Japanese domination. As noted previously, the network of the Republic of South Africa stands out prominently in a continent that has few railways elsewhere. Latin America supplies a number of anomalies, mainly technically developed countries such as Uruguay, Argentina, and Chile. Mexico and some of the Central American republics are likewise above the world mean for railway density.

There are many internal variations in railway development within those countries on the periphery of the world heartland. This is especially true in Latin America, where the focality of rail systems is extreme. Routes usually converge upon the capital city and the main area of economic concentration, which are normally one and the same. With the exception of Mexico, whose capital and principal rail hub is in the midst of the central plateau, the most economically active areas of Latin American countries are decidedly eccentric in location, usually fronting on the sea. For example, the rail lines of Brazil focus upon the São Paulo region, and those of Uruguay and Argentina concentrate in the Rio de la Plata area.

Road systems   In the early years of motorized highway transportation, trucks were used for the short-haul traffic; and roads, such as they were, served local areas or acted as feeders to rail lines. Today, highway freight moves over the longer hauls too, especially where limited-access intercity routes are available. Likewise, in more prosperous societies a major share of the passenger traffic is carried by motorcars, true symbols of Rostow's age of high mass consumption. In many societies buses have an important place also.

In the world at large, road patterns resemble railways somewhat in their relative densities, but with important differences. Like railways, road networks are decidedly denser in the world heartland than elsewhere; and, indeed, only one-third of the countries have densities above the world mean (Ginsburg, 1961, p. 70). The poorest countries are at the bottom of the scale of road densities, with several notable exceptions. As in the case of the railways, certain former British and Japanese colonies in south and east Asia have much better road systems than their per capita incomes would suggest.

Among the differences between roads and railways in most poor areas is the additional emphasis now being given to road building in development schemes. Roads currently tend to be preferred to railways in such regions largely because of the smaller amounts of capital needed for their construction and the greater flexibility in routes that they permit. Another distinction between road and rail patterns is found in certain technically advanced lands that stress railways at the expense of road systems; in others the reverse is true. Within countries, still other differences appear between one region and the next, especially in areas of difficult terrain, where motor vehicles are better able to negotiate steep grades than railway trains are. Finally, in many parts of the world road systems tend to have proportionately greater total mileage than other forms of transportation as a result of the finer mesh of the road network, especially if all classes of roads are included. At this point it should be cautioned that international figures on road densities are always suspect because of variations in quality. In many places the roads are mere tracks and hardly to be compared with multilane expressways.

Heartland   Several countries of Western Europe lead the world in road densities (Ginsburg, 1961, pp. 70–71). The Continent as a whole, including the U.S.S.R., produces a concentric road pattern that much resembles that of the railways, except, perhaps, that road densities in Scandinavia are relatively greater than those of railways. European countries have fewer motorcars per capita than the United States, and there is a greater reliance on buses instead. The road system of the Soviet Union is one of the most sparse in the world, despite the great size of the economy and a comparatively high per capita gross national product. This, of course, can be attributed to the long-time policy favoring railways rather than motor traffic in national planning. Until recently there were very few passenger cars; today this attitude is rapidly changing and such vehicles are at last being mass-produced in that country.

The United States is second to Europe in overall road density, even though per capita auto and truck registrations lead the world. Motor freight traffic has experienced a rapid growth in the United States, although it now appears stabilized at slightly more than one-fifth of the total ton-miles transported by all forms. By comparison, the railways still receive more than two-fifths of the total freight business, although this proportion is slowly decreasing. The fastest growth of all has been that of highway passenger traffic. Currently, private automobiles account for about seven-eighths of the total passenger traffic, although this figure is down from the peak year of 1961, owing to incursions by the airlines. In the United States buses now carry a mere 2 percent of the total.

The road pattern of the United States as a whole is similar to that of the railways, with the greatest densities in the most populous areas. The road system is less subject to restriction by barriers, however, and is represented better in some mountainous districts. Furthermore, the interstate highway system is somewhat more evenly distributed over the country than the railways or, for that matter, other classes of roads. There are, in fact, several layers of road systems in the United States which form a hierarchical structure. At the top is a relatively thin mesh of limited-access expressways, which resemble railways in many of their characteristics and also in their locational effects. These routes tend to emphasize linkages among major metropolitan centers. Below this is the system of federal and state intercity routes, a denser network which provides close ties between small places as well as large; and at the bottom are the innumerable county and other local roads and streets.

Canada ranks fairly low among countries in the density of her road system owing to the vast negative areas lacking traffic-generating possibilities (Ginsburg, 1961, p. 70). As in the United States, the road system is hierarchical and densities are greatest in the more heavily populated areas in the southernmost parts of the country, especially southern Ontario. Motor vehicle densities also resemble those of the United States.

Other areas In other regions of the world only Japan ranks as a leader in road densities. Several of the former British and Japanese colonies of the Far East also have denser networks than their neighbors, although the difference is less than in the case of railways. Australia, with its extensive desert barriers, is similar to Canada in its low ranking despite high road densities along its economically active eastern and southern margins. Most of Asia, Africa, and Latin America have poorly developed road systems. This is true even of some comparatively advanced Latin American countries, as, for example, Argentina and Mexico, both of which have emphasized rail transportation in the past. Nevertheless, there is much internal variation in most of these areas. Thus the central plateau region of Brazil has a large road network despite a dearth of such routes elsewhere in the country.

Transmission systems So new and unobtrusive that they are often overlooked in discussions of transportation are networks of a very different sort: pipelines and electric power distribution systems. These are much too important to neglect, however. As a result of exceedingly rapid growth since World War II, they have come to rank among the principal means of transportation in most developed areas and even in some less developed ones. The recency of their expansion is related to an accelerating demand for the products they carry and to modern advances in techniques of construction and transmission.

Both pipelines and power lines are highly specialized modes of transportation; normally they are designed for moving a single commodity, or at the least a limited number of related items. Their competitive strength, with respect to other media, reflects their favorable cost structures. Although they incur heavy initial capital outlays for construction, transmission systems require only small labor inputs once installed. Indeed, they are virtually automatic in operation.

There is a tendency for transmission systems to assume treelike forms, which particularly lend themselves to analysis by means of graph theory. Their spatial patterns are little affected by physical barriers, and they readily cross high mountains and go beneath lakes, rivers, and seas. Altogether they are among the most flexible of transport media.

Pipelines   Although a given system is usually designed for a particular type of commodity, pipelines are used for moving a wide range of liquids, gases, and even suspended solids such as coal. Pipelines are generally more economical than railways and trucks but more expensive than water transportation. With their great flexibility, pipelines can be built over the most direct routes, with little circuitry and with wide areal coverage.

Often there is much branching of pipeline networks at both ends of the journey. A gas pipeline system may tap various wells and even different gas fields and connect with many markets at the distribution end. Oil pipelines are customarily of two kinds, those which carry crude from the field or from a break-of-bulk point to the refinery and those which transport to market the various products such as gasoline, fuel oils, or chemical feedstocks. This form of transportation is little noticed in the areas through which it passes, since the pipes are usually below ground. Although pipelines are usually better represented in technically advanced lands, they are found also in less developed countries situated in areas of raw-material sources such as North Africa and the Middle East.

The most elaborate development of pipelines has taken place in the United States, where total mileage of all types is double that of railways. As carriers of cargo they are second only to the railways. Oil pipelines alone have overtaken motor trucks in ton-miles of intercity freight movements. It is difficult to find a comparable measure for natural gas moved by pipeline, but it should be noted that gas accounts for more than one-third of the energy consumption in the country.

The growing market for oil and gas in Anglo-America has been served by a rapidly spreading pipeline network incorporating important innovations in pipe design, pipeline construction, and pumping methods. Today the flow of liquids and gases is remotely controlled by means of electronically operated valves. This method of transportation has also benefited from its aptness for economies of scale. Some of the strongest incentives for long-range pipeline construction have come from government, however, particularly during the crash programs of pipeline construction of the World War II era, when enemy submarines were decimating the tanker fleet.

In Canada and the United States there is a convergence of oil pipelines upon the North American manufacturing belt. The prime energy markets are widely separated from major source areas in the western sections of both countries, and the pipelines must therefore cover great distances. Within the market area there is still another pipeline network which distributes petroleum products from the various refineries. The pipelines carrying natural gas have similar patterns.

In spite of promising new oil discoveries in the North Sea, the European countries must still import the greater part of their crude oil needs. Typically the refineries are located at coastal points for ease of receiving the raw material, and product pipelines connect these to markets in the continental interior. More recently a number of refineries have sprung up at large interior market areas such as the German Ruhr, and the crude oil is then piped in from the Mediterranean and Baltic coasts. The major market for oil in the U.S.S.R. is the Moscow region, which is linked by pipelines to the principal fields, particularly those in the Volga and Caspian areas. More recently, Soviet pipelines have been built to carry petroleum to eastern Europe and are being extended into central and southern Europe as well.

In other parts of the world, pipelines serve mainly to connect oil and gas fields of producing countries, such as those in North Africa and the Middle East, to coastal points for loading on board tankers.

Electric power   So closely related are electric power consumption and economic development that the former is frequently used as a measure of the latter. It is to be expected, therefore, that those countries in the industrial heartland will predominate in power use. Since there is as yet a definite limit to the range of power transmission, this means that power generation and the world network of power lines is likewise heavily concentrated in the most highly industrialized lands. For this same reason there is a close correspondence within countries between the location of markets for electricity and the patterns of power transmission systems.

More recently, however, a new technology has greatly extended the economically feasible transmission range from its former limit of 300 miles to several times that distance. Not only can electricity travel farther over the new high-voltage lines, but its distribution is further aided by the trend toward interconnected grid systems between different regions and even different countries. At last, therefore, it has become possible for a spatial separation of electric power production and consumption. Thus thermally generated electric power is increasingly being produced at the fuel source, such as coal, gas, and oil fields, and transmitted to markets in distant regions. For example, generators have been set up on the lignite fields of the rural Dakotas, and the power they produce is shipped to midwestern markets. This means, in essence, that interregional shipments of coal or lignite are being replaced by movements of electricity. There is the beginning of a trend, therefore, toward a closer approximation of electric power transmission systems to the kinds of spatial patterns we have noted in the case of pipelines, with long-range power links connecting the great metropolitan areas to source areas of fossil fuels.

AIR TRANSPORTATION

Commercial aviation has been with us since the mid-1920s; yet this dynamic industry has experienced its greatest growth in the period following the Second World War. The airlines of the United States, for example, have attained seven-eighths of their current total annual domestic revenue-miles since 1946, and they have added 97 percent of their present revenue-miles in international service during this same period. Indeed, nearly three-fifths of these totals was acquired during the 1960s alone. Air transport is peculiarly subject to rapid technological change, and it is especially advantageous for any airline to be the first to introduce a radically new plane. Those companies which led in offering jet service, for example, quickly reached 100 percent load factors at the expense of their competitors. Commercial aviation, for all its rapid growth, is now apparently reaching maturity. In many parts of the world it is already the principal means of commercial passenger transportation; and although commodity traffic has been slow to develop, even this is beginning to surge upward.

Political considerations, though prominent in most forms of transportation, are especially so in aviation. Air transport holds a special place in the political realm, partly because it has proved such a strong force for the unification of large territories. Civil aviation has also been an invariable handmaiden of military aviation in the larger countries. Even some of the smaller and more backward countries feel constrained to have their own national airlines, if only for prestige; and most countries, large and small, find their airlines an important stimulus to tourism. With this political interest in aviation, the industry has been able to depend upon governments to provide airport construction and maintenance, navigation and safety aids, patronage in the form of airmail contracts, and research and development, the last being a frequent spin-off of military aviation. Civil aviation has customarily been much subsidized. In the case of the United States this has mostly been of the indirect types cited above; but in much of the rest of the world, government participation takes the form of direct involvement and even outright ownership of airlines.

Several different types of service are provided by commercial carriers. There are scheduled airlines, which follow set route patterns and observe predetermined hours of arrival and departure, and nonscheduled airlines, which operate under various kinds of charter arrangements. A further distinction is made between domestic airlines and international airlines. There are also differences in the kinds of traffic carried, as between those flights transporting both passengers and freight and those moving cargo only. In fact, since it is vital to keep expensive craft in the air for as much of the time as possible, the same plane may often be used for passengers during the daylight hours and for all-cargo flights at night.

Commercial route patterns Commercial air transport has acquired a distinctive set of network characteristics. Being independent of the ordinary barriers to transportation, and therefore capable of direct movement between origin and destination, air networks tend to have a large degree of focality. Of the several network types that prevail, therefore, one of the most common is the radial or spoke pattern. This is much favored in Europe, where national airlines tend to center upon their own capital cities. The spoke design is characteristic also of regional airlines within the United States, although commercial air route patterns of this country commonly include three other types as well: circular, grid, and linear.

International airline routes strongly resemble the pattern of shipping routes. This is apparent, first of all, in the heavy route densities connecting the principal components of the world industrial heartland, especially those crossing the North Atlantic. Second, there is evidence of a high degree of focality of routes. Large numbers of these converge upon such important international centers as New York, London, Amsterdam, Paris, and Tokyo from outlying regions of the globe. Also similar to ocean patterns is the notable absence of air routes over the southern seas except in the vicinity of Australia and New Zealand. Surprising, too, are the concentrations of routes meeting at such sea-lane crossroads as the Middle East, Panama, and Singapore.

Domestic and intraregional air patterns also bear some similarities to those of other forms of transportation. Airline route densities are thus greater in developed than in less developed countries, and such densities are especially concentrated in those parts of the technically advanced lands that are most active economically and therefore have the greatest traffic-generating potential. Air routes, especially those of the regional airlines, focus in large numbers upon major centers such as New York, Chicago, Denver, Dallas–Fort Worth, Washington, Columbus, San Francisco, and Los Angeles. In another respect, however, patterns of airlines and of other forms of domestic travel tend to differ somewhat. Air service in underdeveloped countries is likely to be more advanced than highway or railway service. Many newly developing lands have stepped directly into the air age, since large sums of capital are not required for construction of rights-of-way for this form of transportation. Indeed, in some countries air transport provides the only links to their remoter sections.

TRANSPORTATION IN PERSPECTIVE

Transportation has been viewed by economic geographers from a number of vantage points, but today it is regarded increasingly as an integral part of the world spatial economic system. As we have seen here, transportation is the invariable companion of commercial production and of the distributive trades. It serves as a link between spatially separated supply and demand, and as such it is a fundamental type of spatial interaction. In the study of transportation as a system, one of the principal tools is network analysis, which relies upon the mathematical theory of graphs in determining the spatial properties of a pattern composed of nodes and links.

Since it has been shown that the characteristics of a given network are capable of exerting a strong influence on the location of economic activity, it is no surprise that network properties vary fairly consistently with level of development. Furthermore, the experience of several regions now regarded as technically advanced indicates that the various modes of transportation have tended to contribute to the development process in different ways.

Looking at particular networks at several levels of observation, we have seen that transport systems are highly focal in nature. The most accessible nodes, and those which accommodate the greatest amount of traffic, are situated in the most economically active parts of the world, particularly those regions we have designated as the industrial heartland. Upon these centrally located nodes, routes converge from the remoter areas with which spatial interaction takes place. Transport ties weaken with distance, however, as shown by the fairly systematic decline in route densities as one moves farther away from these central points of focus.

Viewed from the perspective of time, growth of the world economic system and its outward spread away from its places of origin have been accompanied and at times preceded by the growth and diffusion of transport networks. Expansion and development of the system have depended in large measure upon advances in transport technology—improvements in old modes and the introduction of new ones. With increasing maturity of the system a division of labor among the various forms of transportation has begun to appear as competition among them has tested their innate capabilities more and more severely.

The emphasis here has been upon transportation regarded as a physical means for conveying people and merchandise. The next chapter will examine another side of this problem, namely, the flows between regions, which we call trade. There we shall look at the factors that tend to generate this form of spatial interaction and to influence the volume, content, and direction of the resulting interregional and international flows.

INTERNATIONAL TRADE: THEORY AND PATTERNS

The flow of goods between countries reflects spatial variations in capabilities, goals, ideas, cultures, and levels of development. In view of the spatial character of commodity movements, the subject of trade is of particular interest to geographers. It forms an integral part of economic geography because of the way in which it is interwoven with other aspects of the study: production, consumption, transportation, and regional development. A country whose farms and factories are capable of producing more goods than the domestic market can absorb may seek foreign outlets for its surpluses. The earnings from these exports can then be used to pay for the importation of other commodities that can be more cheaply or easily produced elsewhere. In this way, trade serves to balance production and consumption and at the same time helps to use the world's resources more efficiently. There is an especially close relationship between trade and transportation. A transport network is made up of a number of nodes and the links that connect them; the flow of goods passing through that network constitutes trade.

The welfare of countries and regions is closely related to the amount of trade they are able to generate as well as to the kinds of goods making up that trade. The interdependence of areas has grown at an accelerating rate in recent years, as a result of rising levels of production and consumption, the voracious demands of an expanding technology, the exhaustion of local resources, and the discovery of new ones elsewhere. So intimate is the relationship between national prosperity and the nature of a country's trade that many nations have turned to new forms of international cooperation in an effort to solve their trade problems and at the same time to stimulate their rate of economic growth.

There is a reciprocal relationship between *trade* and the *location* of economic activities. The volume, direction, and composition of trade between one area and another directly reflect the location of particular types of production and of the markets for such goods. At the same time, the nature of the trading connections between two places helps to determine the kinds of production and consumption that are possible in each. This can be seen in the history of the development of trade between the eastern seaboard of the United States and the more recently settled areas west of the Appalachians. Separated by the barriers of distance because of inadequate transport connections, the two regions remained self-sufficient during the first quarter of the nineteenth century. Throughout this early period the settlers of the Ohio territory were forced to live largely at a subsistence level, despite the richness of the farmlands they occupied. With the opening of the Erie Canal in 1825 and the subsequent appearance of the railway, trade between the Midwest and Atlantic states quickly developed. As a result of this trade, Middle Westerners were relieved of the necessity of making everything they needed and were able to develop a very efficient and productive type of commercial agriculture. Cash received from the sale of their produce in the East could be spent on manufactured goods such as shoes and clothing made better and more cheaply in New England factories than they could make for themselves. For consumers in the Eastern states the opening of trade provided less expensive and higher-quality grain than they had obtained locally, and it gave them profitable markets for their manufactures. New England farmers, however, could not compete with the western grain and were forced to specialize in dairy products, vegetables, and other commodities of Thünen's first ring. For both regions the net result of interregional trade was higher incomes and improved standards of living.

Trade is the same in principal whether it occurs locally, regionally, or internationally. The major distinction between domestic and international trade is that flows between countries encounter more serious barriers. Many of these barriers are man-made. National governments tend to interfere (both intentionally and inadvertently) with flows of goods across their borders in ways that make international shipments more complicated and sometimes affect their makeup as well. International borders may influence trade in more subtle ways, too. There is less movement of populations across international boundaries than between regions of a country, and this tends to make the residents of nations different from each other in their consuming habits and even in their ways of doing business. Most of our attention in this chapter will be focused upon the trade between countries, for which a large body of literature has accumulated.

THEORY

During the course of its long history, the theory of international trade has become elaborate and highly abstract. Several aspects of this theory are of importance to geographers, especially those parts which attempt to explain why countries engage in foreign trade, how they select their trading partners, and which commodities they are likely to trade and in what quantities. In the following pages we shall first consider the nature of those factors affecting international trade and then summarize briefly the theory that combines these elements. Finally, we shall examine the relationship between the theories of international trade and location and note the attempts that have been made to reconcile the two bodies of theory.

FACTORS AFFECTING INTERNATIONAL TRADE

Commodity movements between nations are subject to a great many influences. Some of them tend to increase the flow, while others restrict it, alter its composition, or direct it into particular channels. These factors include the physical attributes of countries, certain characteristics of their populations, the availability of capital, distance from suppliers and customers, the nature of political control, and levels of development.

Physical characteristics of countries A country's physical attributes affect its trade with the rest of the world both directly and indirectly. One such characteristic is areal extent, which can have either positive or negative implications for trade. Among the principal trading countries (see Figure 9-1), for example, are three of great size: the United States, which ranks first in value of trade; the Soviet Union, eighth; and Canada, sixth. Within their immense territories all three have abundant

FIGURE 9-1 EXPORTS OF TEN PRINCIPAL TRADING NATIONS, 1970. (UNITED NATIONS *YEARBOOK OF INTERNATIONAL TRADE STATISTICS.*)

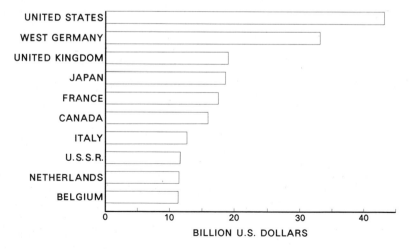

BILLION U.S. DOLLARS

resources, possess the technical capabilities to develop these resources, and are thus able to send large volumes of products into the world market. Several other large countries are not on this list, however. Thus Brazil and communist China are not sufficiently developed economically to have become important traders. On the other hand, seven of the top ten trading nations have small areas, especially Belgium, Luxembourg, and the Netherlands, which together are smaller than the state of West Virginia. It should be noted, however, that much of the trade among the small European states is comparable to the large domestic movements of freight within countries such as the United States and the Soviet Union. There is no choice for the small yet economically active countries of Western Europe but to import the raw materials and other requirements their own limited resources cannot provide and to sell their goods in the larger world market.

So erratic is the spatial distribution of the world's natural resources that even the larger countries lack certain commodities essential to their economies, while other countries have more of these materials than they can use. The United States does not have enough of the nonferrous and alloying metals that modern industry must have, but Canada's supply of some of these is greater than her small labor force and inadequate capital can use effectively. Many less developed countries have great reserves of valuable minerals that they are unable to exploit for themselves and therefore export to more industrialized lands. This is true of Indian and Liberian iron ore, Malaysian and Bolivian tin, and Congolese copper. One vital group of minerals, the fossil fuels, are distributed among the world's nations in a particularly uneven fashion, thus helping to account for the large and growing trade in coal, petroleum, and natural gas.

The major world regions differ likewise in their agricultural capabilities and biotic resources, reflecting variations in world climates, physical relief, natural vegetation, and soils. Thus Canadian wheat, produced on rich soils in the subhumid western prairies, is shipped to the Caribbean in exchange for bananas, sugar, and other crops of the humid tropics. Similarly, low-lying Denmark and the Netherlands export vegetables and small fruits to mountainous Austria and Switzerland. Biotic resources form a basis for trade too, as shown by Iceland's fish and Sweden's forest-products exports. A related aspect of the physical environment that accounts for an increasing volume of trade is the variability of harvests. In a given year one major growing region may have a crop failure while another may be reaping a bountiful harvest. Thus the Soviet Union, which in some years produces a surplus of wheat, has been forced to import much grain at other times.

Population   In addition to the physical differences among countries, there are also a number of important determinants of trade that have a nonphysical origin. One such element is the variable character of populations, which plays a multiple role in international trade. First of all, it is the source of the labor supply. The size and quality of a country's labor force has much to do with its ability to exploit its resources and with the kinds of goods it will export and import. A country that is short of labor but has ample physical resources will tend to produce and export goods obtained from the land with a minimum application of labor. Canada exports land-intensive commodities such as paper, wood products, and minerals, and Australia exports wheat and wool, while the imports of both countries tend to be high in labor content. At the other extreme are countries having a bountiful supply of labor but few natural resources. The Japanese import land-intensive raw materials, add to these the skills of a large, industrious labor force, and export finished products. This formula works less well with certain other populous countries, since labor costs involve not only wage rates but also labor quality. Many underdeveloped countries have an abundance of labor that is cheap but lacks the skills, work habits, and incentives needed for economically staffing a modern industrial establishment.

A country's population provides not only its work force but also its market. The size, per capita income, and cultural traits of the population determine how good a market that country will be for its foreign suppliers. The largest and most sought-after markets today are those of Anglo-America and Western Europe, where large numbers of prosperous consumers with varied tastes provide an effective demand of great size. Although communist China has one-fourth of the world's population, her estimated per capita gross national product is only $100; the Chinese market has therefore proved disappointingly small to foreign suppliers. In some places the kinds of products that will be imported are limited by cultural attributes of the population. The dietary laws of the Jews of Israel, the Moslems of Pakistan, and the Hindus of India affect the food imports of those countries. Even food *habits* may exert a considerable influence, as shown by the commercial effects of the British fondness for tea and the American preference for coffee.

Capital   The significance of capital to international trade has been apparent from the above examples of countries where it was conspicuously present or absent. Capital affects both the kinds of goods traded and their quantity. Most highly developed countries tend to export products having a high content of capital, that is, goods requiring much expensive plant and equipment in their production. This is especially true of the exports of the United States, West Germany, and the United Kingdom. It is said that Japan's changeover to high-quality, high-value merchandise such as optical equipment, electronics, and motorcars can be attributed at least in part to a greater availability of capital in that country.

In the absence of artificial restraints, however, money capital is highly mobile, and this can have either positive or negative effects on the total flow of merchandise. When a company starts a branch plant in a country to which it formerly exported, the usual effect is to reduce trade. In effect the company is replacing its exports of goods with exports of capital, and the only return is the repatriation of profits from the new foreign operation. Often a company is given little choice in such decisions. The importing country may have imposed a high tariff on the company's goods, thereby forcing the management to begin manufacturing in that country or lose a profitable market to competitors. On the other hand, new trade may be created if a company invests in foreign resource development for the purpose of acquiring raw materials for its operations elsewhere. An American steel company opening new iron ore mines in Venezuela or a British rubber company starting a plantation in Malaysia is initiating a substantial flow of such commodities into international channels.

Distance It is due largely to modern innovations in transportation that such remotely located markets as Australia and New Zealand are able to have any profitable trade with Western Europe and Anglo-America. The long-term downward trend in transport costs has substantially widened the range of commodities entering international trade. This cost reduction has been made possible by a number of technological developments, including the steel-hulled ship, the screw propeller, diesel engines, bulk carriers, and refrigeration. The last of these has been of special importance for Oceania's exports of chilled meats, butter, and cheese. Australia and New Zealand benefit also from the fact that their main producing areas are located close to cheap ocean transport, which has a greater long-haul advantage than any other transport mode. Many other features of the freight-rate structure have affected the flow of trade and location of production.

The effect of distance on trade has been demonstrated by W. Beckerman, who studied the pattern of Western European trade to determine its relationship to the distance separating trading partners (Beckerman, 1956). As a substitute for actual distance, Beckerman used transport cost as a measure of "economic distance." He ranked the countries of Western Europe in order of their relative economic distances from other countries and also in order of the amount of trade with each country (after adjusting for size of country). He found a fairly strong correlation between the two rankings, which showed that trade and distance are indeed closely associated. Several other studies have similarly confirmed the importance of distance as an influence on trade. One of these examined the exchange of goods among eighty countries and found that gross national product and distance were the two determinants that affected trade most of all (Linnemann, 1966). Another study examined the trade of each of several selected countries with the rest of the world and was likewise able to demonstrate the importance of these two factors (Yeates, 1969).

Political element Governments customarily play an important role in matters relating to their trade with other countries. Because trade is so important to national economies, governments watch closely the state of that trade and try wherever possible to influence it in their favor. One standard by which the condition of a country's foreign commerce is gauged is the *balance of trade*. This is the difference between the total value of all merchandise exported and imported by the residents of one country in their trade with all other countries. It is usually reckoned over a specified period of time, most often a year. An excess of exports over imports is customarily referred to as a "favorable" balance of trade, and the opposite is termed an "unfavorable" balance of trade.

Although a few countries manage to export more than they import, many others run chronic balance-of-trade deficits. Some of these, such as Israel and some of the less developed nations, manage to bridge at least some of this gap by means of long-term loans from abroad, while others accomplish this by providing services to foreigners. Norway, for example, depends heavily upon income from its merchant fleet, which is one of the world's largest. The United Kingdom earns important amounts by supplying banking, insurance, and transportation services to the world. Practically all Western European countries benefit handsomely from tourist expenditures within their borders, but the United States experiences a substantial net loss from tourism.

Important as the trade balance may be to a country's financial condition, therefore, it usually accounts for only a part of its international monetary transactions. The remainder includes expenditures and receipts for such items as transportation, tourism, investments, gifts, government aid, military operations, and gold. The net effect of all these items constitutes a country's *balance of payments*, which can be defined as the difference between the total of all payments and receipts by residents of one country and those of all other countries within a specified period. The significance of this gauge is shown by the fact that, although the United States usually has a trade surplus, it has had a sizable deficit in its balance of payments over a period of several years, resulting in a very large overseas flow of United States dollars and severe strains on the international monetary system.

Because of their ability to control the points of entry and exit along their borders and to influence their residents by means of taxation and police authority, governments hold a certain amount of power over the quantity and character of exports and imports. In their exercise of this prerogative, they have a growing list of regulatory devices from which to choose. Perhaps the oldest of these is the *tariff*, the principal measure used before World War I. A tariff is a list of taxes or duties that must be paid against various categories of merchandise when these are transferred across the border of a country. The term *tariff* may be used also to refer to the duty applicable to an individual commodity. Tariffs may be levied against imports or exports, but the former is much more common because most countries hesitate to handicap their own products in the competitive world market.

According to the purposes for which they are intended, tariffs are of two types, *protective* and *revenue*. As the name implies, tariffs for revenue serve as sources of governmental income. Although a common device in less developed countries, this class of tariffs is of little importance elsewhere. More usual is the protective tariff, which is used to provide special help to some sector of the home economy. The latter may be an "infant industry," that is, one that is becoming newly established, or it may be an older activity that is weak and declining. By imposing high duties on certain imports, a country may be able to acquire new domestic industries making those products.

A *quota* is a regulatory device by which a country limits directly the specific quantities of goods it will import or (less commonly) export. More drastic than the tariff, quotas produce an instantaneous effect. This technique was much favored during the Depression of the 1930s and it is still widely used, especially for regulating the flow of agricultural commodities, such as sugar.

Some countries troubled with persistently unfavorable trade balances impose *exchange controls*, another drastic measure. Where this practice is followed, all foreign currencies earned by the country's residents are funneled into a central agency, which parcels them out to its importers according to the type of foreign merchandise that is desired, preference usually going to essential items. *Multiple exchange rates* are sometimes maintained in cases of this type. These are usually fixed in such a way that the buyer has to pay a higher price for foreign currencies that are to be used for purchasing luxuries than for importing necessities. Certain Latin American countries maintain two or even three such rates of exchange. Quotas and exchange controls are usually enforced by means of government licensing arrangements.

The most severe distortions to normal trading patterns are those produced by national animosities and wars. Rivalries, whether ideologically inspired or otherwise, tend to impede trade and may cut it off entirely. Examples are the iron curtain between Eastern and Western Europe, the disputes between the Israelis and the Arabs, and the enmity between India and Pakistan. War, or even the threat of it, halts the flow of merchandise between combatants and promotes efforts for national self-sufficiency. Sugar beets and synthetic rubber were originally developed under such stimuli. Neutral countries cut off from normal supply sources may be led to develop diversified secondary production of their own, as demonstrated by Argentina during World Wars I and II.

Not all governmental effects on trade are negative, however. To increase their exports, countries sometimes engage in trade-promotion activities such as fairs, exhibits, and foreign trade missions, together with different types of financial and technical aid to exporters. Participation in trade blocs is another way governments attempt to increase their foreign trade.

Stage of development   It has already been suggested that a country's level of development has much to do with the extent to which it participates in trade and the nature of that participation. The kind of market that a country offers to prospective foreign suppliers can be gauged with some accuracy by the amount of its per capita income. The best possibilities for sales are clearly to be found in those lands that have reached a high level of mass consumption, while the prospects are poor among people living at a subsistence level. It should be noted, however, that certain very large populations at low levels of development present fairly tempting markets simply because of the total aggregate demand these appear to constitute.

As suppliers to the world market, the less developed countries tend to share a number of distinctive characteristics and problems. One common trait is excessive specialization in the production and exporting of a limited number of primary goods, particularly agricultural commodities. For technically advanced countries specialization is generally considered advantageous, since it results in greater production efficiencies and lower unit costs. But the advanced countries ordinarily specialize in manufactured goods, which do not present the problems of primary specialization. The kinds of commodities in which less developed countries specialize usually encounter a world demand that grows very slowly if at all.

Consequently the prices of these goods tend to be weak on the world market. Added to this are uncertainties of production due to crop failures and other unforeseen circumstances. Often the production facilities are owned and operated by foreigners, while the unskilled labor is supplied locally. This can give the country an unbalanced labor force, the great majority being low-paid agricultural workers.

The trade problems of less developed countries are not made easier by the fact that they are ordinarily dependent upon technically advanced countries as trading partners. In many cases such trade ties are between former colonies and the imperial powers by whom they had been controlled. Britain, France, and Portugal retain many links of this sort with their old colonies. Because their production is so similar, less developed lands tend to trade very little with each other. Their imports from the advanced countries consist largely of manufactured goods, which they require in considerable variety. Most underdeveloped lands thus present a contrast between diversified imports and narrowly specialized exports. This places the less developed countries at a further disadvantage in that over the long run manufactured goods tend to rise steadily in price while primary commodity prices change but little. Hence it is often said that the *terms of trade* are unfavorable for underdeveloped lands.

For these reasons such countries are turning increasingly to industrialization as a solution to their trade problems. Many of them now undertake more of the initial processing of their domestic raw materials, especially petroleum and mineral ores, in order to increase the total value of their exports. They are also attempting to make more of the consumer goods they have been accustomed to import. All this is part of the general effort to acquire a manufacturing sector that will lift them higher in the scale of development. Even in this, however, they face many difficulties. One of these is the lack of a manufacturing tradition, a shortage of the necessary labor and managerial skills, and insufficient capital.

A further problem is posed by what is termed the "technological gap." In the competition for world markets there are decided advantages to those countries with a lead in the technology required for introducing new products or for making old products more cheaply and better. Less developed countries cannot compete in this race. They can only borrow and imitate, and while they are doing this, the leaders have gone on to new achievements. Finally, there is the further problem that the home market for manufactured goods is often inadequate to provide a sufficiently large supporting base for new industries to become established.

PRINCIPAL THEORIES OF INTERNATIONAL TRADE

Many of the features of trade described in the preceding paragraphs have been incorporated in the large body of international trade theory that has grown up over a period of more than two centuries. This theory had its beginning in the practical needs of political decision makers, but it has since evolved into an academic specialty of fundamental importance to a number of disciplines, including geography. We will consider three periods in the development of this theory, each of them corresponding to a particular school of thought (Chipman, 1965, 1966).

Classical theory   The classical theorists emphasized the advantages of a country's specializing in its production and trade. Ricardo had much to do with the development of classical theory, which treated a country's industries as though each branch yielded only one product and employed but one factor of production, namely, labor. Labor served as the unit of value, and all output was measured in terms of the labor it required. Labor was considered completely mobile within countries but entirely immobile between countries. The classical theorists ignored the cost of transportation, as have most of those theorists who followed them.

From the classical school came two important ideas that have remained a fundamental part of subsequent theories. These are the *law of comparative advantage* and the *theory of international values*. To illustrate this idea, we may begin with the simple case of two countries, each of which is capable of producing only two products. Assuming the absence of transport costs and of any artificial restraints on the international movement of goods, trade will arise between two countries out of the differences in their respective production costs. As an example, let us assume both that the United States requires fewer man-hours than Canada to make cloth, and that Canada has lower labor requirements for paper. Clearly, less total labor would be required in the two countries if Canada were to specialize in paper manufacturing and the United States in the making of cloth. Each would then exchange its surplus with the other—an arrangement that benefits both countries.

It is not necessary, however, that these cost advantages be absolute for the two countries to gain from trade. Suppose that the United States can produce *both* cloth and paper cheaper than Canada, and that the difference between the Canadian and United States costs is greater for cloth than it is for paper, as follows:

	CANADA	UNITED STATES
Cloth	130	90
Paper	110	100

In *comparative* terms paper is thus cheap in Canada and cloth is cheap in the United States ($\frac{90}{130} < \frac{100}{110}$).   Despite its absolute advantage in each of the two goods, the United States will still be better off to specialize in producing and exporting cloth while Canada concentrates on supplying paper for both countries. The law of comparative advantage may therefore be stated as follows: *In the absence of barriers to trade, a country will specialize in the production and export of those commodities that it can produce at a comparatively low cost and import those goods that can be produced at a comparatively lower cost in other countries.*

The law of comparative advantage does not give the exact ratio at which goods will be exchanged (i.e., the "barter terms of trade"), but merely the limits within which such a value lies. In 1852 John Stuart Mill proposed his *theory of international values* as a way of arriving at this figure. This theory shows how the interaction of supply and demand in the two countries will produce a point of equilibrium representing the value at which trade takes place. Mill determined the equilibrium point algebraically by means of a series of proportions. Alfred Marshall later developed a graphic technique involving *reciprocal demand and supply curves* to find this point. Marshall's solution was still confined to two countries and two commodities, but later authors have found ways to extend this idea to the multicountry, multicommodity case.

Neoclassical theory That body of thought usually termed neoclassical trade theory typically solves theoretical problems with the aid of geometric techniques. In addition to Marshall's reciprocal demand curves, geometry has been used to develop the concept of *opportunity cost*. This involves substituting one commodity for another, based on their relative costs, through a shift in the means of production. Another neoclassical development of particular interest to geographers is the concept of *external economies*, which helps to explain the existence of trade between areas that do *not* have significant physical or cultural differences. A major part of the world's trade fits this description. A prominent example is the exchange of manufactured goods among the countries of Western Europe and between Europe and North America. The idea of external economies is based on Adam Smith's work on the division of labor and the advantages of specialization. External economies refer to the efficiencies gained by an industry (or industries) owing to the expansion of the entire industry. These are the benefits that an industry enjoys as a result of the better and cheaper transportation and communications, larger and more skilled labor supply, greater exchange of business information and technical knowledge, and other savings that the growth of an industrial complex brings. This concept has many implications for problems of economic development and trade policy.

Modern theory Classical theory has been much criticized for emphasizing only one factor of production, labor. The other factors are clearly of much importance and in some modern industries may be decidedly more important than labor. Modern theory therefore follows the lead of Heckscher (1919) and Ohlin (1933) by treating the problem of intercountry differences in terms of their *factor endowments*. Thus we may speak of the degree to which a country is "endowed" with the various factors of production, capital, labor, land, or entrepreneurship. Of special importance in this context is the Heckscher-Ohlin *law of factor-price equalization*, which refers to the tendency of the income accruing to particular factors of production in different countries to become equalized when trade is permitted to flow freely among them. If, for example, an agricultural and an industrial country engage in trade, the agricultural country can expect a rise in its previously low land rents and a decrease in its relatively high industrial labor costs. In the industrial country the reverse will take place. According to Ohlin, only a partial adjustment of this sort occurs, and this contention appears to be confirmed by the trading history of numerous countries.

INTERNATIONAL TRADE THEORY AND LOCATION THEORY

Trade theory and location theory have had entirely separate development, and those writers concerned with the one have largely ignored the other. The reader will nevertheless have noticed that certain elements of international trade discussed above resemble concepts that appeared in earlier chapters dealing with the location of primary, secondary, and tertiary activities. We have seen, for example, that raw materials often flow from a source in one country to a place of manufacture in another, while the product is sold to a third. This is Alfred Weber's location figure at an international scale. Furthermore, the external economies of trade theory are related to Weber's agglomeration factor. These are but a few of the many points of coincidence that could be cited. This has been summarized by Walter Isard: "(1) Location cannot be explained unless at the same time trade is accounted for and (2) trade cannot be explained without the simultaneous determination of locations" (Isard, 1956, p. 53), and "trade and location are as the two sides of the same coin" (Isard, 1956, p. 207).

Weber was one of the first to point out the critical omission of distance from the theory of international trade (Weber, 1911). As indicated earlier, trade theory usually treats countries as though no space separated them. With distance thus held constant, trade is assumed to take place in a spaceless world. In drawing attention to this deficiency in trade theory, Weber also noted the many international manufacturing firms whose locations have been chosen mainly because of the savings in transport cost they afforded. We might cite numerous examples, including oil and sugar refineries, chemical works, steel mills, aluminum refineries, and many other kinds of production drawing upon raw materials and serving markets in countries other than that in which the manufacturing facilities are located. Thus it seems clear that trade theory is not complete without a consideration of distance, which is another element that location and trade theories appear to have in common.

The first concerted effort to unite the two theories was made by Bertil Ohlin, who attempted to show that trade theory is but a part of general location theory—that the former is to a considerable degree concerned with the international location of production (Ohlin, 1933). Ohlin constructed a trade theory in which he replaced the classical labor theory of value with the concept of factor endowments. From this basis he then analyzed domestic and international movements of the factors of production and their relation to the movement of commodities. He observed that movements of capital and labor are greater within countries than between countries and that international trade is much affected by this difference. In his analysis he incorporated both the Thünen and Weber approaches to the location of production. Among his conclusions, Ohlin indicated that trade and the location of production are inextricably interrelated. It was Ohlin, moreover, who noted that domestic trade and international trade are basically similar, differing mainly in the greater impediments to international trade.

Numerous subsequent attempts have been made to bring location theory and international trade theory into harmony. One of the most notable of these was undertaken by Walter Isard, who constructed an international trade model including three countries and two commodities (Isard, 1956, pp. 207–220). Treating "transport inputs" as though they were commodities, Isard was able to calculate the final place of production of each good, the composition of each country's trade, and even the country that provided the transportation.

To date, the attempts to reconcile the two theories have not been wholly successful, despite general recognition that a relationship exists between them. One of the obstacles is that trade theory has been developed to a higher level of abstraction and treats countries as points instead of areas, whereas location theory emphasizes space, is less abstract, and is thus somewhat closer to reality. Moreover, both theories are subdivided into separate schools of thought and need to be unified internally before they can be joined. Haberler suggests that more attention be given to the spatial dimension and transport cost in trade theory and that location theory be made more general (Haberler, 1961). A fully unified theory is a goal toward which several individuals are now working actively.

REGIONAL INTEGRATION

Trade and location are linked in still another, related body of literature referred to as customs union theory (Viner, 1950) or, more recently, as the theory of regional integration (Balassa, 1961; Thoman and Conkling, 1967, chap. 7). By regional integration is meant the joining together of two or more sovereign countries to form a single economy. The purpose of such an association is to promote increased trade among the members of the group through economic cooperation and other common efforts, all having the ultimate aim of raising the standard of living in each nation concerned. A union of this type, if it is successful, results in a reorientation of trade, which in turn means a reordering of the location of production and consumption as well. There are several types of degrees of regional integration, each of which is represented to some extent in the numerous experiments of this sort taking place today throughout the world. The lead in this movement has been taken by certain of the technically advanced nations, although the greatest promise of beneficial results appears to be in the less developed countries.

Integration was first tried during the nineteenth century, but it was not until after World War II that the idea gained wide acceptance. In part its recent popularity in Europe reflects a general reaction to the political and commercial rivalries of the interwar period, when many countries had sought economic self-sufficiency and had traded as little as possible with each other. It has been the hope of European leaders that such cooperation will help to prevent a return to the economic stagnation and general dissension that preceded and no doubt helped to bring about the war. In that politically fragmented continent, it became widely accepted that unity not only would strengthen the general economy and raise the standard of living but also would give these small countries greater bargaining power in world economic affairs. Introduced at a time when Europeans much feared the growing military power of the Soviet bloc, economic integration was also regarded as a way of achieving the economic strength needed to resist aggression. Among poorer countries elsewhere in the world, integration has been seized upon as a means for achieving economic development.

It has been suggested that five different degrees of integration are possible, ranging from the most tentative steps toward trade cooperation to complete economic, social, and even political unification (Balassa, 1961, p. 2). The five categories are the free trade area, customs union, common market, economic union, and full economic integration. The loosest form of economic integration, the *free trade area*, calls merely for removing barriers to the movement of goods between member countries. No attempt is made to coordinate trading relations with the outside world. The *customs union* implies a somewhat closer type of cooperation in which obstacles to the exchange of merchandise among members are removed and in addition a common tariff wall is erected to imports from nonmember countries. The *common market* not only has all the features of the customs union but also permits the factors of production, particularly capital and labor, to flow freely among members. This is the most preferred type of integration at present, and it is best exemplified by the European Economic Community. *Economic union* goes a step beyond the common market in specifying coordination of other aspects of economic policy among members, including such things as currency controls, tax policy, and patent and licensing arrangements. Complete *economic integration* has the characteristics of economic union plus coordination of social policies and in addition calls for a supranational authority including executive, judicial, and legislative branches, all with binding authority over member countries. Note that each step requires the surrender of a progressively greater amount of sovereignty by the countries that belong to the group.

WORLD PATTERNS OF TRADE

In the previous section we have seen that many influences affect a country's selection of trading partners and determine the amount and kinds of goods that will be exchanged. Thus prepared, we can now examine more meaningfully the complex pattern of world commodity flows. We shall begin with a general view of trade in the world as a whole, observing the various ways in which such trade has changed over time and noting the extent to which each of the "three worlds" is able to share in it. Following this we turn to an examination of trade among individual countries and blocs of countries. Finally we look at certain international organizations to which most of the world's trading nations belong. Before undertaking this analysis of specific patterns, however, it is necessary to have a brief introduction to two practical aspects of trade that will aid our interpretation. These are the organizational arrangements of international trade and the problems of measuring world trade data.

Organization of trade　There is a side of the trading scene that does not appear in official government reports. Between its place of production in one country and its final destination in another, a consignment of goods threads a maze of great complexity. During its journey it receives the attention of freight forwarders, customs house brokers, transport agencies, financial institutions, and innumerable government officials, all of whom serve, or are charged with regulating the activities of, those basic units of the international trading system, the individual exporters and importers.

It is common to think of international trade as an exchange that takes place between governments. In some parts of the world this is literally true, but in others—the most active trading areas of all—this simple view is not accurate. In noncommunist countries the actual initiative for trade and the daily functioning of it are the province of many commercial firms, who are concerned with obtaining a profit and whose success depends upon their ability to meet the exacting demands of a highly competitive international market. The trade statistics of a capitalist country, then, represent the aggregate results of countless individual transactions into which its exporters and importers have entered.

In the communist lands, trade with other countries is a monopoly of the government. *State trading* is the method by which all merchandise enters or leaves the country. Decisions to buy or sell on the foreign market are made by central agencies whose activities are governed by the dictates of the official plan and the need to supplement its shortfalls or to dispose of its surpluses. Prices are often set not so much by competitive conditions as by sometimes arbitrary government decisions reflecting the Marxist labor theory of value. To develop a reliable system of cost accounting is a task in which communist economics has yet to succeed. State trading is not confined to the communist world, however. To a limited degree it is found even in capitalist countries wherever certain classes of exports and imports are reserved to the government. A wheat board may collect and arrange for the sale abroad of a country's grain, or a government tobacco, sugar, or alcoholic beverage monopoly may control the importation and domestic distribution of these commodities.

GROWTH AND CHANGE IN WORLD TRADE

World trade has undergone remarkable changes in total volume in modern times, and the rate of growth appears unabated in recent years. The overall composition of that trade has undergone also a number of important shifts recently, although this transition has tended to be more gradual and orderly. When viewed at the global scale, however, the patterns of trade flows have remained remarkably constant. Year after year the same groups of countries maintain their decidedly unequal shares of the total and continue clinging to their traditional trading partners.

Total world trade   In 1969 the combined exports of all the world's nations totaled $272 billion. This was actually $100 billion more than was exported by the world only five years previously, an increase of nearly three-fifths. If the 1969 total is compared with that of still earlier years, we discover almost equally startling changes. The figure for 1969 is five times that of 1948, for example, and nearly twelve times the trade of 1938, the last normal year before World War II. If we allow for the declining value of the dollar, the change appears somewhat less dramatic; even so the growth since 1938 has been something in the order of 4 1/2 times.

How do we explain this resurgence of world trade after long years of stagnation between the two world wars? First of all, there were the combined effects of recovery from a severe depression and a devastating war. This was followed by a prolonged period of almost uninterrupted world prosperity during which the technically advanced countries attained new heights of economic activity. At the same time, the countries of the world were coming to depend increasingly upon each other for a greater variety of raw materials and products. At least as important as any of these, however, was the change in general attitude toward trade, a spirit of cooperation replacing one of commercial rivalry and economic nationalism. Indeed, it is difficult to say which was more cause than effect, the rise in world prosperity or the expansion of trade; each seems to have been an inseparable accompaniment of the other.

The general outline of world trade as it appears today has been long in developing, and there have been several significant changes in the composition of that trade over the years. One of these was the rise of manufactured products as articles of world commerce, a development that gained importance during the nineteenth century and has been gathering momentum ever since. Matching the innovations in manufacturing technology that made this growth possible were other technological advances in the shipping industry that permitted industrial raw materials and other primary commodities to extend their range of movement. Transport technology, especially refrigeration, also made possible the entry of whole new classes of goods into world channels, especially foodstuffs such as animal products and tropical fruits. Between the two world wars the makeup of international trade changed little except for the significant appearance of petroleum. Despite the world depression, manufactured goods continued to increase as a proportion of total exports, accounting for an ever greater share of the exchange between North America and Europe in particular.

The years following World War II have seen manufactured goods maintain their steady growth in relation to other internationally traded merchandise. Since the end of World War II the proportion of finished and semifinished products has increased from two-thirds of the world total to four-fifths. The largest component of this group, and the most rapidly growing one, is machinery and transport equipment, which alone now constitutes more than two-fifths of all exports. Mineral fuels and lubricants have increased also, having apparently stabilized at approximately one-tenth of the total. A marked decline has taken place since World War II, however, in the relative place of raw materials and foods. In 1950 the two categories together accounted for 46.5 percent of all shipments, but within a decade and a half this proportion had fallen to less than a third. Considering the degree to which less developed countries rely on such commodities for their export earnings, as noted earlier in this chapter, we shall turn next to a comparison of the trade performances of countries in the developed, less developed, and communist groups.

Trade of the three worlds   Although total world trade has been rising steeply for more than two decades, the increase has not been shared equally by all countries. The technically advanced nations have long dominated world trade, and in recent years they have succeeded in capturing an even greater portion of it. Whereas in

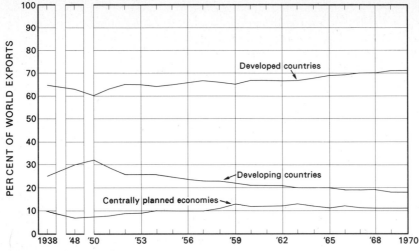

FIGURE 9-2 SHARES OF DEVELOPED, LESS DEVELOPED, AND COMMUNIST COUNTRIES IN WORLD
EXPORTS, 1938, 1948, AND 1950–1970 (PERCENT OF WORLD EXPORTS). (INTERNATIONAL BANK FOR
RECONSTRUCTION AND DEVELOPMENT.)

1950 these countries accounted for 60 percent of world exports, by 1970 they were
to supply 71 percent (see Figure 9-2). This has occurred even though the advanced
countries have well under one-quarter of the world's population.

The communist countries, with one-third of the people of the world, are being
eagerly sought as trading partners. Yet this bloc of countries contributes a
surprisingly small flow of goods to the world market. The low point in communist
trade occurred in 1948, when they shipped only 7 percent of the world's exports.
The proportion rose slowly to 13 percent by 1959, but since that time the
communist share has slipped to only 11 percent in 1970. Other problems of
communist trade will be reviewed later in connection with the Comecon countries
and China, since this group varies so greatly in levels of development that they
cannot be treated successfully in summary fashion.

The noncommunist countries of the less developed world benefited temporari-
ly from the Second World War and the subsequent period of recovery, when their
commodities were much in demand and some of them had currency surpluses
accumulated during the hostilities. As a group their peak year was 1950, when they
supplied 32 percent of the goods moving into international channels. Since then,
however, their exports have declined steadily, reaching a low of 18 percent by
1970, despite the fact that they have nearly 45 percent of the world's population.

There are several reasons for this disappointing trade performance of the less
developed countries; some of these have been cited earlier in the chapter. One
problem is illustrated in Figure 9-3, which shows the direction of trade movements.
The diagram confirms our earlier observation that a major part of the trade of
technically advanced countries takes place with other countries at similarly high
levels of development while most of the trade of less developed countries is

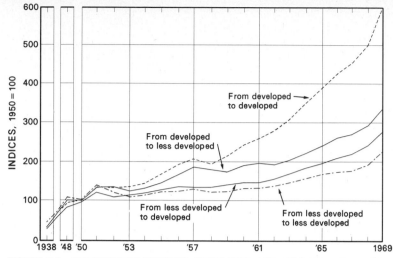

FIGURE 9-3 DIRECTION OF EXPORTS, DEVELOPED AND LESS DEVELOPED COUNTRIES, INDICES 1938, 1948, AND 1950–1960. (INTERNATIONAL BANK FOR RECONSTRUCTION AND DEVELOPMENT.)

likewise directed toward the advanced nations. Many trade linkages of the latter sort grew out of former colonial ties. Comparatively little trade occurs between less developed countries. Moreover, Figure 9-3 shows that the disparities between these different kinds of linkages are becoming greater. For example, trade between developed countries increased sixfold in value between 1950 and 1969, while shipments from developed to less developed lands increased a little more than threefold. Meanwhile, exports of less developed countries to developed ones rose somewhat less than threefold, and trade between underdeveloped nations a little more than doubled. This tells us something about the relative decline in the less developed countries' share in total trade, but why did the decline occur?

An examination of the composition of that trade gives part of the answer. As we have seen, one of the problems of less developed countries is their excessive dependence on a limited number of primary exports. Figure 9-4 helps to show why such specialization can be harmful to an underdeveloped country's interests. This diagram compares the trade performance over a twenty-year period of three groups of products as measured by dollar value: manufactured goods (Standard International Trade Classification sections 5 to 8), primary commodities (SITC sections 0, 1, 2, and 4), and petroleum (SITC section 3). The first of the three, manufactures, is overwhelmingly dominated by the advanced countries. Note the steady and rapid rise in manufactured goods, which has been such a boon to the technically advanced countries and helps to explain much of their increased share in total trade. By comparison, primary exports, upon which the underdeveloped countries are so dependent, have risen only modestly. Only those few less developed countries that export oil have fared well. Although the less developed countries must rely mainly on primary exports, paradoxically these nations are not the chief suppliers of this class of goods. As Figure 9-5 shows, more than half

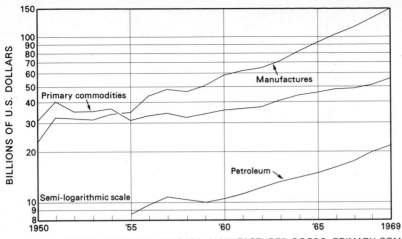

FIGURE 9-4 TREND IN WORLD EXPORTS: MANUFACTURED GOODS, PRIMARY COMMODITIES, AND PETROLEUM 1950–1969. (INTERNATIONAL BANK FOR RECONSTRUCTION AND DEVELOPMENT.)

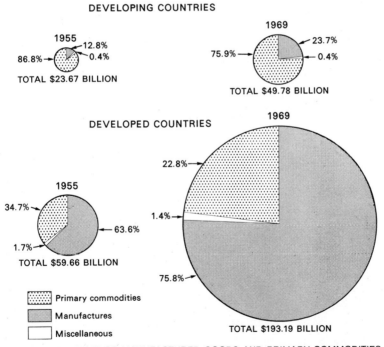

FIGURE 9-5 VALUE OF MANUFACTURED GOODS AND PRIMARY COMMODITIES AS A PERCENTAGE OF EXPORTS FROM DEVELOPED AND LESS DEVELOPED COUNTRIES, 1955 AND 1969. (INTERNATIONAL BANK FOR RECONSTRUCTION AND DEVELOPMENT.)

of the world's primary goods entering trade is supplied by technically advanced lands. Such countries as the United States, Canada, France, and Australia are the main shippers of grains; the United States leads in coal exports; Sweden and Canada are important suppliers of metallic ores. Nevertheless, we observe from Figure 9-5 that more than three-fourths of the advanced countries' exports is manufactured goods, an increase from 64 percent in 1955. At the same time, well over three-fourths of the exports from less developed countries are primary commodities. Even so, this represents an encouraging change from 1955, when primary exports were seven-eighths of the total, since it suggests that more of the underdeveloped lands are acquiring import-competing industries.

As noted earlier, another serious trade problem of less developed countries is the unfavorable price trends they encounter in the international market. From Figure 9-6 we see that, while the total quantity of developed countries' exports was experiencing a more than fourfold increase, the value of those exports was increasing sixfold. This difference reflects both rising prices and a higher degree of processing of such goods. On the other hand, the exports of less developed countries were increasing threefold in total quantity, while total value was rising at almost the same rate. This indicates that there was no significant change in unit prices.

What this shows is that less developed countries are having to pay higher prices for the goods they buy from the advanced countries while getting no more for their own merchandise. The effect of this is summarized in Figure 9-7, which contrasts the changes in the terms of trade of the two groups of nations. To measure a country's terms of trade, we divide the unit value of its exports by the

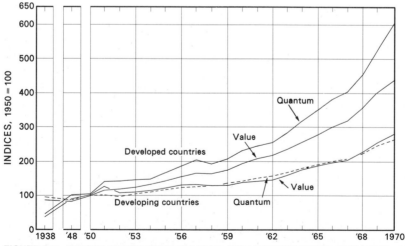

FIGURE 9-6 EXPORT INDICES OF DEVELOPED AND LESS DEVELOPED COUNTRIES, BY VALUE AND QUANTUM, 1938, 1948, AND 1950–1970. (INTERNATIONAL BANK FOR RECONSTRUCTION AND DEVELOPMENT.)

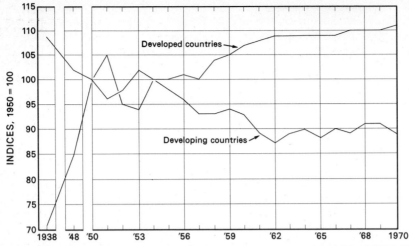

FIGURE 9-7 TERMS OF TRADE OF DEVELOPED AND LESS DEVELOPED COUNTRIES, 1938, 1948, AND 1950–1970. (INTERNATIONAL BANK FOR RECONSTRUCTION AND DEVELOPMENT.)

unit value of its imports. As the diagram indicates, the terms of trade of the developed group rose by 11 percentage points during the past twenty years at the same time that the terms of trade of the less developed lands were falling by that same amount.

This trend is made still plainer by tracing the performance of the six leading commodities exported by less developed countries, as in Figure 9-8. During the twenty-year period the relatively small number of oil-exporting countries did very well. Note, however, the wide fluctuations in the export value of metallic ores and

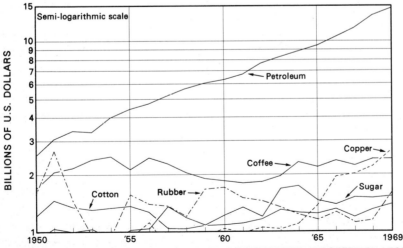

FIGURE 9-8 VALUE OF SIX MOST IMPORTANT COMMODITIES EXPORTED BY LESS DEVELOPED COUNTRIES, 1950–1969. (INTERNATIONAL BANK FOR RECONSTRUCTION AND DEVELOPMENT.)

tropical plantation crops. Since the world market for such goods is relatively stable, these variations reflect the effects of changes in their supply periods of glutted markets alternating with shortages. As this series of drawings has illustrated, trade presents difficult problems for less developed countries, and their uncertain performance in the world market continues to be a source of concern.

PRINCIPAL TRADING COUNTRIES AND BLOCS

Next we shall examine the trade patterns of particular countries and closely associated trade groups. Special attention will be given to the ways in which the trade of these countries has been shaped by the basic influences outlined earlier in this chapter. In view of their overwhelming dominance in the world trading scene, three major centers of trade will receive the principal emphasis: Anglo-America, Western Europe, and Japan. The discussion will be organized by major world regions, partly as a matter of convenience but also in recognition of the role of distance in world trade.

Anglo-America   Together Canada and the United States contribute approximately one-fifth of the world's exports. These countries are inhabited by some 230 million persons, whose exceedingly high level of economic activity makes this region a prime market and at the same time a vital source of goods for the international market. The great volume of this activity is shown by the per capita gross domestic products of $3,960 in the case of the United States and $2,621 for Canada (1969). This output per person is greater overall than that of Western Europe, which ranges between $1,573 (United Kingdom) and $2,905 (Sweden) in the core area but falls to as low as $479 (Portugal) on the periphery.

The Anglo-American nations are unusually interdependent in their trading relations, and each is the other's best customer. This dependence is especially great in the case of Canada, which in 1969 received 72 percent of its imports from the United States and sent 71 percent of its exports to that country in return. For the United States the dependence is relatively less but still very important. In 1969 imports from Canada represented 28 percent of the United States total, while exports were approximately 24 percent. Moreover, this interdependence of the two economies continues to grow stronger each year.

The nature of the commodities flowing between these countries gives further insight into this relationship. Leading the list of merchandise supplied by the United States to Canada are machinery, transport equipment, and parts; a great variety of other manufactured goods; coal; and fruits, vegetables, and other foodstuffs. Moving from Canada to the United States are paper, wood pulp, and other forest products; refined metals; metallic ores and concentrates; and machinery, transport equipment, and parts.

Much of this flow is due to the contiguity of the two countries, both very large and sharing a 2,600-mile border. Canada imports American coal, for example, because her own substantial deposits of high-quality coal are located in the far east and far west of the country, whereas the Appalachian coal deposits of the

United States are only a short distance from Canada's economic heartland centering on Toronto. This distance effect is enhanced further by the fact that most of Canada's population live within 300 miles of the United States boundary. To a great extent, however, the makeup of this two-way trade can be attributed to the complementarity of the two economies. Canada's land-intensive exports of wood products and metallic ores and American shipments of machinery and other capital-intensive goods illustrate this. Complementarity is also demonstrated by Canada's imports of winter vegetables and citrus fruits, which come from regions of subtropical climate in the United States that Canada cannot duplicate. The similarity of cultures in the two countries is an additional aid to commerce between them.

The high percentage of American commercial control of Canadian industry further influences the character of this trade, as shown by the automobile agreement between the United States and Canada. This pact represents a rather tentative sectoral approach to economic integration, involving as it does the raw materials and products of a single giant industry. Motor vehicle production on both sides of the border is under the same ownership and makes identical products by the same methods. Before the agreement the Canadian portion of the industry was protected by a high tariff wall and had operated at a considerable cost disadvantage. With a domestic market only slightly larger than that of California, the Canadian branches were hampered by short model runs and high unit costs. Under the new arrangement manufacturers can transport parts and assembled vehicles duty-free between the two countries (although private citizens cannot do so), thereby permitting greater specialization and increased economies of large-scale production in both countries. Not all aspects of the Canadian–United States production and trade are so closely interrelated as the automobile industry, however, and each country has trading connections beyond Anglo-America.

United States Approximately one-seventh of the world's commerce is generated by the United States, which remains the world's leading trading nation. In recent years, however, United States foreign trade has not grown at the world rate. For more than three decades the country had enjoyed a substantial surplus of exports over imports, but by 1971 even this had disappeared. As Figure 9-9 indicates, this reversal reflects a continuing rise in imports and a simultaneous decline in exports as inflation eroded the country's ability to compete in the world market. Even so, the United States retains a commanding lead over second-place West Germany and third-place Japan.

Despite the great volume of goods traded abroad by the United States, the nation depends upon its trade earnings for a surprisingly small proportion of its trillion-dollar total output of goods and services. In most years the value of exports represents only 4 to 5 percent of the country's gross domestic product, as compared with 18 to 20 percent for Canada and as much as 40 percent for some Western European lands. In large measure this low rate of trade participation by the United States can be attributed to the size of the economy and the per capita purchasing power of the population. Then too, the country is able to provide a

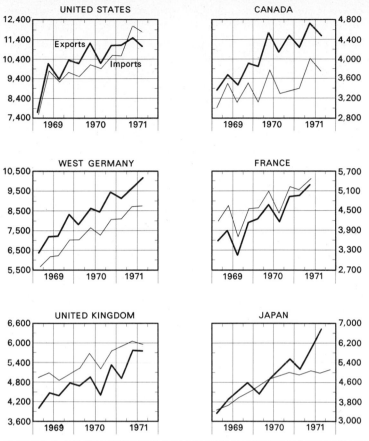

FIGURE 9-9 VALUE OF EXPORTS AND IMPORTS OF SIX LEADING TRADING NATIONS, 1969, 1970, AND 1971. (UNITED NATIONS *YEARBOOK OF INTERNATIONAL TRADE STATISTICS.*)

large part of its own needs by reason of its unusually generous and varied resource endowment. The wide range of climatic and soil types and large expanse of arable farmland permit food production far in excess of domestic requirements. Many of the most important minerals occur within the country in ample quantities—especially coal—and manufacturing is highly developed and exceedingly varied. These are some of the reasons why the importance of foreign trade is greatly underestimated by most citizens of the United States, who are unaware of the need for large export earnings to pay for certain vital imports required by the complex domestic economy and to finance other expenditures abroad (including overseas military outlays, tourist spending, and foreign aid).

Foreign trade has been essential to the United States from the start. The original Colonies, with their coastal location and isolation from the great undeveloped continental interior, depended upon Europe and the West Indies for economic survival. Before the twentieth century the United States was mainly an exporter of foodstuffs and crude materials, particularly cotton, tobacco, grains, coal, and later, oil. Manufactured goods continued to gain in importance, however, and since about 1910 they have constituted the larger part of total exports. Today the country's exports are highly diverse, including an almost infinite variety of both manufactured and primary goods. In each category are certain commodities for which American producers have an important comparative advantage. Corn, wheat, soybeans, and coal, for example, are produced at lower unit costs than in most other lands, owing not just to a superior natural endowment but also to efficient, capital-intensive production techniques. For many years the United States has likewise held an absolute advantage in high-technology manufactures—goods requiring much research and development. The country continues to maintain a technological lead in such products as aircraft, computers, and chemicals; but certain others, such as motorcars, electronics, machine tools, and photographic equipment, have passed out of the country's grasp. The United States also remains competitive in various other lines owing to the external economies a large and varied manufacturing concentration is able to command.

After Canada, the most important customers of the United States are Japan, the United Kingdom, and West Germany. As a whole, Western Europe takes nearly a third of United States exports, and well over half of that amount goes to the EEC countries alone. Imports of the United States have a similar pattern, the chief suppliers being Canada, Japan, West Germany, and the United Kingdom. In recent years, trade with Latin America has actually declined absolutely while that with Western Europe and Japan has risen.

Canada For a country with so small a population, Canada ranks high among the world's trading nations: sixth in exports and seventh in imports (1970). Canada's exports represent a far greater proportion of its domestic output than those of the United States do. This high rate of trade participation is attributable to the small size of Canada's population, which enjoys a high level of technical advancement and occupies a vast territory offering an abundance of minerals, forest products, and grains for exploitation and sale on the world market. Although most of Canada's farms are very productive, agriculture is confined largely by climatic and other physical conditions to a narrow belt near the United States border, which limits the variety of agricultural output. The Canadian domestic market is too small to support certain types of manufacturing with a high order of entry. Thus, although the Canadian economy produces a large surplus of certain goods, it is not able to provide a sufficient variety to meet the full range of needs and wants of its own people. The result is a high level of exchange with the outside world, and this trade continues to grow at a rapid rate (see Figure 9-9).

It should not be supposed that Canada supplies only food and industrial raw materials directly from the mine, forest, or farm in unchanged form. A majority of Canada's exports are processed at least to some degree before leaving the country. Many of the metallic ores are first smelted or even fabricated into useful shapes; the greater part of the wood is converted to lumber, wood pulp, or paper; and much of the grain is milled into flour or animal feed. To these land-intensive goods are added a number of finished products, including such consumer durables as motorcars. As a class, therefore, manufactured products form a relatively high proportion of the goods sent abroad.

Although the United States is Canada's principal supplier and market, trade with other countries is important too. The United Kingdom, Japan, and the EEC countries are Canada's best customers; these same countries plus Venezuela are the principal suppliers. The United Kingdom's prominence as a trading partner reflects in large part Canada's British Commonwealth ties. The highest rate of trade increase has been with Japan, an important customer for western Canada's coal, wood products, and grain. The Soviet Union and China occasionally import very large quantities of Canadian grain and flour during years of poor harvests in those communist lands. As a bloc the EEC is rapidly assuming a larger place in Canada's exports and imports. Venezuela remains an important source of petroleum for Montreal's refineries. That portion of Canada's trade remaining from its huge exchange with the United States is thus beginning to shift to new partners on the continent of Europe and in the Far East. The rapidly growing sales of grain foreshadow the future role for which Canada appears to be destined in the critical war against world hunger.

Noncommunist Europe   The second major world trading region is more than twice as active as the first. Nearly half of the world's commerce is generated by Western Europe. Six of the ten leading trading nations—all highly industrialized—are in this region, which has become very productive and prosperous. Its dense population provides a superb labor force and a rich market, and it is here that per capita trade reaches the world's highest levels. The exports-GDP ratio is also very high, especially within the Benelux group.

It must be recognized, of course, that much of this great flow of trade is merely a function of Europe's political fragmentation—twenty countries occupying less than half the area of the United States. Indeed, two-thirds of the trade of these countries moves within Western Europe. If a United States of Western Europe were formed, all this intra-European movement would be counted as domestic trade, leaving a trade with the rest of the world not much greater than that of the United States alone. This confirms the logic of economic integration, a concept of European origin.

European Economic Community   In 1944, near the end of World War II, the three Benelux countries formed a customs union, which was subsequently to become quite successful. The Benelux group, together with France, West Germany, and Italy, joined together in 1953 to establish the European Coal and Steel Community (ECSC), an experiment in the sectoral approach to economic integration. Being concerned only with these two closely associated activities, the ECSC provided for the free movement of the raw materials and products of those industries and of their factors of production. All this took place under the control of a supranational authority. So effective was this test of the integration principle that in 1957 the six countries agreed under the terms of the Treaty of Rome to expand the arrangement to include all other facets of their economies. The new organization, which was called the European Economic Community, or European Common Market, was in fact more than just a common market. In addition to the usual provisions, it called for harmonization of economic policies, cooperation in social affairs, and the creation of a supranational executive, judiciary, and legislature. Internal barriers among the six have gradually been removed and a common tariff wall to nonmembers has been erected.

Several circumstances favored the new organization. Being relatively small, they had much to gain from the economies of large-scale operation that an enlarged market would bring; being contiguous and forming a compact shape, they could achieve important economies by uniting their efficient, well-developed transport systems; having a wide range of primary and secondary production, they could form a single economy of great strength and diversity.

At the time the EEC was formed, much was made of the advantages that the group would have by virtue of their complementarities, each with a special contribution to make to the union: France, its important iron ore deposits and large agricultural acreage; West Germany, its large reserves of high-quality coal; Italy, its subtropical agriculture and surplus labor; and the Netherlands, its efficient, very intensive vegetable and animal industries. More recently it has become recognized that one of the EEC's greatest strengths is the competitive nature of the industrial sectors. Union has forced individual firms to become more efficient in their operations in order to survive, and everyone has benefited from the lower unit production costs that have resulted.

Formation of this union has brought profound changes to its member countries, particularly their trade. Although European trade has risen steadily during the period of postwar recovery, it was beginning to lose momentum at the time of the signing of the Treaty of Rome. Since then it has surged upward once more, much more rapidly than the trade of most nonmembers. Especially notable have been the trade-diversion effects of this union, shown by the growth of trade among EEC members at the expense of their trade with others. In 1958 intra-EEC exports were 32 percent of the total exports of the six; by 1969 they had exceeded 48 percent of the total. Thus the people of West Germany were buying Dutch vegetables and animal products instead of Danish, and they were importing French wheat instead of American. All six members have participated in the general rise in trade, and all are numbered among the top ten trading nations of the world. Note in Figure 9-9, for example, the recent strong trade performance of the two leaders of this group, West Germany and France. This intrabloc trade gives clear evidence of the effects of integration on production, which has become increasingly specialized within industry groups. Thus all six have their steel industries, but each country's steel mills tend to emphasize the production of particular types of steel goods, such as structural steel, flat-rolled sheet products, or high-alloy tool steels.

Although these trade-diversion effects were widely anticipated and feared by nonmembers, the operation of the EEC has unexpectedly resulted in a great deal of trade creation as well. The rise in per capita incomes of EEC members and the rapid growth of their industries has greatly increased the demand for goods from the rest of the world. Consequently there has been a substantial absolute growth of external trade by EEC members. In its commerce with nonmembers the EEC trades most with the EFTA group and to a lesser degree with Anglo-America. There is also substantial exchange with former French and Belgian colonies in Africa. Middle Eastern oil occupies an important place in the imports of the six. On the whole, however, the less developed countries have a declining place in the EEC's total trade. Except for goods from Anglo-America, most of the EEC's imports from non-European sources are industrial raw materials, fuels, and agricultural goods, whereas the EEC's exports are predominantly industrial products.

The demonstrated value of membership in the EEC has led a number of other nations to seek economic ties with the group. Most important of all was the recent agreement which added three new full members to the Common Market, two of them former members of a rival group, the European Free Trade Association (EFTA).

European Free Trade Association   Although the United Kingdom had participated in the negotiations that resulted in the Treaty of Rome and the formation of the EEC, the British declined membership in the EEC because of their reluctance to accept such a high level of integration. Britain thereupon joined with six other European nations—Austria, Denmark, Norway, Portugal, Sweden, and Switzerland—in a free-trade area (ultimately including Finland and Iceland as well). Aside from the difficulty of administering an organization lacking control over the external trade of its members, the European Free Trade Association encountered problems because of the scattered locations of several of its members.

From the inception of the EFTA in 1960, one of its prime purposes was to eventually achieve some form of association with the EEC. To facilitate such a rapprochement, the EFTA group used the same gradual approach as the EEC in removing barriers to the movements of goods among members. All intra-EFTA tariffs on industrial products were finally reduced to zero on December 31, 1966. One of the strongest incentives for forming a connection with the EEC was the tradition of close trading ties between individual members of the two groups— those between Denmark and Germany and between the United Kingdom and Benelux, for example. The EFTA as a whole came to depend heavily upon its trade with EEC countries, much more than the EEC relied upon the EFTA. Indeed, EEC became EFTA's chief trading partner, taking more than one-fourth of EFTA's exports and supplying one-third of its imports. This interbloc trade was much greater, in fact, than the trade among EFTA members.

All of this underlay the decision of Britain and Denmark to withdraw from the EFTA and join the EEC. After lengthy negotiations, these two countries were finally admitted to the Common Market on January 1, 1973, together with Ireland, thereby increasing the EEC to a total of nine full members. In addition, a number of nations in Africa and southeastern Europe have acquired associate membership.

Despite its problems, the EFTA had enjoyed some modest success. Trade within the bloc had benefited from the complementarity of production among its various members. Norway, Sweden, and Finland had provided the forest products and minerals, and Denmark and Portugal had supplied the agricultural commodities, needed by Britain; at the same time, several members contributed their particular industrial specialties. One of the EFTA's lasting dividends has been the sharp rise in trade among its Scandinavian members, which enjoy the advantage of contiguity.

Before 1973, the United Kingdom had accounted for nearly half of EFTA's total trade, although its share had been diminishing for some time. The United Kingdom was the world's third largest importer until 1968, when Japan surged ahead. Britain's exports are lower than its imports, causing a serious trade imbalance (Figure 9-9). As indicated earlier, Britain has relied upon "invisible exports," such as tourism and financial and transport services, to bring its international payments into balance, but with diminishing success in recent years. The British trading pattern still evidences the long-standing commercial links with the Commonwealth, which includes the country's remaining colonies and most of its former possessions. Except for Canada, which is more closely associated commercially with the United States, most of the Commonwealth countries belong to the sterling bloc. Members of the latter group base their currencies on the British pound sterling, maintain monetary reserves in sterling, and depend on London for their banking. Commercial links with the Commonwealth are weakening, however, and British trade growth is not keeping pace with that of the rest of the world.

Other noncommunist trade Outside of Anglo-America and Western Europe, there is only one major supplier of industrial goods to the world market, Japan. Although the Soviet Union has the second largest economy in the world, only a minor part of its industrial output leaves the country. With this important exception, most of the rest of the nations of the world—even including several at high levels of technical advancement—are suppliers mainly of crude materials and foodstuffs.

Latin America The trade of Latin America is increasing but slowly. In large measure this low rate of growth is due to the types of commodities exported, which are mainly primary goods. Because of the limited demand and weak prices for many of these items, the export earnings of their suppliers are not sufficient to pay for needed imports. In their levels of economic development the Latin American countries range from very low to moderately advanced. Bolivia's per capita gross domestic product is only $165 while the per capita figures for Argentina and Venezuela are $657 and $977 respectively (1969).

One notable feature of Latin American trade is the role of the United States as both a market and supplier to many of these countries. In 1969 the United States accounted for 30 percent of all Latin American exports and 37 percent of its imports. This dependence on the United States is steadily diminishing, however, as trade with other parts of the world becomes relatively more important. Indeed, more than one-third of Latin America's exports now go to Western Europe, the EEC countries being the most important customers. Trade with Japan and the Soviet Union is rising also. On the other hand, only 11 percent of Latin American trade is with other Latin American countries.

For this reason the current experiments in economic integration are especially significant. Of the three integrated groups of the region, the Central American

Common Market (CACM) shows the greatest promise. Integration is being used deliberately as a device for achieving economic development, as the CACM countries attempt to foster individual manufacturing specialties to add to their traditionally competitive exports of minerals and tropical foods. Each of the five member countries is too small to provide a viable market for most modern industries, but together they have a population that numbers more than 15 million and is growing rapidly. The CACM is a highly integrated organization with a supranational authority, a development bank, and much-needed cooperative educational and training facilities. Among the several encouraging results thus far is the establishment of a number of new manufacturing plants. While the total trade of the group has risen steadily since formation of the union in 1961, trade among members of the bloc has grown even more rapidly.

A second integration attempt, the Latin American Free Trade Association has made little noticeable progress. Among its many problems are the great distances separating the effective territories of member countries, the near absence of connecting overland routes, and highly competitive production of both primary and secondary goods. Similar difficulties confront the efforts to implement a customs union in the Caribbean.

Northern Africa and the Middle East Except for Israel, all the Middle Eastern countries are at a low level of development. Nevertheless, total exports of the group have risen more rapidly than those of the world as a whole owing to fast-growing petroleum exports from the region. The Moslem countries of this area have tentatively formed integrated groups, but no concrete results are apparent as yet. The only technically advanced nation in the Middle East, Israel has a diversified economy and exports both primary commodities and manufactured goods. There is a high degree of complementarity between the output of Israel on the one hand and the Arab states on the other, but trade has failed to develop because of the intense enmity that separates the two sides. Indeed, there is very little trade within the Moslem bloc itself.

Africa south of the Sahara The most advanced country in the continent, South Africa, has diverse production and is a very active trader. Not only is it the world's largest source of gold and gem-quality diamonds, it is also an important exporter of subtropical foods and animal products. The remaining countries of Africa south of the Sahara are at low levels of development, although there is a substantial outpouring of tropical agricultural products and minerals, in some cases from foreign enclaves within these countries and in other cases from native production. Most of these political entities have recently gained their independence, but a large part of their trade continues to be channeled to the colonial powers to which they were formerly attached. One notable integration experiment in the region was the East African Federation, comprising Kenya, Tanzania, and Uganda.

Noncommunist South and East Asia Throughout much of the Orient, the characteristics of trade are much affected by the nature and distribution of human populations. In most eastern countries high population densities are associated with a subsistence type of production that does not permit many people to participate in the commercial economy. Nevertheless, in a few places—Taiwan, Singapore, Hong Kong, and especially Japan—large populations have been mobilized in such a way as to yield high levels of output and to allow active participation in world trade.

Japan's seemingly miraculous performance in the modern commercial world is unprecedented. One by one Japan has overtaken the leaders of world trade until the country has now attained third place behind the United States and West Germany. Faced with the formidable problem of supporting more than 100 million people on a meager physical resource base, Japan has achieved a high degree of efficiency in (1) transporting the imported raw materials, fuels, and food required by its economy and in distributing finished products to foreign markets, (2) utilizing a well-disciplined and highly skilled labor force, and (3) mobilizing a large and growing body of capital.

Japan entered the postwar period with a reputation for being clever at copying the technology of the leading industrial nations and for producing mainly labor-intensive nondurable consumer goods that were cheaply produced and sometimes shoddy in quality. Today Japan has gone a long way toward closing the technology gap and is becoming an innovator exercising close quality control. The nature of goods produced for export has changed markedly, and the emphasis is now being given to goods requiring more engineering, a higher order of labor skills, and greater capital input. So far has this transformation proceeded that Japan now sends far more high-technology goods to the United States than she receives in return.

One important category of Japanese exports is consumer durables, such as radios, television sets, tape recorders, cameras, and motorcars. The country has been aided in developing overseas markets for these goods by the growing domestic market for consumer products as per capita incomes have risen, thereby making possible economies of large-scale production and lower unit costs. The Japanese have also become leading suppliers of other types of transport equipment, locomotives and ships in particular. Here the advantages of industrial agglomeration have been important, especially the well-developed steel and engineering industries of the islands. Finally there is a wide range of producer goods, including such items as machine tools and textile machinery. Japan has thus further developed her role as an importer of basic raw materials and an exporter of finished goods. As Figure 9-9 indicates, Japan has acquired an uncommonly large surplus of exports over imports.

Another distinctive characteristic of Japanese trade is the unusual diversification of trade linkages, that is, the large variety of markets and sources of supply. Slightly more than one-half of Japan's trade is with other technically advanced nations. The United States is the largest single market, taking nearly one-third of Japanese exports while supplying about 28 percent of that country's imports. Collectively the nations of Western Europe represent the second largest trading partner of the Japanese, accounting for 13 percent of her exports and 11 percent of her imports (1969). One of the unique aspects of Japan's foreign commerce, however, is the large proportion of it that takes place with less developed countries, more than either of the other major trading regions. Well over two-fifths of Japanese trade is of this sort. Most of the less developed countries of Latin America, Africa, and the Middle East are linked in trade with Japan. Japan obtains more than 13 percent of her imports from the Middle East alone, the major source of all important petroleum supplies for the modern Japanese economy. One of Japan's largest markets, however, is found among the less developed countries of Asia, which contribute more than one-quarter of the country's trade. Japan is the single largest supplier to other Asiatic countries, including those of the communist bloc. This clearly illustrates the trade effects of distance, since Japan is easily able to undercut competitors from Europe and North America, owing to lower transport costs. The influence of distance also shows up in trade with Australia, which now supplies nearly one-tenth of Japan's imports.

With certain exceptions, the rest of the Far East contrasts starkly with Japan's trading experience. These exceptions, as noted earlier, are Taiwan, Singapore, and Hong Kong, which are replacing Japan increasingly as suppliers of cheaply produced consumer goods of a labor-intensive nature, such as toys, lower grades of textiles, and ready-to-wear clothing. Other than these, the noncommunist less developed countries of Asia have failed to participate equally in the general rise in world trade. Most of the exports of these countries are unprocessed primary commodities, although Malaysia now ships smelted tin, and India is exporting low-grade cotton cloth and jute fabrics. The principal communist country of Asia, China, has a particularly low rate of trade participation despite a population of more than 800 million.

Oceania Australia and New Zealand rank high among the world's technically advanced countries in per capita GDP and both have acquired secondary industries of some diversity. Most of their manufactured goods are for home consumption, however, and exports continue to be land-intensive, with a particular emphasis on grains and high-value animal products, such as chilled meat, wool, butter, and cheese. This concentration on agricultural exports of high transportability reflects the peripheral location of these two countries with respect to the principal markets for such goods in Western Europe, especially the United Kingdom and the EEC. Australia also trades importantly with the United States. Communist China and the Soviet Union are occasionally customers for large quantities of Australian grain. The most rapidly growing market for Australia's minerals, sugar, and wheat, however, is Japan, as indicated above. With the hope of increasing their comparatively minor sales to each other, the two principal nations of Oceania in 1966 signed the Australia–New Zealand Free Trade Agreement.

Eastern Europe and the Soviet Union Earlier we noted that the communist countries have a different approach to international trade. Throughout the Stalin regime trade was deemphasized and national economic self-sufficiency was stressed by the Soviet Union and its tightly reined satellites. A new impetus was given to trade in the post-Stalin period, with the result that the countries of the

Soviet bloc are beginning to trade more actively both with one another and with the outside world.

This change is seen in the altered character and role of the Communist Council for Mutual Economic Assistance (CMEA or Comecon). Originally intended as a device to encourage the development process in the communist countries, Comecon was reorganized in 1958 in reaction to the formation of the EEC, which the communists regarded as an economic threat. Although the new Comecon was supposedly recast in the image of the EEC, it differs from the latter in many essential respects, particularly in its lack of supranational authority and the absence in the communist world of tariffs as such. At Khrushchev's insistence the group attempted to assign specific production roles to individual members, but the less developed members, Romania and Bulgaria, refused to accept their delegated tasks as suppliers of primary goods in exchange for the manufactured goods of the more highly developed countries of the bloc, such as Czechoslovakia and East Germany. Thus little has been accomplished by the CMEA despite their apparent advantages for integration. Nevertheless, intra-Comecon trade represents two-thirds of the group's total. Communist China was formerly a Comecon customer, but now purchases very little from the bloc.

Recently the communist countries have been seeking to broaden their trading connections throughout the world. One area with which CMEA trade has grown rapidly is Western Europe, a good market for the bloc's coal, petroleum, forest products, and metallic minerals. Comecon trade with the less developed nations has also been increasing, and these countries now account for more than 10 percent of the bloc's foreign sales. Approximately two-fifths of Comecon's trade is provided by the Soviet Union, which usually ranks eighth or ninth among the world's exporting nations. This is a much poorer showing than would normally be expected of the world's second largest economy.

WORLD ORGANIZATIONS

In noting the strong post-World War II trend toward economic integration, we have observed that the truly successful unions have tended to expand their intrabloc trade more rapidly than their trade with the rest of the world. Carried to its ultimate conclusion, this trend would produce a world in which trade was largely compartmentalized. Because of widespread concern on this point, efforts are being made to obtain world agreements to reduce or eliminate barriers to trade generally. The main vehicle for this movement has been the General Agreement on Tariffs and Trade (GATT), to which most of the trading nations of the world subscribe. Six successful negotiating rounds of GATT have been completed since the group came into being in 1947. The sixth series of negotiations (called the Kennedy Round after the enabling act of Congress sponsored by the late President of the United States) was completed in 1967. Its principal result was the reduction of most tariffs by approximately one-third. It was the hope of those who signed this agreement that world trade might continue its long and steady postwar climb and that world prosperity would thereby be enabled to increase and spread more widely.

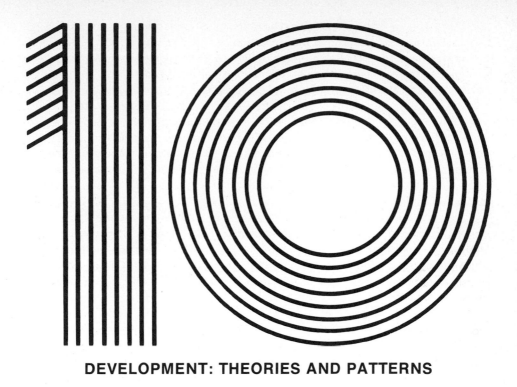

DEVELOPMENT: THEORIES AND PATTERNS

Preceding chapters have indicated some of the reasons why certain places are chosen for the location of production and distribution of goods and as foci for transport networks and trade flows. But what of those areas passed by in this selection process? The contrasts between the blooming prosperity of the chosen and the deepening poverty of the neglected are beginning to arouse greater concern, owing in large measure to an awakened social consciousness. Internationally the widening disparities between rich and poor countries have been dramatized by the end of colonial rule and the appearance of a world "population explosion." Within more prosperous countries attention has been directed toward the plight of those persons living in regions that have failed to participate in the general rise in affluence. Although certain problems of economic development have been suggested earlier, this dynamic aspect of the spatial economic system will be our main focus in this final chapter.

Development may be defined as a rapid rise in total and per capita income, sustained over a considerable time and affecting most segments of a society, together with related demographic, economic, and technological changes. There are several important elements in this definition. Note first of all that growth and change occur rapidly, are sweeping in character, and appear endless. All facets of society are transformed in this process. High rates of invention and innovation result in the rapid adoption of new techniques of production, transportation, and distribution. Output rises in volume and diversity, bringing changes in the composition of the labor force and, in particular, a decline in the proportion employed in agriculture. An increasing division of labor occurs as the growing complexity of the economic system demands higher levels of specialization. All this means rising levels of efficiency and a greater productivity of all factors—land, labor, capital, and entrepreneurship.

Development not only produces a rise in total income, but more particularly it brings growth in per capita incomes and a redistribution of incomes. With increasing individual prosperity, per capita consumption levels rise, diets improve, and more personal income remains for the purchase of luxuries. Changes likewise occur in population growth characteristics as mortality rates and, eventually, birth rates decline, causing a reduction in family size and altering of the age structure. The population becomes increasingly mobile, both horizontally and vertically as barriers to such movement fall. Accompanying these economic and social changes are the loosening of old folkways and mores and an increasing secularization of society. Development is, therefore, a many-faceted phenomenon, affecting a region in nearly every respect. Most important of all, however, is the material well-being it brings. "Fundamentally, [economic development] means rising per capita incomes" (Higgins, 1968, p. 147).

Yet, as we have already noted, this prosperity does not come in equal measure to all places at the same time. At the international level it is customary to refer to the wealthier lands as being "developed," "advanced," or "technically advanced," and to label the poorer ones as "underdeveloped," "less developed," or "lagging." It should not be thought, however, that all countries fall into either of these two extreme categories. Actually there is a continuum, or graduated scale, of development along which the countries of the world are arrayed at various intervals, suggesting the many possible degrees of prosperity or poverty. These variations are recognized in some of the terminology appearing in the literature, as, for example, use of the expression "developing" to distinguish those poorer countries that are making genuine progress from "backward" countries that are making little or no visible headway (Linder, 1967). Moreover, it is presumed that the developmental process is never complete.

The concern of this chapter, therefore, is with a problem that exists in both time and space. In the next section we shall examine some of the leading theories that attempt to provide an orderly explanation of the sequence of events leading from a state of underdevelopment to one of development and to account for the ways in which development and underdevelopment vary spatially. We shall then note certain specific problems of development, measure their scope, and review a few of the efforts to apply the insights of theory to overcoming these problems.

Whether it is the development of districts, regions, or countries that is of interest, it will be found that most of the same principles apply. The main differences between the national and international scales of observation, as in the case of trade, relate to the barriers to the movement of labor, capital, and entrepreneurship, which are greater between countries than between other regions.

THEORIES OF DEVELOPMENT

No single overall theory of development has received general acceptance at this time, an indication of the extreme complexity of the problem. Nevertheless, the various theories appear to fall mainly within a limited number of categories representing particular lines of thought. Two main vantage points tend to be expressed in the theoretical literature on development as such: the historical and the spatial. *Historical* theories are intended to explain and predict the changes that happen to a given society along the path of development. This is the temporal view of events in a single area. On the other hand, *spatial* theories attempt to discern a meaningful spatial pattern of the various levels of development at a given point in time. The concern here is with all places on a given date. In addition to these theories of development, *underdevelopment* is the subject of an accumulating third body of thought. The theories in this last group relate specifically to the problems of those areas that have as yet been passed by in the developmental process.

HISTORICAL THEORIES OF DEVELOPMENT

Although the subject of development has gained prominence in recent decades, it is by no means a new topic. Theorists of the late eighteenth and early nineteenth centuries were much preoccupied with matters of economic growth and progress; they included such great names as Adam Smith, John Stuart Mill, Thomas Malthus, and Karl Marx. All had directly experienced the effects of the first industrial revolution in the United Kingdom. Although the topic lay dormant between 1870 and about 1935, under the label "economic development" it has received considerable impetus since World War II as the problems of less developed areas have been thrust upon our attention. Historical theories of development fall under two headings, the general theories, with origins in the classical period, and the stage theories, having to do with a sequence of steps through which a region is presumed to pass in the developmental process.

General theories The classical theorists were interested in learning how incomes could be made to continue rising and how technological advances could outpace population growth without falling into stagnation. Despite their differences in details, the general theorists have agreed that increased income depends upon four factors: population growth, resource discovery, technological progress, and capital accumulation. For output to rise, at least one of these is essential (Higgins, 1968, p. 188).

Population As the source of labor supply and as the market for a region's output, population can affect development in a number of ways, some positive and others negative. On the positive side, labor functioned as the chief factor of production during the long period of handicrafts and before the modernization of agriculture. During that era growth in total output bore a direct relationship to increases in the size of the labor force. The industrial and agricultural revolutions greatly reduced this dependence. Beneficial effects likewise result from an increase in the size of a high-income population, since the growing market permits economies of large-scale production, which in turn stimulate employment. Both conditions are illustrated by the history of development in the United States during the colonial period and afterwards, when rapid growth of an initially sparse population played an essential part in the expansion of the economic system.

From the negative viewpoint, population growth can mean having to divide a finite amount of income, capital, and resources among larger numbers of people. If population grows at an excessive rate, it can outpace increases in total income and capital and strip the region of its resources. These are grave problems today. Rapid population growth also results in large numbers of dependent children to be supported by the work force.

To the classical writers population size was ultimately a function of workers' incomes. The first to address this problem was Thomas R. Malthus, whose famous statement appeared in 1798. According to Malthus, population tends to grow at an ever-increasing rate, while the means of subsistence (the food supply) tends to rise at a steady rate. The result is that population will at some point in time outstrip the food supply and the increase in numbers will thereupon be halted by famine. This outcome is inevitable unless population growth is checked in some manner, either by positive checks such as war, famine, or plague or by the preventive check of "moral restraint" (abstinence from marriage). Because of a number of fortuitous events Malthus could not have foreseen, his dread predictions for Europe and the Europeanized lands of the New World never materialized, but they are proving tragically all too true in many of today's less developed lands. Karl Marx strongly disagreed with Malthus's assessment, claiming that an equitable distribution of output and income would remove any population problem. This position has not been confirmed in the grossly overpopulated countries; even communist China has had to place severe restrictions on population growth.

Resource discovery As a factor of production, land is considered to include not only arable or crop land but also mineral deposits, forests, and other useful items associated with it. Although in the absolute sense land is fixed in quantity, some of its attributes are not. Advancing technology brings new uses for minerals, as in the case of uranium, and new methods of using reserves that were previously considered uneconomical—lean iron ores, for example. At the same time, new discoveries may add to the total stock of known reserves while the depletion of old deposits reduces those reserves.

Clearly the development of an area may be importantly affected by the amount and kind of resources it possesses. The influence of resource discovery was understandably stressed by the classical theorists, who were writing at the time of the opening of new worlds overseas. Resources were thus important in the past, and they are likewise proving vital to the development plans of some areas at present, especially the oil-producing lands of the Middle East, Africa, and Latin America.

Technological progress   The classical theories, conceived as they were after the first industrial revolution, gave a central role also to technology. Much has been made of the effects on development of invention (the conceiving of fundamentally new ideas) and innovation (putting those ideas to practical use) and the key role of the entrepreneur in promoting these. Technological advances serve to increase the unit output of the factors of production. Thus the agricultural revolution increased the amount produced by each farm worker and each acre of land. Similarly, the advances in industrial technology expanded the productivity of factory labor and increased the efficiency of resource use. These increases in the productivity of labor and land translate, of course, into increased per capita income.

Social overhead   Capital refers not only to the supply of liquid financial assets but also to the stock of man-made means of production, such as machinery, tools, and factories. The necessity of adding to the supply of capital lies at the heart of the developmental process as seen by the classical theorists, and it is still viewed that way in communistic as well as capitalistic countries. The accumulation of capital in its various forms is regarded as essential to technological progress. Development requires investment in the means of production—factory construction and land clearance, for example—as well as financial support for invention and innovation. Investment must also be made in what is called "social capital," facilities that are used by the whole society, such as roads, utilities, schools, and ports. The money required for these may be obtained through savings of individuals, government taxes, borrowing at home or abroad, or foreign aid grants.

Stages of development   Some theorists have maintained that development generally occurs through an orderly and predictable sequence of events that can be assigned to a number of distinct phases or stages. The region or country can be expected to exhibit a unique set of characteristics while passing through each phase. Some of the earlier attempts to distinguish such a set of developmental stages date to the nineteenth century, and such writers as Weber (1909), Hoover (1947), and Isard (1956) have subsequently outlined such schemes, especially with respect to the evolution of regional economies.

Hoover, for example, identifies the first stage as the *primitive region*, which, because of high transport costs, is forced to be self-sufficient in its production. Only subsistence types of hunting, fishing, grazing, and agriculture are feasible under these conditions. As transport rates fall, trade with other areas can take place and the stage of *regional specialization* commences. During this phase production emphasizes primary commodities for which there is the greatest comparative advantage in national or world markets. Subsequently the region enters a phase of *intensified rural land use* as the need for greater and greater output is felt. Eventually agriculture proves to be an inadequate base for continued growth owing to the limited market for primary goods and the inability of primary activities to continue absorbing population increases. Manufacturing must therefore be introduced if economic growth is to continue. Industrialization occurs in stages also, the first of these being devoted to *processing agricultural or forest products*. Later, smelting, refining, chemical, or other *heavy industries* are introduced, using fossil fuels obtained locally or nearby. Alternatively, industries using imported raw materials may become established in response to some local processing-cost advantage such as cheap or highly skilled labor. In the final phase a *service sector* appears and, if it thrives and develops sufficiently, it may even bring in income from outside the region, as has happened in the case of London, New York City, and Washington, D.C.

Rostow's stages The most celebrated attempt to devise a stage theory is that of Walt W. Rostow (1962), whose work was concerned mainly with the development of countries but, as he himself indicated, could equally well be applied to the economic growth of regions within countries. Unlike some of his predecessors, Rostow explicitly took into account, noneconomic as well as economic behavior in devising a theory of economic growth that was intended to explain the historical development of today's technically advanced economies and provide a basis for predicting the future of particular economies that are as yet undeveloped. His method was to break down the developmental history of national economies into five stages that appear to be common to all societies: the "traditional society," "establishing the preconditions for take-off," the "take-off," the "drive to maturity," and the "age of high mass consumption."

The "traditional society" is one that has severely limited production, mainly subsistence agriculture and other simple primary activities. Knowledge of modern science and technology is lacking, and there is a prevalent attitude that the physical environment is not susceptible of human management. Attitudes, like both social and political organization, generally tend to be rigid. Extreme conservatism dominates all thought, and there is a resistance to change born of a fear of the unfamiliar. The social structure is rigidly hierarchical, based on family, clan, or tribal groupings. Political control is firmly held by the landowners.

Overcoming these obstacles to economic growth is the main function of the second stage, called "establishing the preconditions for take-off." Rostow regards this as a transitional period during which the society is preparing itself (or being prepared by some outside authority) for sustained growth. Because of the strong resistance to change of any kind, much time is usually required for this transformation of the traditional society. The kinds of changes required are (1) a shift of emphasis from agriculture into secondary and tertiary activities; (2) achievement of national unity; (3) a decline in birth rate to reduce the numbers in the nonproductive ages and to permit a rise in per capita incomes; (4) the rechanneling of savings into productive uses, especially modern types of production; (5) the elimination of caste or rigid class lines; (6) learning to manipulate the physical environment. Note that farming is not to be abandoned, only to be made more productive, with the proceeds invested in modern kinds of activities. During this period much investment must be allocated to transportation, schools, housing, and other forms of social capital.

If all this can be accomplished, conditions may be right for the economy to experience the "take-off." The first take-off occurred in the United Kingdom, followed in time by neighboring countries of Western Europe and by the United States and other lands settled by large numbers of Europeans. The take-off is defined as that period during which growth becomes a normal condition, a self-reinforcing kind of growth. One of the essential conditions for this is a substantial rise in the rate of productive investment, a rate that must be greater than the rate of population growth. At least some of the capital for this may be imported, as indeed was the case in the United States, Canada, and several others of the newer lands. It is necessary also for one or more high-growth manufacturing industries to become established at this time. Equally essential is the existence of the kinds of political, social, and institutional frameworks conducive to high growth.

The "drive to maturity" is a long period of sustained progress during which the modern forms of technology gradually reach into all parts of the economy. To avoid lapsing into stagnation, the economy must continue to receive a high rate of investment—higher than the rate of population growth. During this period the country assumes a place in the international economy. Although there is more domestic production of goods formerly imported, there is a need for new types of imports such as machinery and industrial raw materials, and additional exports must be developed to pay for these. There is much shifting of emphasis during this interval of change, as one after another industry jockeys for a leading place. Much time is required for modern technology to be fully absorbed, however, and Rostow suggests that most countries have needed at least three generations (about sixty years) after the beginning of the take-off for maturity to be reached. When it at last arrives, maturity is characterized by a wide range of industrial activity and a complex technology.

Finally comes the "age of high mass consumption." According to Rostow the United States is just emerging from this era, while Western Europe and Japan have only recently entered it and the Soviet Union is gingerly contemplating its possibilities. This stage is defined as one in which the leading sectors of the economy have shifted toward the production of durable consumers' goods and services. This shift is made possible by generally high per capita incomes that permit a large proportion of the population to make consumer purchases above the bare essentials. Composition of the labor force changes to include a larger percentage of clerical and other service workers and industrial workers with higher orders of skill. Characteristically, activities of these kinds are highly agglomerated; hence the rapid growth of urbanization during this period. Since modern technology has at last been fully absorbed, resources are increasingly allocated to social welfare and security. Because of the emphasis upon consumer durables, Rostow is led to suggest the mass-produced motorcar as the symbol of this era. Such a choice seems appropriate when one remembers how rapidly the number of automobiles in the United States grew after World War I, or the enthusiasm with which Western Europeans expanded their use of the motorcar in the 1950s and the Japanese in the 1960s.

When it first appeared, Rostow's theory elicited a thunderous response. It quickly became the subject of a voluminous critical literature—some favorable, much unfavorable—and several international conferences. The unfavorable comments fall into three categories: (1) that no such stage model of growth is possible, (2) that Rostow's particular attempt is flawed, and (3) that the real-world evidence is inadequate to support it. Under the first heading, some claim that no two economies are precisely alike and that it is impossible to generalize their experiences in a single model, let alone isolate clearly distinguishable phases of growth that are common to all. Others criticize the way Rostow's model is drawn. Although most agree that it emphasizes the essential elements in the developmental process, they feel it does not truly analyze causes but merely describes development as such. One common criticism is that Rostow does not provide any clear method for measuring the turning points, that the transitions between stages are blurred. It is also said that he fails to specify the mechanism by which the stages are linked to each other. Finally there is the criticism that empirical tests have so far failed to confirm discrete stages in the growth of those countries that now reached technical advancement. There are also numerous questions about the specific facts Rostow cites, particularly the dates when various economies experienced their take-offs.

Despite the furor over Rostow's theory, it has not yet been successfully replaced, and even his most ardent critics have adopted his terminology, which is now a firm part of the literature. With all its limitations, the theory remains a useful conceptual device for viewing the development process historically. Most modern countries seem to have undergone something like this in reaching their present states even though they may not all have done it in precisely the same manner or in discrete steplike fashion. A larger question is whether or not the countries now undergoing development are likely to follow this particular path, as Rostow insists. Already there is evidence that certain of these stages may be bypassed by today's newly developing lands. Moreover, as we shall see subsequently, some of the problems they encounter are of a different sort.

Economic base theory   In discussing his preconditions stage, Rostow presents his "leading sector" theory, referring to the circumstances under which an economy can acquire some dynamic activity to initiate its take-off. This theory is closely akin to the "staple export" theory devised by Innis to explain the development of Canada's economy (Innis, 1930). Innis's ideas have since been elaborated into an "economic base" theory, often used to represent the past experience of today's developed countries.

It has been pointed out that, while the traditional society was of great duration in many parts of the world (preindustrial Europe, Asia, Africa, and Latin America), it was exceedingly brief in those lands settled by the British, especially the United

States, Canada, Australia, and New Zealand (North, 1955). These latter areas were opened with the express purpose of expanding commerce with the mother country, and attention was directed immediately to fostering some "staple" export. This was a product for which the region had a comparative advantage with respect to other places and which could therefore be depended upon to bring income into the region. What this product might be was often determined through experimentation with various alternatives. To engage in such trade, it was necessary to have good transport connections to other markets; and to retain those markets in the face of competition, continual improvements in production techniques were necessary. The more attention thus given to the regional export specialty, the more firmly established it became in the local economy.

A careful distinction is made between the export industry, producing for foreign markets, and "residentiary" industry, whose products were intended for local consumption. Some writers refer to the export production as "basic" industry and the domestic type as "nonbasic." As this terminology suggests, it is the success of the export activities that determines the level of per capita incomes in the region, while the residentiary industry is mainly of a derived nature. Thus a region's rate of growth depends upon the success of its export base; any deterioration in that base causes the region to decline.

SPATIAL THEORIES

In recent years there has been an increasing emphasis upon building a body of theory to explain variations in level of development among different areas at any given time. A growing recognition of the close relationship that exists between the temporal and spatial dimensions leads us to expect that some systematic spatial pattern of development does indeed exist and is subject to logical explanation.

Center-periphery concept Earlier chapters have emphasized the universal tendency for human activities to focus upon some central point or node. This was the basis for classical land use theory as explained in Chapter 2, and it was an essential part of the analysis of transportation and trade patterns presented in Chapters 8 and 9. Many theorists argue that the fundamental ordering principle in all space relations is the center-periphery arrangement, the contrast between a central point of focus and areas on the margins of the region. From this center the benefits of economic growth are diffused outward into the surrounding region. Ray (1971) has developed a strong empirical argument that the entire Canadian economy can be viewed in a center-periphery context.

It has been observed, however, that the influence of spread effects diminishes with increasing distance from the center until at some point they cease to provide any positive stimulus at all. Thus we have a dichotomy in the use of earth space, with intense activity at the center and a tendency for that intensity to grow, and a much lower level of activity on the margins, where stagnation may actually prevail. This contrast is one that seems to appear early in the developmental process and to persist tenaciously.

Origins of spatial variation in development   How does one area gain the ascendancy over another in this way? By the processes described earlier certain regions begin to develop economically and are led in time to industrialization. Industries do not locate in all feasible places, however, owing to the compelling influence of agglomeration factors. Having gained a start in one particular place, for whatever reason the choice may have been made, secondary activities attract others in a cumulative fashion. This self-reinforcing growth of manufacturing results in falling unit costs because of large-scale production and other internal economies. External economies in the form of "backward linkages" likewise appear, as suppliers of the original firms locate in the area to be near their markets. Similarly, "forward linkages" take place when customers of the first group set up operations in the area to be near their raw-material sources. Firms of all types, whether related or not, enjoy the "urbanization" economies to be found in a large center with its transport features, financial institutions and other services, communications, and police and fire protection. Added to these multiplier factors are a number of less tangible considerations, such as the reputation for success and the presence of various amenities in the largest and most advanced places.

Other areas passed by in the industrialization process must continue to rely upon primary production. Consequently they fail to grow at a pace equal to that of the manufacturing regions and in fact are inclined to stagnate. The resulting spatial structure represents a dichotomy between a vital center that is intensifying its growth and development and a periphery that badly lags behind.

Spatial contrasts at different scales of observation   The dichotomy is apparent at several geographic levels. In the urban region the urban center is the focal point not only of manufacturing and commerce but also of the social, cultural, and political life of the entire region tributary to it. It is likewise the prime destination for rural-urban migration. This magnetic attraction of the great city is seen in the influence of Chicago, which pervades the entire American Midwest. At the national level certain regions tend to gain ascendancy over all others and to set the basic conditions for economic growth in the entire country. The megalopolis region of the northeastern United States illustrates an area that achieved national dominance through an early start.

At the continental scale, the dominant area of Europe centers upon the valleys of the Thames and the Rhine. The intense activity of this core region, which includes Britain, the Low Countries, northern France, and West Germany, contrasts starkly with the retarded development of Iberia and the Balkans on the southern and eastern margins of the Continent. Even at the global scale we can distinguish two main core areas, northwestern Europe and northeastern North America, which dominate the world economic system. The level of economic activity tends to diminish with increasing distance from these two foci until, on the periphery, we reach areas of persistent economic backwardness—much of Asia, Africa, and Latin America. It should be noted, however, that this pattern of stagnation at the margins is not entirely consistent, since we find several new growth poles appearing there as well. Most notable of these is Japan, the dominant center of the Far East, but there are others as well, such as Australia, New Zealand, and Argentina.

THEORY OF UNDERDEVELOPMENT

It is an explicit assumption of the historical theories of development (though not necessarily of the newer spatial theories) that, once the development process has begun, today's underdeveloped countries will follow along the same way taken previously by the present advanced countries. This notion has been increasingly questioned in recent years. Numerous writers point to the very different circumstances of most underdeveloped countries in a world where the first take-off occurred more than two centuries ago and where the contrasts between rich and poor have become so great. Because of the difficulty of applying the past experience of the advanced countries to these problems, a new body of theory is emerging: a theory of *underdevelopment*. In the next few pages we shall consider the special problems of underdeveloped countries and regions today and note some of the theoretical ideas that have appeared for explaining these.

Disadvantageous relationship with advanced areas One of the first problems of underdeveloped areas is that they often contribute more than they receive in return. There is a perverse tendency for capital, entrepreneurship, and the best labor to flow from the poorer areas to the richest, along with a stream of primary commodities consisting of unprocessed or only partially processed foodstuffs and industrial raw materials. As we noted in the previous chapter, much of the trade between underdeveloped and advanced countries is of a bilateral nature, representing connections established during the era when the poorer land was a colony of the richer.

Moreover, trade relations between the rich and the poor are frequently unfavorable to the latter. One of the expectations of traditional theory is that trade will serve as an "engine of growth" to newly developing regions, based on the experience of the New World during the nineteenth century. Under the conditions that then prevailed, the spread effects of development did seem to flow outward with the opening of trade. But the experience of the underdeveloped lands of today is different: trade is not automatically beneficial to them. Indeed, less developed areas may sustain largely unfavorable, or backwash, effects from their trade with more advanced areas that will in the end leave them weakened (Myrdal, 1957).

One such problem of poorer lands is that the long-run terms of trade tend to turn against them. As we observed in Chapter 9, the world demand for manufactured goods and the prices they can command tend to rise steadily while the demand for primary goods, especially certain agricultural commodities, rises more slowly and their prices fluctuate widely. This means that primary producers must continually pay more for what they buy and receive less relatively for what they sell. This results in a deteriorating balance of trade and diminishing resources for use in developmental purposes.

In addition, trade with advanced areas often has the effect of locking less developed regions into a permanent role as suppliers of primary goods. Because these lagging areas cannot develop manufactures that can compete with those of advanced lands, they are forced into the straitjacket of excessive specialization in the production and sale of commodities with unstable prices and employing only unskilled labor. At the same time, their imports of mass-produced manufactured items may kill off such small-scale manufacture as they have. This is especially true of traditional handicrafts, as in the case of India.

Persistence of disparities between the rich and poor The dichotomy between wealthy and impoverished lands we have pictured is a tenacious one: the rich get richer and the poor get poorer. Why is this? What are the special advantages of the developed regions, and what is it that holds back the underdeveloped areas? We have mentioned the unfavorable relationships between the two kinds of regions, but there are other inherent characteristics in each that cause the disparities to persist and increase.

Advantages of technically advanced areas One of the expectations of traditional theory now being questioned is that advanced regions will eventually experience diminishing returns. Supposedly they will reach a maximum size, at which point they will encounter a number of inefficiencies, including problems of congestion. According to Weber (1929), this would then bring about a trend toward deglomeration. In practice this has not usually happened. Areas that have gained an early start and built up a large momentum of growth characteristically retain their attraction to manufacturing and commerce if only because of their reputations for success, the familiarity of entrepreneurs with their conditions, and the many amenities they manage to accumulate. In addition, established areas tend to hold the industries they have because of inertia; it is just too costly and too much trouble to pick up and move elsewhere. Moreover, economies of large-scale production continue to rise to higher levels with advancing technology, rather than to diminish, and new optimal sizes and limits to growth are always being set.

One persistent attraction of advanced countries and metropolitan regions alike is that they happen also to represent the richest international or national markets, as the case may be. It is here that the highest incomes are concentrated, with the best-developed demand for manufactured goods. Thus they constitute irresistible magnets for market-oriented forms of production. These are usually the later stages of manufacture, which add the greatest value to the product and pay the highest wages. Unfortunately for the backward regions, there is a strong trend for most industries to become increasingly market-oriented.

The most highly developed areas form the largest concentrations of quaternary services, too. These are the highest-order types of service activities, such as finance, research, planning, and corporate and political control. They also include certain educational and cultural institutions. Taken together, these concentrations of many kinds of secondary, tertiary, and quaternary activities attract to them an accumulation of very diverse and highly qualified people. This produces an in-migration of the most capable foreigners seeking the highest returns for their services. A locational advantage of this sort cannot be overestimated.

Obstacles confronting less developed areas   The technically advanced regions seem to have everything going for them. Once development is well under way, success breeds more success in a continuous upward spiraling of growth. But the situation facing the less developed areas is of a different sort. Conditions there conspire to produce a downward spiral that has been termed "interlocking vicious circles of poverty" (Singer, 1949, p. 5). This tendency has been described by Myrdal (1957) as the "principle of circular and cumulative causation." He likens the circumstances of underdeveloped countries to the problem of the vicious circle in individual human affairs: people get sick because they are poor and they become poorer because they are sick. The result is a circular and cumulative process that continues to press them ever downward.

What are some of the conditions that contribute to the downward spiral? As suggested, these include the difficulty of attracting capital. Investment opportunities tend to be overlooked by outsiders, who lack sufficient knowledge of isolated areas. They find it simpler merely to continue investing in familiar enterprises in their own areas. Furthermore, they often have a distorted perception of the opportunities in underdeveloped areas because poverty conditions conceal or disguise them. Savings accumulated domestically by elite members of the underdeveloped society often leave the area for what is considered to be safer investment in technically advanced regions.

Characteristics of the population and labor force present still other obstacles to growth. As noted previously, the dire predictions of Malthus are being realized in many of today's underdeveloped countries. The nature of the problem is explained by *transition theory*. "Demographic transition" refers to the changes in population growth characteristics that occur during the development process, as observed in the past experience of countries now classified as technically advanced.

Phase 1 of transition theory (see Figure 10-1) corresponds to conditions within Rostow's traditional society. The birth rate is very high and the death rate is similarly high, though fluctuating because of variations in the food supply and natural calamities of various kinds. The result is a population that is roughly in equilibrium. When some event occurs to initiate the development process, the society enters phase 2 of the demographic transition. Public health improvements

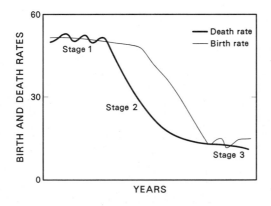

FIGURE 10-1   TRANSITION THEORY.

and other favorable events accompanying technical advancement cause the death rate to drop sharply; but meanwhile the birth rate remains high because people are naturally reluctant to change their traditional attitudes toward marriage and the family. Consequently, the birth rate and death rate curves begin to diverge and the "demographic gap" appears, giving rise to a population explosion. When at last the age of high mass consumption is reached, the society experiences phase 3 of the transition. With the attainment of economic maturity, the birth rate is brought under control, mainly through voluntary means. With birth and death rates once more back in balance, a condition of population equilibrium is regained, except for relatively minor fluctuations of the birth rate in accordance with movements of the business cycle.

Another kind of problem of poor areas is the disruptive effect of the selective out-migration they experience. Those who leave are mainly the youngest and the most skilled, talented, vigorous, and venturesome—in short, those with the highest leadership potential. This is a particular problem of the less developed countries, where it takes the form of the so-called "brain drain," but it is equally serious for the lagging regions of technically advanced countries, where it may be less noticed. In either case this migration of the most able persons leaves behind the very old and the very young. It produces a conservative leadership in the poor areas affected by this, and it tends to exacerbate the shortage of skills and entrepreneurship from which they already suffer.

It is no wonder, then, that less developed areas are faced with still another, related problem, the lack of a concept of change among the indigenous population. As Rostow noted, prevailing social attitudes and formal and informal institutions are attuned to conditions of stability and the maintenance of tradition. Trades are held in low esteem, and there is a suspicion and even fear of anything new.

Dual economies   One paradoxical feature that is commonly found in underdeveloped countries is the "dual economy." By this is meant the existence side by side of modern, highly efficient production and primitive subsistence agriculture and other traditional ways of gaining a livelihood. The modern production usually consists of well-organized forms of primary resource exploitation, financed and managed by foreign enterprise and producing for the world market. This may consist of mineral production, as in the case of oil exploitation in Libya, Algeria, or Iraq, or the iron mining in Liberia, Mauritania, or Venezuela. On the other hand, it may represent various types of plantation agriculture, such as rubber production in Malaysia and Indonesia, banana culture in Central America, or sugar growing in the Caribbean.

In either case there tends to be little connection between the foreign-dominated modern production and the indigenous subsistence forms. Characteristically there are dual wage structures and very little occupational mobility from the one to the other. The modern enterprise is ordinarily a self-contained enclave with its own shops, transport systems, power generation, and so forth. Such economic dualism may continue indefinitely without contribution materially to the development of the country as a whole. Although this is not always a negative feature, it can have harmful effects, as in those cases where the modern enterprise results in the final exhaustion of valuable natural resources with little or no domestic benefit to compensate.

Poor as they are, even some of the less developed countries vary internally from one place to another in levels of per capita income and economic opportunity. Within a country so small as Guatemala—which is about the size of Ohio and has a population of only 5 million—factories, commerce, entrepreneurship, and political control are concentrated in the central highland basins. Outlying areas, especially in the east and north, are almost untouched by modern development except for the United Fruit Company's enclave at Bananera and a few isolated mineral ventures and limited port activities on the Caribbean.

These are some of the elements now entering the literature and accumulating to form a theory of underdevelopment. In the remainder of this chapter we shall be looking at the global dimensions of development and noting briefly some examples of what is being done about these problems.

DEVELOPMENT PROBLEM: DIMENSIONS, PATTERNS, AND SOLUTIONS

The theoretical writings on development and underdevelopment suggest a great many ways in which areas of wealth and poverty differ from each other. Many of these characteristics can be measured and, with varying degrees of reliability, can serve as indicators of level of development. As we examine and compare these variables, we find a strong tendency for them to coincide spatially. Based largely on this kind of information, a number of strategies have been devised for attacking the problems both of less developed countries and of lagging regions within advanced countries.

A WORLD VIEW OF POVERTY

Despite a popular inclination to lump the world's nations into two distinct and sharply contrasting groups, the advanced and the underdeveloped, the objective evidence does not support such a simplistic view. By nearly every indicator of social and economic well-being the 100-odd countries are found distributed with surprising evenness along a scale leading from the poorest to the richest. Spatially as well as historically, then, development appears to occur in the form of a continuum, as we have noted previously. The large variety of conditions this implies suggests also a number of possible approaches to solving problems of growth and development.

Measuring development Three different categories of development measures are implied by the literature on this subject: those referring to the nature of domestic economies, to characteristics of populations, and to relations with the world at large. At the international scale of observation quantitative data can be found for a large number of these variables, although there are several problems in using them. One difficulty is that information for certain countries is frequently missing from the total. Since these countries also tend to be the least developed, their omission tends to bias the results. Another problem is the difficulty of getting accurate data in a consistent form from a large number of countries differing both in ideology and administrative sophistication.

There are compelling reasons to use countries as statistical units for international comparisons, since a greater homogeneity of culture, language, business practices, systems of measurement, and political control can be expected to obtain within countries than between them. Moreover, national entities are the most common reporting units for quantitative information. Nevertheless, it should not be forgotten that much variation exists within the borders of such large territorial units as Brazil, Canada, and the Soviet Union, and even within some of the smaller countries, especially those with dual economies. Distortions also arise in the case of those exporters of valuable mineral fuels, such as Libya and Venezuela, whose very large national incomes serve to mask certain persistent features of underdevelopment.

Measures of production and consumption Gross national product (GNP), defined as the sum of all goods and services produced by a population, is much used as an indicator not only of output but also, by implication, of consumption as well. Total GNP is especially valuable as a gauge of the possibilities for achieving economies of large-scale production. In this form GNP can be misleading, however, especially when it must be divided among a very large population, as in India and China. More commonly, therefore, this is expressed in the form of per capita GNP, which implies much more about the well-being of the average citizen (though admittedly concealing wide variations in personal income).

When we compare the per capita GNP of the less developed countries as a group to certain of the advanced countries (see Figure 10-2), we are struck by the extreme degree of variation. First there is the towering position of the United States, whose per capita GNP was $4,241 in 1969, followed, in Figure 10-2, by Canada with $2,654 (Sweden's figure of $2,915 was even higher in that year). On the other hand, the per capita GNP of the eighty less developed countries came to only $218, slightly more than one-twentieth that of the United States. Note also that the per capita GNP of this group increased by only 26 percent between 1960 and 1969, while that of the United States rose by a third and that of Japan grew by an incredible 137 percent.

Even so, there is much variation among these eighty countries and between continental groupings (Figure 10-3). Viewed in this manner, Africa and Asia appear to be much worse off than other underdeveloped regions. Southern Europe (Cyprus, Greece, Malta, Portugal, Spain, Turkey, and Yugoslavia in this example) are in a much better position and are experiencing a high rate of growth (55 percent between 1960 and 1969). Note also the effect of newly acquired oil income in the Middle East. The global pattern that emerges, therefore, is one in which the United States and Canada, Western Europe, Australia and New Zealand, and the Soviet Union are arrayed near the upper end of the scale of per capita GNP, with Asia and Africa and certain of the Latin American countries at or near the lower end. The other countries of the world are distributed fairly regularly between.

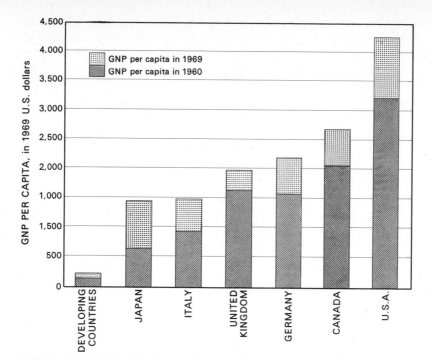

FIGURE 10-2 PER CAPITA GNP, LESS DEVELOPED AND SELECTED ADVANCED COUNTRIES, BY REGION, 1960 AND 1969. (INTERNATIONAL BANK FOR RECONSTRUCTION AND DEVELOPMENT.)

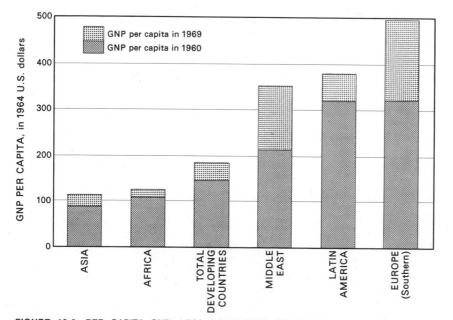

FIGURE 10-3 PER CAPITA GNP, LESS DEVELOPED COUNTRIES, BY REGION, 1960 AND 1969. (INTERNATIONAL BANK FOR RECONSTRUCTION AND DEVELOPMENT.)

Demographic and social variables As we noted earlier, one of our theoretical expectations is that demographic characteristics will change with rising levels of development. This is confirmed by the data on world population growth (Figure 10-4), which show that the less developed areas of Asia, Africa, and Latin America have been assuming a larger part of the world total and will continue doing so between now and the year 2000.

Diet is similarly considered to be a function of development. Based on standards established by the United Nations Food and Agricultural Organization (shown as 100 percent in Figure 10-5), the populations of advanced countries tend to eat much too well. The majority of the less developed peoples are undernourished, however, especially those of Africa, Asia, the Caribbean, and Andean South America. The picture would become even worse if we were to examine qualities of diet, as, for example, daily protein consumption. A number of other demographic and social variables we might have considered are fertility rates, number of physicians per capita, levels of education, school enrollments, and literacy.

Basic dimensions of development It has often been noted that these many economic, demographic, and social variables behave with uncommon consistency. Whichever of these measures may be used, they seem to produce virtually the same groupings of countries. Berry (1961, pp. 110–119) concluded that, since many variables seem to be saying the same things, there must be some way to economize in making a quantitative description of development. Using statistical techniques capable of simultaneously analyzing the relationships among many variables, he tested this notion on forty-three indices of development for ninety-five countries and colonies. The purpose of this exercise was to see whether or not

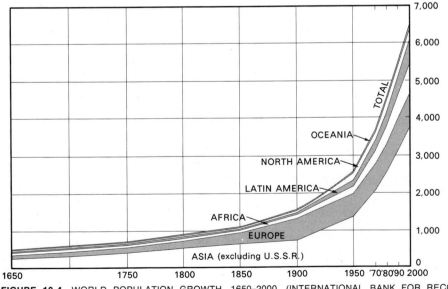

FIGURE 10-4 WORLD POPULATION GROWTH, 1650–2000. (INTERNATIONAL BANK FOR RECONSTRUCTION AND DEVELOPMENT.)

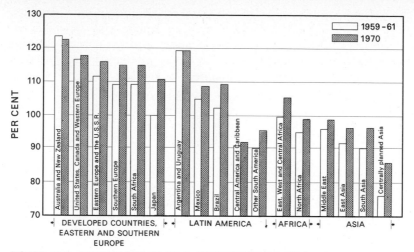

FIGURE 10-5 CALORIE INTAKE AS A PERCENTAGE OF ESTABLISHED STANDARDS, BY MAJOR REGIONS AND COUNTRIES, 1959–1961 AND (PROJECTED) 1970. (INTERNATIONAL BANK FOR RECONSTRUCTION AND DEVELOPMENT.)

the variables could be summarized or condensed to disclose a fundamental spatial pattern.

These calculations resulted in four basic dimensions of development that explained almost as much of the variation among the ninety-five countries as the forty-three individual measures did together. The first and much the strongest of the four dimensions was labeled the "technology scale." Closely associated in this basic pattern were measures of accessibility, transportation, trade, external relations, technology, industrialization, urbanization, GNP, and organization of the population. When the ninety-five countries were plotted according to their performance on this scale, they were found to be spaced fairly regularly along a continuum. These countries also produced a consistent spatial pattern when mapped (see Figure 10-6).

The second strongest set of associations was labeled the "demographic scale." Positively related to it were a number of population measures, including birth and death rates, infant mortality rates, population growth rates, and population densities. Other positive relationships were obtained from population per unit of cultivated land, rice yields, and percentage of export trade with the North Atlantic region (Anglo-America and Western Europe). Contrasting negative relationships were indicated by per capita foreign trade, per capita energy consumption, per capita newspaper circulation, per capita GNP, per capita telephone use, and per capita automobile ownership. In other words, this dimension disclosed the effects of population pressures and other population problems associated with poverty and low rates of economic participation. A map of the demographic pattern (Figure 10-7) closely resembles that of the technological pattern except that in this case the highest rank actually refers to the lowest levels of development, indicating the effects of high population densities, high growth rates, and so forth. Again the demographic pattern forms a linear scale.

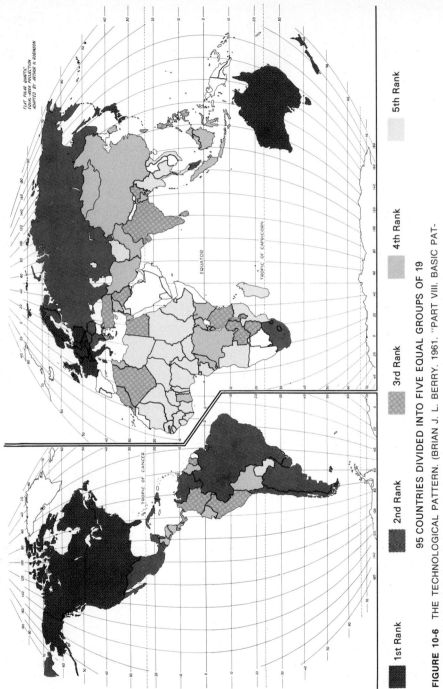

1st Rank   2nd Rank   3rd Rank   4th Rank   5th Rank

95 COUNTRIES DIVIDED INTO FIVE EQUAL GROUPS OF 19

FIGURE 10-6 THE TECHNOLOGICAL PATTERN. (BRIAN J. L. BERRY. 1961. "PART VIII. BASIC PAT-TERNS OF ECONOMIC DEVELOPMENT." IN NORTON GINSBURG, *ATLAS OF ECONOMIC DEVELOP-MENT.* CHICAGO: UNIVERSITY OF CHICAGO PRESS. PP. 110–119.)

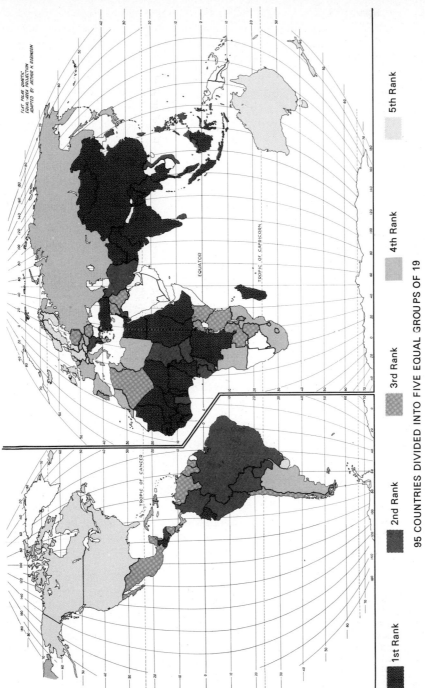

FIGURE 10-7 THE DEMOGRAPHIC PATTERN. (BERRY, 1961.)

95 COUNTRIES DIVIDED INTO FIVE EQUAL GROUPS OF 19

1st Rank   2nd Rank   3rd Rank   4th Rank   5th Rank

Although the third and fourth dimensions were much weaker, they too provided significant information about development. The third one, termed "contrasts in income and external relations," highlighted differences between low-technology countries with much trade (Central America, for example) and large countries poorly integrated into the international economy (the Soviet bloc countries, India, Pakistan, and others). The fourth dimension was called "the large and the small" and contrasted very large countries, mostly at high levels of development, with very small countries having high densities and little mechanical energy use.

Planning for national development Viewed optimistically, today's underdeveloped countries have several special opportunities. For one thing, the development process can be more deliberate and orderly than it was in the case of the present advanced countries, where development came spontaneously, "almost accidentally" (Hirschman, 1968, p. 8). This means that carefully prepared plans are possible and, in fact, necessary. The current group of underdeveloped nations are further aided by the accumulated experience and the reservoir of technical progress that the advanced lands can offer. They do not have to wait for the unpredictable appearance of invention and innovation as their predecessors did. Yet the disadvantages of a delayed start along the route of development probably outweigh the advantages. As we have seen, the problems of underdevelopment are numerous and vary considerably from one case to another. Not least is the great magnitude of the task, since the underdeveloped countries as a group have a per capita GNP not much more than one-twentieth that of the richest country. Most of all, there is the difficulty of just getting started, of finding that one critical element that is needed to provide the initial "kick."

Goals and strategy The per capita GNP is the most widely used measure of development, and the prime goal of development is to raise the level of income per person, to erase the grinding poverty that is itself an obstacle to development. Although this is seldom explicitly admitted, it seems likely that few, if any, of the present underdeveloped nations can hope to catch up with the leaders, unless the latter stumble badly. One obvious reason for this is that by all objective measures the world does not possess enough resources to support its entire population at current levels of consumption in the North Atlantic countries. For example, the United States, with only 6 percent of the world's population, now accounts for one-third to one-half of the total annual resource use. Realism would thus seem to dictate more modest goals.

The proposed means for achieving the goal of rising per capita output and consumption are as numerous as the writers suggesting them, and as the wide range of developmental problems to be overcome, but certain key elements are common to most strategies. Most of these relate to the GNP/population ratio in one way or another, since the national output per person can be increased either by expanding the numerator or contracting the denominator. Thus, one of the most common strategies is to attack the population problem in an effort to reduce the denominator of the fraction, or at least to keep it from growing at a faster rate than the numerator, GNP. The most direct approach is to find ways to reduce birth rates, a strategy used successfully during the post-World War II period by Japan and more recently by communist China. Results from this tactic have been exceedingly slow, however, in those lands where the populations are less mobilized and which are burdened with the encrustations of traditional social attitudes, poor communications, and low levels of education, as in India and Pakistan.

In other parts of the world where religion or other considerations intervene— Latin America, for example—even this approach is denied planners. There, the only expedient remedy is to accept high population growth rates and try to provide new jobs more rapidly for the unemployed and underemployed, a formidable task in most cases. Neither approach is likely to work rapidly or surely enough, however, in the usual underdeveloped economy based on agriculture or other forms of primary production. Nor can traditional kinds of labor-intensive handicraft industries be counted upon, since they are ordinarily much too inefficient to compete with machine-made imports. Only modern types of industry can be expected to provide the necessary jobs and at the same time yield the output required to increase the numerator of the GNP/population fraction.

But modern industry is capital-intensive, and with few exceptions the underdeveloped countries are capital-poor. Consequently, another common element in developmental schemes is some mechanism for increasing the rate of capital formation. There must be an investment not only in factories but also in roads, railways, airports, communications, port works, and the other social overhead required for a manufacturing economy. Not the least of these is the need for schools and the staff to man them, since high literacy rates are an unavoidable requirement for modernization. This capital will have to be acquired through hard domestic saving as well as intergovernmental aid.

A third key part of most developmental strategies is some provision for determining priorities for investment among the many claimants for such funds. Although industrialization is generally regarded as unavoidable for the development of a country, this is not usually regarded as sufficient by itself. Agriculture must also be modernized in order to yield a higher output and thus provide an enlarged tax base and to generate export earnings to pay for the larger quantity and variety of imports that development entails. Necessities entailed by development include factory machinery and equipment, industrial raw materials, transport equipment, and other goods that have to be imported from advanced countries, since underdeveloped lands lack the means for producing these sophisticated goods themselves.

Finally, as we have noted earlier, even the poorest countries have a great deal of internal variation in their economic health. Although Brazil has a fairly low per capita GNP, for example, concealed within this figure are the extreme contrasts between the rich, modern São Paulo region and the poverty-stricken northeast. Development planners are seldom allowed to forget this. Human misery in such areas is too great to overlook. Moreover, conditions of this sort leave far too large a proportion of the population outside the national economy making no contribution to it. And, it is politically dangerous to ignore these poorest districts. Hence Brazil established her new capital in a poor and comparatively isolated western region to provide that area with a ready-made growth point, and she is now constructing a trans-Amazonian highway to relieve conditions in the north and northeast. Similar considerations have prompted Guatemala to include important elements of regional development in her official plan. Though much favored by government officials, these approaches to relieving regional disparities in underdeveloped countries have met opposition in the development literature. In view of the severely limited funds available for development, it is felt that the regional approach spreads these moneys too thin. Investment should be concentrated in established areas of high growth, and the others should be permitted to rely upon spread effects for their eventual salvation.

REGIONAL DISPARITIES WITHIN COUNTRIES: THE LAGGING REGION

Just as the world has its problem with countries that have failed to participate in the general rise in incomes accompanying technological advancement, so even the wealthiest countries have their own domestic problems with regions that lag behind the rest in the growth of the national economy as a whole or that have declined from a former condition of prosperity and become "strained." Appalachia and the Ozarks are the two best-known cases of lagging regions in the United States. Britain has had her stranded regions on the northeast coast, in South Wales, on Merseyside, and in the Scottish Midlands, all industrial areas of former booming growth. These problems are found not only in the United States and the United Kingdom, but also in France, Italy, Canada, and nearly every other advanced country.

Although there are many similarities among these regions, they differ considerably in their particular circumstances. The question thus becomes quite complex, calling for a variety of strategies that depend upon local causes and effects. For example, there is the strategy of industrial diversification for an area considered to have been overly specialized in the past (South Wales), of providing improved access to isolated pockets of poverty (Appalachia), and of establishing new growth centers in areas of rural overpopulation and poverty (southern Italy). As our example of regional development problems and planning in a technically advanced country, let us review the Canadian experience.

Regional development issues in Canada Though Canada has the second highest per capita income in the world, there are tremendous inequalities of wealth, income, and opportunity contained within its borders. It is well, however, to recognize from the outset that the range of the inequalities found within Canada is nowhere near as great as that found between the different countries of the world. In fact, a relatively well-off person from southeast Asia might regard the living conditions in some of the less developed parts of Canada as quite high, and the poorer people from this same part of the world would definitely regard the life of even the poorest segment of the Canadian population as enviably prosperous.

The existence of economic inequalities which give rise to demands for development are, then, relative things. In Canada the situation is particularly recognized because economic inequalities exist in a number of dimensions (Ray, 1971). First, there is the spatial element, which is of fundamental interest to economic geographers. Some parts of the country have been poor relative to other sections since the nineteenth century. This has been well documented by Green (1971), who indicates that the Maritime Provinces (Prince Edward Island, Nova Scotia, and New Brunswick) and Quebec have always had per capita incomes less than the national average whereas Ontario and British Columbia have persistently been above the national average. The Prairie Provinces (Alberta, Saskatchewan, and Manitoba) have usually been around the national average, occasionally above it, but more often below it.

This persistent existence of the regional location of inequalities is matched by a second element, which, though it happens to be spatial in content, is more interesting in a political context. Within the provinces, the largest urban areas appear to be wealthier than the rural areas. Furthermore, the job-creating activities are located in these larger metropolitan areas, and the more rural communities appear to be gaining very little economic activity. This is surprising in a country which developed on the crutches of an export staple economy. Before the First World War, the chief characteristic of the country was that it depended upon the export of wheat and other grains from a rapidly expanding agricultural frontier. The export of staple commodities such as these provided the money which was used to purchase manufactured products. This is the classic basic economy situation which has been discussed previously.

The whole operation of the grain trade—transportation, financing, and marketing—was undertaken via Montreal, with Toronto gaining in importance as time progressed. These two cities, in effect, accrued the wealth and economic activity to be derived from the processing, marketing, and financing of an economy which depended upon the export of staple products and the import of manufactured materials. They became the hub of the rail transport network that spread its iron fingers across the country and knit the nation. But the wealth that was derived from these activities was not spread evenly throughout the nation, for the country developed under a cutthroat capitalist system which prized the advantages to be gleaned from domination and control. These prizes are, in effect, measured by the size of the profits that can be gained from eliminating risk through monopolistic or oligopolistic control. The very simplicity of this early Canadian economy encouraged these trends, and that is why most of the benefits were received by the two urban areas that dominated the trade.

The period following World War I was one in which the export of staples, both agricultural and mineral, was still fundamentally important, and in which Montreal still controlled the bulk of the trade. The experience of that war encouraged the government to promote manufacturing within the confines of the country, and the stimulative mechanism adopted was a protective tariff. A high tariff was placed on the import of manufactured goods in order to raise the price level to that which could be met by domestic producers. Though the tariff was criticized vehemently by the farmers, it was maintained as a vital aspect of national policy. The important feature of this policy was the attempt to replace by domestic capacity some part of the manufacturing capacity which Canada, in a sense, generated beyond its borders.

The question that arises, therefore, is where this manufacturing capacity would locate. Given many of the locational principles discussed in previous chapters, it would be expected that much of the capacity would locate in the larger urban areas, for it is here that is located a large labor force, ancillary industries, a capital market, and a local consumer market. The structure of rail freight rates that were developed and developing during this period also encouraged the new manufacturing capacity to locate in the large urban areas, particularly in Montreal, and the area embracing Oshawa, Toronto, and Hamilton. The freight rates, which were controlled by the major railroad companies who had their headquarters and considerable investments in Montreal and Toronto, favored the flow of raw materials and agricultural products to these two cities and manufactured products out from them. In other words, the freight rate structure discriminated against manufacturers who might have located elsewhere.

Thus, the existing urban-rural wealth differential strengthened into a center-periphery dichotomy, with the areas surrounding Montreal and Toronto gleaning much of the new manufacturing capacity. During the last thirty years, Toronto has managed to gain control of much of the business deriving from the mining industry, and has also managed to obtain a disproportionately large share of the high-growth industries. Montreal, on the other hand, adopted a more cautious attitude to the financing of the mining industry, and became quite specialized in the textile and clothing industry, which is low-wage and labor-intensive, and the petroleum-refining industry, which is capital-intensive but creates little employment.

The development of a more diverse industrial economy, which has been described briefly in the preceding paragraphs, is accompanied by a proliferation of specialized jobs and a more complex stratification of society according to occupation. This gives rise to the third (and final) dimension of economic inequality, for the different occupations receive levels of income related to their scarcity value and level of training. The managerial, professional, and technical occupations, which require the most training, receive a greater average income than clerical workers, and these, in return, receive higher incomes than others, such as miners. The resultant hierarchy of occupations, which appears very much related to the amount of training or education received by the worker, is urban-oriented, with the higher-level occupations being concentrated in the major urban areas.

The result is that there exists a persistent geographic distribution of regional economic inequalities within Canada. These inequalities crystallized at an early stage in the development of the country into a center-periphery dichotomy, and the dichotomy was accentuated in the Maritimes by a most unproductive agricultural and primary industry sector. The maturing of the country into a more diverse array of manufacturing industries did not reduce these inequalities, but reinforced them, because the two large urban regions already controlled the transportation, marketing, and financial needs of the nation.

In this type of situation the inequalities matter because they are persistent. The people living in poorer regions are always poorer and underemployed compared with those in the wealthier areas, and the social attitudes along with the restricted opportunities that result are of national concern (Brewis, 1970). This concern is accentuated by the fact that a disproportionately large number of French Canadians are involved, whether they are in the low-wage industries of Montreal, the declining parts of rural Quebec, or the Acadian area of New Brunswick. As a result, a major aim of the federal and provincial governments of Canada has been to reduce the existence of these regional inequalities.

The policy is clear, but a policy needs a program if its aims are to be fulfilled. The programs that have been developed are as many as the number of governments and years involved, for they range from local job-finding schemes to federal industrial incentive programs. Only recently has there been any attempt at program coordination, and this has proved to be an administratively complex cooperation. Rather than detail the many programs that have been tested, for these are discussed elsewhere (Brewis, 1969), in this section the discussion will focus briefly on a few examples.

Area Development Agency   In 1965 the federal government introduced an Area Development Incentives Act, to be administered by an Area Development Agency within the Federal Department of Industry. Areas within the country were designated as zones in which new or expanding manufacturing firms could receive incentives, and the criterion for designation was basically unemployment. Though the criterion and terms of the act were changed during the ensuing five-year period, the basic incentive premise and criterion for designation remained intact. All large urban areas, and nearly all medium-sized cities (30,000 to 150,000 people) were automatically excluded from designation. Thus the aim was to take manufacturing jobs to people in small towns and rural areas. The incentive, or bribe, paid to firms for locating or expanding in these designated areas, which embraced almost the entire country outside of southern Ontario, the St. Lawrence Valley between Montreal and Quebec City, Edmonton, Calgary, Winnipeg, Halifax, and Vancouver, was a capital grant or tax allowance on new plant, buildings, or both.

Thus, the incentives program, in effect, implied that the problems of unemployment in rural areas were related to the shortage of productive capital in these areas. This is, of course, related to one of the indicators of underdevelopment discussed previously. But the movement of capital into an area does not imply that jobs will be created, and the program was effective only in those areas that were marginal to the major growth poles within the country. For example, the program was effective for a short time in the southern Georgian Bay area (Yeates and Lloyd, 1970), Windsor, and Cornwall. But it was not really effective in the Maritimes, where a great deal of induced investment succeeded in creating very few jobs of the type required.

Area Rehabilitation and Development Agency The Area Rehabilitation and Development Agency, which was established by the ARD Act in 1961, was directed toward alleviating the readjustment problems of agricultural areas within the country. As a result of innovations in technology, farmers were now able to produce more food than could be consumed at prevailing price levels, the requirements for labor were continuously decreasing, and marginal farms that were usually small in size, on poor land, or both, were being forced out of business. The result was that the per capita income of the rural community was well below that of urban areas, though a few farmers with large farms in fertile areas were quite well off.

The programs approved under the act as interpreted by the agency included a study of land capability in Canada as a prelude to the development of a program to improve land use; a comprehensive rural redevelopment program involving the rehabilitation and retraining of the unemployed; and soil and water conservation. One of the important features of the program was that it required all schemes to be operated with full provincial cooperation with federal-provincial cost sharing. This, naturally, incurred provincial favor, whereas the ADA did not.

But though the act had many sound objectives, it could not fulfill its aims because it was only a partial attempt at alleviating the problems of low income and unemployment in rural areas. If farms are uneconomic, and located in areas which are demonstrably marginal for any kind of agricultural purpose, the only real solution is to move the people off the land and allow the property to convert to forest or scrub. This involves complete family retraining, and numerous problems concerning social dislocation, for the people can only go to urban areas. The kinds of assistance required, therefore, involve far more than rehabilitation within rural areas, for they also require readjustment to urban living as well. This type of complete relocation and social restructuring implies much more cooperation and coordination between the various levels of federal and provincial governments than could be mobilized by the agency.

Resettlement One of the characteristics of many depressed areas is that the inhabitants are remote from any basic services, and have lost their basic source of employment. This is particularly true in many remote coastal villages in Newfoundland, where the inhabitants can no longer gain a livelihood from fishing because their boats are too small, harbors too shallow, and locations too remote to compete with the "factory" fishing based on the larger ports. The situation is made worse by the fact that there is no alternative source of income in these villages, and that they are too small to support any of the educational and medical facilities that are generally considered necessary.

The lack of services is particularly hard on the young people of these communities, for they have to leave their village to gain employment, and when they do obtain employment, they find they lack the basic education necessary to hold a reasonable job. As a result of the negative aspects of remoteness, unemployment, and deprivation, the provincial government initiated the resettlement scheme. This scheme is designed to transfer the inhabitants of the smaller villages to larger villages and towns, and to provide the necessary medical, housing, educational, and employment opportunities in these designated growth areas. To achieve this end, the provincial agency takes advantage of any and all federal schemes available.

Although the resettlement scheme involves considerable readjustment for the people involved, it does make a great deal of sense. The Newfoundland resettlement scheme is one of the few examples of a situation where the government has decided that there are areas which cannot be redeveloped, and that the only solution is to remove the inhabitants lock, stock, and barrel, to larger and better-located units. The criticism that can be leveled is that the scheme is expensive, and has not really gone far enough, for it has tried to promote alternative locations that, in themselves, may not be tenable in the long run.

Department of Regional Economic Expansion   The piecemeal schemes that have been outlined thus far proved to be self-defeating or limited because they were not part of a more general program designed to tackle the problem of low income and unemployment in all its many facets. In recognition of this, the federal government established the Department of Regional Economic Expansion in 1968, and by 1970 it had detailed a broad-based program designed to reduce regional inequalities. This program recognized that the problems of rural and urban poverty were intertwined and redevelopment could probably be promoted best by the recognition and establishment of growth centers. These growth centers are selected in cooperation with the provincial government involved, and federal and provincial governments are empowered to facilitate the operation of these centers with schemes designed to upgrade the entire urban infrastructure.

Preliminary indications suggest that the entire program is extremely expensive compared with the number of jobs created directly and indirectly by the economic activities induced to the area. Though a firm is granted a cash incentive based on the number of jobs created, it would appear that this incentive has frequently been abused. Furthermore, the very nature of the Canadian economy, which is fundamentally oriented toward Montreal and southern Ontario, means that most of the direct employment lured to these peripheral areas accrues larger indirectly linked benefits to the Toronto-Montreal area. Furthermore, the only positive success is seen in areas where the latent advantages of large local metropolises, such as Halifax, can be utilized.

Thus, regional development is a complex and expensive problem. Regional inequalities, as well as inequalities of any other kind, cannot be accepted by a sane society. But, unfortunately, the remedies utilized thus far have yielded disappointing results. This is, perhaps, because the remedies have been implemented within an economy which still fosters these discrepancies (Gonick, 1970). The brief discussion of the development of the Canadian economy that has been presented in this section suggests that the regional inequalities arose naturally out of the monopolistic-oligopolistic nature of the capitalist system which favored the concentration of economic power in a few areas. It would be wise to examine this contention, for it appears that all the previous schemes have been doomed to failure within a few years.

REFERENCES

Abiodun, J. O. 1967. "Urban Hierarchy in a Developing Country," *Economic Geography*, **43:**347–367.

Ahmad, E. 1952. "Rural Settlement Types in Uttar Pradesh," *Annals of the Association of American Geographers*, **42:**228–237.

Alonso, W. 1960. "A Theory of the Urban Land Market," *Regional Science Association, Papers and Proceedings*, **6:**149–157.

———. 1964. *Location and Land Use: Toward a General Theory of Land Rent*. Cambridge, Mass.: Harvard University Press.

Arnold, J. H., and F. Montgomery. 1918. *Influence of a City on Farming*. Washington: U.S. Department of Agriculture, Bulletin 678.

Baade, F. 1972. "Einhundert Jahre steigende Ernten durch die Anwendung von Handelsdünger," Seminar on the Use of Fertilizer and its Effects on the Agricultural Economy, Vatican City, April 10–16, 1972. (Unpublished.)

Balassa, B. 1961. *The Theory of Economic Integration*. Homewood, Ill.: Richard D. Irwin, Inc.

Barnum, H. G. 1966. *Market Centers and Hinterlands in Baden-Württemberg*, Research Paper 103, Department of Geography. Chicago: University of Chicago Press.

Bauer, P. T., and B. S. Yamey. 1957. *The Economics of Underdeveloped Countries*. Chicago: University of Chicago Press.

Beavington, F. 1963. "The Change to More Extensive Methods in Market Gardening in Bedfordshire," *The Institute of British Geographers, Transactions and Papers,* **33:**89–100.

Beckerman, W. 1956. "Distance and the Pattern of Intra-European Trade," *Review of Economics and Statistics*, **38:**31–40.

Berry, B. J. L. 1959. "Ribbon Developments in the Urban Business Pattern," *Annals of the Association of American Geographers*, **49:**145–155.

———. 1961. "Part VIII. Basic Patterns of Economic Development," in Norton Ginsburg, *Atlas of Economic Development*. Chicago: University of Chicago Press.

———. 1963. *Commercial Structure and Commercial Blight*, Research Paper 85, Department of Geography. Chicago: University of Chicago Press.

———. 1967. *Geography of Market Centers and Retail Distribution*. Englewood Cliffs, N.J.: Prentice-Hall.

———, H. G. Barnum, and R. J. Tennant. 1962. "Retail Location and Consumer Behavior," *Papers and Proceedings of the Regional Science Association*, **9:**65–106.

———, and W. L. Garrison, 1958a. "The Functional Bases of the Central Place Hierarchy," *Economic Geography*, **34:**145–154.

———, and ———. 1958b. "Recent Developments in Central Place Theory," *Papers and Proceedings of the Regional Science Association*, **4:**107–120.

———, and A. Pred. 1961. *Central Place Studies: A Bibliography of Theory and Application*. Philadelphia: Regional Science Research Institute. With *Supplement*, 1965.

Blumenfeld, H. 1954. "The Tidal Wave of Metropolitan Expansion," *Journal of the American Institute of Planners*, **20:**3–14.

Borchert, J. R. 1963. *The Urbanization of the Upper Midwest: 1930–1960*. Upper Midwest Economic Study, Urban Report No. 2. Minneapolis: University of Minnesota.

———, and R. B. Adams. 1963. *Trade Centers and Trade Areas of the Upper Midwest*. Upper Midwest Economic Study, Urban Report No. 3. Minneapolis: University of Minnesota.

Bourne, L. S. (ed.) 1971. *Internal Structure of the City*. Toronto: The Oxford University Press.

Bracey, H. E. 1962. "English Central Villages: Identification, Distribution and Functions," *Lund Studies in Geography, Series B, Human Geography*, **24:**169–190.

Bredo, W., and A. S. Rojko. 1952. *Prices and Milksheds of Northeastern Markets*. University of Massachusetts Agricultural Experiment Station, Bulletin No. 470.

Brewis, T. N. 1969. *Regional Economic Policies in Canada*. Toronto: The Macmillan Company of Canada.

———. 1970. "The Problem of Regional Disparities," in W. E. Mann (ed.), *Poverty and Social Policy in Canada*. Toronto: The Copp Clark Publishing Co.

Brinkmann, T. 1935. *Theodor Brinkmann's Economics of the Farm Business*, trans. E. T. Benedict. Berkeley: University of California Press.

Brunn, S. D. 1967. "The Inertia Effect in Measuring Threshold Populations," *The Southeastern Geographer*, **7:**6–12.

———. 1968. "Changes in the Service Structure of Rural Trade Centers," *Rural Sociology*, **33:**200–206.

Burgess, E. W. 1925. "The Growth of the City: An Introduction to a Research Project," in Robert E. Park, Ernest W. Burgess, and Roderick D. McKenzie, *The City*. Chicago: The University of Chicago Press.

Chipman, J. S. 1965, 1966. "A Survey of the Theory of International Trade," *Econometrica*, **33:**477–519 and 654–760; **34:**18–76.

Chisholm, M. 1962. *Rural Settlement and Land Use: An Essay in Location*. London: Hutchinson University Library.

Christaller, W. 1933. *Die Zentralen Orte in Suddentschland*. Jera: Gustav Fischer Verlag. Trans. C. W. Baskin. 1966. *Central Places in Southern Germany*. Englewood Cliffs, N.J.: Prentice-Hall.

Clark, C. 1951. "Urban Population Densities," *Journal of the Royal Statistical Society*, A, **114:**490–496.

Clarke, W. A. V. 1968. "Consumer Travel Patterns and the Concept of Range," *Annals of the Association of American Geographers*, **58:**386–396.

Conkling, E. C., and B. J. L. Berry. 1976. *The Geography of Land Use: Theory and Empirical Evidence*. New York: Wiley.

Daggett, S. 1955. *Principles of Inland Transportation*. New York: Harper.

Davies, W. K. 1967. "Centrality and the Central Place Hierarchy," *Urban Studies*, **4:**61–79.

Dunn, E. S. 1954. *The Location of Agricultural Production*. Gainesville: University of Florida Press.

Estall, R. D. 1963. "The Electronic Products Industry of New England," *Economic Geography*, **39:**189–216.

Eyre, J. D. 1959. "Sources of Tokyo's Fresh Food Supply," *Geographical Review*, **49:**455–474.

Fetter, R. A. 1924. "The Economic Law of Market Areas," *Quarterly Journal of Economics*, **39:**520–529.

Foster, G. J., and H. J. Nelson. 1958. *Ventura Boulevard: A String-Type Shopping Street*. Los Angeles: University of California at Los Angeles, Real Estate Research Program.

Garner, B. J. 1966. *The Internal Structure of Retail Nucleations*. Department of Geography, Evanston: Northwestern University.

———. 1967. "Models of Urban Geography and Settlement Location," in R. J. Chorley and P. Haggett (eds.), *Models in Geography*. London: Methuen.

Garrison, W. L. 1959. "Spatial Structure of the Economy II," *Annals of the Association of American Geographers*, **49:**471–482.

Gasson, R. 1966. "The Changing Location of Intensive Crops in England and Wales," *Geography*, **51:**16–28.

Ginsburg, N. 1961. *Atlas of Economic Development*. Chicago: The University of Chicago Press.

Gonick, C. W. 1970. "Poverty and Capitalism," in W. E. Mann (ed.), *Poverty and Social Policy in Canada*. Toronto: The Copp Clark Publishing Co.

Green, A. G. 1971. *Regional Aspects of Canada's Economic Growth*. Toronto: University of Toronto Press.

Greenhut, M. L. 1956. *Plant Location in Theory and Practice: the Economics of Space*. Chapel Hill: The University of North Carolina Press.

Haberler, G. 1961. *A Survey of International Trade Theory*, Special Papers in International Economics No. 1. Princeton: Princeton University Press.

Hägerstrand, T. 1952. "The Propagation of Innovation Waves," *Lund Studies in Geography, Series B, Human Geography*, **4**. Department of Geography, Lund: Lund University.

———. 1953. *Innovationsförloppet ur korologisk synpunkt*. Lund: Gleerup. Trans. and postscript A. Pred. 1967. *Innovation Diffusion as a Spatial Process*. Chicago: The University of Chicago Press.

Haggett, P. 1965. *Locational Analysis in Human Geography*. London: Edward Arnold.

———, and R. J. Chorley. 1969. *Network Analysis in Geography*. New York: St. Martin's Press.

———, and K. A. Gunawardena. 1964. "Determination of Population Thresholds for Settlement Functions by the Reed-Muench Method," *Professional Geographer*, **16–24:**6–9.

Hall, P. (ed.) 1966. *Von Thünen's Isolated State*. Oxford: Pergamon Press.

Harvey, D. W. 1966. "Theoretical Concepts and the Analysis of Agricultural Land Use Patterns in Geography," *Annals of the Association of American Geographers*, **56:**361–374.

Heady, E. O., and M. Skold. 1965. *Projections of U.S. Agricultural Capacity and Interregional Adjustments in Production and Land Use with Spatial Programming Models*. Ames: Agricultural and Home Economics Experiment Station, Iowa State University, Research Bulletin 539.

Heckscher, E. 1919. "The Effects of Foreign Trade on the Distribution of Income," *Ekonomisk Tidskrift*, **21**. Trans. in H. S. Ellis and L. A. Metzler (eds.), *Readings in the Theory of International Trade*. Philadelphia: Blackiston, 1949.

Higgins, B. 1968. *Economic Development: Problems, Principles, and Policies*. New York: W. W. Norton & Company, Inc.

Hirschman, A. O. 1958. *The Strategy of Economic Development*. New Haven: Yale University Press.

Hodge, G. 1965. "The Prediction of Trade Center Viability in the Great Plains," *Papers and Proceedings of the Regional Science Association*, **15:**87–118.

———. 1966. "Do Villages Grow? Some Perspectives and Predictions," *Rural Sociology*, **31:**183–196.

Hoover, E. M. 1937. *Location Theory and the Shoe and Leather Industries*, Harvard Economic Studies, Vol. LV. Cambridge: Harvard University Press.

———. 1963. *The Location of Economic Activity*. New York: McGraw-Hill.

———, and R. Vernon. 1959. *Anatomy of a Metropolis*. Cambridge: Harvard University Press.

Horvath, R. J. 1969. "Von Thünen's Isolated State and the Area Around Addis Ababa, Ethiopia," *Annals of the Association of American Geographers*, **19:**123–140.

Hoyt, H. 1933. *One Hundred Years of Land Values in Chicago*. Chicago: University of Chicago Press.

———. 1939. *The Structure and Growth of Residential Neighborhoods in American Cities*. Washington: Federal Housing Administration.

Huff, D. L. 1960. "A Topographic Model of Consumer Space Preferences," *Papers and Proceedings of the Regional Science Association*, **6:**159–173.

———. 1962. "A Topographical Model of Consumer Space References," *Papers and Proceedings of the Regional Science Association*, **6:**160–173.

Hunt, D. T. 1959. "Market Gardening in Metropolitan Auckland," *New Zealand Geographer*, **15:**130–155.

Hurd, R. M. 1924. *Principles of City Land Values*. New York: The Record and Guide.

Iklé, F. C. 1954. "Sociological Relationship of Traffic to Population and Distance," *Traffic Quarterly*, **8:**123–136.

Innis, H. A. 1956. *Essays in Canadian Economic History*, ed. M. Q. Innis. Toronto: University of Toronto Press.

Isard, W. 1956. *Location and Space Economy*. New York: Wiley.

Jonasson, O. 1925. "Agricultural Regions of Europe," *Economic Geography*, **1:**277–314.

Judge, G. G., and T. D. Wallace. 1958. "Estimation of Spatial Price Equilibrium Models," *Journal of Farm Economics*, **40:**801–820.

Kalbach, W. E., and W. W. McVey. 1971. *The Demographic Bases of Canadian Society.* Toronto: McGraw-Hill Company of Canada.

Kansky, K. J. 1963. *Structure of Transportation Networks*, Research Paper 84, Department of Geography. Chicago: University of Chicago Press.

Kennelly, R. A. 1954, 1955. "The Location of the Mexican Steel Industry," *Revista Geografica*, **15:**109–129; **16:**199–213; **17:**60–77.

Kerr, D. 1965. "Some Aspects of the Geography of Finance in Canada," *Canadian Geographer*, **9:**175–192.

Kielczewska-Zaleska, M. 1964. "Geographical Studies on Rural Settlement in Poland," *Geographia Polonica*, **1:**97–110.

King, L. J. 1961. "The Functional Role of Small Towns in Canterbury," *Proceedings of the Third New Zealand Geography Conference*, New Zealand Geographical Society, pp. 139–149.

———. 1969. *Statistical Analysis in Geography.* Englewood Cliffs, N.J.: Prentice-Hall.

Knos, D. S. 1962. *Distribution of Land Values in Topeka, Kansas.* Center for Research in Business, Lawrence: University of Kansas Press.

Krzymowski, R. 1928. "Graphical Presentation of Thünen's Theory of Intensity," *Journal of Farm Economics*, **10:**461–482.

Kuhn, H. W., and R. E. Kuenne. 1962. "An Efficient Algorithm for the Numerical Solution of the Generalized Weber Problem in Spatial Economics," *Papers and Proceedings, Regional Science Association*, **8:**21–33.

Latham, R. F., and M. H. Yeates. 1970. "Population Density Growth in Metropolitan Toronto," *Geographical Analysis*, **2:**177–185.

Lindberg, O. 1953. "An Economic-Geographical Study of the Localization of the Swedish Paper Industry," *Geografiska Annaler*, **35:**28–40.

Linder, S. B. 1967. *Trade and Trade Policy for Development.* New York: Frederick A. Prager, Publisher.

Linnemann, H. 1966. *An Econometric Study of International Trade Flows.* Amsterdam: North Holland Publishing Co.

Lösch, A. 1938. "The Nature of Economic Regions," *Southern Economic Journal*, **5:**71–78.

———. 1954. *The Economics of Location*, trans. W. H. Woglom. New Haven: Yale University Press. Originally published by Gustav Fischer Verlag.

Lowenstein, L. K., and D. Bradwell. 1966. "What Makes Desirable Industrial Property," *The Appraisal Journal*, **34:**263–267.

Lowry, I. S. 1964. *A Model of a Metropolis.* Santa Monica, Calif.: The Rand Corporation, RM-4035-RC.

Marshall, J. U. 1969. *The Location of Service Towns.* Toronto: University of Toronto Press.

Martin, J. E. 1966. *Greater London: An Industrial Geography.* Chicago: The University of Chicago Press.

Mayfield, R. C. 1967. "A Central-Place Hierarchy in Northern India," in W. L. Garrison and D. F. Marble, *Quantitative Geography. Part I: Economic and Cultural Topics.* Evanston: Northwestern University Press.

Merriam, W. B. 1962. "The Mushroom Industry at Kennett Square, Pennsylvania," *The Journal of Geography*, **41:**68–71.

Morrill, R. L. 1965. *Migration and the Spread and Growth of Urban Settlement.* Lund: Gleerup.

Moses, L. N. 1958. "Location and the Theory of Production," *Quarterly Journal of Economics*, **72:**259–272.

———. 1960. "Growth and Change in Metropolitan Areas and Their Relation to Metropolitan Transportation: A Summary of Findings" (mimeographed). The Transport Center, Evanston: Northwestern University.

Moses, L. F., and H. F. Williamson, Jr. 1967. "The Location of Economic Activity in Cities," *American Economic Review*, **52:**211–222.

Moyer, M. S., and G. Snyder. 1967. *Trends in Canadian Marketing*. Ottawa: Statistics Canada.

Mueller, E., and J. N. Morgan. 1962. "Location Decisions of Manufacturers," *American Economic Review, Papers and Proceedings*, **502:**204–217.

Murdie, R. A. 1965. "Cultural Differences in Consumer Travel," *Economic Geography*, **41:**211–233.

———. 1969. *Factorial Ecology of Metropolitan Toronto, 1951–1961*, Research Paper No. 116, Department of Geography. Chicago: University of Chicago Press.

Murphy, R. E., and J. E. Vance. 1954. "A Comparative Study of Nine Central Business Districts," *Economic Geography*, **30:**301–336.

Myrdal, G. 1957. *Economic Theory and Underdeveloped Regions*. London: Duckworth and Co., Ltd.

Newling, B. E. 1966. "Urban Growth and Spatial Structure: Mathematical Models and Empirical Evidence," *The Geographical Review*, **56:**213–225.

———. 1969. "The Spatial Variation of Urban Population Densities," *The Geographical Review*, **59:**242–252.

North, D. C. 1955. "Location Theory and Regional Economic Growth," *Journal of Political Economy*, **63:**243–258.

Norton, W., and E. C. Conkling. 1974. "Land Use Theory and the Pioneering Economy," *Geografiska Annaler*, **56:**44–56.

Nourse, H. O. 1968. *Regional Economics*. New York: McGraw-Hill.

Ohlin, B. 1933. *Interregional and International Trade*, Harvard Economic Studies, 39. Cambridge: Harvard University Press.

———. 1935. "Some Aspects of the Theory of Rent: Von Thünen vs. Ricardo," in N. E. Himes (ed.), *Economics, Sociology and the Modern World: Essays in Honor of T. N. Carver*. Cambridge: Harvard University Press.

Olsson, G. 1964. *Distance and Human Interaction*. Philadelphia: Regional Science Research Institute.

Peet, J. R. 1969. "The Spatial Expansion of Commercial Agriculture in the Nineteenth Century: A Von Thünen Interpretation," *Economic Geography*, **45:**283–301.

Ray, D. M. 1967. "Cultural Differences in Consumer Travel Behavior in Eastern Ontario," *Canadian Geographer*, **11:**143–156.

———. 1971. *Dimensions of Canadian Regionalism*, Geographical Paper No. 49, Policy Research and Coordination Branch. Ottawa: Department of Energy, Mines and Resources.

Reeder, L. G. 1954. "Industrial Location Trends in Chicago in Comparison to Population Growth," *Land Economics*, **30:**177–182.

———. 1955. "Industrial Deconcentration as a Factor in Rural-Urban Fringe Development," *Land Economics*, **31:**275–280.

Rees, P. H. 1968. "The Factorial Ecology of Metropolitan Chicago, 1960," unpublished master's thesis, Department of Geography. Chicago: University of Chicago.

Rogers, A. 1967. "Theories of Intra-Urban Spatial Structure: A Dissenting View," *Land Economics*, **63:**108–112.

Rostow, W. W. 1960. *The Stages of Economic Growth*. Cambridge: Cambridge University Press.

Rushton, G. 1966. *Spatial Pattern of Grocery Purchases by the Iowa Rural Population*, Bureau of Business and Economic Research, Studies in Business and Economics, No. 9. Iowa City: The University of Iowa.

Schlebecker, J. T. 1960. "The World Metropolis and the History of American Agriculture," *Journal of Economic History*, **20:**187–208.

Simpson, J. K. 1968. "A Geographical Analysis of Grain Flows Through Eastern Canada," unpublished master's thesis, Department of Geography. Kingston: Queen's University.

Singer, H. W. 1949. "Economic Progress in Underdeveloped Countries," *Social Research*, **16:**1–11.

Skinner, G. W. 1964–1965. "Marketing and Social Structure in Rural China," *Journal of Asian Studies*, **24:**3–43, 195–228, 363–399.

Skold, M. D., and E. O Heady. 1966. *Regional Location of Production of Major Field Crops at Alternative Demand and Price Levels, 1975*. Technical Bulletin 1354, Washington: U.S. Department of Agriculture Economics Research Service.

Smith, D. L. 1966. "Market Gardening at Adelaide's Urban Fringe," *Economic Geography*, **42:**19–36.

Smith, D. M. 1966. "A Theoretical Framework for Geographical Studies of Industrial Location," *Economic Geography*, **42:**95–113.

———. 1971. *Industrial Location: An Economic Geographical Analysis*. New York: Wiley.

Snyder, D. E. 1962. "Commercial Passenger Linkages and the Metropolitan Nodality of Montevideo," *Economic Geography*, **38:**95–112.

Sobel, I. 1954. "Collective Bargaining and Decentralization in the Rubber Tire Industry," *The Journal of Political Economy*, **62:**12–25.

Stafford, H. A. 1963. "The Functional Bases of Small Towns," *Economic Geography*, **39:**165–175.

Stevens, B. H. 1961. "Linear Programming and Location Rent," *Journal of Regional Science*, **3:**15–26.

Taaffe, E. J. 1962. "The Urban Hierarchy: An Air Passenger Definition," *Economic Geography*, **38:**1–14.

———, R. L. Morrill, and P. R. Gould. 1963. "Transport Expansion in Underdeveloped Countries," *The Geographical Review*, **53:**503–529.

Thoman, R. S., and M. H. Yeates. 1966. *Delimitation of Development Regions in Canada: With Special Attention to the Georgian Bay Area*. Ottawa: Area Development Agency, Department of Industry.

———, and E. C. Conkling. 1967. *Geography of International Trade*. Englewood Cliffs, N.J.: Prentice-Hall.

Ullman, E. L. 1957. *American Commodity Flow*. Seattle: University of Washington Press.

Vance, J. E., Jr. 1970. *The Merchant's Word: The Geography of Wholesaling*. Englewood Cliffs, N.J.: Prentice-Hall.

Viner, J. 1950. *The Customs Union Issue*. New York: Carnegie Endowment for International Peace.

Weber, A. 1911. "Die Standortslehre und die Handelspolitik," *Archiv für Sozialwissenschaft und Sozialpolitik*, **32:**667.

———. 1929. *Theory of the Location of Industries* (trans. of 1909 German edition). Chicago: University of Chicago Press.

Wingo, L., Jr. 1961. *Transportation and Urban Land*. Washington: Resources for the Future, Inc.

Winsborough, H. H. 1961. "A Comparative Study of Urban Population Densities," unpublished doctoral dissertation, Department of Sociology. Chicago: University of Chicago.

Wolpert, J. 1964. "The Decision Process in a Spatial Context," *Annals of the Association of American Geographers*, **54:**537–558.

Yeates, M. H. 1963. "Hinterland Delimitation: A Distance-Minimizing Approach," *The Professional Geographer*, **15:**7–10.

———. 1965. "Some Factors Affecting the Spatial Distribution of Chicago Land Values, 1910–1960," *Economic Geography*, **41:**55–70.

————. 1969. "A Note Concerning the Development of a Geographic Model of International Trade," *Geographical Analysis*, **1**:399–404.

————, and B. J. Garner. 1976. *The North American City* (2d ed.). New York: Harper & Row.

————, and P. E. Lloyd. 1970. *Impact of Industrial Incentives: Southern Georgian Bay Region, Ontario*. Ottawa: The Queen's Printer.

Zipf, G. K. 1949. *Human Behavior and the Principle of Least Effort*. Reading, Mass.: Addison-Wesley Press.

INDEX

Density:
    of ocean routes, 212
    population, 77, 200
Denver, Colorado, 71
Denver and Rio Grande Western Railway, 214
Department of Regional Expansion, 285
Depressed areas, 284
Desire line maps, 188, 189
Destinations, 198, 201, 203, 208
Detroit, Michigan, 55, 126, 127, 131
Development, 114, 257, 259
    basic dimensions of, 274
    process, 278
    spread effects of, 267
    stages of, 261
    in United States, 260
Developmental phases, 132
Developmental process, 258, 264, 265
Diagonal linkages, 124
Diesel power, 121
Diet, 274
Dietary quality, 43
Diminishing returns, 18, 19, 268
Discrimination in rate setting for carriers, 208
Disparities between rich and poor countries, 257
Distance, 200, 202, 207, 208
    barriers of, 225
    decay, 203
    exponent of, 202, 203
    friction of, 160
    influence of, 40, 41
    minimization, 203
Distressed areas, 98
Distribution:
    cost, 100
    technology of, 80
Distributive occupations, 153
Diversification, 12, 67, 254
    of trade, 254
Dividends, 84
Docking basins, 213
Docks, 212
Dow Chemical Company, 123
Drive to maturity, 262, 263
Dual economy, 270
Dubuque, Iowa, 76
Dunkerque, 116
Dunn, Edgar S., 15
Du Pont Corporation, 123
Durango, Mexico, 116
Dust bowl, 70

East Chicago, Indiana, 115
Eastern Ontario, 190
Ecology, human, 77
Economic base theory, 264
Economic growth, 262
Economic inequalities, 281, 282
    regional, 282, 283
Economic integration, 237, 249, 252
Economic location, 9
Economic man, 13, 28, 30, 108
Economic maturity, 269
Economic self-sufficiency, 236
    of Soviet Union, 255

Economic space, 9
Economic union, 237
Economies:
    agglomeration, 100
    external, 86, 113, 119, 234, 235, 266
    internal, 79, 86, 113, 119, 150, 266
    of large-scale operation, 97, 100, 113, 115, 118, 121, 122, 127-129, 131, 142, 144, 200, 246, 250, 260, 268
    localization, 97, 122
    of scale, 97, 100, 113, 115, 118, 121, 122, 127-129, 131, 142, 144, 200, 246, 250, 260, 268
    scale of, 85
    urbanization, 87, 97, 114, 123
ECSC (European Coal and Steel Community), 249
Eden Valley, 128, 129
Edmonton, 283
Educational level, 43
EEC-EFTA trade (European Free Trade Association), 251
Eggs, 65
Egypt, 73
Electric power, 220
    consumption, 220
    distribution systems, 218
    thermally generated, 220
Electricity, 119, 121, 220
    high voltage lines, 220
Electronics, 133
    industry, 132
Elevators, country, 40, 106, 107
Employment, industrial, 78
Energy, 119, 121, 145
    consumption, 219
    inputs, 83
Engel's law, 27
Engineers, 133
England, 53, 63, 64, 138
    southeast, 146
    (See also Great Britain)
English Channel, 139
English Midlands, 139
Ensilage, 58
Entrepreneur(s), 57, 108-111, 131
    motives of, 88
Entrepreneurial capacity, 109
Entrepreneurial limitations, 109
Entrepreneurial profits, 29
Entrepreneurial skill, 54, 57, 100
Equal access, 21
Erie, Lake, 52, 55, 67, 119
Erie Canal, 51, 52
Essex, 56
Essex Peninsula, 55
Establishments, 159
Estall, R. D., 132
Ethiopia, 42
Ethyl, 123
Europe, 41, 44, 56, 70, 121
    eastern, 140
    political fragmentation, 249
    southern, 138
    western, 32, 40, 53, 55, 62, 67, 138, 140, 144, 145, 213, 217
European Coal and Steel Community (see ECSC)

Railway(s):
  Japanese, 216
  Latin America, 216
  passenger flows, 206
  passenger service, 215, 216
  Soviet, 215
  terminals, 78
  United States and Canada, 215
  world pattern, 214
Range of a good, 159-160
  ideal limit, 160, 162
  maximum, 160
Rapeseed, 72
Rate-making practices, 98
Rate structure, 210
Raw material:
  inputs, 83
  quality of, 103
  source, 98
Ray, D. M., 191, 265, 281
Real estate, 77
Reciprocal demand and supply curves, 234
Reclamation, 67
Reed-Meunch method, 175
Rees, P. H., 76
Refineries, 219, 220
Refrigeration, 64
Regional development, 280, 285
Regional inequalities, 285
Regional integration, 236
Regional specialization, 261
Regulation, 114
Rent, 19, 28, 39, 74, 75, 79, 103
  contract, 15
  curve, 43, 58
  economic, 15, 17, 27, 33, 34, 70
Rentals, 84
Rents, 94
Republic of South Africa, 70, 143
Reputation, 126
Research and development, 133
Resettlement, 284, 285
Residential land use, 75
Resource(s), 261
  biotic, 227
  discovery, 260
  endowment of the United States, 247
  endowments, 201
Retail, 79
Retail center, 75
Retailing, 76, 78
Reynosa, 116
Rhine Delta, 138, 139
Rhine-Ruhr district, 138, 139
Rhine Valley, 140
Ribbon development, 79, 81
Ricardo, D., 15, 70
River navigation, 213
Rivers, 213
Road patterns:
  density of, 217
  of United States, 218
Road system, 218
Rochester, New York, 51, 126
Root crops, 50
Rostow, W. W., 262-264, 269
Rotation, 50, 67, 71
Rotterdam, 139

Routes, 128, 132, 198
  spacing of, 200
Rubber:
  crude, 74
  synthetic, 123
  tire industry, 124-127
Rural redevelopment, 284
Rural unemployed, 284
Rural-urban migration, 266
Rushton, G. R., 188

Saar basin, 140
Sabinas, 116
St. Clair River, 123
St. Lawrence River, 40, 50, 58, 119, 214
St. Lawrence Valley, 283
St. Louis, Missouri, 126
Sales:
  territory, size of, 103
  volume of, 103
Salt, 124
San Francisco, California, 79, 81
São Paulo, 280
Sardinia, 41, 199
Sarnia, Ontario, 123
Saskatchewan, 281
Satisficers, 30, 109
Scale:
  economies, 97, 100, 113, 121, 122, 131,
    200, 246, 250, 260, 268
  of operation, changing, 100
Scandinavia, 44, 138
Scandinavian industry, 140
Schlebecker, J. T., 53, 70
Scientific research, 132
Scottish midlands, 139
Scrap metal, 115, 116
Seaports, 212
  Antwerp, 212
  break of bulk points, 213
  commercial functions of, 213
  European, 212
  hinterlands of, 212
  Hong Kong, 212
  industries of, 213
  London, 212
  New York, 212
  Rotterdam, 212
  Singapore, 212
  United States, East Coast, 212
Seattle, Washington, 80
Sectoral growth, 151
Sectors, 79, 81
Seed, 73
Seedbed hypothesis, 78
Service sector, 262
Services, 79, 263
Shanghai, 143
Sheep, 63
Shell Oil Company, 123
Shippers, 208
Shipping, ocean, 211
  (See also Steamship)
Shoe factories, 126
Shoe industry, 124-126
Shoemaking, mechanization of, 126
Shopping centers, 81
  complete, 180, 195